Towards the Critique of Violence

Bloomsbury Studies in Continental Philosophy

Bloomsbury Studies in Continental Philosophy presents cutting-edge scholarship in the field of modern European thought. The wholly original arguments, perspectives and research findings in titles in this series make it an important and stimulating resource for students and academics from across the discipline.

Other titles in the series

Towards the Critique of Violence

Walter Benjamin and Giorgio Agamben

Edited by Brendan Moran and Carlo Salzani

Bloomsbury Academic
An imprint of Bloomsbury Publishing Plc

B L O O M S B U R Y

LONDON • OXFORD • NEW YORK • NEW DELHI • SYDNEY

Bloomsbury Academic

An imprint of Bloomsbury Publishing Plc

50 Bedford Square   1385 Broadway

London   New York

WC1B 3DP   NY 10018

UK   USA

www.bloomsbury.com

BLOOMSBURY and the Diana logo are trademarks of Bloomsbury Publishing Plc

First published 2015
Paperback edition first published 2017

British Library Cataloguing-in-Publication Data
A catalogue record for this book is available from the British Library.

ISBN: HB: 978-1-47252-324-2
PB: 978-1-47424-189-2
ePDF: 978-1-47252-928-2
ePub: 978-1-47253-349-4

Library of Congress Cataloging-in-Publication Data
A catalog record for this book is available from the Library of Congress.

Series: Bloomsbury Studies in Continental Philosophy

Typeset by Fakenham Prepress Solutions, Fakenham, Norfolk NR21 8NN

Contents

Abbreviations

References to the work of Benjamin and Agamben are made parenthetically in the text according to the following conventions.

Benjamin

All references to the *Arcades Project* are to the convolute number without further specification, for example (M5,9).

AP   *The Arcades Project*, trans. Howard Eiland and Kevin McLaughlin (Cambridge, MA: Belknap Press of Harvard University Press, 1999).

BA   *Briefwechsel 1938–1940: Theodor W. Adorno, Walter Benjamin*, ed. Gershom Scholem (Frankfurt a.M.: Suhrkamp, 1994).

BS   *Briefwechsel 1933–1940: Walter Benjamin, Gershom Scholem*, ed. Gershom Scholem (Frankfurt a.M.: Suhrkamp, 1985).

C   *The Correspondence of Walter Benjamin 1910–1940*, eds. Gershom Scholem and Theodor W. Adorno, trans. Manfred R. Jakobson and Evelyn M. Jakobson (Chicago, IL: University of Chicago Press, 1994).

CA   Theodor Adorno and Walter Benjamin, *The Complete Correspondence 1920–1940*, ed. Henri Lonitz, trans. Nicholas Walker (Cambridge, MA: Harvard University Press, 1999).

CS   *The Correspondence of Walter Benjamin and Gershom Scholem*, ed. Gershom Scholem, trans. Gary Smith and André Lefevere (Cambridge, MA: Harvard University Press, 1992).

GB   *Gesammelte Briefe*, 6 vols., eds. Christoph Gödde and Henri Lonitz (Frankfurt a.M.: Suhrkamp, 1995–2000).

GS   *Gesammelte Schriften*, eds. Rolf Tiedemann and Hermann Schweppenhäuser (Frankfurt a.M.: Suhrkamp, 1974 ff.).

OT   *The Origin of the German Tragic Drama*, trans. John Osborne (London: Verso, 1998).

SW   *Selected Writings*, 4 vols., ed. Michael W. Jennings (Cambridge, MA: Belknap Press of Harvard University Press, 1997–2003).

Agamben

When reference is made both to the Italian text and the English translation, a slash separates the page numbers of the different editions, for example (*HS* 7/5).

CC   *La comunità che viene* (Turin: Einaudi, 1990, then Turin: Bollati Boringhieri, 2001) / *The Coming Community*, trans. Michael Hardt (Minneapolis, MN: University of Minnesota Press, 1993).

EP   *Categorie italiane. Studi di poetica* (Venice: Marsilio, 1996) / *The End of the Poem: Studies in Poetics*, trans. Daniel Heller-Roazen (Stanford, CA: Stanford University Press, 1999).

HP   *Altissima povertà. Regole monastiche e forma di vita* (Vicenza: Neri Pozza, 2011) / *The Highest Poverty: Monastic Rules and Form-of-Life*, trans. Adam Kotsko (Stanford, CA: Stanford University Press, 2013).

HS   *Homo sacer. Il potere sovrano e la nuda vita* (Turin: Einaudi, 1995) / *Homo Sacer: Sovereign Power and Bare Life*, trans. Daniel Heller-Roazen (Stanford, CA: Stanford University Press, 1998).

IH   *Infanzia e storia. Distruzione dell'esperienza e origine della storia* (Turin: Einaudi 1978) / *Infancy and History: On the Destruction of Experience*, trans. Liz Heron (London: Verso, 1996).

IP   *Idea della prosa* (Milan: Feltrinelli, 1985, then Macerata: Quodlibet, 2002) / *Idea of Prose*, trans. Sam Whitsitt and Michael Sullivan (Albany, NY: SUNY Press, 1995).

KG   *Il Regno e la Gloria. Per una genealogia teologica dell'economia e del governo* (Vicenza: Neri Pozza, 2007 then Turin: Bollati Boringhieri, 2009) / *The Kingdom and the Glory: For a Theological Genealogy of Economy and Government*, trans. Lorenzo Chiesa (with Matteo Mandarini) (Stanford, CA: Stanford University Press, 2011).

LD   *Il linguaggio e la morte. Un seminario sul luogo della negatività* (Turin: Einaudi, 1982) / *Language and Death: The Place of Negativity*, trans. Karen Pinkus and Michael Hardt (Minneapolis, MN: University of Minnesota Press, 1991).

LOV   'Sui limiti della violenza', in *Nuovi Argomenti* 17 (1970): 159–73 / 'On the Limits of Violence', trans. Elisabeth Fay, *diacritics* 39.4 (2009): 103–11. This translation is reprinted in the appendix to this volume, so page numbers in the text refer to the appendix.

MC   *L'uomo senza contenuto* (Milan: Rizzoli, 1970, then Macerata: Quodlibet, 1994) / *The Man Without Content*, trans. Georgia Albert (Stanford, CA: Stanford University Press, 1999).

ME   *Mezzi senza fine. Note sulla politica* (Turin: Bollati Boringhieri, 1996) / *Means without End: Notes on Politics*, trans. Vincenzo Binetti and Cesare Casarino (Minneapolis, MN: University of Minnesota Press, 2000).

N   *Nudità* (Rome: Nottetempo, 2009) / *Nudities*, trans. David Kishik and Stefan Pedatella (Stanford, CA: Stanford University Press, 2011).

O   *L'aperto. L'uomo e l'animale* (Turin: Bollati Boringhieri, 2002) / *The Open: Man and Animal*, trans. Kevin Attell (Stanford, CA: Stanford University Press, 2004).

OD   *Opus Dei. Archeologia dell'ufficio* (Turin: Bollati Boringhieri, 2012) / *Opus Dei: An Archaeology of Duty*, trans. Adam Kotsko (Stanford, CA: Stanford University Press, 2013).

PO   *La potenza del pensiero. Saggi e conferenze* (Vicenza: Neri Pozza, 2005) / *Potentialities: Collected Essays in Philosophy*, trans. Daniel Heller-Roazen (Stanford, CA: Stanford University Press, 1999).

PR   *Profanazioni* (Rome: Nottetempo, 2005) / *Profanations*, trans. Jeff Fort (New York: Zone Books, 2007).

RA   *Quel che resta di Auschwitz. L'archivio e il testimone* (Turin: Bollati Boringhieri, 1998) / *Remnants of Auschwitz: The Witness and the Archive*, trans. Daniel Heller-Roazen (New York: Zone, 1999).

S   *Stanze. La parola e il fantasma nella cultura occidentale* (Turin: Einaudi, 1979) / *Stanzas: Word and Phantasm in Western Culture*, trans. Ronald L. Martinez (Minneapolis, MN: University of Minnesota Press, 1993).

SE   *Stato di Eccezione* (Turin: Bollati Boringhieri, 2003) / *State of Exception*, trans. Kevin Attell (Chicago, IL: University of Chicago Press, 2005).

SL   *Il sacramento del linguaggio. Archeologia del giuramento* (Rome-Bari: Laterza, 2008) / *The Sacrament of Language: An Archaeology of the Oath*, trans. Adam Kotsko (Cambridge: Polity Press, 2011).

ST   *Signatura rerum. Sul metodo* (Turin: Bollati Boringhieri, 2008) / *The Signature of All Things: On Method*, trans. Luca di Santo and Kevin Attell (New York: Zone Books, 2009).

TR   *Il tempo che resta. Un commento alla 'Lettera ai romani'* (Turin: Bollati Boringhieri, 2000) / *The Time that Remains: a Commentary on the Letter to the Romans*, trans. Patricia Dailey (Stanford, CA: Stanford University Press, 2005).

Contributors

Amir Ahmadi is an Adjunct Research Fellow at the School of Languages, Literatures, Cultures and Linguistics, Monash University, Australia. He is the author of *The Daēva Cult in the Gāthās: An Ideological Archeology of Zoroastrianism* (2015).

Paolo Bartoloni is Professor and Head of Italian at the National University of Ireland, Galway. He is the author of *Interstitial Writing: Calvino, Caproni, Sereni, and Svevo* (2003), *On the Cultures of Exile, Translation, and Writing* (2008), and of the forthcoming volumes *Sapere di scrivere. Svevo e gli ordigni di* La coscienza di Zeno (2015), and *Things that Matter: Objects in Italian Life and Culture* (2016).

Antonia Birnbaum teaches at the Department of Philosophy, University of Paris 8. She has written on Nietzsche, Descartes, Foucault, Rancière, and others. Her work is concerned with the relation between courage and thought. Among her publications are *Trajectoires obliques* (2013), *Bonheur Justice. Walter Benjamin* (2008) and *Nietzsche. Les aventures de l'héroïsme* (2000).

Vivian Liska is Full Professor of German Literature and Director of the Institute of Jewish Studies at the University of Antwerp, Belgium. She is also, since 2013, Distinguished Visiting Professor in the Faculty of the Humanities at Hebrew University in Jerusalem and on the Visiting Staff at the German Center of NYU University. Her research focuses on modernist literature, German-Jewish literature and culture, and literary theory. She is the editor or co-editor of numerous books, among them the two-volume ICLA publication *Modernism*, and *What does the Veil Know?* (with Eva Meyer). She is the editor of the book series 'Perspectives on Jewish Texts and Contexts' (De Gruyter, Berlin) and the co-editor of the comparative literature journal *arcadia* and the *Yearbook of European Jewish Literature*. She is the author of, among other books, *Die Nacht der Hymnen* (on Paul Celan) and *Das schelmische Erhabene* (On Else Lasker-Schüler), *Giorgio Agamben's leerer Messianismus* and *When Kafka Says We. Uncommon Communities in German-Jewish Literature*. Her most recent book is *Fremde Gemeinschaft. Deutsch-jüdische Literatur der Moderne*.

James R. Martel teaches in the department of political science at San Francisco State University. He specializes in political theology, anarchism and critical legal studies. He is the author, most recently, of *The One and Only Law: Walter Benjamin and the Second Commandment*.

J. Colin McQuillan is Assistant Professor of Philosophy at St. Mary's University in San Antonio, Texas. He is the co-editor, with Joseph Tanke, of the *Bloomsbury Anthology of Aesthetics* and the author of *Immanuel Kant: The Very Idea of a Critique of Pure Reason* (forthcoming) and *Early Modern Aesthetics* (forthcoming).

Bettine Menke is Professor and Chair of Comparative Literature at the University of Erfurt, Germany. Her publications include *Das Trauerspiel-Buch. Der Souverän – das Trauerspiel – Konstellationen – Ruinen* (2010), *Prosopopoiia. Stimme und Text bei Brentano, Hoffmann, Kleist und Kafka* (2000) and *Sprachfiguren. Name – Allegorie – Bild nach Walter Benjamin* (1991). Her fields of research span from literary theory to deconstruction, gender and rhetoric.

Brendan Moran is Associate Professor of Philosophy, and Adjunct Associate Professor of German, at the University of Calgary, Canada. His publications include *Wild, Unforgettable Philosophy in Early Works of Walter Benjamin*, *Philosophy and Kafka* (co-edited with Carlo Salzani), and articles on Benjamin, Kafka, Agamben and Salomo Friedlaender. He has just completed a study titled *Philosophy as Renegade. Benjamin's 'Kafkan' Politics*.

Alex Murray teaches in the School of English at Queen's University Belfast. He works primarily on Decadent and Modernist literature. He is the author of *Giorgio Agamben* (2010) and co-edited two collections on Agamben for Edinburgh University Press.

Alison Ross is an Australian Research Council Future Fellow in Philosophy at Monash University (Australia). She is the author of *The Aesthetic Paths of Philosophy: Presentation in Kant, Heidegger, Lacoue-Labarthe and Nancy* (2007) and *Walter Benjamin's Concept of the Image* (2014).

Carlo Salzani holds a degree in philosophy from the University of Verona (Italy) and a PhD in Comparative Literature from Monash University (Australia). He has published *Constellations of Reading: Walter Benjamin in Figures of Actuality* (2009), *Crisi e possibilità: Robert Musil e il tramonto dell'Occidente* (2010), and *Introduzione a Giorgio Agamben* (2013), and co-edited *Essays on Boredom and Modernity* (with Barbara Dalle Pezze, 2009) and *Philosophy and Kafka* (with Brendan Moran, 2013). He has translated into Italian some works by Walter Benjamin and Slavoj Žižek.

William Watkin is Professor of Contemporary Literature and Philosophy at Brunel University, West London. He is the author of *The Literary Agamben* (2010) and *Agamben and Indifference* (2014). He is currently writing a two-volume study of both volumes of Badiou's *Being and Event* as part of a wider project or re-describing the current philosophical and political moment in terms of indifference.

Thanos Zartaloudis is an academic, a lawyer and a writer who teaches and researches at the University of Kent, Kent Law School and at the Architectural Association, School of Architecture in London. His early monograph was dedicated to the thought of Giorgio Agamben and is titled *Giorgio Agamben: Power, Law and the Uses of Criticism* (2010). He is currently completing a short book titled *The Idea of Justice* (EUP) and is working on another titled *The Use of Things: In Law, Art and Architecture*.

Introduction: On the *Actuality* of 'Critique of Violence'

Brendan Moran and Carlo Salzani

1

One of the most quoted entries of Walter Benjamin's unfinished *Arcades Project* reads as follows:

> For the historical index of the images not only says that they belong to a particular time; it says, above all, that they attain to legibility [*Lesbarkeit*] only at a particular time. And, indeed, this acceding 'to legibility' constitutes a specific critical point in the movement at their interior. Every present day is determined by the images that are synchronic with it: each 'now' is the now of a particular recognizability [*Erkennbarkeit*]. In it, truth is charged to the bursting point with time. (N3,1)

This historical indexing could conceivably also apply to the 'images' proposed and developed in works of art or philosophy. One could well ask whether Benjamin's essay, 'Towards the Critique of Violence', is entering a period of legibility, at least in comparison with the several decades in which it was relatively dormant. Written and published in 1921, it might seem to have attained greater 'legibility' only in the past twenty-five years or so, when it has become a central and, for many, unavoidable reference in philosophico-political debates. Its compelling 'actuality' does not very often entail, however, utilitarian 'usefulness' for the analysis and comprehension of very specific historico-political phenomena so distant and so different from the time of its composition and the mind of its author. Yet something that might be called the world's 'present' may involve a 'now' of the essay's recognizability. The essay has entered a much contested 'legibility' in the sense that it has quite influentially entered recent and contemporary debates. It has entered a 'constellation' of attention for current readers and commentators.

Benjamin has a view that the 'truth' of a work – or an event – becomes legible only after a temporal and critical process has been undergone. This is a tenet to which he remains faithful throughout his whole career and which he applied to the most diverse fields, from literary criticism to the reading of history. He developed and deployed the concept of criticism in works such as *The Concept of Criticism in German Romanticism* (1919), 'Goethe's *Elective Affinities*' (1919–22) or *The Origin of German Tragic Drama* (1925, 1928). In the words of the latter study, the 'material content' [*Sachgehalt*] is 'mortified' and the 'truth content' [*Wahrheitsgehalt*] can emerge (*GS* 1.1:357/*OT* 182). The 'truth' of a work can only emerge in its critical 'afterlife', and it is the present, as Benjamin writes again in a note for the *Arcades Project*, 'that polarizes the event into fore- and after-history' (N7a,8). According to this line of analysis, the 'truth content' of 'Critique of Violence' might resonate as it enters a 'force field' with the present and possibly the future, a force field in which this polarization happens 'always anew, never in the same way' (N7a,1).

2

The reader of a book of essays pertaining to Benjamin's 'Critique' could well expect at least a brief account of its genesis and reception. Our first paragraphs above presuppose in some way a broad familiarity with certain details, and that presupposition might be mistaken. From his correspondence we know that in the early 1920s Benjamin planned a large study on politics, to which he generally referred with the simple working-title *Politik*.[1] The first mention of the project appears in a letter to Bernd Kampfmeyer from September 1920, in which Benjamin asks for 'bibliographic information' for a 'line of political studies' that he is developing (part of which he named 'Der Abbau der Gewalt', 'The Decomposition of Violence'). He mentions too for the first time (in his available letters) Georges Sorel's *Réflexions sur la violence* (*GB* 2:101). It is, however, to Gershom Scholem that Benjamin describes, in several letters, the development of the project, whose general outline is provided in a letter from December 1, 1920: it would consist of three main sections. The first part would be named 'Der wahre Politiker' ('The True Politician'). The second part (on which he was working at the time) would be called 'Die wahre Politik' ('The True Politics'), and would be divided into 'Der Abbau der Gewalt' and 'Teleologie ohne Endzweck' ('Teleology without Final Purpose').[2] Finally, the third part would be a philosophical critique of Paul Scheerbart's utopian novel *Lesabéndio* (1913) (*GB* 2: 109).[3] On December 29, 1920 he writes that the first part has been completed and that he hopes to see it soon in print (*GB* 2: 119). In January 1921 he mentions for the first time 'Zur Kritik der Gewalt', which he was asked to write by Emil Lederer for the latter's journal *Weißen Blätter* (*GB* 2: 130); the editors of the *Gesammelte Briefe* surmise that this piece ultimately coincides with 'Der Abbau der Gewalt' (*GB* 2: 111n). In the following letter, he says that the piece has finally been written, and that Lederer has rejected 'Der wahre Politiker' for his journal (*GB* 2: 131). In a letter from February 14, 1921, he tells Scholem that Lederer has rejected 'Zur Kritik der Gewalt' for die *Weißen Blätter* (he found it too long and too difficult for the journal), but accepted it instead for the *Archiv für Sozialwissenschaft und Sozialpolitik*, the prestigious journal founded in 1904 by Max Weber, Werner Sombart and Edgar Jaffé, which Lederer also edited, and where the piece finally appeared in issue August 3, 1921 (*GB* 2, 138).[4] As far as 'Der wahre Politiker' is concerned, Benjamin sent it to Scholem on March 26, 1921, asking for advice on where to publish it (*GB* 2: 148). In letters from July 26 and August 4, 1921 he says he is working again on the *Politik* (*GB* 2: 174). He mentions 'Der wahre

Politiker' once more in 1923 in some letters to Martin Buber and Gottfried Salomon-Delatour (*GB* 2: 360, 382, 385), but could not find a way to publish it. The essay is now considered lost. Benjamin finally abandoned the project, but as late as January 24, 1926 he mentions again, to Salomon-Delatour, 'Der wahre Politiker' and 'Zur Kritik der Gewalt'; these, he says, contain the 'arsenal' of his 'political works' (*GB* 3: 9).

'Critique of Violence' is, therefore, the only surviving part of a greater and unfinished project. In Benjamin's oeuvre, it might in some ways seem an isolated experiment, almost a 'fragment' or even a 'ruin' of an unfinished and abandoned construction. There exist, however, various notes (dated by editors at around 1918–20) that document further related philosophic explorations concerning politics, ethics and law (*GS* 6: 91–3, 98–100, 104–8). Themes in 'Critique of Violence' echo, moreover, in texts such as the so-called 'Theological-Political Fragment', 'Goethe's *Elective Affinities*', the *Trauerspiel*-book, Benjamin's writings on Kafka, and perhaps even the various versions of 'On the Concept of History'. Upon publication, however, it did not seem to produce any great effect and – in that sense – it might appear correct for Beatrice Hanssen to write that it remained 'virtually unnoticed by Benjamin's contemporaries (except for a handful of close friends and intellectual allies)'.[5] Hanssen's next claim – that Derrida's 1989 'Force of law' 'pulled the essay out of relative obscurity'[6] – is more clearly a slight overstatement. It is certainly the case, however, that 'Critique of Violence' did not occupy a very prominent position in the first waves of the posthumous Benjamin-reception. It did, in fact, open the first two-volume edition of Benjamin's *Schriften*, edited in 1955 by Theodor W. and Gretel Adorno,[7] but it was only in the mid-1960s that it acquired some conspicuous critical attention: in 1965, there appeared a slim selection of Benjamin's writings under the title *Zur Kritik der Gewalt und andere Aufsätze*.[8] Herbert Marcuse's (brief) afterword might seem – in a sense – to give the tone for the openly revolutionary interpretations of the late 1960s. Marcuse reads 'Critique of Violence' as an unambiguous revolutionary text unmasking and criticizing the violence 'of the Establishment, that which preserves its monopoly on legality, truth, and justice'. He also stresses that Benjamin's messianism concerns 'historical truth' and 'societal categories'.[9] This reading fits very well in the context of the social and political unrest of the so-called 1968-period: Oskar Negt, among others, uses Benjamin's essay in a critical analysis of the German predicament in the aftermath of the assassination attempt on Rudi Dutschke, the so-called *Springerblockade*, and the student revolts.[10] And it is perhaps because of the predominance of this allegedly 'Sorelian'[11] interpretation at the time that Benjamin's essay is conspicuously absent from Hannah Arendt's 1969 treatise *On Violence*.[12]

Reacting to the dominant 'revolutionary' reading of the 1960s, Jürgen Habermas in the early 1970s places 'Critique of Violence' in the context of the (failed) Surrealist aesthetics and politics, and dismisses Benjamin's messianic project as 'conservative-revolutionary'.[13] Habermas' 1972 essay was somewhat influential. Particularly among readers already enthusiastic about Habermas, it may have contributed to a kind of non-reading of Benjamin's essay. Continuing to some extent still today, this negligent reading places Benjamin in a linear conception of progress whereby Benjamin, along with Adorno and Horkheimer, is surpassed by a culmination involving Habermas, his cohorts, or his successors (usually in Frankfurt am Main). Within this 'liberal' camp, Habermas's essay might also, however, have given rise to, or made explicit, what Richard Bernstein calls a 'nervousness' about 'Critique of Violence', and in particular about the issue of 'pure' or 'divine violence'.[14] This nervousness has recently spawned the erroneous claim that Benjamin's notion of divine violence involves advocacy of corporal punishment of children by educators and parents.[15]

Such 'nervousness' was possibly further fuelled in 1971 as Jacob Taubes made public a previously suppressed letter that Benjamin wrote in 1930 to Carl Schmitt acknowledging his indebtedness to the latter's theory of sovereignty for his *Trauerspiel*-book (cf. *GB* 3: 558–9). Even Benjamin's usage, in the *Trauerspiel*-book, of Schmitt's work had been rendered invisible in the edition put out in 1955 by Theodor and Gretel Adorno. The passages quoting and paraphrasing Schmitt appear without the endnotes indicating their source as Schmitt's *Political Theology*.[16] Although Benjamin's usages of Schmitt are ultimately critical, the so-called 'dangerous liaison'[17] between Benjamin and the *Kronjurist* of the Third Reich was a scandal for many, particularly for self-proclaimed 'democratic' interpreters of Benjamin; this was so much the case that Habermas stepped up his criticism when, fifteen years after his first essay on Benjamin, he practically inscribed Benjamin in the conservative, antiliberal camp by cursorily mentioning 'Critique of Violence' (reduced to an 'essay on Sorel') in a fierce critique of Schmitt and associating it with the latter's aesthetics of violence and thrust towards the 'violent destruction of the normative as such'. In this passage, Habermas's rhetoric reaches the point of fabricating a claim that Schmitt wrote a letter to Benjamin to congratulate him on 'his essay on Sorel'. There is no record of such a letter.[18] Even the somewhat more informed Axel Honneth proclaims Benjamin's 'questionable' critique of parliamentarism to be in 'astonishing proximity to the antidemocratic thinking of Carl Schmitt'.[19] Unlike Schmitt, or Sorel for that matter, Benjamin never endorses a *myth* of political action. Regardless of what one might think of it, Benjaminian politics is philosophically impelled and thus *largely* opposed to the closed forms in which both Schmitt and Sorel imagine politics. With regard to Schmitt, there may be philosophic reasons not to follow the attempt, made recently by David Pan, to integrate Benjamin's work into Schmitt's notion of 'decision that is used in the state of exception to establish the system of norms'.[20] Schmitt provides an answer precisely where Benjamin continues to question.

At the end of the 1970s there was in fact an attempt by Günter Figal and Horst Folkers to provide a relatively unbiased, 'philosophical' analysis of 'Critique of Violence', in particular by focusing on its Neo-Kantian context and language and its relations to Kant's politics and ethics.[21] Although this effort was well received, the effect on the Benjamin-reception and the international debate about his works remained comparatively slight.[22] In this regard, Hanssen is right to describe Derrida's 1989 'Force of law' as a decisive factor in magnifying the reception of Benjamin's essay – despite the (very influential) 'nervousness' Derrida expresses apropos 'divine violence': Derrida's reading literally sparked a wide and intense debate and had the effect of placing 'Critique of Violence' in the forefront of many discussions of Benjamin's works. This is perhaps especially the case for the reception in the English language.[23] As is often the case, however, this development in the Anglo-American world quite quickly echoed in the German-language reception.[24] Since the appearance of Derrida's discussion, Benjamin's essay has been more and more minutely scrutinized, analysed, dissected, and has provoked a wide range of different and diverse, and often conflicting, interpretations by thinkers as distinct as the aforementioned Axel Honneth, Judith Butler, Simon Critchley and Slavoj Žižek (to name just a few).[25] During this period, an essay that had a particularly strong influence was Werner Hamacher's 'Afformative, strike'; this influence was and remains so strong that it has sometimes been the default-reading for some readers who are perhaps hesitant about entering the labyrinth of Benjamin's 'Critique of Violence'.[26] This does not, of course, apply to all readings that are sympathetic to Hamacher's arguments. In any case, during the past two and half decades it has increasingly become as if, in Bernstein's words, '[i]n seeking to make sense of violence and to distinguish types of violence (and non-violence) there is an almost irresistible obsession to return to Benjamin's essay and to take one's stand in regard to it'.[27]

3

Besides Derrida's reading in 'Force of law', one of the major factors accounting for the 'actuality' of 'Critique of Violence' is undoubtedly Giorgio Agamben's recurrent borrowings from, and interpretative takes upon, Benjamin's essay. The importance of Benjamin for Agamben's philosophy is comparable maybe only to that of Heidegger, and the simultaneous encounter with these two figures in the mid-1960s (Heidegger in person, Benjamin in the books) marked, in Agamben's words, his 'true encounter with philosophy'.[28] In a 1985 interview with Adriano Sofri he said: 'I read him [Benjamin] for the first time in the 1960s in the Italian edition of *Angelus Novus*, edited by Renato Solmi. He immediately made the strongest impression on me: for no other author have I felt such an unsettling affinity'.[29] 'Critique of Violence' opened the *Angelus Novus* collection and it must have contributed to the 'strongest impression' this book made on Agamben, to the point that it inspired and informed (together with Arendt's *On Violence*) one of his first academic articles, 'On the Limits of Violence' (1970), which we reproduce in the appendix to this volume. This text is to be read within the context of the late 1960s' often violent uprisings and the politico-philosophic debate they initiated; the emphasis on Benjamin's not yet popular essay is perhaps to be ascribed to the aforementioned debates that were happening in Germany at the time. Surprisingly, though, when mentioning his own 1970 essay in the 1985 interview with Sofri, Agamben does not refer to Benjamin:

> I haven't been totally at ease with 1968. In those years I was reading Hannah Arendt, whom my leftist friends considered a reactionary author, and one could not speak about her …
>
> An essay of mine on the limits of violence, which dealt with Arendt's thought, was rejected by a journal of the [student] movement and had to be published in a literary journal.[30]

The presence of Benjamin in Agamben's work remained massive throughout the 1970s and 1980s, though in this time 'Critique of Violence' did not appear, explicitly at least, as a central reference. The latter qualification is important, for there are a few implicit but fundamental references at key moments. In the very final paragraph of *Language and Death* (1982), Agamben mentions for the first time, together with the expression *homo sacer*, the syntagm '*nuda vita*' (bare life), without acknowledging that it is the translation of Benjamin's usage of the formulation *bloßes Leben* in 'Critique of Violence' and 'Goethe's *Elective Affinities*' (*LD* 133/106). A few years later, in *The Coming Community*, he mentions the syntagm twice again (*CC* 52/64–5, 68/86). 'Critique of Violence' is briefly mentioned, moreover, in the 1982 essay 'Walter Benjamin and the demonic: Happiness and historical redemption'. An increasing political focus in the early 1990s brought 'Critique of Violence' to the forefront of Agamben's elaborations, until it finally became the key reference for *Homo Sacer* (1995).

Adam Kotsko has written that 'Critique of Violence' provides the 'primary impetus' for, and 'supplies the basic structure of [Agamben's] project in *Homo Sacer*'.[31] One could even argue, as Kotsko and Leland de la Durantaye have intimated,[32] that this book (or at least the whole second part of it, precisely entitled 'Homo Sacer') can be read as an attempt at following a suggestion Benjamin makes in the second-last paragraph of 'Critique of Violence':

> It might be well worthwhile to track down the origin of the dogma of the sacredness of life. Perhaps, indeed probably, it is relatively recent, the last mistaken attempt of the weakened Western tradition to seek the saint it has lost in cosmological impenetrability. (*GS* 2.1:202/*SW* 1:251)

Though only a (very compressed) reading of 'Critique of Violence' is proposed in the first 'threshold' of *Homo Sacer* (cf. *HS* 72–6/63–7), the theses and the language of Benjamin's essay become something like the grid through which Agamben approaches the political.

This will remain true for the rest of Agamben's *Homo Sacer* series – and for the volumes not 'officially' belonging to it. The 1996 collection of essays *Means without End: Notes on Politics*, which collects a number of preparatory studies for *Homo Sacer*, even takes its title from a concept Benjamin introduces in 'Critique of Violence'. Agamben's most extensive analysis of 'Critique of Violence' is, however, enacted in a fundamental chapter of *State of Exception* (2003), entitled 'Gigantomachy concerning a void' (cf. *SE* 68–83/52–64). In this chapter, he analyses in detail what he outlines as a debate between Benjamin and Carl Schmitt on the state of exception, and proposes a thesis that completely reverses the traditional view of 'Critique of Violence' as an isolated and finally failed 'torso' of a project with no real impact on debates during its time. Agamben notes that Schmitt was a regular reader of the *Archiv für Sozialwissenschaft und Sozialpolitik*, and that he quotes the issues immediately preceding and following the one containing Benjamin's essay (issue 47.3). Agamben argues that Schmitt could not have missed a text like 'Critique of Violence'. He accordingly attempts to read Schmitt's theory of sovereignty as a response to Benjamin's essay.

Even if the scope of Agamben's following books widens from an analysis and critique of sovereignty to a more comprehensive analysis of power, and even if Agamben does not offer further readings of 'Critique of Violence', it is almost certain that the theoretical framework and the vocabulary of Benjamin's text are still woven into the fabric of Agamben's whole project: notions like 'bare life', 'pure means', 'pure violence', 'deposition', and the critique of law will remain central for Agamben and might well continue to permeate his own philosophical parlance.

4

Apart from the appendix containing Agamben's 'On the Limits of Violence', this volume contains thirteen essays. The essays provide a considerable array of perspectives. The editors saw it as their task not to constrain the authors beyond fairly conventional editorial criteria. It did occasionally happen that the editors were in disagreement with parts of an essay. After one or two nudges, however, they did not insist. The views expressed in any given essay are, therefore, above all those of the author. The essays do not follow an editorial line, other than the editorial request that they be philosophic.[33] The result is a book in which essays are often in at least implicit disagreement with one another. Given the difficulty of Benjamin's 'Towards the Critique of Violence' and the provocative character of Agamben's usages of Benjamin's work, it did not strike the editors as regrettable that such a varied collection of essays has emerged.

The essays are divided quite simply into two parts. The first part, 'Benjamin's Critique of Violence', offers five essays exclusively, or almost exclusively, focused on Benjamin's 'Towards the Critique of Violence' and related writings by him. The second part, 'Agamben's Readings of Benjamin', contains eight essays dealing with, and sometimes debating, Agamben's usages of Benjamin's works, particularly 'Towards the Critique of Violence' but also other related works by Benjamin.

The volume commences with Bettine Menke's 'Techniques of Agreement, Diplomacy, Lying', which is quite unique in addressing Benjamin's endorsement of certain comparatively non-violent practices in political, governmental and legal affairs. Further adding to the distinctness of Menke's essay is that she discusses these practices against the backdrop of similarities and differences of Benjamin's views with those of the twentieth-century philosopher and sociologist, Helmuth Plessner, whose work – especially in the non-Germanic world – is relatively neglected.

The second essay is Alison Ross's 'The Ambiguity of Ambiguity in Benjamin's "Critique of Violence"', which is a critical analysis of Benjamin's quite varied conceptions of the role of ambiguity in law and in mythic constructions more broadly. Ross focuses primarily on 'Towards the Critique of Violence' and the thematically and chronologically akin 'Goethe's *Elective Affinities*', but also provides comparative remarks on Benjamin's late work.

Ross's study is followed by Amir Ahmadi's 'Benjamin's Niobe', which is a critical examination of Benjamin's 'Towards the Critique of Violence' in the context of its usage of the story of Niobe. Drawing on analyses of ancient Greek myth, and providing comparative analysis of the role in Benjamin's essay of the biblical story of the company of Korah, Ahmadi argues for a reconsideration of various nuances in Benjamin's distinction of divine violence and mythic violence.

In Brendan Moran's 'Nature, Decision and Muteness', analyses of passages from 'Towards the Critique of Violence' are supplemented by extensive examination of 'Goethe's *Elective Affinities*', where Benjamin provides considerable discussion of nature, the human, and decision. Benjamin is shown to distinguish mythic nature, which instils resignation to alleged fate, from destructive, liberatory nature that helps decision to be critical of myth. Moran criticizes aspects of Benjamin's vilification of entities and people that are supposedly beneath the human.

The final essay of Part 1 is Antonia Birnbaum's 'Variations of Fate'. Primarily examining 'Towards the Critique of Violence' and the *Trauerspiel*-book (1928), Birnbaum detects views that fate is accompanied by interruptive forces involving struggle and gaps. These forces indicate either a concern with justice or an apprehension of ruinous time that enables philosophy to decipher incompleteness. Birnbaum examines these different interruptive forces in terms of their implications for class struggle and for possibilities of interjection against alienation.

Part 2 begins with Carlo Salzani's 'From Benjamin's *bloßes Leben* to Agamben's *Nuda Vita*: A Genealogy'. Salzani traces the genealogy of the notion of 'bare life' from Benjamin's 'Towards the Critique of Violence' to Agamben's writings. He discusses the distinct cultural and philosophical context for Benjamin's remarks on 'bare life', and he shows how 'bare life' took on a very different permutation in works by Agamben. Salzani contends Agamben develops 'bare life' into a correlate of the Schmittian exception. He also outlines how vastly important 'bare life' is for Agamben's project as a whole.

J. Colin McQuillan's essay, 'Agamben's Critique of Sacrificial Violence', revolves around the contention that sacrifice has been a recurrent theme for Agamben because it enables him to address the problem of violence. The essay proposes that Agamben's discussions of sacrificial violence are modelled on Benjamin's critique of mythic violence. McQuillan outlines not only Agamben's critique of sacrifice, but also some of the ways – such as government, *désœuvrement*, profanation and form-of-life – in which Agamben conceives alternatives to sacrifice.

William Watkin's essay, 'Agamben, Benjamin and the Indifference of Violence', focuses on Agamben's reading of Benjamin's concept of divine violence. Watkin considers how divine violence, in Agamben's writing, inflects with notions such as sovereignty and *homo sacer*. Divine violence becomes a mode of rendering indifferent distinctions, such as that between state-founding violence and state-protecting violence. On the basis of Agamben's reading of Benjamin, Watkin criticizes the reading of Benjamin offered by Slavoj Žižek and concludes that divine violence is a form of rendering state-violence inoperative.

The next contribution, Paolo Bartoloni's 'Suchness and the Threshold between Possession and Violence', concentrates on Agamben's notion of 'suchness'. Bartoloni examines 'suchness' in its aesthetic, ethical and political implications, and links it to Benjamin's advancement of a certain kind of non-violence called 'pure means'. Agamben and Benjamin's emphases on non-possessive non-violence are discussed by Bartoloni as indicative of an emergent aesthetic and ethical ecology.

Thanos Zartaloudis's 'Violence Without Law? On Pure Violence as Destituent Power' responds to the question of whether there can be violence without law and law without violence. Zartaloudis reads Benjamin's 'Towards the Critique of Violence' alongside various readings by Agamben, particularly his early essay on violence (the appendix of this volume) and his recent essay on destituent power. Zartaloudis attempts to provide a provisional response to the question that forms the leitmotif of his essay.

This is followed by James Martel's 'The Anarchist Life we are Already Living: Benjamin and Agamben on Bare Life and the Resistance to Sovereignty'. From Benjamin, Martel elicits the view that there are practices in life, 'anarchistic' practices, that elude myth and thereby partake in pure means. He argues that Agamben's notion of bare life, in some respects, facilitates an enrichment of Benjamin's approach to politics. Agamben thereby helps us to trace variants of life that exist under capitalism and sovereignty, but avoid attendant constraints.

Vivian Liska's 'Benjamin and Agamben on Kafka, Judaism and the Law' compares Benjamin and Agamben on the question of law in Kafka's writings. Benjamin's Kafka-analyses contain passages that are very close to 'Towards the Critique of Violence', so they are an obvious site for further consideration of Benjamin on law. Agamben recognizes this. Liska argues that Benjamin and Agamben are akin concerning secular legal systems, but diverge on the question of religious – specifically, Jewish – law. She contends that this difference may highlight some problems with the 'Paulinian turn' in contemporary philosophy.

Supplementing the volume with a concern that is only ostensibly a diversion, the final essay (before the appendix containing Agamben's early essay on violence) is Alex Murray's 'Expropriated Experience: Agamben Reading Benjamin, Reading Kant', which considers the possible relevance of Benjamin's critique of Kant to Agamben's early work, especially *Infancy and History* and *Stanzas: Word and Phantasm in Western Culture*. Murray argues that, however obliquely at times, Agamben pits Kant and Benjamin against one another. Murray contends that Benjamin's emphasis (via Johann Georg Hamann) on language provides Agamben with the basis for a critique of Kant's project.

Notes

1   On the historical, cultural and philosophical background of the project see Uwe Steiner, 'The true politician: Walter Benjamin's concept of the political', trans. Colin Sample, *New German Critique* 83 (Spring–Summer 2001): 43–88.

2   Beatrice Hanssen, among others, argues that this might be the 'Theological-Political Fragment'; Beatrice Hanssen, *Critique of Violence: Between Poststructuralism and Critical Theory* (London and New York: Routledge, 2000), 261n.

3   Paul Scheerbart, *Lesabéndio. Ein Asteroiden-Roman* (Munich-Leipzig: Georg Müller 1913). Peter Fenves suggests that all of the proposed titles derive directly from Kant: 'the title of the middle section, "The True Politics," comes from the aforementioned passage in "Toward Eternal Peace," where Kant distinguishes the "moral politician" from the "political moralist" …; and the title of the first section, "The True Politician," represents a middle term that presumably takes both sides of the Kantian dichotomy to their respective extremes. In addition, the chapter

entitled "True Politics" is itself divided into two subsections, the second of which is entitled "Teleology Without Final Purpose" ... and thus represents a bisection of the *Critique of Judgement*, the first part of which revolves around two famous formulas for beauty, "lawfulness without law" and "purposiveness without purpose" ..., while the second part, as a critique of teleological judgement, culminates in a reflection on the "final purpose of the existence of the world, that is, of creation itself" .... The only title not drawn directly from Kant is that of the first subsection of "The True Politics," which was to be called "Die Abbauung [sic] der Gewalt" (The dismantling of violence; or: The deconstruction of power). This subsection, however, would probably consist in a revision of "Toward the Critique of *Gewalt*," which expresses the Kantian character of the entire enterprise more effectively than any of the others' (Peter Fenves, *The Messianic Reduction: Walter Benjamin and the Shape of Time* [Stanford, CA: Stanford University Press, 2011], 208–9).

4   Cf. *Archiv für Sozialwissenschaft und Sozialpolitik* 47.3 (1921): 809–32. Gershom Scholem argues that 'it appeared in 1921 in a sociological journal among whose articles Benjamin's seemed quite out of place' (Gershom Scholem, *Walter Benjamin – die Geschichte einer Freundschaft* [Frankfurt a.M.: Suhrkamp, 1975], 119 / *Walter Benjamin. The Story of a Friendship*, trans. Harry Zohn [Philadelphia: The Jewish Publication Society of America, 1981], 93).

5   Hanssen, *Critique of Violence*, 3.

6   Hanssen, *Critique of Violence*, 8.

7   Cf. Walter Benjamin, *Schriften*, eds. Theodor W. and Gretel Adorno (Frankfurt a.M.: Suhrkamp, 1955), vol. 1, 3–30.

8   Walter Benjamin, *Zur Kritik der Gewalt und andere Aufsätze*. Mit einem Nachwort von Herbert Marcuse (Frankfurt a.M.: Suhrkamp, 1965).

9   Herbert Marcuse, 'Nachwort', in Walter Benjamin, *Zur Kritik der Gewalt und andere Aufsätze*, 99, 100–1.

10   Oskar Negt, 'Rechtsordnung, Öffentlichkeit und Gewalt', in *Die Auferstehung der Gewalt: Springerblockade und politische Reaktion in der Bundesrepublik*, eds. Heinz Grossmann and Oskar Negt (Frankfurt a.M.: Europäische Verlagsanstalt, 1968), 168–85.

11   Richard J. Bernstein deems Marcuse's reading '"Sorelian" insofar as it highlights the radical revolution that is required to bring about emancipation from existing legal violence', and notes how this 'revolutionary reading' has always attracted supporters (Richard J. Bernstein, *Violence: Thinking Without Banisters* [Cambridge: Polity Press, 2013], 57).

12   Cf. Hannah Arendt, *On Violence* (New York: Harcourt Brace & Company, 1969). It is perhaps also significant that Arendt did not include 'Critique of Violence' in the 1968 volume *Illuminations*, the first English collection of Benjamin's writings. The first English translation of 'Critique of Violence' appeared only ten years later in *Reflections*, a new collection of Benjamin texts edited by Peter Demetz in 1978, although Demetz implies that Arendt had some influence on the choice of texts for *Reflections* (xv).

13   Jürgen Habermas, 'Bewußtmachende oder rettende Kritik. Die Aktualität Walter Benjamins', in *Zur Aktualität Walter Benjamins*, ed. Siegfried Unseld (Frankfurt a.M.: Suhrkamp, 1972), 212–15, 220 / 'Consciousness-raising or redemptive criticism: the contemporaneity of Walter Benjamin', trans. Philip Brewster and Carl Howard Buchner, *New German Critique* 17 (Spring 1979): 54–6, 59.

14   Bernstein, *Violence*, 74–5.

15 Axel Honneth, 'Zur Kritik der Gewalt', in *Benjamin-Handbuch,* eds. Burkhardt
    Lindner with Thomas Küpper and Timo Skrandies (Stuttgart: Verlag J. B. Metzler,
    2006), 193–210, especially 208. See too the comments on education in Honneth,
    'Eine geschichtsphilosophische Rettung des Sakralen', in *Pathologien der Vernunft.*
    Geschichte und Gegenwart der Kritischen Theorie (Frankfurt a.M.: Suhrkamp, 2007),
    154 / 'Saving the sacred with a philosophy of history', in *Pathologies of Reason:*
    On the Legacy of Critical Theory, trans. James D. Ingram (New York: Columbia
    University Press, 2009), 124.

16 See Benjamin, *Schriften*, eds. Theodor W. Adorno and Gretel Adorno, vol. 1
    (Frankfurt a.M.: Suhrkamp, 1955), 183–4. Cf. *GS* 1.1, 245–6 / *OT*, 65–6. In these
    pages, Benjamin borrows from Schmitt's portrayal of a seventeenth-century outlook.
    He also indicates interest in Schmitt's accompanying critique of Kantian 'rationalism'
    in the latter's disregard for exception. For the relevant remarks in Schmitt's portrayal,
    see Schmitt, *Politische Theologie. Vier Kapitel zur Lehre von der Souveränität* (Berlin:
    Duncker & Humblot, 1990), 15–22 / *Political Theology. Four Chapters on the Concept
    of Sovereignty*, trans. George Schwab (Cambridge, MA: MIT Press, 1985), 9–15.

17 This is the title of a book on Benjamin and Schmitt: Susanne Heil, *'Gefährliche
    Beziehungen': Walter Benjamin und Carl Schmitt* (Stuttgart & Weimar: J. B. Metzler,
    1996).

18 Cf. Jürgen Habermas, 'Die Schrecken der Autonomie: Carl Schmitt auf Englisch',
    Eine Art Schadensabwicklung (Frankfurt a.M.: Suhrkamp, 1987), 112 / 'The horrors
    of autonomy: Carl Schmitt in English' (1987), in *The New Conservatism: Cultural
    Criticism and the Historian's Debate*, ed. and trans. Shierry Weber Nicholsen
    (Cambridge: Polity Press, 1989), 137.

19 Honneth, 'Eine geschichtsphilosophische Rettung des Sakralen', *Pathologien der
    Vernunft*, 144 / 'Saving the sacred with a philosophy of history', *Pathologies of
    Reason*, 115. For disregard of the anti-mythic usage of a Sorelian 'construction' in
    Benjamin's essay, see 138–9/110–11.

20 David Pan, 'Against biopolitics: Walter Benjamin, Carl Schmitt, and Giorgio
    Agamben on political sovereignty and symbolic order', *The German Quarterly* 82.1
    (Winter 2009): 54; see too: 56–7. Pan's article is an attempt to draw on Carl Schmitt's
    decisionism to offset Benjamin's relatively strict wariness of complacency about
    law-positing.

21 Cf. Günter Figal and Horst Folkers, *Zur Theorie der Gewalt und Gewaltlosigkeit bei
    Walter Benjamin: Aufsätze und Diskussionen* (Heidelberg: F.E.S.T., 1979); the slim
    volume consists of two essays, Figal's 'Die Ethik Walter Benjamins als Philosophie
    der reinen Mittel', 1–24, and Folker's 'Zum Begriff der Gewalt bei Kant und
    Benjamin', 25–57.

22 Also noteworthy in this context are: Figal, 'Recht und Moral bei Kant, Cohen und
    Benjamin', in Heinz-Ludwig Ollig, ed., *Materialien zur Neukantianismus-Diskussion*
    (Darmstadt: Wissenschaftliche Buchgesellschaft, 1987), 163–83; and Figal, 'Vom
    Sinn der Geschichte: Zur Erörterung der politschen Theologie bei Carl Schmitt
    und Walter Benjamin', in *Dialektischer Negativismus: Michael Theunissen zum
    60. Geburtstag*, eds. Emil Angehrn, Hinrich Fink-Eitel, Christian Iber and Georg
    Lohmann. (Frankfurt a.M.: Suhrkamp, 1992), 252–69.

23 As Robert Sinnerbrink notes (Robert Sinnerbrink, 'Violence, deconstruction, and
    sovereignty: Derrida and Agamben on Benjamin's "Critique of Violence"', in *Walter
    Benjamin and the Architecture of Modernity*, eds. Andrew Benjamin and Charles
    Rice [Melbourne: re.press, 2009], 77–8).

24   See Anselm Haverkamp, ed., *Gewalt und Gerechtigkeit. Derrida-Benjamin* (Frankfurt a.M.: Suhrkamp, 1994). The volume contains translations of many essays that originally appeared in English, as well as a few original German-language contributions.

25   Cf. Axel Honneth, 'Eine geschichtsphilosophische Rettung des Sakralen', in *Pathologien der Vernunft*, 112–56 / 'Saving the sacred with a philosophy of history', in *Pathologies of Reason*, 88–121; Judith Butler, 'Critique, coercion and sacred life in Benjamin's "Critique of Violence"', in *Political Theologies: Public Religions in a Post-Secular World*, eds. Hent de Vries and Lawrence E. Sullivan (New York: Fordham University Press, 2006), 201–19; Simon Critchley, *The Faith of the Faithless: Experiments in Political Theology* (New York: Verso, 2012), 213–21; Slavoj Žižek, *Violence* (New York: Picador, 2008).

26   Werner Hamacher, 'Afformativ, Streik', *Was heißt "Darstellen"?* ed. Christiaan Hart Nibbrig (Frankfurt a.M: Suhrkamp 1994), 340–74 / 'Afformative, strike', trans. Dana Hollander, *Cardozo Law Review* 13.4 (1991): 1133–57.

27   Bernstein, *Violence*, 48.

28   Adriano Sofri, 'Un'idea di Giorgio Agamben', interview with Giorgio Agamben, *Reporter* (November 9–10, 1985), 32.

29   Sofri, 'Un'idea di Giorgio Agamben', 32.

30   Sofri, 'Un'idea di Giorgio Agamben', 32. As he recounts in a much later interview, during a seminar with Heidegger at Le Thor in 1968 they used to discuss the events of the student revolts and authors like Arendt and Marcuse; Heidegger gave Arendt's New York mailing address to Agamben, who wrote to her, also sending 'On the Limits of Violence' (Hannah Leitgeb and Cornelia Vismann, 'Das unheilige Leben. Ein Gespräch mit dem italienischen Philosophen Giorgio Agamben', in *Literaturen* 2.1 [2001], 18). Arendt will cite this text in a note of the German translation of *On Violence* (cf. Hannah Arendt, *Macht und Gewalt*, trans. Gisela Uellenberg [Munich: Piper, 1970], 35).

31   Adam Kotsko, 'On Agamben's use of Benjamin's "Critique of Violence"', in *Telos* 145 (Winter 2008), 120. Anselm Haverkamp has described *Homo Sacer* as 'the most important of all the books influenced by the "Critique of Violence" or produced in its wake' (Anselm Haverkamp, 'Anagrammatics of violence: the Benjaminian ground of *Homo Sacer*', in *Politics, Metaphysics, and Death: Essays on Giorgio Agamben's Homo Sacer*, ed. Andrew Norris [Durham, NC: Duke University Press, 2005], 137).

32   Kotsko, 'On Agamben's use of Benjamin's "Critique of Violence"', 119; Leland de la Durantaye, *Giorgio Agamben: A Critical Introduction* (Stanford, CA: Stanford University Press, 2009), 354.

33   This specifically philosophic focus distinguishes the book from the broad approach taken in *Benjamin-Agamben: Politics, Messianism, Kabbalah*, eds. Vittoria Borsò, Claas Morgenroth, Karl Solibakke, and Bernd Witte (Würzburg: Verlag Königshausen & Neumann, 2010).

Works cited

Arendt, Hannah. *On Violence*. New York: Harcourt Brace & Company, 1969.
—*Macht und Gewalt*. Translated by Gisela Uellenberg. Munich: Piper, 1970.

Benjamin, Walter. *Schriften*. Edited by Theodor W. and Gretel Adorno. 2 volumes. Frankfurt a.M.: Suhrkamp, 1955.

—*Zur Kritik der Gewalt und andere Aufsätze*. Mit einem Nachwort von Herbert Marcuse. Frankfurt a.M.: Suhrkamp, 1965.

—*Illuminations: Essays and Reflections*. Edited by Hannah Arendt. Translated by Harry Zohn. New York: Schocken, 1968.

—*Reflections: Essays, Aphorisms, Autobiographical Writings*. Edited by Peter Demetz. Translated by Edmund Jephcott. New York: Harcourt Brace & Company, 1978.

—*Angelus Novus. Saggi e frammenti* (1962). Translated and edited by Renato Solmi. Turin: Einaudi, 1995.

Bernstein, Richard J. *Violence: Thinking Without Banisters*. Cambridge: Polity Press, 2013.

Borsò, Vittoria, Claas Morgenroth, Karl Solibakke and Bernd Witte, eds. *Benjamin-Agamben: Politics, Messianism, Kabbalah*. Würzburg: Verlag Königshausen & Neumann, 2010.

Butler, Judith. 'Critique, coercion and sacred life in Benjamin's "Critique of Violence"'. In *Political Theologies: Public Religions in a Post-Secular World*, edited by Hent de Vries and Lawrence E. Sullivan. New York: Fordham University Press, 2006. 201–19.

Critchley, Simon. *The Faith of the Faithless: Experiments in Political Theology*. New York: Verso, 2012. 213–21.

de la Durantaye, Leland. *Giorgio Agamben: A Critical Introduction*. Stanford, CA: Stanford University Press, 2009.

Demetz, Peter. 'Introduction', in Benjamin, *Reflections*, vii–xliii.

Derrida, Jacques. 'Force de loi: Le "fondement mystique de l'autorité" / 'Force of law: The "mystical foundation of authority"'. Translated by Mary Quaintance. *Cardozo Law Review* 11.5–6 (July/August 1990): 919–1045.

Fenves, Peter. *The Messianic Reduction: Walter Benjamin and the Shape of Time*. Stanford, CA: Stanford University Press, 2011.

Figal, Günter. 'Recht und Moral bei Kant, Cohen und Benjamin', in *Materialien zur Neukantianismus-Diskussion*. Edited by Heinz-Ludwig Ollig. Darmstadt: Wissenschaftliche Buchgesellschaft, 1987, 163–83.

—'Vom Sinn der Geschichte: Zur Erörterung der politschen Theologie bei Carl Schmitt und Walter Benjamin', in *Dialektischer Negativismus: Michael Theunissen zum 60. Geburtstag*. Edited by Emil Angehrn, Hinrich Fink-Eitel, Christian Iber and Georg Lohmann, Frankfurt a.M.: Suhrkamp, 1992. 252–69.

Figal, Günter and Horst Folkers. *Zur Theorie der Gewalt und Gewaltlosigkeit bei Walter Benjamin: Aufsätze und Diskussionen*. Heidelberg: F.E.S.T., 1979.

Habermas, Jürgen. 'Bewußtmachende oder rettende Kritik. Die Aktualität Walter Benjamins'. in *Zur Aktualität Walter Benjamins*. Edited by Siegfried Unseld. Frankfurt a.M.: Suhrkamp, 1972, 173–223.

—'Consciousness-raising or redemptive criticism: The contemporaneity of Walter Benjamin'. Translated by Philip Brewster and Carl Howard Buchner. *New German Critique* 17 (Spring 1979): 30–59.

—'The horrors of autonomy: Carl Schmitt in English' (1987). In Jürgen Habermas, *The New Conservatism: Cultural Criticism and the Historian's Debate*. Edited and translated by Shierry Weber Nicholsen. Cambridge: Polity Press, 1989, 128–39.

—'Die Schrecken der Autonomie. Carl Schmitt auf Englisch', *Eine Art Schadensabwicklung*. Frankfurt a.M.: Suhrkamp, 1987, 101–14.

Hamacher, Werner. 'Afformative, strike'. Translated by Dana Hollander. *Cardozo Law Review* 13.4 (1991): 1133–57.

—'Afformativ, Streik'. In *Was heißt "Darstellen"?* Edited by Christiaan Hart Nibbrig. Frankfurt a.M.: Suhrkamp 1994, 340–74.

Hanssen, Beatrice. *Critique of Violence: Between Poststructuralism and Critical Theory*. London and New York: Routledge, 2000.

Haverkamp, Anselm, ed. *Gewalt und Gerechtigkeit. Derrida-Benjamin*. Frankfurt a.M.: Suhrkamp, 1994.

—'Anagrammatics of violence: the Benjaminian ground of *Homo Sacer*'. In *Politics, Metaphysics, and Death: Essays on Giorgio Agamben's Homo Sacer*. Edited by Andrew Norris. Durham, NC: Duke University Press, 2005, 135–44.

Heil, Susanne. *'Gefährliche Beziehungen': Walter Benjamin und Carl Schmitt*. Stuttgart & Weimar: J. B. Metzler, 1996.

Honneth, Axel, 'Zur Kritik der Gewalt', in *Benjamin-Handbuch. Leben – Werk – Wirkung*. Edited by Burkhardt Lindner with Thomas Küpper and Timo Skrandies. Stuttgart: Verlag J. B. Metzler, 2006, 193–210.

—'Eine geschichtsphilosophische Rettung des Sakralen'. *Pathologien der Vernunft. Geschichte und Gegenwart der Kritischen Theorie*. Frankfurt a.M.: Suhrkamp, 2007, 112–56.

—'Saving the sacred with a philosophy of history'. In Axel Honneth, *Pathologies of Reason: On the Legacy of Critical Theory*. Translated by James D. Ingram. New York: Columbia University Press, 2009, 88–125.

Kotsko, Adam. 'On Agamben's use of Benjamin's "Critique of Violence"'. In *Telos* 145 (Winter 2008): 119–29.

Leitgeb, Hannah, and Cornelia Vismann. 'Das unheilige Leben. Ein Gespräch mit dem italienischen Philosophen Giorgio Agamben'. In *Literaturen* 2.1 (2001): 16–22.

Marcuse, Herbert. 'Nachwort'. In Walter Benjamin, *Zur Kritik der Gewalt und andere Aufsätze*. Frankfurt a.M.: Suhrkamp, 1965. 98–107.

Negt, Oskar. 'Rechtsordnung, Öffentlichkeit und Gewalt'. In *Die Auferstehung der Gewalt: Springerblockade und politische Reaktion in der Bundesrepublik*. Edited by Heinz Grossmann and Oskar Negt. Frankfurt a.M.: Europäische Verlagsanstalt, 1968, 168–85.

Pan, David. 'Against biopolitics: Walter Benjamin, Carl Schmitt, and Giorgio Agamben on political sovereignty and symbolic order'. *The German Quarterly* 82.1 (Winter 2009): 42–62.

Scheerbart, Paul. *Lesabéndio. Ein Asteroiden-Roman*. Munich-Leipzig: Georg Müller, 1913.

Schmitt, Carl. *Political Theology. Four Chapters on the Concept of Sovereignty*. Translated by George Schwab. Cambridge, MA: MIT Press, 1985.

—*Politische Theologie. Vier Kapitel zur Lehre von der Souveränität*. Berlin: Duncker & Humblot, 1990.

Scholem, Gershom. *Walter Benjamin – die Geschichte einer Freundschaft*. Frankfurt a.M.: Suhrkamp, 1975.

—*Walter Benjamin. The Story of a Friendship*. Translated by Harry Zohn. Philadelphia: The Jewish Publication Society of America, 1981.

Sinnerbrink, Robert. 'Violence, deconstruction, and sovereignty: Derrida and Agamben on Benjamin's "Critique of Violence"'. In *Walter Benjamin and the Architecture of Modernity*. Edited by Andrew Benjamin and Charles Rice. Melbourne: re.press, 2009, 77–91.

Sofri, Adriano. 'Un'idea di Giorgio Agamben'. Interview with Giorgio Agamben. *Reporter*, 9–10 (November 1985): 32–3.

Sorel, Georges. *Réflexions sur la violence*. Paris: Marcel Rivière et Cie, 1908.

Steiner, Uwe. 'The true politician: Walter Benjamin's concept of the political'. Translated by Colin Sample. *New German Critique* 83 (Spring–Summer 2001): 43–88.
Žižek, Slavoj. *Violence*. New York: Picador, 2008.

Part One

Benjamin's Critique of Violence

Techniques of Agreement, Diplomacy, Lying

Bettine Menke
(trans. Carlo Salzani and Brendan Moran)[1]

Benjamin's essay 'Critique of Violence' has gained, in the past ten or fifteen years, decisive importance for the discussion of the Benjaminian concept of the political in relation to right and justice and their reliance on *the* other instance, that of a striking God.[2] I would like here to concern myself, however, with the *techniques of agreement* (or the 'pure means' which these techniques are an instance of), with *language* and *technique*, *lying* and *diplomacy*, which have gone somewhat unnoticed in the analysis of Benjamin's essay.

While Benjamin's analysis, like Derrida's, of the concept of the sovereign decision for developing the concept of the positing and foundation of the law was conducted with reference to Carl Schmitt,[3] for the perspective on the 'techniques of agreement' another name might be mentioned: that of Helmuth Plessner. In the years 1920–1, when Benjamin wrote and published 'Critique of Violence', Plessner addressed the art of politics and (among other things) of diplomacy in a series of short publications.

In his 1924 eponymous book (*Grenzen der Gemeinschaft*), Plessner deals with the *Limits of Community*, whereby the 'community' is limited from outside and the demarcation of the community is distinguished in the sense of a 'culture of distance'.[4] This happens in the inversion of the order of values proposed, for instance, by Ferdinand Tönnies in *Community and Society* (*Gemeinschaft und Gesellschaft*, 1887):[5] so Plessner recognizes and values artifact over organism, contract over comprehension [*Verständnis*], statecraft, diplomacy and form over humaneness. In the years 1920 and 1921, Plessner published a series of little contributions[6] in which he addresses statecraft and diplomacy, *inter alia* 'Staatskunst und Menschlichkeit' ('Statecraft and humanity', 1920), 'Politische Kultur' and 'Politische Erziehung in Deutschland' ('Political culture', and 'Political education in Germany', both 1921).[7] A contiguity of Benjamin's 'Critique of Violence' and Plessner's above-mentioned texts can be recognized in their respective praise of diplomacy.[8] It is the last of the works by Plessner that we have mentioned, 'Politische Erziehung in Deutschland', with its programme of 'education to politics' as a teaching in the art of government [*Staats-Kunst-Lehre*], which shows the closest and at times literal parallels to Benjamin's 'Critique of Violence' (published a few months earlier), namely with regard to the 'pure means' themselves, and not only to one of them, 'diplomacy'. With his 'project of a school for political thinking', Plessner wants to counter the 'opposition between power-politics and politics of under-standing [*Verständigung*]'.[9] Politics should adopt the form of an 'art of government' [*Staats-Kunst*][10] in order to counteract its degradation, which it has suffered since the eighteenth century under the postulate of the priority of goals or ideals, and under the postulate of the overcoming of politics through community.[11] The 'opposition between power-politics and politics of understanding' would found the proviso that such a 'school' would be an institute that serves 'the interests of power-politics in contrast to the interests of a sincere politics of understanding and reconciliation'.[12] Hence Plessner turns against this failed opposition by giving the contrast a different form:

> The opposition between power-politics and the politics of understanding has a definite meaning only when it names the difference between a politics of pure means and one of impure means. Impure means are those which originate in violence and flow into violence, the police and the army. They characterize a politics of threat.[13]

In contrast to the so-characterized 'impure means, which originate in violence and flow into violence', Plessner defines the 'politics of pure means' as a 'politics of persuasive arguments and voluntary agreement'. However, this politics and its deter-mination are established only indirectly, from the outside, as a necessity imposed 'anyway' on Germany:

> Bereft of military means, Germany is anyway forced to avow a politics of pure means, a politics of persuasive arguments and voluntary agreement, based on the natural interests of the countries and on an accurate self-assessment of one's own country, and whose supreme tenet is no longer the development of the spirit of military capability, but rather the respect for peace.[14]

This argument, however, does not address the dissolution of the 'threat' whose *inside* instrument is the police; after naming it, Plessner forgets about it – and it remains forgotten also in the text that follows. In contrast, Benjamin's 'Critique of Violence' is not concerned with the 'politics of threat', but rather with the 'indeterminate' threat-ening by law [*des Rechts*], an 'indeterminacy' in which the law shows itself as partaking of the mythical cohesion or of fate. It is these traits of the law that Benjamin identifies in the specific function of police in the modern state. Benjamin's argument is that this 'indefinite' threat belongs *systematically* to the law, which thus shows itself as an 'order which imposes itself as fate' [*schicksalhafte Ordnung*]: all and every possible infringment of the legal regulations stands, in each particular case, under *this* threat, which aims essentially at the protection of law *as such*; and vice versa, critique would be insufficient if it only directed itself against 'particular laws or legal practices',

> that the law, in fact, takes under the protection of its power, which resides in the fact that there is only one fate and that the existing [*das Bestehende*], and in particular the threatening [*das Drohende*], belongs indissolubly [*unverbrüchlich*] to its order. For law-preserving violence is a threatening violence. (*GS* 2.1:187–8/ *SW* 1:242, translation modified)

The systematically *indefinite* 'threatening' of the law [*das 'Drohende' des Rechts*] is what makes the power of law [*Recht*] as such and aims at the protection of the legal order as a whole.[15] The 'indeterminateness' that constitutes the threatening [*das Drohende*] originates, according to Benjamin, in the 'sphere of fate'. Into this sphere has lapsed the law-preserving violence, and with it the law as such, which, *as power*, manifests itself in the 'indeterminateness of the legal threat' ['*Unbestimmtheit der Rechtsdrohung*'] (*GS* 2.1:188/*SW* 1:242, translation modified). Therefore, with the indeterminate 'legal threat' [*Rechtsdrohung*] is announced 'something rotten in the law' (*GS* 2.1:188/*SW* 1:242). For instance, capital punishment does not so much have the purpose to 'punish the infringement of law'; rather, in capital punishment the law itself as 'violence over life and death' is 'reaffirmed'. It is not only because in the formulation 'something rotten in the law' – as in Benjamin's formula of the *ghostly presence* of the police – one can read an allusion to Hamlet, that the definition of law as cohesion of *fate* stands in the closest relation to Benjamin's rejection of the police as an 'abominable' institution of the modern state. For the police show themselves to be the institution of a 'kind of spectral mixture' [*gleichsam gespenstische ... Vermischung*] of the 'two kinds of violence' (a 'far more unnatural combination' [*weit widernatürlicheren Verbindung*] than the death penalty) (*GS* 2.1:189/*SW* 1:242, translation modified):

> The ignominy of such an institution [*Behörde*] ... lies in the fact that in it the separation of law-positing [*rechtsetzender*] and law-preserving [*rechtserhaltender*] violence is suspended. If the first is required to prove itself in victory [*daß sie im Siege sich ausweise*], the second is subject to the restriction that it may not set itself new ends. Police violence is emancipated from both conditions. ... True, this is a violence for legal ends [*Gewalt zu Rechtszwecken*] (it includes the right of disposition [*mit Verfügungsrecht*]), but with the simultaneous authority [*Befugnis*] to posit these ends itself within wide limits (it includes the right of decree [*mit Verordnungsrecht*]). (*GS* 2.1:189/*SW* 1:242–3, translation modified)

The police, which Plessner calls an 'impure means' insofar as it is a means of a politics of threatening with violence, is distinguished, according to Benjamin, by the 'impurity' of a precisely defined 'intermixture': insofar as this institution of the preservation of law, of the protection of the juridical order, latently amounts to the unjustified and irredeemable *positing* of legal ends, this positing is distinguished as a violence threatening to intervene anywhere and anytime. The police are 'spectral' in this precise sense. Precisely in distinction from the law's '"decision" determined by place and time', which is the decision that raises a claim to 'essentiality'[16] (even though this does not amount to anything other than a tautological, retroactively maintained founding of law-positing as victorious imposition or instatement [*Einsetzung*] of law and power), 'spectral' is the violence of a non-'essential' but manifesting indefinite intervention, which creates law: 'Its power [*Gewalt*] is formless [*gestaltlos*], like its nowhere-tangible, all pervasive, ghostly presence [*gespenstische Erscheinung*] in the life of civilized states' (*GS* 2.1:189/*SW* 1:243).[17] The 'impurity' of police violence, as specifically 'ignominious' and 'spectral', is expression of the systematic bond between the law-positing [*rechtsetzende*] and law-preserving violence, which Benjamin identifies as 'mythic' immediate manifestation of violence, the immediate manifestation that renders law-positing [*Rechtsetzung*] as 'imposition of power' [*Machtsetzung*]. Derrida finds here the *tautology* of the foundation of law. All law-positing [*Rechtsetzung*] is imposition of *power* [*Macht*setzung], *insofar as* it is able to authenticate [*beglaubigen*] itself retroactively as *im*-position [*Ein*-setzung] of a juridical order, insofar as it is 'victorious'. The juridical order not only – in the mode of *law-positing* [*rechtsetzend*] – applies violence as (its) *means*, but rather, as threatening power, it intimately attaches – in a law-preserving mode – to violence itself its *ends*, which then might be called protection of the law (*GS* 2.1:198/*SW* 1:248–9).

If Benjamin's argument attempts to keep apart '*rechtsetzende*/law-positing' and '*rechtserhaltende*/law-preserving' violence, and in particular differentiates between 'mythic' and 'pure' violence,[18] he still makes clear that, in opposition to the 'impure genealogy' of law,[19] by no means must one seek – in the name of justice – a 'purer' genealogy. He attempts rather to take into consideration something 'completely other' than the law. For *all* juridical institutions and the juridical order as such, which seeks to preserve itself as a whole, refer back to violence(s) and to 'impure combinations' of violence(s). The *oppositional* pair – presupposed by, and at the basis of, the modern state – of '*rechtsetzender*/law-positing' and '*rechtserhaltender*/law-preserving' violence only and constantly founds the 'impure' interaction of the two poles.[20] Measured according to its own notion – founded in the opposition law-positing/law-preserving – law is, according to Benjamin, 'impure'. Therefore, Benjamin's 'critique' applies not only 'both to law-positing and law-preserving violence' (*GS* 2.1:188/*SW* 1:242), but to the interrelation or 'cycle' of both, which constitutes law as such.[21] Insofar as the law founds and manifests itself only in the circularity of law-positing and law-preserving violence, positing of law as 'power-imposition' [*Machtsetzung*] is – according to Benjamin – *mythic*, a repeatedly circular self-endorsing 'immediate manifestation of violence':

> For the function of violence in law-positing is twofold, in the sense that law-positing pursues as its end, with violence as the means, *what* is being established as law, but at the moment of imposition of its purposes as law, violence does not abdicate; rather, at this very moment, it is made, in a strict sense and immediately, into a law-positing violence, insofar as it establishes as law not an end unalloyed by violence, but one necessarily and intimately bound to it, under the title of power. Law-positing is imposition of power, and to that extent an act of immediate manifestation of violence.
>
> [*Die Funktion der Gewalt in der Rechtsetzung ist nämlich zwiefach in dem Sinne, daß die Rechtsetzung zwar dasjenige, was als Recht eingesetzt wird, als ihren Zweck mit der Gewalt als Mittel erstrebt, im Augenblick der Einsetzung des Bezweckten als Recht aber die Gewalt nicht abdankt, sondern sie nun erst im strengen Sinne und zwar unmittelbar zur rechtsetzenden macht, indem sie nicht einen von Gewalt freien und unabhängigen, sondern notwendig und innig an sie gebundenen Zweck als Recht unter dem Namen der Macht einsetzt. Rechtsetzung ist Machtsetzung und insofern ein Akt von unmittelbarer Manifestation der Gewalt*]. (*GS* 2.1:197–8/*SW* 1:248, translation modified)

Benjamin's text does not refer to the concept of 'impure means', which are for Plessner 'impure' insofar as they partake in violence;[22] his text aims rather at the possibility of 'non-violent means', which he identifies as 'pure means': 'Legal and illegal means of every kind that are all the same violent may be confronted with nonviolent ones as pure means' (*GS* 2.1:191/*SW* 1:244, translation modified).This happens at the decisive bifurcation in the argument of 'Critique of Violence', which is prepared through the following formulation:

> All violence as a means is either law-positing or law-preserving. If it lays claim to neither of these predicates, it forfeits all validity [*Geltung*]. It follows, however, that all violence as a means, even in the most favorable case, partakes in the problematic nature of law itself. (*GS* 2.1:190/*SW* 1:243, translation modified)

Consequently, Benjamin will pursue, *on the one hand*, the question of a 'nonmediate [*nicht mittelbare*] function of violence' (*GS* 2.1:196/*SW* 1:248), thus of a *violence* that *cannot* be considered a *means*. It is 'immediate manifestation': either as the *mythic* violence of threatening power, which circularly founds and justifies itself, or rather as (the manifestation of) a divine intervention, which is and remains empty and 'is' nothing but interruption itself.[23] But, *on the other hand*, it firstly and conversely becomes pressing to consider the question of 'whether there are no other than violent means for regulating conflicting human interests' (*GS* 2.1:190/*SW* 1:243).

Benjamin's attempt to identify 'other than violent means' is a decisive point for his analysis of law and for the relation, i.e. the break, between law and justice. For these 'other than violent means', according to Benjamin, can in no case be found in the law,[24] neither in a single regulation nor in the juridical order as a whole, which monopolizes violence and must fear and reject as threat (to itself) all that is other than its own violence, and precisely as a competing law-positing. The finding 'that all violence as a means, even in the most favorable case, partakes in the problematic nature of law itself' (that is, in its 'moral ambiguity'), necessarily leads to the conclusion 'that a totally nonviolent resolution of conflicts can never result in a legal contract' (*GS* 2.1:190/*SW* 1:243, translation modified). The 'legal contract' is, rather, that to which Benjamin's 'pure means' are precisely opposed: contracts, however peacefully concluded, correspond in Benjamin's formulation to Plessner's definition of 'impure means', which are not utterly violent, but rather 'originate in violence and flow into violence'.[25] Every contract refers to law-violence both in the 'outcome' and in its 'origin' (*GS* 2.1:190/*SW* 1:243), claims the right to resort to violence, and is thus bound in its 'origin and outcome' to violence, which lies 'latent' in it.[26]

The non-violent, i.e. 'pure means', are (on the one hand) thus *negatively* defined through the exclusion of the legal contract and of 'legal and illegal means of every kind' (*GS* 2.1:191/*SW* 1:244). To this negative definition (on the other hand), there are corresponding positive definitions of their 'objective manifestation [*Erscheinung*]'; to these belongs the formula of the 'technique of agreement':

> Their objective apparition [*Erscheinung*], however, is determined by the law ... that pure means are never those of direct solutions but always those of indirect solutions. They therefore never apply directly to the arbitration [*Schlichtung*] of conflict between man and man, but only by the way of things [*Sie beziehen sich*

daher niemals unmittelbar auf die Schlichtung der Konflikte zwischen Mensch und Mensch, sondern nur auf dem Wege über die Sachen]. The realm of nonviolent means opens up in the most 'factual' relationship of human conflicts to goods [*In der sachlichsten Beziehung menschlicher Konflikte auf Güter eröffnet sich das Gebiet der reinen Mittel*]. For this reason, technique in the broadest sense of the word is their most particular area. (*GS* 2.1:191–2/*SW* 1:244, translation modified)

The definition of the 'most proper realm' of the 'pure means' by 'technique' as the indirect way mediated by 'things' also concerns *language as* technique, which, as Benjamin says further, constitutes, 'perhaps', the 'profoundest example' of technique: 'the interlocution, considered as a technique of civil agreement' [*die Unterredung als eine Technik ziviler Übereinkunft betrachtet*] (*GS* 2.1:192/*SW* 1:244, translation modified). We have to think here, of course, of the *techné* or *ars* called rhetoric.[27] Plessner explicitly names rhetoric as a part of political 'art' [*Kunst*] and of its doctrine,[28] but indeed he never uses the concept of 'technique' other than in a pejorative way.[29]

If, according to Benjamin, 'the interlocution, considered as a technique of civil agreement' can be taken as the 'profoundest example' of 'pure means', whose sphere opens up 'in the *most factual* [*sachlichsten*] relationship of human conflicts to goods' (*GS* 2.1:191–2/*SW* 1:244, translation modified), it then depends though – perhaps surprisingly – on *lying* (which allegedly is in no way irreconciliable with 'objectivity' [*Sachlichkeit*]). It is a commonplace to link lying and the technique of *rhetoric*. But that language as such is not to be separated from saying it differently (translating or feigning, *inter alia*), constitutes its initial rhetoricity. The possibility of lying belongs 'originally' to language. Decisive for the characterization of language as medium of 'non-violent agreement' – which is what interests Benjamin – is however the 'impunity of lying' [*die Straflosigkeit der Lüge*]:

> For in it [language] not only is nonviolent agreement possible, but also the exclusion of violence in principle is quite explicitly demonstrable by one significant factor: the impunity of lying. Probably no legislation on earth originally punished it. This makes clear that there is a sphere of human agreement that is nonviolent to the extent that it is wholly inaccessible to violence: the proper sphere of 'understanding', language. Only late and in a peculiar process of decay has it been penetrated by legal violence in the penalty placed on fraud.
>
> [*In ihr (der Sprache) ist nämlich gewaltlose Einigung nicht allein möglich, sondern die prinzipielle Ausschaltung der Gewalt ist ganz ausdrücklich an einem bedeutenden Verhältnis zu belegen: an der Straflosigkeit der Lüge. Es gibt vielleicht keine Gesetzgebung auf der Erde, welche sie ursprünglich bestraft. Darin spricht sich aus, daß es eine in dem Grade gewaltlose Sphäre menschlicher Übereinkunft gibt, daß sie der Gewalt vollständig unzugänglich ist: die eigentliche Sphäre der 'Verständigung', die Sprache. Erst spät und in einem eigentümlichen Verfallsprozeß ist die Rechtsgewalt dennoch in sie eingedrungen, indem sie den Betrug unter Strafe stellte*]. (*GS* 2.1:192/*SW* 1:244–5, translation modified)[30]

The 'impunity of lying' is, therefore, what makes language a 'sphere' released from the order of law and thus from power, in whose imposition [*Einsetzung*] law-positing has been victoriously realized.[31] The fact that, according to Benjamin, 'originally' there is no sanction for lying vouches for the fact that speech and interlocution [*Unterredung*] are not based – either explicitly or implicitly – on contractual relations, that neither in 'origin' nor in 'outcome' is a contract, which produces or modifies legal relations, given, presupposed, or resultant. In this way, speech and interlocution are withdrawn from the 'sphere of fate' to which the 'legal threat' belongs (*GS* 2.1:188/*SW* 1:242). In this respect, Benjamin's argument about interlocution as a 'technique of civil agreement' constitutes precisely the counter-position and objection to Habermas's model of an implicit and necessary assumption of truthfulness as a quasi-contractual presupposition of any agreement, indeed of all interlocution.

The specificity of Benjamin's argument about the 'impunity of lying' is highlighted also by the fact that Plessner very carefully attempts to avoid this and all proximity between diplomacy and lying, whereas Benjamin is concerned with this proximity, when he mentions *diplomacy* as one of the 'pure means in politics … analogous to those which govern peaceful intercourse between private persons' (*GS* 2.1:193/*SW* 1:245), that is, to the already analysed 'techniques of interlocution'. Plessner fears the attribution of lying when he advocates for an 'art' of politics and diplomacy, and dismisses lying in advance as 'tricks', as 'ruses and dodges'.[32]

As noted above, Helmut Lethen identifies the kinship of Plessner's *Limits of Community* and Benjamin's 'Notizen zu einer Arbeit über die Lüge II' ('Notes for a Work on Lying II', c. 1922). In these notes, however, Benjamin does not limit himself to counterposing the 'unrestrained speaking out of everything [*schrankenloses Alles-Heraus-Sagen*]' to the 'well-groomed type of the diplomat' (*GS* 6:62),[33] and thus does not limit himself – as does Plessner – to counterposing to the injunction of (self-) expression the 'outwardness' of forms, or more precisely, the 'pure' *surface*: to abide by the 'pure' surface is what constitutes Benjamin's '*Sachlichkeit*' – in reference to Paul Scheerbart, Paul Klee or Robert Walser; it is the detachment from 'inwardness' or 'motives'.[34] The 'Notes for a Work on Lying II' agree with 'Critique of Violence' more precisely on another point – that in the commandment of 'honesty' the impotence [*Ohnmacht*] and with it the untenability of authority, which wants to create obligation to this commandment, show themselves:

> Not the demand of truth, but rather that of honesty is what one has to contest in principle as procurator [*Sachwalterin*] of powerless [*ohnmächtiger*] and therefore unjustified authorities. Everywhere the disarray of honesty reveals a factually and morally untenable claim of the one demanding. (*GS* 6:63)

According to 'Critique of Violence', fraud was sanctioned only by 'the law of a later period, [which,] lacking confidence in its own power, no longer felt itself [as did the law in the Roman and ancient Germanic periods] a match for all other instances of violence. Rather, fear of the latter and mistrust of itself indicate its shakiness [*seine Erschütterung*]' (*GS* 2.1:192/*SW* 1:245, translation modified).[35] Benjamin's argument, that in the sanctioning of fraud there is the il-legitimacy of law's own authority (and of its distrust in itself) showing, implicates a problematic genealogical pattern of decline. It is problematic because this pattern of decline presupposes a lost but formerly given self-empowered and thus 'legitimate' authority. The sanctionability of lying as fraud, based on a contractual framework, however implicit this may be, identifies in contrast an inner shakiness [*Erschüttertheit*] of the juridical order, which is to be detected as its violent character [*Gewaltsamkeit*], as the insecurity of its acting, when it approaches actions in terms of motives.[36] Language, which is not subordinated to the threat of law [*Drohung des Rechts*], is determined by the 'impunity of lying' as that medium which releases as such from the logic (i.e. from the spell) of the circular foundation of the imposition – of something.

The premise of interlocution as the 'sphere' of 'civil agreement' is that no recourse to law will be sought and that it is not kept under the 'threat' of law. This makes plausible Benjamin's characterization of *diplomacy* as a field which is granted to the 'techniques of agreement' in politics. Diplomacy seeks solutions, on the one hand, in the sense of the *Sachlichkeit* (factuality) of 'pure means', which 'are never those of immediate/direct solutions but always those of mediated/indirect solutions', and 'never apply directly to the resolution of conflict between man and man, but only by the way of things [*Sachen*]', and, on the other, '*von Fall zu Fall*', from case to case (*GS* 2.1:195/*SW* 1:247, translation modified).[37] The diplomatic negotiating in language not only does not rely on any juridical order, but also does not aim (as a rule) at 'modifying legal systems'; it posits no law [*kein Recht*] and in this respect does not need to become a power im-position, in which law has to stabilize itself:

> [So] the means of nonviolent agreement have developed in thousands of years of the history of states. Only occasionally does the task of diplomats in their transactions consist of modifying legal systems. Fundamentally they must, entirely on the analogy of agreement between private persons, resolve conflicts case by case, in the name of their states, peacefully and without contracts. A delicate task that is more resolutely performed by referees, but a method of solution that in principle is above that of the referee because it is beyond all legal systems and therefore beyond violence. Accordingly, like the intercourse of private persons, that of diplomats has engendered its own forms and virtues, which, even though they have become outward [*äußerlich*], need not always have been so. (*GS* 2.1:195/*SW* 1:247 translation modified)[38]

These 'forms and virtues' were not mere outward formalities insofar as they did not succumb to the opposition between inwardness and outwardness. They are the medium of *release* from that which (in 'conflicts between man and man' [*Mensch und Mensch*]) may be ascribed to 'humans' as interiority, as intentions or motives. This release corresponds to the *delicateness* of the 'delicate task' that is diplomacy.[39] It imparts itself to the 'method of solution': 'beyond all legal systems and therefore beyond violence',[40] beyond the 'violence' that is all positing, which either will have become 'victorious' imposition (of power), or would be nothing but a violent means, not even partaking in the problematic of legal violence.

If this abstention from all law-positing finds in diplomacy its established and at the same time enclosed field, 'lying' in contrast enacts yet another move, which can be called *deposing* [*Entsetzen*]. This brings lying close to that other 'pure means' of politics which Benjamin identified in the proletarian general strike.[41] If we consider 'lying' as a speech-act of deposing, then *not* (only) insofar as it, by lying, says something, but rather *insofar as*, through lying, the order of law or a regime of truthfulness, under whose sanctioning-threat it would stand, is, as power, de-posed [*ent-setzt*]. Lying would be understood as a de-posing of the regime(s) of truth, that not only protects this order of truth 'as a whole' in the face of *all* its infringements, but with the notion of lying also seizes the motives, a presupposed constitutive interiority. In the diffuse obligation to 'honesty' or veracity, this order would have already revealed itself as being as impotent as it is untenable. Lying always also lays claim, besides all that it can otherwise do, to the possibility of a speech freed from referential framings, and backs a speech that is setting (itself) free from the ties to any referent – and also from preceding motives.[42]

With the concept of deposing[43] I have referred to Benjamin's concept of the 'proletarian general strike', which he sets in precise opposition to the law-positing revolutionary act, identified as a means to an end. The proletarian general strike 'clearly announces', according to Benjamin, 'its indifference toward material gain through conquest' (into which law-positing violence must convert and authenticate itself) – and this as 'revolt' in which 'all these fine things' ('every kind of program, of utopia – in a word, of law-positing [*Rechtsetzungen*]') 'disappear'.[44] The proletarian general strike is '*as* pure means nonviolent', *insofar as* it is not subordinated to the 'gain' as its end, but rather is that 'upheaval that this kind of strike not so much causes as performs [*vollzieht*]' (*GS* 2.1:194/*SW* 1:246, translation modified). Therefore, it is not that, according to a binary model, *through* a 'means' we achieve an end independent from this means; rather, in the consummation or execution [*Vollzug*], which turns out to be the 'pure means' itself, the 'end' is both already achieved *and* suspended as *telos* (detached from means, and both redeeming the means and transcending them).[45] The upheaval is enacted just *in* the general strike *as* the general strike: as *event* of deposing (without a result which would confirm the act). And this is what defines Benjamin's concept of *politics* – as well as his concept of *technique(s)*. Whether the event of deposing exists as such, i.e. *whether* it can remain 'free' from appropriation, *whether* deposing does name an act, a move, a gesture, without the possibility, in the end, to restrain it from the imposition[46] – these are the questions that this notion of 'pure means' marks without giving an answer. Conceived as *Vollzug*, the enactment of that which cannot be its *telos*, the 'pure means', which among other things or, in particular, is *language*, cannot be separated from the *immediacy* [*Unmittelbarkeit*] of language's imparting [*Mitteilung*], that is, the imparting of the impartability [*Mitteilbarkeit*] of language, as enunciated in Benjamin's earlier essay 'On Language as Such and on the Language of the Man' (1916). The term *medium* [*Medium*] underlines this: what is achieved in language's imparting [*Mitteilung*] is not communicated *through* it and not as its meaning or sense, but rather it is a *Vollzug*, an enactment, *in* it: the imparting [*Mitteilung*] of language *in* language. *This* is what Benjamin characterizes as the mediality of language – language as medium.[47] Precisely here, where the mediality of 'pure means' can be conceived, is annulled the discriminability between the 'pure means' that is language and the *immediacy* of the imparting of and in language.[48] Thereby is challenged the purity of *that* distinction [*Unter-Scheidung*] upon which 'Critique of Violence' seems to rely with its alternative – marked through the decisive bifurcation of its argumentation – between 'pure (nonviolent) means' and 'immediate' 'manifestations' (which are no means) of violence.[49] On the one hand, however, the application of violence as an (alleged) *means* lapses into, as Benjamin argues, its mythic immediacy in which violence coincides with its end: when law-positing affirms itself 'victoriously' as power-imposition.[50] On the other hand, 'pure means' in their moment of deposing [*Entsetzung*] correspond to the 'manifestation' of violence, which as 'pure' or divine 'violence' does not posit, but is rather striking.[51] For 'pure means' *are* what they consummate or enact, and namely *in that* they *suspend* the ends which they precisely will *not* have established retroactively.

The field of differentiations of 'Critique of Violence' gets into such displacements which I will not pursue further now, because here still, in the scope of 'pure means', I want to emphasize a countermovement: I mean the countermovement to and in that trait of the argument exposing the *de-posing* in which *lying* is analogous to the proletarian general strike as 'pure means' of politics: in which *lying* is not considered an act of positing or imposition, and not with regard to a (false) reproduction of something, but rather is analogous to the enactment, *Vollzug*, of the 'upheaval' that is the 'proletarian general strike'. To lying as deposing of the regime of truthfulness, however unpunished it might have been in origin, a 'heroic' trait is attributed. This trait can be recognized in a sentence in Benjamin's 'Notes for a Work on Lying' which immediately follows the above-quoted insight that the powerlessness [*Ohnmacht*] and untenability of the imposing authority show themselves in the commandment of honesty:

> On the other hand, any revolutionary movement that would not methodically make lying a duty of its supporters as foundation of their struggle, denounces itself as unfree and captivated by the most dangerous suggestions of the rulers. (*GS* 6: 63)

The 'duty' to lying participates in a heroics of freedom. A *heroism* of lying would, however, itself be caught up in the mythic, in the perpetuation of guilt, which is fate.[52] For it is the *hero* (or more precisely his death) in tragedy, that stands in for the imposition of sense in the end.[53] Therefore, it is of some concern to conceive lying not as heroism, not even as that of depositing, but to let it show the entirely non-heroic trait of a lower mode of lying, as illustrated in the deceiver as leading character of comedy,[54] or in the intriguers of the *Trauerspiele* and their at times comic characters. With the lying, the *ruses and dodges*, which Plessner only considers as denunciations of the statecraft and diplomacy that he recommends as 'art', this anything but heroic liar, the schemer and intriguer as known by the baroque *Trauerspiel* and by Benjamin's *Origin of German Mourning Play*, enters the theoretical scene.[55] Benjamin's *Trauerspiel*-book shows that the politics of the 'sovereign decision' in the frenzy of the autocrat's affects, at which the 'schemes' of the intriguers aim, are not at all distinguishable from undecidability. These 'machinations', which expose the powerlessness [*Ohnmacht*] of the creature, show at the same time *Komik* [comicalness] as the 'reverse side' of the melancholy or the sadness proper to this insight, i.e. the 'obligate inner side of mourning which from time to time, like the lining of a dress at the hem or lapel, makes its presence felt' [*die 'obligate Innenseite der Trauer, die ab und zu wie das Futter eines Kleides im Saum oder Revers zur Geltung kommt'*] (*GS* 1.1:304/OT

125–6, translation modified).[56] *Komik* belongs to the *Trauerspiel* itself in the moment of *play* in it[57] and of it: as (exposed) 'deliberateness' of the *intrigue* (*GS* 1.1:261–2/*OT* 82–3, translation modified) as well as 'deliberateness' of the (mourning-)*play*'s joining [*Fügung*], in which one can recognize, still and precisely in chance, the force of 'fate'.[58] Thus instead of committing Benjamin's 'Critique of Violence' to the 'heroics' of the decision (however empty it might be), lying, whose 'impunity' evidences language as 'pure means', allows us to perceive in the field of 'Critique of Violence' the 'fun or lark' [*Spaß*],[59] the laughable [*Lächerliche*] in the mean as well as poor tricks that give the action and the tricky actor away to chance.

Notes

1   An earlier version of this essay was published in German as 'Zur Kritik der Gewalt: Techniken der Übereinkunft, Diplomatie, Lüge', in *Techniken der Übereinkunft. Zur Medialität des Politischen*, eds., Hendrik Blumentrath, Katja Rothe, Sven Werkmeister, Manuela Wünsch, Barbara Wurm (Berlin: Kulturverlag Kadmos, 2009), 37–56. The translators thank Bettine Menke for her very helpful suggestions and advice.

2   Cf. Jacques Derrida, 'Force de loi: Le "fondement mystique de l'autorité"'/ 'Force of Law: The "Mystical Foundation of Authority"', in *Cardozo Law Review* 11.5–6 (July/ August 1990): 919–1045.

3   These are questions of the foundation of the law and of the decision, the differentiation between the mythic violence of law and divine violence (which is determined through/by its incognizability), the act of positing [*Setzung*] becoming 'victorious' as imposition/instauration [*Einsetzung*] of a juridical order countered by the concept of de-posing [*Ent-setzen*], and the impossibility of providing a foundation for decision.

4   Cf. Helmut Lethen, *Verhaltenslehren der Kälte. Lebensversuche zwischen den Kriegen* (Frankfurt a.M.: Suhrkamp, 1994), 77–9 / *Cool Conduct: The Culture of Distance in Weimar Germany*, trans. Don Reneau (Berkeley CA: University of California Press, 2002), 53–5.

5   According to Joseph Vogl, Tönnies' 'typological juxtaposition' established at the same time 'a historical-evolutionary relation between organic unities and contractual mergers', with a 'dualistic pointed emphasis: "community" versus "society", "natural will" versus "arbitrariness", "organism" versus "artifact", "self" versus "person", "comprehension" versus "contract"' (Joseph Vogl, 'Einleitung', in *Gemeinschaften. Positionen zu einer Philosophie des Politischen*, ed. Joseph Vogl [Frankfurt a.M.: Suhrkamp, 1994], 11).

6   Alexander Garcia Düttmann first drew my attention to the relation between Benjamin's 'Critique of Violence' and Plessner's texts several years ago.

7   Helmuth Plessner, 'Staatskunst und Menschlichkeit', first published in *Volkswacht für Schlesien*, Breslau, 9 November 1920, now included in Helmuth Plessner, *Politik – Anthropologie – Philosophie. Aufsätze und Vorträge*, eds. Salvatore Giammusso and Hans-Ulrich Lessing (Munich: Fink, 2001), 47–50; 'Politische Kultur. Vom Wert und Sinn der Staatskunst als Kulturaufgabe', in *Frankfurter Zeitung*, April 1921, reprinted in *Deutsche Universitätszeitung* 8.2 (1953): 6–7, now included in *Politik*

– *Anthropologie – Philosophie*: 51–6; 'Politische Erziehung in Deutschland', in *Die Zukunft* 30.6 (1921): 149–65, now included in *Politik – Anthropologie – Philosophie*, 57–70.

8   Their contiguity can be invoked with the keywords 'New Objectivity' [*Neue Sachlichkeit*], within whose horizon Helmut Lethen places Plessner's *The Limits of Community*, and in turn, he also applies this label to Benjamin, though not to 'Critique of Violence' but rather to the slightly later composed and never published 'Notizen zu einer Arbeit über die Lüge II' (*GS* 6:62–64; 'Notes for a Work on Lying II', c. 1922). Lethen characterizes Plessner's 1924 work as an 'early manifesto [which] attacks the "tyranny of intimacy" …. Plessner shares his aversion for the cult of authenticity with Walter Benjamin' (Lethen, *Verhaltenslehren*, 79 / *Cool Conduct*, 54–5). The ambivalences of Plessner's work on *The Limits* lead, according to Lethen, to the fact that, on the one hand, it constitutes a manifesto of the '*Neue Sachlichkeit*' and, on the other, is an 'advice-giver … meant to fortify the "ethos of rulers and leaders". Plessner consigns the rest of the public to the dark schema of oppression' (Lethen, *Verhaltenslehren*, 94/ *Cool Conduct*, 67, translation modified).

9   Plessner, 'Politische Erziehung', 64. The 'utopia' of the 'overcoming of politics and of its replacement through a purely morally-oriented ethics for states and peoples' has always raised 'a fundamental either-or': 'peace agreement through means of statecraft, indirect and on the basis of opposition … or without any means, purely through the power of trust in the magnanimity and rationality of the enemy, thus in the relinquishment of all one's own power – that is, through humanity' (Plessner, 'Staatskunst und Menschlichkeit', 47–8).

10   *Staatskunst* is usually translated as 'statecraft' or 'statesmanship', but the hyphen here separating the two terms emphasizes that statecraft is originally an 'art' [*Kunst*], politics as the 'art' of government; *trans*.

11   Pre-eminence has always been given to the 'utopia' of the 'overcoming of politics and of its replacement through a purely morally-oriented ethics for states and peoples' (Plessner, 'Staatskunst und Menschlichkeit', 47–8); 'in their appraisal of the political, civil servants and parliamentarians of every orientation are, even today, the same: you get your hands dirty, you do your duty and serve what you identify as the good and true idea. As a consequence, in Germany, at least since Bismarck, the concept of political culture could not arise and even today is nowhere to be found' (Plessner, 'Politische Kultur', 51). Plessner observes the dichotomy between the state-norm [*Staatsnorm*] and the reality of the state [*Staatswirklichkeit*] in its various historical developments (as 'Platonism of our political Romanticism'), in order to counterpose to it the formation of a 'political culture' (Plessner, 'Politische Kultur', 55–6).

12   Plessner, 'Politische Erziehung', 64.

13   This quotation and the following are from Plessner, 'Politische Erziehung', 64.

14   Plessner, 'Politische Erziehung', 64–5. Here we could compare Plessner's theses with the parallel case of Benjamin's arguments about 'military law', 'militarism', 'conscription', and pacifism, which aim at a 'really effective critique' of 'law-preserving violence' as well: 'Rather, such a critique coincides with the critique of all legal violence – that is, with the critique of legal or executive force – and cannot be performed by any lesser program' (*GS* 2.1:187/*SW* 1:241).

15   To this trait corresponds conversely the fact that '[i]n the great criminal' (according to a tradition that can be traced back to Hölderlin and Hegel) this foreign, not state-owned or state-controlled, violence confronts the state and modern law 'with the

threat of positing a new legal order [*neues Recht zu setzen*], a threat that even today, despite its impotence, in important instances makes the public shiver [*erschauern*] as it did in primeval times. The state, however, fears this violence simply for its law-positing [*rechtsetzenden*] character' (*GS* 2.1:186/*SW* 1:241, translation modified). Also about the strike and martial law cf. *GS* 2.1:183–6/*SW* 1:239–41.

16 Cf.: 'Unlike law [*Recht*], which acknowledges in the "decision" determined by place and time a metaphysical category that gives it a claim to critical evaluation, a consideration of the police institution encounters nothing essential at all'. It shows rather that the state 'can no longer guarantee through the legal system [its] empirical ends' (*GS* 2.1:189/*SW* 1:243).

17 Here we can identify another literary model, E.T.A Hoffmann's *Das Fräulein von Scuderi* (*Mademoiselle de Scudéri*), which intimately links the birth of police to the uncanniness of the widespread secret suspicion of clandestinity. In the list of the works read by Benjamin, it is listed as no. 697, in chronological proximity to 'Critique of Violence', reflected in the reading of Georges Sorel's works, in particular no. 734 (Georges Sorel, *Réflexions sur la violence*, Paris, 1908), and of no. 735 (Erich Unger, *Politik und Metaphysik*, Berlin 1921). Cf. 'Verzeichnis der gelesenen Schriften', *GS* 7.1:437–76, here 446–7.

18 Benjamin's formulas of the 'impure' or 'unnatural combination', of the 'ignominious mixture', of the bastardization (of forms) in the law have been read by Derrida as an emphasis on purity or purification. See, for instance, the following formula by Benjamin: 'Once again all the eternal forms are open to pure divine violence, which myth bastardized with law' (*GS* 2.1:203/*SW* 1:252). On the basis of Derrida's interpretation, such formulas have been in turn discussed with reference to the premise and modality of Benjamin's 'critique'. On this debate see *Cardozo Law Review* 11.5–6 (July–August 1990), 'Deconstruction and the possibility of justice'; *Cardozo Law Review* 13.4 (December 1991), 'On the necessity of violence for any possibility of justice'. In particular, among others, see Samuel Weber, 'In the name of the law', in *Cardozo Law Review* 11.5–6 (July/August 1990): 1515–38; Samuel Weber, 'Deconstruction before the name. Some preliminary remarks on deconstruction and violence', in *Cardozo Law Review* 13.4 (December 1991): 1181–90; for the transposition of the debate into the German context, see Anselm Haverkamp, ed., *Gewalt und Gerechtigkeit. Derrida-Benjamin* (Frankfurt a.M.: Suhrkamp, 1994).

19 Derrida, 'Force of law', 1037.

20 Cf. *GS* 2.1:185–7/*SW* 1:240–2. On the one hand, the violence of law as 'law-positing' must have become also 'law-preserving' and, vice versa, there is no 'law-preserving' violence without the act of founding (of law), which is inaccessible to conservation [*Erhaltung*]. On the other hand, as law-preserving, this violence must exclude all (other) law-positing violence, and vice versa, as law-positing violence it must contest the right of law-preserving violence.

21 Benjamin talks about the 'cycle maintained by mythic forms of law' when he considers their 'breaking' (*GS* 2.1:202/*SW* 1:251).

22 Plessner, 'Politische Erziehung', 64.

23 Cf. *GS* 2.1:196/*SW* 1:248. *This* distinction was what provoked Derrida's reading, and the questioning of the type and (im)possibility (of the purity) of this decisive distinction. But it is precisely from this that, according to Benjamin, results the strict 'ultimate indecidability of all legal problems': 'For it is never reason that decides on the justification of means and the justness of ends: fate-imposing violence

[*schicksalhafte Gewalt*] decides on the former, and God on the latter. An insight that is uncommon only because of the stubborn prevailing habit of conceiving those just ends as ends of a possible law – that is, not only as generally valid (which follows analytically from the attribute of justice) but also as capable of generalization, which, as could be shown, contradicts this attribute. For ends that in one situation are just, generally to be accepted, and valid are so in no other situation, no matter how similar the situations may be in other respects' (*GS* 2.1:196/*SW* 1:247–8, translation modified).

24 Also in Plessner's works which are not actually concerned with a strict analysis of the law, the law [*Recht*] does not present the defence against the 'impure means' of politics. Cf. Plessner, 'Politische Erziehung', 62–4.

25 Plessner, 'Politische Erziehung', 64.

26 Benjamin talks about the 'latent presence of violence in a legal institution'; if the awareness of this fact disappears, the institution 'falls into decay'. This is Benjamin's critique of parliamentarianism: 'what a parliament achieves in vital affairs can be only those legal decrees that in their origin and outcome are afflicted with violence'. By this Benjamin also rejects parliamentarianism as a possible candidate in his quest for 'means of political agreement that are in principle nonviolent': parliamentary debates, and especially 'compromises', only crystallizes the (self-) misjudgement of this legal institution, which is a law-positing one. Cf. *GS* 2.1:190–91/*SW* 1:244.

27 The keywords rhetoric and 'technique of interlocution [*Unterredung*]' emphasize that the 'pure means' *language* and *technique* are not in conflict with each other.

28 Plessner looks for 'points of contact' for the instruction of those whose tasks consist 'in the disposition of the social and political-economic means of power [*Machtmittel*] of the nation, such as money, industry, science, press, public opinion, sympathies and antipathies, cultural productivity as colonizing and persuasive power', explicitly also in the 'old and almost forgotten university discipline of rhetoric', 'the science and art of speech and interlocution [*Unterredung*]', 'methods of negotiation (bargaining is only one among many), leading a discussion, polemics and defense' (Plessner, 'Politische Erziehung', 67–8).

29 In 'Politische Kultur' (1921) Plessner strives to distinguish between 'political culture' and politics, which, 'detached from definite ends with regard to content', only counts 'as mere technique and matter of skill, it [politics] has nothing to do with culture as embodiment of the over-ordinary [*Über-Alltäglichen*], as is today often asserted; it belongs to civilization like all technique(s)' (Plessner, 'Politische Kultur', 51). Plessner correspondingly argues for a 'political culture' of great politicians, who would be 'not mere virtuosos and old hands [*Routiniers*], but rather artists' (Plessner, 'Politische Kultur', 55–6).

30 Also Derrida briefly notes that this point is noteworthy. Cf., Derrida, 'Force of law', 1019.

31 Through the 'impunity of lying' the use of language is delivered from logic or from the ban, from the circular foundation of im-position [*Ein-setzung*] of something. Cf. Peter Fenves, 'Testing right – lying in view of justice', in *Cardozo Law Review* 13.4 (December 1991): 1081–113, in particular 1108–12.

32 Plessner, 'Politische Erziehung', 64.

33 Benjamin writes: 'It is not accidental that the unrestrained speaking out of everything [*schrankenloses Alles-Heraus-Sagen*] is not infrequently found in people, who are also often externally unkempt (the vegetarian type)[;] the contrast to these is the well-groomed type of the diplomat'. But this seems to be 'not accidental'

because 'lying is a dietary vital necessity for all those people for whom the last strong intention to the truth is not constantly present without interruption'. This 'intention' obviously must be distinguished from 'honesty', the commitment to which is failed (*GS* 6:63). Benjamin also writes: 'lying presents a constitutive relation to speech (so that lying through silence is immoral)' (*GS* 6:64).

34   Cf. the solution through '*nur auf dem Wege über die Sachen*', by being concerned with 'things' or 'matters', instead of the 'direct' 'resolution of conflict between man and man' in 'Critique of Violence' (*GS* 2.1:191/*SW* 1:244). Paul Scheerbart's novel *Lesabéndio* (1913) exposes the 'most outward, purest surface' [*äußerste, reinste Oberfläche*], to which *Deutung* or reading has to abide, so that 'all relations that could mislead to a confused inwardness, to interpretation and explanation, are kept away'. Scheerbart's novel thereby presents the 'frame of a rigorous *Sachlichkeit*'; Benjamin, 'Paul Scheerbart: Lesabéndio', *GS* 2.2:618–20. See also Benjamin's essay 'Robert Walser', *GS* 2.1:324–8/*SW* 2:257–61, in particular *GS* 2.1:326–7/*SW* 2:258–9, and Benjamin's letter to Martin Buber of 17 July 1916, *GB* 1:325–7.

35   'For whereas the legal system at its origin, trusting to its victorious power, is content to defeat law-breaking wherever it happens to appear, and deception, having itself no trace of power about it, was ... exempt from punishment ... the law of a later period, lacking confidence in its own power, no longer felt itself [as did the law in Roman and ancient Germanic periods] a match for all other instances of violence' (*GS* 2.1:192/*SW* 1:245, translation modified).

36   Benjamin provides some clues for this: 'the law of a later period, lacking confidence in its own power ... turns against fraud, therefore, not out of moral considerations but for fear of the acts of violence [*Gewalttätigkeiten*] that it might unleash in the defrauded party. Since such fear conflicts with the violent nature [*Gewaltnatur*] of law derived from its origins, such ends are inappropriate to the justified means of law. They evince not only the decay of its own sphere but also a diminution of pure means. For in prohibiting fraud, law restricts the use of wholly nonviolent means because they could produce reactive violence' (*GS* 2.1:192/*SW* 1:245 translation modified).

37   Also according to Plessner, lawyers (not though judges or public prosecutors) who proceed case by case can present the type of an 'art of politics'. Cf. Plessner, 'Politische Erziehung', 62–4. He is not thereby interested, however, in a critique of and, with it, strict rejection of, law.

38   The discussion of diplomacy is followed by the sections on 'law-positing' and 'law-preserving violence' and furthermore on the positing [*Setzung*] as im-position [*Einsetzung*] ('*what* is being established [*eingesetzt*] as law'), then by the quest for the detachment from that 'grave problematic of all legal violence' [*schweren Problematik jeder Rechtsgewalt*], as 'the quest for ... other kinds of violence than all those envisaged by legal theory' [*Frage nach andern Arten der Gewalt ... als alle Rechtstheorie ins Auge faßt*]: i.e., violence as 'manifestation' (*GS* 2.1:196–8/*SW* 1:247–9, translation modified).

39   Plessner, to the contrary, talks about the 'education towards the understanding of politics ... inwardly and outwardly ... [education] towards statecraft [*Staatskunst*]', and says 'these things are somewhat too important that one would cloak delicate defensive movement with demands to do nothing, but rather let it develop organically' (Plessner, 'Politische Erziehung', 58).

40   If, according to Benjamin, 'all violence as a means' is 'either law-positing or law-preserving', or otherwise forfeits 'all validity' and therefore 'even in the most

favourable case, partakes in the problematic of law itself', then – despite Benjamin – it does in no way follow that, because techniques of interlocution or diplomacy are means 'beyond all legal systems', they are *therefore* no violence (*GS* 2.1:190 and 195/*SW* 1:243 and 247, translation modified). According to Derrida, it will nevertheless 'soon' be evident 'how this non-violence [of pure means] is not without affinity to pure violence' (Derrida, 'Force of law', 1021): that is, insofar as they withdraw themselves from the legal system and are the de-position [*Ent-Setzung*] of the violence of im-position, of the legal order. Samuel Weber discusses in contrast to '*Setzung*', positing, founding, always a positing of a borderline '*Grenzsetzung*' (*GS* 2.1:198/*SW* 1:248), the undoing [*entsühnend*], expiating divine violence ('Deconstruction before the name', esp. 1184–6).

41   Benjamin introduces some considerations on 'pure means in politics as analogous to those which govern peaceful intercourse between private persons' (*GS* 2.1:193/*SW* 1:245). However near in relation to the 'praise of diplomacy' Benjamin's 'Critique of Violence' and Plessner's texts of the same epoch are, the convergence of diplomacy and proletarian general strike as carried out by Benjamin (*GS* 2.1:195/*SW* 1:247) would be entirely foreign to Plessner. The operating of the professional associations [*Standesvereinigungen*] would well be the only category that Plessner would have for the strike, and *this* is by no means the 'proletarian general strike' Benjamin has in mind.

42   Fenves argues that 'the extreme form of lying can only be thought as the striking down of the very form of truth: that form owes its origin to the form-giving power of subjectivity in which veracity is supposed to be secured', also in reference to *mendacity*, which would be the counterpart to (failed mandatory) honesty: 'Extreme mendacity [*Verlogenheit*], which is anything but false representation and which undermines every representational norm, is "objective" to the extent that it strikes at the power to give form and thus, in the end, at legislation in its entirety' (Fenves, 'Testing right', 1113). This is the analogy between lying and the proletarian general strike.

43   Hamacher discusses 'law-imposing violence', its ambiguity (Werner Hamacher, 'Affirmative, strike', in *Cardozo Law Review* 13.4 [1991, 'On the necessity of violence for any possibility of justice'], 1133–57, esp. 1134–6), and indicates a 'break through the cycle of laws and their decay' (1139): 'Pure violence does not posit, it "deposes": it is not performative, but affirmative' (1138). 'In all acts, linguistic as well as political (that is, political in the narrow sense), in all acts of legislation as well as jurisprudence, at least an element of this affirmative function – this deposing, pure violence – is in effect' (1139; and cf. fn. 12). 'Deposing' 'is irreducible to any presentation' (1139).

44   Cf. in contrast the strike, which aims at attaining 'certain ends', and is thus 'violence', which 'is able to found and modify legal conditions' (*GS* 2.1:184–5/*SW* 1:239–40).

45   Benjamin begins 'Critique of Violence' with the discussion of the relation between ends and means (*GS* 2.1:179/*SW* 1:236) and subjects to critique the 'common basic dogma' of all legal theories that 'just ends can be attained by justified means, justified means used for just ends' (*GS* 2.1:180–1, 195–6/*SW* 1:237, 247). In this sense, also the 'factuality' [*Sachlichkeit*], which characterizes 'pure means', technique(s) and diplomacy, would not be a means to the end of conflict resolution; rather, independently of how indirect and mediatorial, it is their mode or *medium* (*GS* 2.1:192, 195/*SW* 1:244–5, 247).

46   Benjamin's argument about the 'pure [divine] violence' is the attempt to withdraw deposing [*Ent-Setzung*] from any hypostatization into presence.

47 'All language imparts itself ... That which in a spiritual entity is impartable is its
    language ... [T]his impartable immediately is language itself. ... What of a spiritual
    entity is impartable, in this it imparts itself. ... [A]ll language imparts itself in itself;
    it is in the purest sense the "medium" of the impartation. The medial, which is the
    immediacy of all mental imparting, is the fundamental problem of linguistic theory'
    [Jede Sprache teilt sich selbst mit. ... (D)as, was an einem geistigen Wesen mitteilbar
    ist, ist seine Sprache. ... (D)ieses Mitteilbare ist unmittelbar die Sprache selbst. ... Was
    an einem geistigen Wesen mitteilbar ist, in dem teilt es sich mit. ... (J)ede Sprache
    teilt sich in sich selbst mit, sie ist im reinsten Sinne das 'Medium' der Mitteilung. Das
    Mediale, das ist die Unmittelbarkeit aller geistigen Mitteilung, ist das Grundproblem
    der Sprachtheorie] ('On Language as Such and on the Language of Man', GS 2.1:142/
    SW 1:63–4, translation modified).

48 In his letter to Martin Buber (of 17 July 1916) Benjamin attempts to think
    the Wirksamkeit [effectiveness] of language: 'not through the communication
    [Vermittlung] of contents', which would be tied to 'motives' (for actions), but through
    'the crystal-clear elimination of the unsayable in language', which 'precisely coincides
    with the properly unadorned and sober writing style [Schreibart]' (GB 1:325–7);
    here however Benjamin uses the concept of means in the limitation of 'language and
    writing demeaned to a mere means': '[the word] taken as means proliferates' (GB
    1:326); cf. the 'pure' breaking away from motives as 'inwardness' in 'Paul Scheerbarts
    Lesabéndio' (GS 2.2:618).

49 The 'manifestation' is negatively determined by the fact that it is not a means (GS
    2.1:196/SW 1:248).

50 To this corresponds – in Benjamin's essay 'On language' – the irony of the
    immediacy of judgment 'on good and evil', which will have generated what
    supposedly it only judges, namely evil first with the distinction between good and
    evil. Cf. GS 2.1:152–4/SW 1:70–2.

51 The (divine) destruction of law would be the abstention from that (and all)
    im-position at the site of the stroke [des Schlags], which would be neither end nor
    means. The status of this manifestation and of this argument has been discussed
    primarily with and following Derrida. Cf. Derrida, 'Force of law' and the literature
    listed in note 19.

52 Peter Fenves points this out, in reference to Benjamin's definition in The Origin of
    German Mourning Play of tragedy through the death of the tragic hero: 'But this
    very heroism and the tragic framework from which it derives its power marks the
    ambiguity in the strike whose features Benjamin draws so selectively from Sorel; such
    ambiguity is radicalized to the point of paradox when one, unlike Benjamin, does not
    remain silent about its essentially mythical character. Perhaps for this very reason the
    mass strike falls prey to the Verfallsprozess itself and thereby falls into precisely that
    sphere which it seeks to destroy – namely, the hold of the mythic. Entirely different
    is the lie. Its mythic character is everywhere apparent, and the denial of the "right" to
    lie is nothing short of its unwitting recognition' (Fenves, 'Testing right', 1112).

53 According to Benjamin (following Lukács and Rosenzweig), the tragic hero is the
    mute hero: as such a hero – the hero mute in death – the hero is still prisoner of
    myth, assigned to the words (not given to him) of his future spectators.

54 So far Fenves alone has noticed this: 'Not without reason does the tragic hero meet
    his other in the principal character of comedy, namely, the deceiver' (Fenves, 'Testing
    right', 1112); however, he examines the status of lying almost exclusively through his
    interpretation of Kant.

55   According to Benjamin's *Origin of German Mourning Play*, 'the insight into
      diplomacy and the manipulation of all the political machinations' on the baroque
      stage had been presented through the intriguer, whom the baroque *Trauerspiel* could
      only develop as busy 'schemer'. This 'insight' explicitly counters a political theology
      of the sovereign (*GS* 1.1:243, 267/*OT* 62, 88, translation modified).

56   Here too we deal in surfaces, the 'inner side' of a dress is itself a surface (no
      interiority). These *comic* sides are shown mainly in the plays by Calderón and
      Shakespeare, which thereby, on the one hand, distinguish themselves from the
      German *Trauerspiele* and, on the other, 'illuminate' them (cf. *GS* 1.1:306–7, 368/
      OT 127–8, 192). 'The finest exemplifications of the *Trauerspiel* are not those which
      adhere strictly to the rules, but where the *Trauerspiel* – by playful transitions – lets
      the *Lustspiel* resonate in it' [*Das Trauerspiel erreicht ja seine Höhe nicht in den
      regelrechten Exemplaren, sondern dort, wo mit spielhaften Übergängen es das Lustspiel
      in sich anklingen macht*] (*GS* 1.1:306/*OT* 127, translation modified).

57   That is the intriguer's play (in the mourning play): an 'accidental' as well as 'planned
      and calculated' play (*GS* 1.1:262/*OT* 83).

58   Cf. Benjamin, 'Calderón's *El Mayor Monstruo, Los Celos* and Hebbel's *Herodes und
      Marianne*: Comments on the problem of historical drama' (1923), *GS* 2.1:260/*SW*
      1:373. Cf. Bettine Menke, 'Reflexion des Trauer-Spiels. Pedro Calderón de la Barca
      El mayor mónstruo, los celos nach Walter Benjamin', in *Literatur als Philosophie.
      Philosophie als Literatur*, eds. Eva Horn, Bettine Menke and Christoph Menke
      (Munich: Fink, 2006), 269–77.

59   In the play of the intriguer, effects of chance [*Zufalls*], the accidental [*Zu-Fall*] of
      (also cheap) effects, the 'Comic – or more precisely: the pure fun or lark' [*Komik –
      richtiger: der reine Spaß*] – belong to the *Trauerspiel* (*GS* 1.1:304/*OT* 125, translation
      modified).

Works cited

Derrida, Jacques. 'Force de loi: Le "fondement mystique de l'autorité"'/ 'Force of law: The
      "mystical foundation of authority"'. Translated by Mary Quaintance. *Cardozo Law
      Review* 11.5–6 (July/August 1990): 919–1045.

Fenves, Peter. 'Testing right – lying in view of justice'. *Cardozo Law Review* 13.4
      (December 1991): 1081–113.

Hamacher, Werner. 'Afformative, strike'. Translated by Dana Hollander. *Cardozo Law
      Review* 13.4 (1991): 1133–57.

Haverkamp, Anselm, ed. *Gewalt und Gerechtigkeit. Derrida-Benjamin*. Frankfurt a.M.:
      Suhrkamp, 1994.

Lethen, Helmut. *Verhaltenslehren der Kälte. Lebensversuche zwischen den Kriegen*.
      Frankfurt a.M.: Suhrkamp, 1994.

—*Cool Conduct: The Culture of Distance in Weimar Germany*. Translated by Don Reneau.
      Berkeley, CA: University of California Press, 2002.

Menke, Bettine. 'Reflexion des Trauer-Spiels. Pedro Calderón de la Barca *El mayor
      mónstruo, los celos* nach Walter Benjamin'. In *Literatur als Philosophie. Philosophie
      als Literatur*. Edited by Eva Horn, Bettine Menke and Christoph Menke. München:
      Wilhelm Fink, 2006, 253–80.

Plessner, Helmuth. 'Politische Erziehung in Deutschland' (1921). In Helmuth Plessner,

Politik – Anthropologie – Philosophie. Aufsätze und Vorträge. Edited by Salvatore
    Giammusso and Hans-Ulrich Lessing. Munich: Fink, 2001, 57–70.
—'Politische Kultur. Vom Wert und Sinn der Staatskunst als Kulturaufgabe' (1921). In
    Helmuth Plessner, *Politik – Anthropologie – Philosophie. Aufsätze und Vorträge*. Edited
    by Salvatore Giammusso and Hans-Ulrich Lessing. Munich: Fink, 2001, 51–56.
—'Staatskunst und Menschlichkeit' (1920). In Helmuth Plessner, *Politik – Anthropologie –
    Philosophie. Aufsätze und Vorträge*. Edited by Salvatore Giammusso and Hans-Ulrich
    Lessing. Munich: Fink, 2001, 47–50.
Vogl, Joseph. 'Einleitung'. In *Gemeinschaften. Positionen zu einer Philosophie des
    Politischen*. Edited by Joseph Vogl. Frankfurt a.M.: Suhrkamp, 1994, 7–27.
Weber, Samuel. 'In the name of the law'. In *Cardozo Law Review* 11.5–6 (July/August
    1990): 1515–38.
—'Deconstruction before the name. Some preliminary remarks on deconstruction and
    violence'. In *Cardozo Law Review* 13.4 (December 1991): 1181–90.

2

The Ambiguity of Ambiguity in Benjamin's 'Critique of Violence'

Alison Ross

For the purposes of analytical clarity it is possible to distinguish a number of different ways that Benjamin's 'Critique of Violence' uses the term 'ambiguity' [*Zweideutigkeit*]. Whereas in Benjamin's late work, 'ambiguity' can mark an equivocal value, as in the formula he uses in 'Paris, the Capital of the Nineteenth Century' (1935) to describe the components of the dialectical image as 'ambiguous' (*AP* 10), the 'Critique of Violence' typifies the way the term is used in the early work to confer an exclusively pejorative meaning. In general, ambiguity in the early work is used to condemn the lack of clarity and absence of truth that Benjamin defines as attributes of 'myth'. The position is put in stark terms in the 1924 essay, 'Goethe's *Elective Affinities*'. In this essay Benjamin links ambiguity to guilt, fate and ritualistic life. One of the significant theses in this essay is Benjamin's critique of ritualistic life. Empty rituals do not provide adequate orientation for human beings; they proffer ambiguous forms, which condemn human beings to a fateful existence. The key to Benjamin's position in this essay is the contrast he draws between mythic life and theological perception. The thesis that mythic life is a life which founders in ambiguity is supported in the essay through the opposition between mythic ambiguity and the clarity of theological perception. In general, the opposition is marked by references to the ambiguous mysticism of word use or silence in the case of myth, and the clarity of logos in the case of theology.

The functions of the lack of clarity that is the defining feature of mythic ambiguity in the 'Critique of Violence', however, are ambiguous. For instance, Benjamin describes the law as 'demonically ambiguous' and he cites as evidence for this description Anatole France's ironic claim that 'Poor and rich are equally forbidden to spend the night under the bridges' (*SW* 1:249). Since only some in fact enjoy this 'right', the 'equality' of the law is shown to pretend to a false universality that disguises its material interest in the protection of class interests. On the other hand, when Benjamin describes the ambiguity of myth in the essay, he refers specifically to its indeterminacy. A further complicating factor in the position of 'ambiguity' in the essay in this respect is the connection that Benjamin tries to make between the features of legal and mythic violence. Benjamin's essay identifies how legal violence is not restricted to the imposition of punishment, but to inducing feelings of anxiety and guilt. As evidence for this claim, Benjamin refers to the earliest legal statutes as 'unwritten' and the 'retribution' their transgression incurs as something that 'befalls' an 'unsuspecting victim': 'A man can unwittingly infringe upon them and thus incur retribution … But however unluckily it may befall its unsuspecting victim, its occurrence is, in the understanding of the law, not chance, but fate showing itself again in its deliberate ambiguity' (*SW* 1:249). The anxiety and dread that 'law' induces points to its intimacy with 'the deliberate ambiguity' of 'fate'. However, this connection between fate and law also points to the difference between the deceitful subjugation that law requires in its 'demonic ambiguity' and the indeterminacy that defines fate's (and law's) 'deliberate ambiguity'.

There are a series of other examples in the essay, which aim to tie law to mythic fate and violence through remarking on law's 'ambiguity'. Thus he claims that the line that neither party may cross established in the peace treaty is an ambiguous line (*SW* 1:249); he also contends that the functioning of the law is ambiguous insofar as the subject's ignorance of the law is no answer to the law (*SW* 1:249); and, as we saw in the case of Anatole France, that law 'enforces' a false equality. Each of these uses of ambiguity to characterize law assists Benjamin's attempt to link 'law' and 'myth' and to characterize both as engendering guilt in their use of violence. Hence he claims that the punishment of Niobe in Greek myth is 'ambiguous' and that it leaves her 'more guilty than before' (*SW* 1:248). The general intent behind this use of ambiguity to link law with mythic fate is the contrast the essay attempts to make between divine and mythic violence in which divine violence would have the 'good' effect of expiation and mythic violence the 'bad' effect of guilt. This opposition between the two kinds of violence seems to mirror in a dense and abbreviated form the well-developed contrast between the pejoratively coded mythic life and the venerated access to theological perception in cases of the moral decision in the essay on Goethe's novel. Although these uses of ambiguity in the violence-essay service this general polemical point regarding myth, they intend by ambiguity quite different things, which range from the deceitful pretence of universal enforcement required for submission to law, to the indeterminacy of law that induces guilt.

Admittedly, the ambiguity in his use of ambiguity may be a consequence of the essay's condensed and inelegant schema of argumentation. Among the accomplished works of his early period – such as his rejected habilitation-thesis on the *Trauerspiel*, the essay on language, his work on the romantic concept of criticism and his essay on 'Goethe's *Elective Affinities*' – the essay on violence does not stand out either as a work of significant merit on its chosen topic, or an important essay within Benjamin's early corpus. In effect, many of the key terms used in the essay are substantially meaningless without the possibility of clarifying references to other pieces from the same period. It is strange, then, that one of the prominent modes of its recent scholarly reception takes the form of commentary that brackets out other pieces from Benjamin's early oeuvre and focuses obsessively on particular phrases from the violence-essay alone. Such commentary has come at the price of distorting Benjamin's position on divine violence, as if he intended by this term to advocate non-violence.[1] Whatever might be said about the essay's conceptual untidiness, Benjamin nowhere states and defends such a position; it would behove those who advance it on his behalf to explain the omission of any statement to this effect in his essay.

In an attempt to provide a defence of the probity of revolutionary violence that would be secure from the claim that this position was merely a partisan perspective, Benjamin's essay takes up the thesis that such violence can be purified of human interests and akin therefore to the justness of divine violence: 'For it is never reason that decides on the justification of means and the justness of ends: fate-imposed violence decides on the former, and God on the latter' (*SW* 1:247). The position of the essay requires that he draw connections between law and myth, on one side, and revolutionary and divine violence on the other. He intends to defend the hope that revolutionary violence is the exercise of wholly 'other violence' than the violence deployed in the means/end schema of the law (*SW* 1:247–8). This 'other violence', which he claims is attested to in the prosecution of just ends in cases of divine violence, would be able to depose legal violence and with it destroy too the 'bloody' mystifications of myth (*SW* 1:249–50). For the purpose of articulating this position, the different characteristics of the phenomena the essay pairs together are less important than the respective grades of the pairings they facilitate and the implacable quality of the opposition between them.

Divine and revolutionary violence have the virtue of clarity; mythic and legal violence the fault of ambiguity. As a corollary, perhaps we should understand the ambiguity of ambiguity as a minor casualty in the complex motivations underpinning Benjamin's articulation of his position on divine violence. On the other hand, the different ways ambiguity is used here may be the consequence of Benjamin's polemical aims regarding law, which overstep the resources he can cite in support of his position. In this case, the manifold uses of ambiguity are significant because they help build the comprehensiveness of his case against law: ambiguity has a general pejorative sense, and it is also defined as a feature of mythic fate. Hence the abundant use of the term, whatever the various specifications in its meaning one could discern, assists in building up the negative image of the law that is one of the main goals of the essay and for which the destructive force of divine/revolutionary violence is warranted. Either way, the various meanings of ambiguity in the essay service a critical position on the law and legal violence: the question to ask is whether, given the use of these different meanings within the essay, this position is warranted.

I would like to defend the thesis that Benjamin's 'Critique of Violence' uses 'ambiguity' in different ways. Further, I would like to argue that the different uses of ambiguity service his essay's overarching polemical goals, but do so without the required conceptual precision. In short: his polemic against the law exceeds the grounds that support it; the seeming cogency of his position profits from an ambiguous account of the connections between law and myth. However, if we consult contemporaneous texts from Benjamin's early writing, it is possible to construct a cogent position regarding his objections to ritualized life, for which 'ambiguity' is the key marker. This position may be used to reconstruct the stakes of his polemic against the ambiguity of law. To make this case I will first provide an analytical account of the different uses he makes of ambiguity in the violence-essay. Next, I will consider the points of coordination between these various uses and the polemic against ambiguity in Benjamin's contemporaneous essay on 'Goethe's *Elective Affinities*', and specifically the opposition that is put forward there between the lack of clarity of mythic life and the theological perception of truth in logos. Finally, I will comment on the use of the concept of ambiguity in Benjamin's later work and consider what the shift in its status tells us about Benjamin's early thinking on the topic of violence and law.

The ambiguity in Benjamin's critique of the ambiguity of legal violence

In 'Critique of Violence' Benjamin claims that the law is itself a type of mythic violence. To defend this assimilation of law to myth, Benjamin makes much of the fact that the earliest legal statutes were not written down. As a consequence it was 'uncertain' when the law was transgressed, or whether acts that did transgress it, would incur 'retribution'. The significance and 'deepest purpose' of this uncertainty lies for Benjamin in 'the sphere of fate in which it originates' (SW 1:242). The reference to the uncertainty of fate foreshadows the essay's later transposition of the components of its objections to law as objections to the features of mythic life. The theme of law's uncertainty understood as the consequence of the non-discursive status of the law raises an obvious objection. If Benjamin wishes to tie law to myth and to do so on the grounds of their shared connection to fate, how does he extend the claim of uncertainty that is the basis of un-articulated rules to the *written* law? The claim that the punitive exercise of the law is ambiguous seems to be the way that he attempts to secure this point. Benjamin argues that it is uncertain whether transgression of the law will end in violent retribution. This ambiguity over whether transgressions elicit penalty aligns law to the uncertainty of myth and through myth to fate. The key point seems to be that such uncertainty is the factor that generates anxiety and guilt.

Law has the authority to punish transgressions. However, the authority to punish what it codifies as a transgression is ambiguous since whether and when it detects the transgression is uncertain. Law exerts a menacing presence precisely in its status as a *potential* threat of detection and punishment. In his treatment of legal statutes, Benjamin draws attention to the fact that ignorance of the law warrants no exemption from the applicability of the law's punitive force. Further, despite its appearance as a neutral broker, the law understands 'equality before the law' in the same way that, as Anatole France ironically comments, 'poor and rich are equally forbidden to spend the night under the bridges' (SW 1:249). Benjamin claims that these latter ambiguities in the law align its operations to those of myth: they reign in a threatening fashion because the boundaries they police are uncertain. As he writes in his 'Paralipomena to "On the Concept of History"': 'The basic conception in myth is the world as punishment – punishment which actually engenders those to whom punishment is due' (SW 4:403). The punitive dimension of myth intensifies the existential effects of the fact that, like the law, what it prohibits is not clear (i.e., it is not articulated) and whether it punishes is not certain ('there is always hope of eluding [the] ... arm [of the law]' [SW 1:242]). This is the import of Benjamin's claim that neither myth nor legal statutes have any relation to truth. The claim rests on the status of articulation as meritorious in Benjamin's thinking. The value of truth and clarity that is attached to the articulate word and opposed to the mystifications of the mute and the taciturn as well as the lack of clarity in 'chatter' can be unpacked in relation to Benjamin's early reflections on language.[2]

Legal violence, he argues, operates according to the 'impurity' or 'bastard form', of instrumental means-end logic (*SW* 1:252). It is alienated from the clarity of truth in much the same way as Benjamin claims that the instrumental category of bourgeois language is alienated from the creative word of God and the naming language of man. His 1916 essay on language contrasts the 'invalid and empty' ... 'bourgeois conception of language' in which the 'means of communication is the word, its object factual, and its addressee a human being', and 'the other conception of language' which 'knows no means, no object, and no addressee of communication'. This 'other' language is man's communication with God: 'It means: *in the name, the mental being of man communicates itself to God*' (*SW* 1:65). Similarly, divine violence is pure violence in Benjamin's view because it is akin to the clarity of 'man's communication with God': it does not prosecute human interests and it annihilates therefore the partial class interests shielded by the 'neutral' operation of the law.

Although the 'Critique of Violence' does not always make the crucial connections, such as the nature of the link between myth and the law, or articulate speech and truth entirely convincing, Benjamin's description of the law as a type of mythic violence helps to specify what he objects to in myth. Myth exerts an imperious and ominous presence. Myth gives an account of nature that relies only on nature's forms to make this account. When they live in the perspective of myth and seek guidance from mythic forms, human beings are caught in a situation where they must decipher the communication of important meaning, e.g., precepts which potentially have punitive consequences, in non-discursive forms. The ambiguity of such forms as precepts is insuperable. Their non-discursive status means that any meaning can be discerned in them. The mythic life is lived in the context of guilt because it takes as the guide for answering demanding questions sensuous forms, which can only offer their interpreter debilitating ambiguity. Guilt is the inevitable consequence since edicts that have been issued will have been disregarded; no exculpation follows from the uncertainty about the content of these edicts and the unintentional feature of their transgression, only the anticipation of retribution. This is the significance of the references to mythic ambiguity as the relevant frame for understanding the *potential* detection of wrongdoing by law.

The connection between ambiguity and guilt is one of the central tenets in Benjamin's characterization of the shared features of legal and mythic violence. However, the grounds for this characterization merge together the two different senses of ambiguity in the essay. For instance, Benjamin claims that one of the features of legal and mythic violence that defines its opposition to the annihilating force of divine violence, is that such violence 'is not ... destructive' (*SW* 1:248). He uses this phrase to describe the case of the violent retribution wrought on Niobe: the violence that 'bursts upon' her 'from the uncertain, ambiguous sphere of fate ... is not', he writes, 'actually destructive' ('*Die Gewalt bricht also aus der unsicheren, zweideutigen Sphäre des Schicksals über Niobe herein. Sie ist nicht eigentlich zerstörend*', GS 2.1:197/*SW* 1:248). Niobe is left behind 'both as an eternally mute bearer of guilt and as a boundary stone on the frontier between men and gods' (*SW* 1:248). The annihilating force of divine violence in the case of God's destruction of the company of Korah, on the other hand, is expiatory. This must mean that what mythic violence does not destroy is what he calls, in 'Fate and Character', 'the guilt context of the living' ('*Schicksal ist der Schuldzusammenhang des Lebendigen*', GS 2.1:175/SW 1:204).[3]

However, in defending this position Benjamin draws not just on the 'deliberate ambiguity' of fate that engenders guilt, but also on the 'demonic ambiguity' of the deceitful universality of the law.

Constitutional law, the establishing of frontiers, 'after all the wars of the mythic age, is the primal phenomenon of all lawmaking violence' (*SW* 1:248–9). Benjamin comments:

> Here we see most clearly that power, more than the most extravagant gain in property, is what is guaranteed by all lawmaking violence. When frontiers are decided, the adversary is not simply annihilated; indeed, he is accorded rights even when the victor's superiority in power is complete. And these are, in a demonically ambiguous [*dämonisch-zweideutiger*] way, 'equal' rights: for both parties to the treaty, it is the same line that may not be crossed. Here appears, in a terribly primitive form, the mythic ambiguity of laws [*mythische Zweideutigkeit der Gesetze*] that may not be 'infringed' – the same ambiguity to which Anatole France refers satirically when he says, 'Poor and rich are equally forbidden to spend the night under the bridges'. (*GS* 2.1:198/SW 1:249).

The 'line' that cannot be crossed is demonically ambiguous because it dissimulates the power differential that underpins the law, engaging in the pretence that the law is an equal broker and that 'it is the same line that may not be crossed'.

There is also another respect in which establishing frontiers is significant for understanding the law: 'Laws and circumscribed frontiers remain ... unwritten laws' (*SW* 1:249). This means that they can be unwittingly infringed and still incur retribution. Such unwitting infringement is the second meaning of ambiguity in the essay, that is, the 'deliberate ambiguity' of fate:

> For each intervention of law that is provoked by an offense against the unwritten and unknown law is called 'retribution' (in contradistinction to 'punishment'). But however unluckily it may befall its unsuspecting victim, its occurrence is, in the understanding of the law, not chance, but fate showing itself once again in its deliberate ambiguity [*planvollen Zweideutigkeit*]. (*GS* 2.1:199/SW 1:249)

Benjamin's essay thus uses an ambiguous series of references to ambiguity to fuse together law and myth and then to set out his opposition between legal and mythic violence, on one side, and divine and revolutionary violence, on the other. The ambiguity in his use of ambiguity can, I will argue below, be clarified in relation to the existential stakes of fate that he attaches to ambiguity in his treatment of ritualized life in 'Goethe's *Elective Affinities*'.

Ritual life and ambiguous forms in 'Goethe's *Elective Affinities*'

'Goethe's *Elective Affinities*', published in two instalments in *Neue Deutsche Beiträge* over 1924/5, was written between 1919–22, contemporaneously with the composition and publication in 1921 of 'Critique of Violence'. Like 'Critique of Violence', in this essay the term 'ambiguity' is given an explicitly pejorative sense. Further, as in the violence-essay, in the piece on Goethe's novel 'ambiguity' is a characteristic attributed to each member of the negatively coded side of a schema of oppositions, which in the essay on Goethe, include: ambiguity/clarity; bourgeois 'free' choice/the moral decision; the semblance/the expressionless; bourgeois civility/critical violence; silence/articulation; myth/revelation; fate/the decision. 'Ambiguity' is used more sparingly and also more consistently in the essay on Goethe's novel than it is in the essay on violence. For Benjamin, 'ambiguity' in the former piece is one of the key indicators of the vacuity of bourgeois, ritualized life. As such, the use of 'ambiguity' in 'Goethe's *Elective Affinities*' can help to clarify the breadth of strategic meanings the word communicates in 'Critique of Violence' but which that essay does not adequately expound.

Benjamin's essay on Goethe's 1809 novel puts forward the thesis that anxiety and guilt are facets of bourgeois, ritualized life. The freedom from tradition that the characters in the novel have won does not lead them anywhere. Rather, it throws these characters into lives of empty, formalized ritual, which he describes, in tandem with the perspective on myth of the essay on violence, as lives lived in the 'pallid light' of myth (*SW* 1:303 and 305). I will not go into all the labyrinthine detail of Benjamin's treatment of the *Elective Affinities* here. The essay has a legitimate claim to being one of Benjamin's most substantial pieces, but it is also one of his most prohibitively difficult essays. In this chapter, I am interested specifically in how Benjamin's analysis of the novel supports the general thesis that bourgeois life has the existential structure of mythic life and his contention that this structure is perceptible theologically. The pivot of this position is 'the knowledge' that the relation between myth and truth 'is one of mutual exclusion. There is no truth, for there is no unequivocalness – and hence not even error – in myth' (*SW* 1:326). Conversely, 'what is proper to the truly divine is the logos: the divine does not ground life without truth, nor does it ground the rite without theology' (*SW* 1:326). The anxiety and guilt of mythic life are presented as consequences of a life reduced to interpreting supposedly significant meaning from irreducibly ambiguous forms. For instance, he treats the category of the symbol in the essay, not as a form that radiates a benign fecundity of meaning, but as a silent form of irreducibly ambiguous significance. Taken as a source of authority, the ambiguity of the symbol traps human beings. When the essay briefly introduces the pivotal concept of the expressionless [*das Ausdruckslose*] as a guard against the seductions of the beautiful semblance, he specifies that it is the 'critical violence' of the expressionless that reduces the ambiguities of the symbol to 'a torso':

> it shatters whatever still survives as the legacy of chaos in all beautiful semblance: the false, errant totality – the absolute totality. Only the expressionless completes the work, by shattering it into a thing of shards, into a fragment of the true world, into the torso of a symbol. (*SW* 1:340)

The violence of the expressionless, like divine violence, is destructive of ambiguity and its accompanying guilt and anxiety; it is destructive of mythic forms.

The symbol is the material form whose plenitude of meaning sustains plural inter-pretations. According to Benjamin's position in this essay, the hermeneutic activity that is required when material forms are given the status of guides for the conduct of human life is pernicious since the meanings they communicate are neither articulate, nor, accordingly, able to be disambiguated. When such forms are taken to be authori-tative they condemn human beings to lives of anxiety and guilt. The anxiety follows from the need to work out what these forms are communicating, when any clarity on the matter is impossible. The guilt is the consequence of the belief that these forms have the authority to impart rules and that it is certain only that these rules will have been transgressed, not when or how, since what they prohibit is unclear:

> Nothing but strict attachment to ritual – which may be called superstition only when, torn from its context, it survives in rudimentary fashion – can promise these human beings a stay against the nature in which they live. ... [I]t is nature itself which, in the hands of human beings, grows superhumanly active. (*SW* 1:303)

Ritual life is excoriated as a life that abides by the precepts of ambiguous, sensuous forms. The absence of truth in sources taken to be authoritative, such as the presumed profundity of nature's inscrutable forms in myth, is the core of the fateful life. If we consider this thesis in relation to the critique of the 'deliberate ambiguity' and 'demonic ambiguity' of law and myth in the violence-essay, it is clear that in these instances too there is an absence of truth (e.g. the 'unknown' and 'unwritten' law) in sources that are taken to be authoritative. Benjamin's call for their destruction may also be understood therefore as the rejection of those institutions and practices unable to offer anything more than an uneasy accommodation with the lack of clarity that breeds anxiety and guilt.

Benjamin opposes to the life that abides by the precepts of ritualized forms, the life that disregards the captivating effects of semblance: the moral decision is the model for the destruction of the bourgeois life, which in Benjamin's view is synonymous not with the 'ease' it aims to cultivate, but with restlessness, anxiety and guilt. Benjamin's essay thus opposes two types of existence: on one hand, there is the life entranced by the free aesthetic arrangement of form that the waning force of tradition enables and which condemns humans to vain attempts to propitiate in ritual the silent forms that they presume to hold authority bearing precepts. On the other, there is the life lived in faith that there is something beyond mere life and that is willing to risk everything, even life itself.[4] This type of life is able to destroy fate. Benjamin patterns the contrast between these two forms of life according to the contrast he sees between the lives of the characters from Goethe's novel and those of the characters of the novella that this novel contains:

> It is the chimerical striving for freedom that draws down fate upon the characters in the novel. The lovers in the novella stand beyond both freedom and fate, and their courageous decision suffices to tear to bits a fate that would gather to a head

over them and to see through a freedom that would pull them down into the nothingness of choice. (*SW* 1:332)

It seems as if it is articulating the decision, that is, making it into the 'object of communication' that alone secures its 'moral' status.[5] 'No moral decision can enter into life without verbal form and, strictly speaking, without thus becoming an object of communication' (*SW* 1:336). Hence Benjamin contrasts the novella lovers – 'The curious tale of the childhood sweethearts' ['*die wunderlichen Nachbarskinder*'] – who ask for their parents' blessing, with the mute conduct of the characters in the novel. Of the latter he writes:

> At the height of their cultivation [these characters] … are subject to the forces that cultivation claims to have mastered, even if it may forever prove impotent to curb them. These forces have given them a feeling for what is seemly; they have lost the sense for what is ethical. This is meant as a judgment not on their actions but rather *on their language*. Feeling, but deaf, seeing, but mute, they go their way. *Deaf to God and mute before the world*. Rendering account eludes them, *not because of their actions* but because of their being. *They fall silent*. (*SW* 1:304–5, emphases added)

Benjamin's description of the decision as 'moral' rests not just on its articulated status. Indeed it needs to be understood in relation to his opposition between fate and the moral decision, in which context the 'moral' status of the decision has the sense of unequivocal opposition to the coercive pressures of the 'cultivated', but empty bourgeois life. The life of the bourgeois is blind to 'the reality that inhabits what they fear' because they inhabit a perspective that is 'unsuited to them' (*SW* 1:303). The effective contestation of this perspective cannot be conducted in silent rebellion. In other essays, Benjamin argues that speaking back to fate is a release from it. Hence, in the 1932 essay on 'Gide's Oedipus' he argues that Oedipus is 'the last of the great escape artists' because he does not mutely submit to fate, but articulates his despair (*SW* 2:580). The status of speech in these positively coded examples does not indicate that the articulate word is, as such, an effective counter to fate. Word use can also founder in deliberate ambiguity, such as the meaningless chatter of bourgeois civility, which the violence-essay describes as the 'civilized outlook' that 'allows the use of unalloyed means of agreement' (*SW* 1:244).[6] The clarity of the word is esteemed, not in the attempts to make peace with civility, but when its articulation undoes the captivations of merely material life, which is fate.

Benjamin's understanding of the relation between clarity in speech and truth is important for our topic since it can help explain how the uncertainty of the unwritten legal codes is sustained and transposed into their written status in the violence-essay.

As we saw, Benjamin refers in his violence-essay to the 'equal rights' in respect to the frontier line as 'demonically ambiguous', and he characterizes such rights as 'a terribly primitive form' of 'the mythic ambiguity of laws that may not be "infringed"' (*SW* 1:249). Benjamin thus uses the pejorative sense of 'ambiguity' to criticize the law-making violence of constitutional law, which, he claims, generates ambiguous frontiers. His description of the 'demonic' ambiguity of the 'frontier line' seems to draw on the hermeneutic conception of ambiguity in the sense that a text or an image, or in this case the possession of 'equal rights' in respect to a frontier, can be interpreted in different ways. This sense is also present in Goethe's conception of the symbol [*Sinnbild*], where material forms carry symbolic meanings insofar as they sustain 'an unending task of interpretation'.[7] In both the essays on Goethe's novel and the essay on violence, Benjamin calls such ambiguity of meaning 'demonic'. Further, Benjamin relates demonic ambiguity to the experience of fate. What sustains the process of interpretation is not therefore, as on the hermeneutic model of ambiguity, benign fecundity of meaning, but the lack of any relation to truth in such forms. Hence what is distinctive about the vocabulary of 'equal rights' is that they dissimulate the mechanisms of 'force' that establish and maintain the frontier and which punish those who infringe it. The exclusion of such forms from truth, which Benjamin marks by calling the consequences of infringement 'retribution' rather than 'punishment', creates the conditions for guilt and anxiety, which thrive under the reign of uncertainty. This is an important point, which can be reconstructed from the pejorative discussion of myth in the violence-essay, but whose significance is only fully explained in the essay on Goethe's novel.

In his essay on violence, Benjamin attempts to link the case of Niobe, whose arrogance challenges the gods, to the principle that 'ignorance of law is no protection against punishment'. This principle of law, he states, dates back to the mythic statutes in which 'laws and circumscribed frontiers' are unwritten and can be unwittingly infringed. In such cases: '"retribution" (in contradistinction to "punishment") … however unluckily it may befall its unsuspecting victim … is, in the understanding of the law, not chance but fate showing itself once again in its deliberate ambiguity (*SW* 1:249).

The uncertainty of apprehension and punishment, seeing that there is always hope of eluding the arm of law, is the aspect of the 'ambiguity' that law shares with myth, which ties them both to the 'deliberate ambiguity' of fate (*SW* 1:242). The uncertainty of legal punishment rules out the liberal interpretation of the law as exercising a function of deterrence. In fact, Benjamin writes, the uncertainty of apprehension 'makes [law] all the more threatening, like fate' (*SW* 1:242). When he discusses uncertainty in the context of myth, this sense of ambiguity as the uncertainty of fate is one that is shown to have concrete existential effects. Life lived under the pallid light of mythic ambiguity produces an anxiety-ridden state in which the fear of punishment at every turn is overwhelming. The evasion of the judgement of fate is not experienced as relief, but only as a postponement of certain, impending punishment. The cycle of transgression, guilt and punishment is closed, since there cannot be any appeal against fate. Aside from knowing that they must be guilty of some transgression because they suffer what they perceive to be 'their' punishment, nothing is known about the whole mechanism by the person who undergoes it. Indeed to reflect on the ancients' conception of fate is to be led to 'the "inescapable realization" that it is, in Hermann Cohen's words, "fate's orders themselves that seem to cause and bring about this infringement, this offense"' (*SW* 1:249). There is no exit from the omnipresent threat of ruinous retribution because fate does not articulate intentions that can be scrutinized, but exerts an ambiguous, uncertain presence. This is why the diffuse sense of guilt feeds the dread of violent punishment.

The different examples that Benjamin uses in the violence-essay to depict the pernicious effects of ambiguity do not give a consistent picture of the problems he finds with mythic violence. On the other hand, his use of ambiguity to describe mythic life in the essay on Goethe's novel does show that what he objects to in the experience of ambiguous meaning is its carriage of the inscrutable punishment that comes from *fate*. There are two key instances in this essay's discussion of the novel – his treatment of the characters' reorganization of the graveyard in the churchyard and the demonic power of the still water that claims the life of the infant – in which Benjamin describes concrete circumstances where the experience of material forms as ambiguously uncertain determines a fateful existence. Benjamin understands myth as a human account (a 'traditional tale'[8]) of what is vital in human life, which only draws on forms and forces of nature. In myth, natural forms and forces are given a human face so that they become approachable for human beings.[9] The ambiguity of myth stems from the potentially infinite meanings that arise once mute nature is given expressive powers. This is a distinctive sense of 'ambiguity', which describes the existential effects of looking to sensuous forms of meaning to guide human life. The modern examples of the Goethe novel make the issues at stake clearer than the mythical example of Niobe's punishment in the violence-essay.[10]

Benjamin describes how the friends in the novel remove the gravestones from the churchyard 'without scruple or consideration' (*SW* 1:302). Benjamin uses this particular example to treat the peculiar settings of bourgeois life where traditional institutions hold no authority. But the real issue in his account of this scene is what may replace tradition as the frame of meaning needed for human life. The friends attempt to substitute for tradition an aesthetic order: 'See how Charlotte has beautified this funeral-ground', comments Eduard to Mittler in the first chapter of the novel.[11] Aesthetic forms, in Benjamin's account, do not provide adequate mechanisms of orientation and existential security, nor can they ward off the omnipresent threat that the mythic perspective on life unleashes. Instead the autonomy of such forms becomes an oppressive regime for human beings.

The 'liberation' from an unquestioning relation to tradition is replaced by ritual whose ubiquity only produces anxiety. The 'freedom' of these friends brings down on their heads a sense of dread and menace that ironically stems from the carefully arranged environment they inhabit. Ritualistic attachment to formal arrangements and procedures turns daily life into an arena of potential infringements and hence dread of retribution. Thus instead of their 'freedom' from tradition fostering an 'authentic' existence, it opens a chasm of potential dangers that crush them.[12] Myth, according to the essay on Goethe's novel, does not make nature approachable but hands over human life to unfathomable, hence threatening, tyrannical forces.

Benjamin argues that it is not natural elements per se that are demonic but their insertion into the semiotic system of myth. He refers to the 'mythic face' of 'sensuous nature' (*SW* 1:315), which is unleashed when humans are blind to the Revelation and the clarity that it gives to nature's forms. Hence the element of water can both destroy human life and be an instrument of salvation. In the novel, Charlotte's infant drowns in the still waters of the lake. On the other hand, the willingness of the lovers in the novella to risk their lives when they throw themselves into the dangerous current seals the truth of their love, which, 'because it risks life for the sake of true reconciliation, achieves this reconciliation and with it the peace in which their bond of love endures' (*SW* 1:342). Benjamin opposes to the supposed freedom of 'bourgeois choice' paraded by the characters of the novel the 'moral decision' of the lovers of the novella. Salvation through faith can only be attained on the other side of uncompromising defiance of natural life. 'Because true reconciliation with God is achieved by no one who does not thereby destroy everything – or as much as he possesses – in order only then, before God's reconciled countenance, to find it resurrected' (*SW* 1:342). Faith in the transcendent source of life reconstitutes nature as responsive to human interests, no longer cut off from the transcendent. Humans are at home in nature only through the knowledge of the intention behind its creation, that is, the Revelation. It is this bond with the transcendent that provides a way out of material totality. Within Goethe's novel, the novella provides a vantage point that allows the destructive effects of mythic nature behind the beautiful semblances of the novel to be recognized: 'If the ambiguity thus leads into the novel's centre, still it points back again to the mythic origin of the novel's image of the beautiful life' (*SW* 1:341–2). What is illuminated is how the still waters of the novel embody the 'power of ambiguity': a bottomless pit of 'primeval' forces that are seemingly 'contained' in a pleasurable, calm, aesthetic reflection (*SW* 1:341). The deceptive appearance of the water as 'reflecting, clear and clarifying' seems akin to the 'ambiguity' of law, which deceptively presents itself as neutral:

> Water as the chaotic element of life does not threaten here in desolate waves that sink a man; rather, it threatens in the *enigmatic calm* that lets him go to his ruin. To the extent that fate governs, the[y] … go to their ruin. Where they spurn the blessing of firm ground, *they succumb to the unfathomable*, which in stagnant water appears as something primeval. … In all this it is nature itself which, *in the hands of human beings*, grows superhumanly active. (*SW* 1:303, emphases added)

Benjamin's essay shows how the deceptive presentation of the surface of the water is demonically ambiguous. When there is no anchor point outside mythic nature, natural forms become omnipotent; they dominate human life. This is the significance of the fact that the lovers in the novella do not take their bearings from nature. In fact, when the lovers decide to jump, he says, they make this decision each 'alone with God' (*SW* 1:344).[13] Thus Benjamin makes the point that nature's sensuous forms can never be adequate grounds for human meaning. The novella lovers stand to the semblance of nature, as revolutionary violence stands to law and divine violence to myth. They each absolutely oppose a false totality, and do so on the grounds of practical faith in something beyond merely natural life. More than this: such practical faith dissolves the ambiguities of myth (and law) because it is attuned to the truth of theological perception. Hence in the cases of both 'deliberate ambiguity' and 'demonic ambiguity' in the violence-essay Benjamin identifies the proliferating force of entrapment that occurs when forms that exclude truth (the line governed by the peace treaty, the statute that proclaims ignorance of the law as no exemption to punishment, the precepts of myth that take nature's forms) enjoy false authority.

Ambiguity and truth in Benjamin's late work

One of the difficult aspects of Benjamin's writing is that it does not have the type of systematic attention to a topic that one ordinarily finds in philosophy and this, together with the compressed style of argumentation and the occasional oracular pronouncements that are threaded through many of his works, makes it hard to pin it down, or at least, distil his writing into core theses or claims. The obscurities of some of his early pieces of writing – including the violence-essay – have made these texts pliable material for the agendas of his commentators. Many of the fundamental commitments of his earliest work – the association of language with the clarity of the creative word of God, i.e., the divine intention; myth with Greek mythology; and truth and revelation with the Judaic God – are skirted over in silence by many Benjamin scholars. I have argued here that the reason 'ambiguity' is coded pejoratively in his early work is because it is the sign of myth's exclusion of truth, which Benjamin understands as the real driver of fate. In bourgeois life, truth is excluded from the very forms that are consulted for guidance and the totalizing trap of the 'superhuman', mythic powers that are devoid of the clarity of divine intention is set (*SW* 1:303). The ambiguities in Benjamin's references to law's 'demonic ambiguity' and the 'deliberate ambiguity' of fate in his violence-essay, can be reconciled if we consider that in each case Benjamin refers to institutions and forms that exclude the clarity of truth and condemn those who follow them to anxiety and guilt.

The 'Critique of Violence' belongs to the period of Benjamin's early writing. Works from this period array a schema of oppositions: ambiguity and clarity; myth and truth; law and revolution; the semblance and the expressionless; and mythic and divine violence. The schema is weighted in his early writing by the opposition between myth and revelation (God), but the hold this opposition has on his thinking has eroded in the later work. What are the consequences of the shift away from this opposition on the terms of his early analysis of ritual life and violence?

In his *Arcades Project*, ambiguity has an equivocal value. Instead of signifying the exclusion of truth that legal violence and myth embody in the early works, ambiguity becomes something of a gateway to the perception of historical truth. For instance, in his formulation of the dialectical image a new optics for the perception of historical meaning is advocated. The dialectical image stages the possibility for the rescue or liberation of residues of meaning from the past. This occurs in a 'flash of recognition' when a moment of the past encounters its meaning in the present and comes thereby to sustain new meaning potentials. Benjamin writes that 'the relation of what-has-been to the now is dialectical', it forms a constellation of a 'suddenly emergent', 'awakened' meaning (N2a, 3). The notion of emancipatory, redemptive meaning potential comes to replace the earlier excoriation of the pernicious ambiguity of forms cut off from communion with God.

Most notably, this shift in the late work resurrects and validates the concept of ambiguity, which is defined in the '1935 Exposé' for the *Arcades* contrary to its pejorative presentation in his early essays, as 'the manifest imaging of dialectic' (*AP* 10). The context of this revaluation is historical: there is, he writes, an

ambiguity peculiar to the social relations and products of this epoch. *Ambiguity*

is the manifest imaging of dialectic, the law of dialectics at a standstill. This standstill is utopia and the dialectical image, therefore, dream image. Such an image
is afforded by the commodity per se: as fetish. Such an image is presented by the
arcades, which are house no less than street. Such an image is the prostitute –
seller and sold in one. (*AP* 10, emphasis added)[14]

Against the value he had placed on a transparent relation to the unequivocal essence of
things in his early discussion of language, the late work seems to assume that material
forms do bear ambiguous meanings and that the negative meaning they carry can be
converted into a positive one. Hence in the commodity form there is a negative form of
meaning that gathers together the semblance characteristics needed for the exigencies
of exchange reified from use and labour; but there is also a positive meaning that is
emancipated from both use and exchange and resistant to any ultimate decryption.
This second meaning is the meaning potential of the commodity form that is trafficked
through its ruined form. The commodity becomes a site of convertible and converted
meaning potentials. On this point, the *Arcades* clearly breaks with Benjamin's early
critique of the pernicious effects of ambiguous meaning potential as he now expects
emancipatory consequences from the fact that such potentials are housed in material
forms. Indeed, if the 'Goethe's *Elective Affinities*' essay emphasizes that the anxious,
guilt-ridden life is the consequence of submitting to the authoritative force of
sensuous forms, such forms now become guides for historical truth.[15] How should we
understand the significance of this shift?

     In relation to Benjamin's essay on violence the question is especially stark since
it was the ambiguity of law, myth and fate that divine/revolutionary violence was
scripted to destroy. His essay on Goethe's novel similarly describes the shimmering
movement of the semblance as the ambiguous form that the critical violence of the
expressionless cuts down. It seems to me that two points can be made in support of the
thesis that there is a continuity underpinning Benjamin's seemingly altered position
on the topic of ambiguity. First, the later position is consistent with the earlier concern
about the pernicious effects of a hopeless hermeneutic relation to authority. After
all, ambiguity may be the feature of the dialectic at a standstill, but it has this status
of the 'standstill' because it does not effectively disguise the truth, but exposes it: for
instance, the 'ambiguity' of the prostitute is that she is 'seller and sold in one'. Second,
to the extent that it is sensuous forms that are consulted to access the historical truth
of the nineteenth century, such forms are able to bear truth because they are the
depository of the human wishes and ideals for emancipation. The vitiated status of
these wishes is what Benjamin intends to lay bare. Hence the shift is away from divine
to human revelation, even though the means of this revelation remains the theological
conception of the perception of truth in the clarity of intention. These wishes are
elevated beyond the partiality of human interests that he identifies in legal violence
and instrumental language since they are the truth as such of human history and they
are detected and 'read' in the 'historical index' of another century.[16] As such, this later
position is also consistent with his perspective on truth as the 'death of intention' in
the *Trauerspiel*-book (*OT* 36), a specific formulation that is also echoed in the *Arcades*
(*N*3,1). Like the emancipatory effect of the knowledge of the transcendent, creative

intention behind nature, the 'intentions' at stake in the *Arcades* are not transitory and partial intentions, but trans-historical and thus liberating ones. Finally, it is the citations in which wishes are lodged and articulated, rather than the sensuous forms themselves, that is the focus of the *Arcades*. This focus sustains the perspective of his early work in which language is cast against mute forms as a vehicle of emancipation.[17]

When the past is thought of as over and complete we are faced with entrapment in the totalizing force of the past (*The Arcades Project*). When law is the arbiter of violent retribution and the only option is submission we are asked to submit to uncertainty ('Critique of Violence'). When the semblance of the beautiful, bourgeois life is held up as the ideal that affords free choice, the mute tyranny of conformity to ritual inculcates guilt and anxiety ('Goethe's *Elective Affinities*'). And when instrumental language replaces the naming language, the reign of arbitrariness forever separates the hold of words on things and suspends the possibility of knowledge of truth ('Language as Such'). In the late work, as in the early, Benjamin advocates for the perception of the truth amidst the ambiguities of sensuous forms. Such perception is the crack in forces of totality that shows such forces to be false and strengthens the courage needed to contest their reign. His opposition to these forces is unwavering: his early work calls for their complete destruction. His later work nuances the militancy of this early call. In the *Arcades* Benjamin uses the resources of theology to look for the crack in the detritus of the past that would be able to sustain redemptive potentials. The case he makes against false totalities and the ambiguity that is their cipher in his early essay on violence can be coordinated with the various positions he takes on history, language and the complicity of bourgeois life with myth. I have argued here, however, that it is only through this coordination with other works of Benjamin's that the meaning of ambiguity in the violence-essay is intelligible. Whether ambiguity is 'deliberate' or 'demonic', what it means for Benjamin is that which is excluded from truth; the destruction of ambiguity is also the destruction of the fear that such inscrutability generates.

Notes

1   An influential articulation of this position can be found in Werner Hamacher, 'Afformative, strike: Benjamin's "Critique of Violence"', in *Walter Benjamin's Philosophy: Destruction and Experience,* eds. Andrew Benjamin and Peter Osborne (Manchester: Clinamen Press, 2000), 108–36. Hamacher's essay is dedicated to Jean-Luc Nancy and the position he defends has more in common with the precepts of Nancy's ontology than it does with Benjamin's argument in his violence-essay. I give critical consideration to this tradition of interpretation of Benjamin's violence-essay in 'The distinction between mythic and divine violence: Walter Benjamin's "Critique of Violence" from the perspective of "Goethe's *Elective Affinities*"', *New German Critique* 41.1 (2014): 93–120.

2   There are specific references to 'clarity' in the *Elective Affinities* essay (see *SW* 1:321, 342, 343), and the concept of clarity is also communicated in the contrast between what is 'brilliantly' 'illuminated' and 'radiant', on one side and that which is 'dark', 'telluric' and 'pallid' on the other (*SW* 1:331, 332, 303). However, the most consistent

reference is to the intimate connection Benjamin sees between speech and clarity (*SW* 1:302). For this reason 'All speechless clarity of action is semblance-like, and in truth the inner life of those who in this way preserve themselves is no less obscure to them than to others' (*SW* 1:337).

3   Compare, 'Goethe's *Elective Affinities*': 'Fate is the nexus of guilt among the living' (*SW* 1:307).

4   Regarding the vocabulary of 'faith': '[T]he certainty of blessing that, in the novella, the lovers take home with them corresponds to the hope of redemption that we nourish for all the dead. This hope is the sole justification of *the faith in immortality*, which must never be kindled from one's own existence' (*SW* 1:355, emphasis added).

5   See Winfried Menninghaus's discussion of this point in 'Walter Benjamin's variations of imagelessness', *Critical Horizons* 14.3 (2013): 407–28, esp. 417–18, Special Issue on *The Image*, eds. Andrew Benjamin and Alison Ross.

6   See the discussion of such 'means' in Ross, 'The distinction between mythic and divine violence', 117–19.

7   See Tzvetan Todorov's account of hermeneutic interpretation of the symbol in his *Theories of the Symbol*, trans. Catherine Porter (Ithaca, NY: Cornell University Press, 1982), 206–7.

8   See Walter Burkert, *Structure and History in Greek Mythology and History* (Los Angeles, CA: University of California Press, 1979).

9   This can be compared with Hans Blumenberg's treatment of this topic in his *Work on Myth*, trans. Robert M. Wallace (Cambridge, MA: MIT Press, 1985). Unlike Benjamin, Blumenberg sees myth as an effective way of managing anthropological deficits. Extending Blumenberg's account, we might say that what Benjamin calls theology and credits with the 'truth' that he claims is excluded from myth is really just another name for the use of myth to deal with anthropological deficits. I defend this comparison with Blumenberg in Chapter 5 of *Walter Benjamin's Concept of the Image* (New York: Routledge, 2014).

10   This is especially so since the contrast in the violence-essay between Niobe's punishment and the destruction of Korah is poorly handled. Niobe is left, in Benjamin's words, as a 'mute boundary stone'; her punishment thus does clearly mark the difference between the powers of the Gods and mortal life, despite Benjamin's description of the punishment of Niobe coming from 'the uncertain, ambiguous sphere of fate' and the meaning of her being rendered 'mute' as a further marker of 'ambiguity' (*SW* 1:248). For further analysis of the function of the Niobe myth in Benjamin's essay see Amir Ahmadi's analysis of Benjamin's distortion of the extant forms of the Greek myth of Niobe in this volume.

11   J. W. von Goethe, *Elective Affinities*, trans. R. J. Hollingdale (London: Penguin Books, 1971), 33.

12   Freud famously analysed the prompts for anxiety that such an un-defined field produces: like Benjamin, in Freud's account what defines anxiety is the absence of a definite object. 'Anxiety [*Angst*] has an unmistakable relation to *expectation*: it is anxiety *about* [*vor*] something. It has a quality of *indefiniteness and lack of object*.' Sigmund Freud, 'Inhibitions, symptoms and anxiety', *The Standard Edition of the Complete Psychological Works of Sigmund Freud*, Volume XX, trans. James Strachey (London: The Hogarth Press and the Institute of Psycho-Analysis, 1973), 164–5.

13   In his gloss on the commandment, 'Thou shall not kill', in his essay on violence, Benjamin says: 'It exists not as a criterion of judgment, but as a guideline for

actions of persons *or* communities who have to wrestle with it in solitude and, in exceptional cases, to take on themselves the responsibility of ignoring it' (*SW* 1:250, emphasis added). His casual placement of the 'or' between 'persons' and 'communities' points to a problem in the essay's account of revolutionary violence: in what sense can a community, which after all is the space of politics, wrestle with the problem of violent acts 'in *solitude*'? (*SW* 1:250, emphasis added). The fudging of the parallel to the lovers' situation, whose decision is made each 'alone with God' [*ein jeder ganz für sich allein vor Gott*] (*GS* 1.1:184/*SW* 1:343), is clear. Even if this problem somehow leaves Benjamin's revolutionary moral faith in a new society intact, one must admit that it compromises the connection between divine and revolutionary violence that the argument of his essay requires.

14   See also for different formulations of the same insistence of the importance of ambiguity his early version of the 1935 Exposé (*AP* 896).

15   The essay refers to Goethe's life as the model of such an anxiety-ridden existence: 'No feeling is richer in variations than fear. Anxiety in the face of death is accompanied by anxiety in the face of life, as is a fundamental tone by its countless overtones (*SW* 1:318). See also the references in this essay to 'dread' (*SW* 1:305).

16   Benjamin's *Arcades Project* refers to historical perception as a type of 'reading' of images; and to the idea that the legibility of these images comes from the 'historical index' between a past moment (i.e., the nineteenth century) and the present (i.e., the twentieth century): 'The expression "the book of nature" indicates that one can read the real like a text. And that is how the reality of the nineteenth century will be treated here. We open the book of what happened' (N4, 2). The 'legibility' of images is what makes the dialectical images 'genuinely historical – that is, not archaic – images' (N3, 1). 'For the historical index of the images not only says that they belong to a particular time; it says, above all, that they attain to legibility only at a particular time' (N3, 1). He writes: 'In the dialectical image, what has been within a particular epoch is always, simultaneously, "what has been from time immemorial". As such, however, it is manifest, on each occasion, only to a quite specific epoch – namely, the one in which humanity, rubbing its eyes, recognizes just this particular dream image as such. It is at this moment that the historian takes up, with regard to that image, the task of dream interpretation' (N4, 1).

17   I develop this reading of the relation between Benjamin's early and later work in more detail in *Walter Benjamin's Concept of the Image* (New York: Routledge, 2014).

Works cited

Blumenberg, Hans. *Work on Myth*. Translated by Robert M. Wallace. Cambridge, MA: MIT Press, 1985.

Burkert, Walter. *Structure and History in Greek Mythology and History*. Los Angeles, CA: University of California Press, 1979.

Goethe, Johann Wolfgang von. *Elective Affinities*. Translated by R. J. Hollingdale. London: Penguin Books, 1971.

Freud, Sigmund. 'Inhibitions, symptoms and anxiety.' *The Standard Edition of the Complete Psychological Works of Sigmund Freud*. Volume XX. Translated and edited by James Strachey. London: The Hogarth Press and the Institute of Psycho-Analysis, 1973, 77–179.

Hamacher, Werner. 'Afformative, strike: Benjamin's "Critique of Violence"'. In *Walter Benjamin's Philosophy: Destruction and Experience*. Edited by Andrew Benjamin and Peter Osborne. Manchester: Clinamen Press, 2000, 108–36.

Menninghaus, Winfried. 'Walter Benjamin's variations of imagelessness'. Translated by Timothy Bahti and David Hensley. *Critical Horizons* 14.3 (2013): 407–28. Special Issue on *The Image*. Edited by Andrew Benjamin and Alison Ross.

Ross, Alison. 'The distinction between mythic and divine violence: Walter Benjamin's "Critique of Violence" from the perspective of "Goethe's *Elective Affinities*"'. *New German Critique* 41.1 (2014): 93–120.

—*Walter Benjamin's Concept of the Image*. New York: Routledge, 2014.

Todorov, Tzvetan. *Theories of the Symbol*. Translated by Catherine Porter. Ithaca, NY: Cornell University Press, 1982.

3

Benjamin's Niobe

Amir Ahmadi

In the 'Critique of Violence' Walter Benjamin uses the story of Niobe to demonstrate what he terms 'mythic violence'. The ultimate concern of the essay is to show the possibility and conditions of a just revolutionary violence, the possibility of 'the existence of violence outside the law' in general. If such a

> pure immediate violence is assured, this furnishes proof that revolutionary violence, the highest manifestation of unalloyed violence by man, is possible, and shows by what means. Less possible and also less urgent for humankind, however, is to decide when unalloyed violence has been realized in particular cases. For only mythic violence, not divine, will be recognizable as such with certainty, unless it be in incomparable effects, because the expiatory power of violence is invisible to men. (*SW* 1: 252)[1]

The conceptual opposition between mythic and divine violence is fundamental. Divine violence, whatever it may be in particular cases and however it may manifest itself, is, minimally, the violence that is *not* mythic. Since divine violence is 'incomparable' in its effects, the opposition to the mythic serves as the sole measure of deciding that the event may indeed be a manifestation of divine violence. In his essay on 'Goethe's *Elective Affinities*', Benjamin underlines the indispensable epistemic service mythology does for 'truth': 'where the presence of truth should be possible, it can be possible solely under the condition of the recognition of myth – that is, the recognition of its crushing indifference to truth' (*SW* 1:326). It is thus important to achieve clarity about myth and, as far as the essay on violence is concerned, about 'mythic violence'.

Neither divine nor mythic violence is a means, but an immediate manifestation of superhuman power that serves nothing ulterior.[2] One cannot evaluate them by invoking the (supposed) different ends they serve. The immediate violence 'has thoroughly objective manifestations in which it can be subjected to criticism' (*SW* 1:248). Divine and mythic violence can be distinguished only in their actual occurrences, in the concrete features they display. The critique of violence (and its 'justness') must rely on a phenomenology of singular events. This is the reason why the 'example' Benjamin gives of 'mythic violence' is not merely an illustration of the concept (*SW* 1:248); it demonstrates its applicability. Mythic violence is thought and defined in reference to the myth of Niobe. But we must go even further. The 'examples' *are* specific forms of experience that ground the concepts in the life-world.[3] They shape experience and thus 'stamp' it with a certain image that is transferrable (i.e., metaphorical) and which underlies the applicability of the concept. For Benjamin at stake in Greek myth and Biblical theology are two basic and opposed forms of experience of the superhuman that fundamentally determine human existence:[4]

> Just as in all spheres God opposes myth, mythic violence is confronted by the divine. And the latter constitutes its antithesis in all respects. If mythic violence is lawmaking, divine violence is law-destroying; if the former sets boundaries, the latter boundlessly destroys them; if mythic violence brings at once guilt and retribution, divine power only expiates; if the former threatens, the latter strikes; if the former is bloody, the latter is lethal without spilling blood. The legend of Niobe may be contrasted with God's judgment on the company of Korah, as an example of such violence. (*SW* 1:249–50)

I leave aside Benjamin's characterization of divine violence in this passage, which seems in its particular aspects derived by reversal from the features he attributes to myth. The story of Niobe is supposed to give us insight into the comprehensive organization of human existence that myth represents. The queen of Thebes drew Leto's wrath for comparing herself favourably with the goddess, who had her children Apollo and Artemis kill Niobe's children as her punishment. Here is Benjamin's account:

> The legend of Niobe contains an outstanding example of this. True, it might appear that the action of Apollo and Artemis is only a punishment. But their violence establishes a law far more than it punishes the infringement of a law that already exists. Niobe's arrogance calls down fate upon her not because her arrogance offends against the law but because it challenges fate – to a fight in which fate must triumph and can bring to light a law only in its triumph. ... Violence therefore bursts upon Niobe from the uncertain, ambiguous sphere of fate. It is not actually destructive. Although it brings a cruel death to Niobe's children, it stops short of claiming the life of their mother, whom it leaves behind, more guilty than before through the death of the children, both as an eternally mute bearer of guilt and as a boundary stone on the frontier between men and gods. (*SW* 1:248)

The existence of the gods is fateful for human beings, who must for their part live under the ascendancy of myth.[5] In the essay 'Fate and Character' Benjamin defines the connection of law and fate in the following terms: 'Law condemns not to punishment but to guilt. Fate is the guilt context of the living. It corresponds to the natural condition of the living ... It is not therefore really man who has a fate; rather, the subject of fate is indeterminable' (*SW* 1:204). Inducement to guilt and reduction to muteness are the two related operations of fate; and the fate of Niobe is an 'outstanding example' of the 'life of the myth'. Three propositions stand out in Benjamin's understanding of the myth: first, the violent action of the sibling gods (Apollo and Artemis) establishes a law; second, the cause of Niobe's misfortune is her having challenged 'fate'; third, the story demonstrates that fate triumphs in the end, shown by the metamorphosis of Niobe to stone, a mute bearer of guilt and a boundary between gods and men.[6] This is the point of the myth according to Benjamin. Let us examine these propositions in the light of the elements of the myth and the meaning they may be assumed to convey, which is dependent to some extent on our theory of myth; for example, on our conception of the function of myth in the life of ancient Greece. Therefore, we have to examine briefly how the mythic mind conceived of the relation of humans with the immortals and the extramundane. We then turn to the various extant traditions of the myth of Niobe. Our aim is to ask whether the myth of Niobe can accommodate the main features of Benjamin's characterization of myth and mythic violence in particular.

Mythic presentation of the divine

The aspiration to be godlike or in some way to rival a god must be assumed for the ancient Greek religious mind. The 'divine man' has access to the underworld, whence he may acquire extraordinary knowledge. While incarnate, he 'purifies' himself through various techniques to become godlike. Empedocles hopes that he is living through his last incarnation before returning to his blessed home. The extant lines of his *Katharmoi* give us a glimpse into his mind: 'from what honor, and from what a height of bliss come I, having left to wander here among mortals' (DK 119).[7] I tell you I am a god immortal, no longer a mortal' (DK 112).[8] He describes a mantic *sophos* (apparently Pythagoras) in a fragment: 'And there was among them a man of rare knowledge, most skilled in all manner of wise works, a man who had won the utmost wealth of thoughts (*prapides*); for whenever he tensed all his *prapides*, he contemplated everything comprised in ten, yea, and twenty lifetimes of men' (DK 129).[9] Marcel Detienne has shown the connection of *prapides* with the ecstatic technique of 'concentrating' the soul in order to separate it from the body and thereby gain access to the invisible source of existence, to truth (cf. *Rep.* 571e–572a).[10] Empedocles (DK 111) promises Pausanias: 'you shall bring back from Hades the life of a dead man'[11] if the disciple 'as an initiate' relies on the *prapides* properly disposed and contemplate the revelations of the master (DK 110).[12] Pausanias will be able to descend into Hades and fetch the dead man's soul back to the world of the living.[13] Pythagoreans and Orphics made it possible for the ordinary person to harbour such grandiose aspirations, which were otherwise limited to the highest types, e.g., aristocrats and prophets (cf. DK 146, 147).[14]

Philosophical life, just like the mysteries, has no other purpose than the attainment of divine state. The rivalry seems to underlie Heraclitus' hostility towards Pythagoras and the mysteries in general (DK 14 and 14a, 81, 129).[15] In Plato, the Orphic motivation of Socratic philosophy is emphasized, while initiation as the basis of qualification for godlike existence gives way to the cultivation of ethical virtues through dialectical and mnemonic practices. The essence of his view is expressed in *Phaedo* 66d–70d as the programme of philosophy: the separation ('purification') of the soul from the body is the necessary condition of wisdom.[16] This conception is fully in line with the Pythagorean doctrine of the reciprocal relation between the purification of the soul and the attainment of true knowledge.[17] The fundamental affinity of philosophy as the true form of 'purification', the 'practice of dying' (*Phaedo* 67e), with the mysteries is clearly expressed in the dialogue: the few (true) initiates 'are those who have been true philosophers' (*Phaedo* 69d).[18] Philosophy (cultivation of virtues) and initiation to the mysteries compete for the same goal. The difference in method therefore has to be set out all the more sharply. In the same text (*Phaedo* 70a–d) Plato also points out the basis of both philosophy and the mystic ideology: the immortality of the soul and its desire to return to its divine nature. For this, he recommends separation of the soul from the body through Pythagorean *askēsis* (*Phaedo* 81b–c, 83a).[19]

This line of thought exists side by side with the 'official' Greek religion centred on *eusebeia* ('piety'), that is to say, keeping one's respectful and cautious distance from the gods.[20] It is not only ridiculous for man to have divine aspirations; it is dangerous. Pindar warns against the folly time and again: 'seek not to become a god' (*Ol.* 5.24).[21] 'Mortal minds must seek what is fitting at the hands of the gods, recognizing what is at our feet, and to what lot we are born. Strive not, my soul, for an immortal life, but do the thing which it is within your power to do' (*Pyth.* 3.59).[22] The warning obviously presupposes the existence of its object (let us call it the Orphic aspiration) in some way. It is in this perspective that the so-called 'hubris' myths are regularly placed. The myths about the members of the house of Tantalos have the theme of rivalry with the gods at their centre. There are two basic ways of interpreting these myths. One can see them as depictions of the human condition, defined fundamentally in contrast to the status of the immortals. 'It is in myth that the limits of the human condition and of proper behaviour and the exploration of its transgression are explored', Sourvinou-Inwood writes; in particular, 'myths of transgression help define the normative'.[23] The tragic stage, according to the Hellenists of the Paris School, presents the very status of man as a question, a topic of contemplation.[24] Myth becomes the medium of reflection on the human condition. The keynote here is the contrast with the gods. But one may also interpret the tragic treatment of the 'myths of transgression' as the reworking of the 'heroic' theme of the rivalry with the gods and possibly of the Orphic aspiration. The boundaries between the divine and the human are blurred in the epic hero, whose aspirations and defiance, whatever the consequences, are not as such an object of censure.

The myth of Niobe

In the epic tradition (in the *Return of the Arteidei*, according to Athenaios), Tantalos socializes with the gods, most notably as their table companion,

> and on one such occasion receives from Zeus a promise to have whatever his heart should desire … he asks to live always the same life as the gods. Naturally Zeus is aghast at this suggestion, yet has no choice but to fulfill it; at the same time, though, so that Tantalos might be unable to enjoy the things set before him, he suspends a rock over the mortal's head.[25]

The aspiration itself draws the divine punishment. In Pindar's *Olympian* 1 the cause of Tantalos' punishment is not the lugubrious banquet that he is supposed to have prepared for the gods from the flesh of his own son Pelops, although describing the feast as a 'most lawful/well-arranged' banquet betrays the awareness of the cannibal-istic theme.[26] Rather, Pindar makes Tantalos' sharing with his friends the food of the gods, with which they made him immortal, the cause of his downfall. Defiance of the gods, the crime of the tongue, is also the cause of his punishment, 'hovering in the air, fearing the rock hanging over his head', in Euripides' *Orestes* (4–10): 'he pays this penalty, as they say, because being a man, and having equal honor at the table of the gods, he could not keep his tongue in check'. According to the scholia to the passage, the offence was specifically that of revealing to men too much of the gods' plans.[27]

Niobe is Tantalos' daughter. In *Iliad* 24 Achilles relates her story in order to convince the grief-stricken Priam to eat. Niobe ate even in her grief. This may be Homer's innovation, however, to make his point.[28] In any case, Niobe calls down the catastrophe by boastfully comparing herself to Leto: whereas she has many children Leto has only two:

> [In] anger Apollo and Artemis, two though they were, slew her twelve offspring, Apollo the six males and Artemis the six females. The dead lay in their own blood for nine days, since there was no one to bury them, Zeus having turned them to stone. Finally on the tenth day the gods themselves buried them, and Niobe took thought of food, when she had tired of weeping. But now, [Achilles] continues, she is among the rocks in the lonely hills of Sipylos, and continues to nourish her grief, although she is stone.[29]

Whatever the peculiarities of the account, the cause of the gods' wrath and the fate of Niobe are found in all the versions of the myth. According to Sappho's single extant line on the topic, 'Leto and Niobe were exceedingly good friends'. According to Gantz, it 'may suggest that Niobe's acceptance by the god as a near-equal brought about her downfall, as it did that of her father'.[30] In any case, one may assume a special relation between the two as the basis of the fateful comparison.

Aeschylus and Sophocles had *Niobe* plays, of which only a few fragments remain. Plato cites a line from the former's play in the *Republic* (380a): 'a god implants a guilty cause in men, when he would utterly destroy a house'.[31] This seems at odds with the general trend of the myth, and the lines immediately following it in the papyrus fragment 'caution against mortals speaking too boldly in the midst of their prosperity'. The words put in Tantalos' mouth point in the same direction: 'Learn not to honor too much the things of man'.[32] In Ovid, too, Niobe's rivalry with the goddess is the cause of her misfortune: 'Niobe finds the Theban women worshipping at Leto's altars, and dares (on the basis of lineage, beauty, and fourteen children) to claim Leto's honors as her own'. Her metamorphosis into stone is the 'result of shock and grief' following the slaughter of her children.[33] Grief as the immediate cause of her turning into a rock, somehow transported to Lydia to be a landmark there, seems to become more common in the classical period and after. But in Pherekydes (and probably in Sophocles), 'Niobe goes back to Lydia by herself … and sees her city destroyed and the rock suspended over her father; in her grief she prays to Zeus to become a stone'.[34] In the version given in the *Iliad* 24, a similar course of events may be assumed, i.e., her grief over the fate of her children is not the immediate cause of her metamorphosis. In Apollodoros and Hyginus, Niobe turns into stone through her weeping, although not immediately in Thebes but in Lydia, having gone there by herself. Niobe's becoming a rock 'landmark' on Sipylos in Lydia, the 'Weeping Rock' shown today, does *not* seem to convey any special point. In Homer, the petrified Niobe is 'now, somewhere, lost on the crags, on the lonely mountain slopes, on Sipylos' (*Il.* 24.723–6).[35] The fact that Niobe's manner of reaching her homeland differs in the various versions that give us information about it shows that what is important is her association with Sipylos. This association must be accommodated in the story told about her. One way or another, Niobe has to end up as a rock formation on the mountain. One is tempted to see in the final metamorphosis an independent toponymic tradition for which the myth must account. In any case, as far as we can tell from the known versions of the myth, the connection between her defiance and punishment, on the one hand, and her turning into stone, on the other, is incidental.

Benjamin's Niobe

Let us go back to Benjamin's interpretation of the myth. He asserts that the gods' 'violence establishes a law', and hence an instance of mythic violence. I have already pointed out that Benjamin's assimilation of law to myth is ambivalent. If we let the 'daemonic ambiguity' of law mean its indeterminacy, then law would be operating in the mode of 'fate' in the sense this 'concept' has for Benjamin in, for example, 'Fate and Character'. The guilty is not so much subjected to the dispensations of fate as entrapped by them. Thus, Benjamin can claim that the 'fate-imposed misfortune' is not the response of the gods to a 'religious offense'. Guilt in the sense of a transgression (or as the psychological accompaniment of an offence) is out of place in the context of fate, just as much as innocence is (see *SW* 1:202–4). In some way, we must understand Apollo's and Artemis' violent outburst as an element in the entrapment of Niobe in the 'net of her fate'. Categories like transgression and punishment are meaningful only with the establishment of the law, and, to that extent, are the consequences of law-making. Does this make law-making similar to fate, since, according to Benjamin, fate brings about the occasion that calls upon the 'guilty' the fateful consequences? The operations of the two are the same; law-making is an entrapment, and both are grounded in mythic violence.

Niobe (or her haughtiness) challenges fate; but, in the end, fate prevails. For Benjamin this is the meaning-effect of the myth, as we saw above. Since the provisions of fate are not clear, one is always liable to feel anxious and guilty of transgression. The death of her children only makes Niobe feel 'more guilty'. The final submission is registered in her stony muteness. It is not clear, however, if one follows the logic of the operation of the 'concept of fate', whether the challenge itself should not be reckoned to her entrapment by fate. It seems to me that Benjamin's 'concept of fate' not just warrants but perhaps also calls for this interpretation, or something in this vein, although it makes the 'challenge' meaningless. The story of the 'triumph' of fate where its challenger is merely its puppet from the beginning would contain no lesson about its crushing 'power'; it would rather be a story of the cunningness of fate.

Defiance requires an object. Fate cannot be the object of Niobe's defiance, since her fate becomes known (to her) only in her eventual misfortune, i.e., after the fact. We must be able to assume this development; otherwise Niobe would only be a fool or a mad woman. If her fate is to be a boundary stone between gods and mortals, in Benjamin's account, it is because her 'defiance' consisted in comparing herself to an immortal, thus disregarding the fundamental difference.[36] In this perspective, one could hardly describe her 'arrogance' as 'challenging fate'. There does not seem to be anything ambiguous in Niobe's haughty comparison, nor about the violent response it draws from the gods. Benjamin's statement that 'violence therefore bursts upon Niobe from the uncertain, ambiguous sphere of fate' does not really describe the cause of Niobe's misfortune.

Let us think back to the myth. The 'arrogance' that causes Niobe's downfall seems to be a family trait. As we saw, her father Tantalos suffers his fate for a similar presumption, comparing oneself with the gods. However one interprets the so-called hubris myths, i.e., whether at issue is the frustration of man's divine aspirations or a general articulation of the human condition in contrast to that of the immortals, the relation ('heroic' rivalry[37] or 'taxonomic' contrast) with the immortals must be the theme of the myth. Gods and men still intermingled in heroic times. Niobe and Leto were good friends. Tantalos shared the table of the gods. Something or other had to happen to bring this commensality to an end. The stories of the house of Tantalos belong to the group of myths (of banishment) that may be understood as defining the human condition in reference to a relatively ideal state, e.g. a very long life without toil, commensality with gods and hence eating the same type of food, and generation without sex.[38] The (Hesiodic) myth of Prometheus, to which Benjamin refers (*SW* 1:248), is the *locus classicus* for this structuralist interpretation.[39] These myths explain a hierarchic reality (the separate stations of gods and men) in narratives of events. This is their *raison d'être*. Whether or not one agrees with the structuralist account, the central theme of these myths (i.e., the separation from the gods) receives its proper due in it. The confusion of stations prior to the precipitous event gives way to clear boundaries. The event is rooted in the confusion, reflects its operation, and occasions its resolution. This is one way the response of the gods to Niobe's 'arrogance' may be understood.

Contra Benjamin's interpretation, there is no indication in the story of Niobe that the cause of her metamorphosis is guilt. In Aeschylus' *Niobe*, she is even excused for the death of her children and the responsibility for her 'arrogance' is ultimately shifted onto the gods, who are the 'cause' of it (*Republic* 2.283b). In none of the versions we have does Niobe feel that it is she who is responsible for the deaths. It is not guilt that precipitates the metamorphosis, but shock and sorrow or weeping, or because she asks for it. In a number of versions (Pherekydes, Homer, Sophocles, Apollodoros and Hyginus) there is even a more or less extended period between the slaughter of her children and Niobe's metamorphosis. In Pherekydes, it is her grief compounded by the predicament of her father (having a rock suspended over his head) that is given as the reason for her praying to Zeus to become stone. Because of her consistent association with Sipylos, her metamorphosis into a rock may plausibly be understood as a geographic or toponymic etiology, as I suggested above.

Benjamin's twofold characterization of the petrified Niobe 'as an eternally mute bearer of guilt and as a boundary stone on the frontier between men and gods' does not find support in the myth. It should rather be explained in reference to Benjamin's own conception of fate and law-making. If the legend of Niobe is to be an 'outstanding example' of mythic violence, it must display the fateful outcome of a 'mythic life'. Niobe has to be the mute bearer of guilt. The 'plant-like muteness' of Ottilie in Goethe's *Elective Affinities* is both the sign and the means by which the daemonic claims her life. Her death proceeds in silence and its 'sacrificial' nature is accentuated by the 'dangerous magic of innocence' given to her by Goethe (*SW* 1:334–8). Her dying is literally a natural decay, just as her 'decision' to die to escape the compromising situation in which she is entrapped is not really a moral decision, clearly articulated and communicable in 'verbal form', 'but a drive'. The emphasis on natural processes and characterizations in describing 'mythic life' is, of course, programmatic. Fateful existence ('the guilt of mere natural life') is the 'natural condition of the living' (*SW* 1:250, 204, respectively), that is to say, life severed from the transcendent. Nature becomes daemonic in the absence of her subordination to the creative intention:

> Death is thus very probably atonement, in the sense of fate but not holy absolution — which voluntary death can never be for human beings and which only the divine death imposed on them can become. Ottilie's death, like her virginity, is merely the last exit of the soul, which flees from ruin. In her death drive, there speaks the longing for rest. Goethe has not failed to indicate how completely it arises from what is natural in her ... Ottilie's existence ... is an unhallowed one, not so much because she trespassed against a marriage in dissolution as because in her seeming and her becoming, subjected until her death to a fateful power, she vegetates without decision. (*SW* 1:336–7)

The 'spirit of language' is the medium of the 'moral world', in which alone human beings can entertain their hope for eternal blessing. The 'merely natural' is daemonic, since its (supposed) meaning, not being grounded in language, must remain indeterminate. Only the creative word can ground genuine knowledge; and only through 'faith in God' can the fallen man master the daemonic, that is to say, the 'mere natural life' (*SW* 1:250; cf. *SW* 1:342, 344–5).[40] To man before the Fall the world appeared as transparent meaning. After the Fall, nature loses its capacity to speak. She becomes 'mute', and because of her incapacity to signify she 'mourns' (*SW* 1:73). In myth, natural phenomena cut off from the creative word grow inscrutable and tyrannical, sources of anxiety, objects of ritual appeasement, and hence the ever-present 'context of guilt'. The absolute opposition of myth and theology shapes Benjamin's interpretation, not only of the 'legend of Niobe', but also of the other stories he treats, Jewish, Greek or modern. This schema informs Benjamin's analysis of Goethe's *Elective Affinities*. The 'subjection to fate' of the lives of the characters in the novel is opposed to the 'fulfilment' and 'redemption' of the lovers of the novella, thanks to their faith in God (*SW* 1:332–3):

> It is the chimerical striving for freedom that draws down fate upon the characters in the novel [*Elective Affinities*]. The lovers in the novella stand beyond both

freedom and fate, and their courageous decision suffices to tear to bits a fate that would gather to a head over them and to see through a freedom that would pull them down into the nothingness of choice. (SW 1:332)

In the novella that *Elective Affinities* contains, the 'true love' between the two characters is sealed in their faith in God, which is shown in their 'shared readiness for death' when, travelling on a boat, they 'dive into the living current' (*SW* 1:332).[41] For Benjamin, the 'meaning of their action' is their elevation through God over the 'mere natural life'. And the natural element thereby becomes an instrument of salvation rather than a daemonic force, 'whose beneficent power appears no less great in this event than the death-dealing power of the still waters in the other' (*SW* 1:332):

> With all this, it can certainly be considered incontrovertible that this novella is of decisive importance in the structure of *Elective Affinities*. Even if it is only in the full light of the main story that all its details are revealed, the ones mentioned proclaim unmistakably that the mythic themes of the novel correspond to those of the novella as themes of redemption. (*SW* 1:332–3)[42]

Faith in God alone releases man from the anxiety and guilt inducing forces of mythic nature, which removed from under the power of God's creative word becomes daemonic. Just as Benjamin says nothing about the fact that the story related in the novella belongs to the past of one of the protagonists in the novel in his account of Goethe's *Elective Affinities*, so in his essay on language he ignores the circumstances in which the 'judging word expels' the human couple from paradise:

> This judging word expels the first human beings from Paradise; they themselves have aroused it in accordance with the immutable law by which this judging word punishes – and expects – its own awakening as the sole and deepest guilt … The Tree of Knowledge stood in the garden of God not in order to dispense information on good and evil,[43] but as an emblem of judgment over the questioner. This immense irony marks the mythic origin of law. (*SW* 1:72)

Benjamin's theodicy must remain blind to the role of the Tree of Knowledge. It is not so much 'an emblem of judgment' as an instrument of fate; or at least, Adam's defiance of the divine word is no less fateful than Niobe's arrogance. Kafka sees this: 'Why do we harp on about Original Sin? It wasn't on its account that we were expelled from Paradise, but because of the Tree of Life, lest we eat of its fruit.'[44] The taunting question that the Lord God addresses to Adam after his transgression, 'where are thou?' (*Gen.* 3.10) is of course not a question at all; it reduces not just him but all his descendants to guilt-ridden silence. It is not meant to be answered by Adam in paradise, but reverberate forever in human existence. The human condition – earthly sufferings and death – is born in the curse of the Lord God.

Ultimately, the expulsion is not the result of Adam's 'rebellion': 'the Lord God said, "Now that the human has become like one of us, knowing good and evil, he may reach out and take as well from the tree of life and live forever"' (*Gen.* 3.22). So, God drove Adam and Eve from the Garden of Eden. The meaning of the original temptation is plainly stated by the serpent: 'you will become as gods' (*Gen.* 3.6). Adam is not expelled because he vitiates the genuinely cognizant language of name and reduces it to 'prattle', the 'true Fall of the spirit of language'. He is expelled lest he become 'as gods'. The proximity with the divine gives rise to the bold temptation. One can see the similarities of the situation with that of Niobe.

Conclusion

The meaning Benjamin attributes to the story of Niobe does not so much reflect the features of the Greek myth as his programmatic and total opposition of 'myth' and 'theology'. For Benjamin, 'mythic life' is a guilt-ridden existence lived under the daemonic power of natural elements and forces. He interprets the story of Niobe in the key of his antagonistic concepts of (Jewish) 'theology' and (Greek) 'myth', language and image. Human life severed from the transcendent, from God's creative intention, succumbs to anxiety and guilt, to the fateful powers of nature. In 'myth' this circumstance achieves its fullest expression. The myth of Niobe is an 'outstanding example' of 'mythic life'. In his essay on violence, Benjamin associates 'mythic violence' paradigmatically with the ancient Greek world and the presence of 'the gods'; it is 'a manifestation of their existence' (*SW* 1:248). I argued that such a view of myth (and mythic life) as represented in Greek culture is untenable. Certainly, any arguable characterization of man's relation with the gods in Greek myths, if one dared to take such a risk, would be very different from what lies in the background of Benjamin's interpretation of the myth of Niobe. The so-called hubris myths, for instance, may be understood as *comptes rendus* of the human condition, as in the structuralist theory of myth. The theme of heroic rivalry with the gods is a commonplace in Greek myths. The structuralist theory is one way of interpreting the theme. Thus we may understand the Hesiodic story of Prometheus' sacrifice as the settlement of the rivalrous relation between mortals and immortals. But Benjamin's conception of mythic life as fateful reduction to guilty silence before the gods – and in the extreme and paradigmatic case, Niobe's metamorphosis to stone – can hardly be an acceptable interpretation of this constellation.

Notes

1   The respective importance given to the 'proof' of the possibility of 'unalloyed violence' in general and to the possible clarity regarding its 'manifestation' in 'particular cases' is puzzling. One can never decide whether a particular act of violence such as the killing of a criminal (cf. *SW* 1:481) is an instance of 'divine violence'. What cognitive or moral purpose does a category serve that has no recognizable feature?

2   'Mythic violence in its archetypal form is a mere manifestation of the gods. Not a means to their ends, scarcely a manifestation of their will, but primarily a manifestation of their existence' (*SW* 1:248).

3   See Hans Blumenberg, *Shipwreck with Spectator: Paradigm of a Metaphor for Existence*, trans. Steven Rendall (Cambridge, MA: MIT Press, 1997), 81–102.

4   Benjamin sets out these basic forms in his essay on Goethe's *Elective Affinities* (see

SW 1:297–360). I refer to his account only to the extent that is required by our topic. Beyond the critique of myth and of the semblance, Benjamin aims at a critique of the image as such. See in particular *SW* 1:322. For an analysis of the essay, see Alison Ross, 'The distinction between mythic and divine violence: Walter Benjamin's "Critique of violence" from the perspective of "Goethe's *Elective Affinities*"', *New German Critique* 41.1 (2014): 93–120.

5   Powerlessness in the face of chaotic forces of 'mythic nature' is the final outcome of the rule of myth, according to Benjamin's 'Goethe's *Elective Affinities*': 'it is nature itself which, in the hands of human beings, grows superhumanly active' (*SW* 1:303). 'To that pass at last leads the life of the myth, which, without master or boundaries, imposes itself as the sole power in the domain of existence ... Mythic humanity pays with fear for intercourse with daemonic forces' (*SW* 1:316–17).

6   In *Elective Affinities*, Ottilie's subjection to the dark forces of fate is the cause of her 'plant-like muteness' (see *SW* 1:336).

7   Empedocles, *The Poem of Empedocles*, trans. Brad Inwood (Toronto: University of Toronto Press, 1992), 255.

8   Empedocles, *The Poem of Empedocles*, 203.

9   Empedocles, *The Poem of Empedocles*, 205.

10 Plato, *The Republic*, trans. Chris Emlyn-Jones and William Preddy (Cambridge, MA: Harvard University Press, 2013), 2: 309. See Marcel Detienne, *La notion de daimon dans le pythagorisme ancien* (Paris: Belles Lettres, 1963), 79–83.

11 Empedocles, *The Poem of Empedocles*, 211.

12 Empedocles, *The Poem of Empedocles*, 211.

13 'The idea of trying to bring someone back from the dead was, in the framework of normal Greek morality, almost unthinkable ... in terms of not only formal and structural analogies but also of historical contacts, there can be no separating the Thracian Orpheus from central-Asiatic shamanic tradition': Peter Kingsley, *Ancient Philosophy, Mystery, and Magic* (Oxford: Clarendon Press, 1995), 226.

14 Empedocles, *The Poem of Empedocles*, 263. On the Pythagoreans see Walter Burkert, *Greek Religion* (Oxford: Blackwell, 1987), and Fritz Graf and Sarah Iles Johnston, *Ritual Texts for the Afterlife* (London: Routledge, 2007) on the Orphic funerary plates. The Orphic initiate lays claim before the rulers of the underworld to a divine status.

15 See M. Marcovich, *Heraclitus* (Mérida: Los Andes University Press, 1967), 464–8, 71–3, 67–70, respectively.

16 Further references to *Phaedo* in the text are from Plato, *Meno and Phaedo*, eds. David Sedley and Alex Long (Cambridge: Cambridge University Press, 2011), 53–8.

17 See Detienne, *La notion de daimon dans le pythagorisme ancien*, 84–92.

18 'The ancients traced *philosophia* – in the sense of a way of life – back to Pythagoras (D.L., *Proem.*, 12). ... Ion of Chios (fr., 2) says that Pythagoras wrote poems under the name of Orpheus; Pythagoras therefore was absolutely an Orphic'. See James Redfield, 'The politics of immortality', in *Orphisme et Orphée*, ed. Philippe Borgeaud (Geneva: Librairie Droz, 1991), 108. Redfield draws a sharp distinction between Pythagoras' and Empedocles' conceptions of the philosophical life. I think the difference is exaggerated, and, generally, Redfield overlooks their shared intellectual horizon. See Detienne, *La notion de daimon dans le pythagorisme ancien*, 79–85. Pythagoras is the link between Orphic themes, and more generally the ideology of the mysteries, and philosophy.

19 Plato, *Meno and Phaedo*, 72–5.

20   See Burkert, *Greek Religion*, 272–5; and Jean-Pierre Vernant, *Mortals and Immortals: Collected Essays*, ed. Froma I. Zeitlin (Princeton, NJ: Princeton University Press, 1991), 269–89.

21   Pindar, *The Complete Odes*, trans. Anthony Verity (Oxford: Oxford University Press, 2007), 15.

22   Pindar, *The Complete Odes*, 50.

23   Christiane Sourvinou-Inwood, 'Crime and punishment: Tityos, Tantalos and Sisyphos in *Odyssey* 11', *Bulletin of the Institute of Classical Studies* 33.1 (1986): 54 and 57, respectively.

24   See Jean-Pierre Vernant, *Myth and Society in Ancient Greece*, trans. Janet Lloyd (New York: Zone Books, 1990), 211–15.

25   Timothy Gantz, *Early Greek Myth: A Guide to Literary and Artistic Sources* (Baltimore, MD: The Johns Hopkins University Press, 1993), II 531.

26   Gantz, *Early Greek Myth*, II 532. See Pindar, *The Complete Odes*, 4.

27   Gantz, *Early Greek Myth*, II 531–6. The passage from *Orestes* can be found in Euripides, *Orestes*; trans. Martin L. West (Warminster: Aris and Phillips, 1987), 63.

28   See Gantz, *Early Greek Myth*, II 536.

29   Gantz, *Early Greek Myth*, II 536–7.

30   Gantz, *Early Greek Myth*, II 537.

31   Plato, *The Republic*, 1: 187.

32   Gantz, *Early Greek Myth*, II 538.

33   Gantz, *Early Greek Myth*, II 539.

34   Gantz, *Early Greek Myth*, II 538.

35   Homer, *The Iliad*, trans. Robert Fagles (New York: Penguin Books, 1998), 608.

36   I emphasize again that despite Benjamin's interpretation the connection between her arrogance and metamorphosis is incidental.

37   Achilles defies Apollo in the *Iliad* (22.23) thus: 'Nothing for you to fear, no punishment to come. Oh I'd pay you back if I only had the power at my command!' (Homer, *The Iliad*, 542)

38   See, for example, Vernant, *Myth and Society in Ancient Greece*, 151–2 and 173–5.

39   See Vernant, *Myth and Society in Ancient Greece*, 183–201. Before the fateful event at Mekone gods and men ate from the same table, the expression *par excellence* of reciprocal trust and community (*Theogony* 530 ff., see Hesiod, *Theogony and Works and Days* [Oxford: Oxford University Press, 2008], 19–21). Men 'lived like gods' then (*Works* 110 ff., see Hesiod, *Theogony and Works and Days*, 40). Vernant (1989) identifies the men of 'gold race' from *Works and Days* with those who share the gods' table before the dispute at Mekone in the *Theogony*. The ostensible antagonist of the supreme god at Mekone is Prometheus, for, seemingly, he deceives the god. But Hesiod says that Zeus' intelligence did not fail him, for 'he recognized the trick and did not mistake it, and he boded evil in his heart for mortal men, which was to come to pass' (Hesiod, *Theogony and Works and Days*, 19). From then on, man (*anēr*) has to work hard for his food hidden in the belly of the earth, which only postpones the inevitable evil of death, and requires the woman, the 'pretty bane', to procreate (*Works and Days* 55 ff., see Hesiod, *Theogony and Works and Days*, 38–9). For men 'desirable things are hidden within evils while evils are sometimes hidden within desirable things and sometimes concealed by their invisibility'. Thus 'human existence is governed, through the gods' "hiding" operations, by a mixture of goods and evils, by ambiguity and duplicity' (Vernant, *Myth and Society in Ancient Greece*, 197). Zeus takes advantage

of Prometheus' deception to determine the woeful human condition. Humans cannot
have divine aspirations. See Hesiod, *Theogony and Works and Days*, 39–40.

40   Although Benjamin never published his 'On Language as Such and on the Language
of Man' (*SW* 1:62–74) in his lifetime, this essay clearly shows the theological
foundation of his thinking: 'With the creative omnipotence of language it [the act
of creation] begins, and at the end language, as it were, assimilates the created,
names it. Language is therefore both creative and the finished creation; it is word
and name' (*SW* 1:68). Things are knowable only in their names as the realized divine
intention (cf. *SW* 1:68). Man knows things through the 'naming word' (*SW* 1:70).
'Things have no proper names except in God. For in his creative word, God called
them into being, calling them by their proper names' (*SW* 1:73). 'Man is the knower
in the same language in which God is the creator' (*SW* 1:68). This is the state of
language in paradise: things communicate their very ipseity through their names.
The 'name-language' (*SW* 1:71) is not an instrument of social communication, but
the medium of communion with things, the 'pure medium of knowledge' (*SW* 1:68).
Naming receives and articulates the 'unspoken word in the existence of things' in
language (*SW* 1:70; cf. *SW* 1:72). Such was the 'task' assigned to man, according to
Benjamin: naming is 'not the prior solution of the task that God expressly assigns to
man himself: that of naming things. In receiving the unspoken nameless language of
things and converting it by name into sounds, man performs this task. It would be
insoluble, were not the name-language of man and the nameless language of things
related in God and released from the same creative word, which in things became
the communication of matter in magic communion, and in man the language of
knowledge and name in blissful mind' (*SW* 1:70). Concrete knowledge consists in a
lexicon of names whose paradigmatic case is the 'paradisiacal language', which was
the language of 'perfect knowledge' (*SW* 1:71).

41   '[E]very love grown within itself must become master of this world – in its natural
exitus, the common (that is, strictly simultaneous) death, or in its supernatural
duration, marriage. Goethe said this expressly in the novella, since the moment of
the shared readiness for death through God's will gives new life to the lovers …
in this pair he depicted the power of true love' (*SW* 1:345). Although it is not the
concern of this essay, I would like to point out that Benjamin's interpretation of the
action of the lovers in the novella is rather tendentious. The female character jumps
overboard in order to end her life in desperation and out of spite and vengefulness.
'She resolved to die, so as to punish him she had formerly hated and now so
passionately loved for his coldness towards her and, since she was not to possess
him, to wed herself eternally to his imagination and remorse. Never should he be
free of the image of her dead face, never should he cease to reproach himself that
he had not recognized, had not fathomed, had not treasured her feelings toward
him' (J. W. von Goethe, *Elective Affinities* [London: Penguin Books, 1971], 240–1).
The male character dives into the river in order to rescue her, having resolved 'the
most agonizing dilemma', since he has to abandon the ship's wheel (Goethe, *Elective
Affinities*, 242). No indication is there until after the rescue that he harbours any
romantic feelings for her. 'His position, his circumstances, his aspirations and
ambitions occupied him so fully he complaisantly accepted the lovely young lady's
friendship as a gratifying supplement without feeling himself involved with her in
any way' (Goethe, *Elective Affinities*, 239). Whatever one makes of his realization of
his feelings for her after rescuing her – underlying *his* action, for example, which is
not clear at all – one cannot overlook the fact that her attempt at killing herself is

not motivated by the spirit of love (by spiritual love) and faith in God in the face of 'mere natural life', but vengeful desperation.

42   Compare: 'only the decision, not the choice, is inscribed in the book of life. For choice is natural and can even belong to the elements; decision is transcendent' (*SW* 1:346).

43   'For – it must be said again – the question as to good and evil in the world after the Creation was empty prattle' (*SW* 1:72).

44   Franz Kafka, *The Zürau Aphorisms*, trans. Michael Hoffmann (London: Harvill Secker, 2006), 82.

Works cited

Blumenberg, Hans. *Shipwreck with Spectator: Paradigm of a Metaphor for Existence.* Translated by Steven Rendall. Cambridge, MA: MIT Press, 1997.

Burkert, Walter. *Greek Religion.* Oxford: Blackwell, 1987.

Detienne, Marcel. *La notion de daimon dans le pythagorisme ancien.* Paris: Belles Lettres, 1963.

Diels, Hermann. *Die Fragmente der Vorsokratiker.* 3 vols. Berlin: Weidmannsche Verlagbuchhandlung, 1959–1960.

Empedocles. *The Poem of Empedocles.* Translated by Brad Inwood. Toronto: University of Toronto Press, 1992.

Euripides. *Orestes.* Edited and translated by Martin L. West. Warminster: Aris and Phillips, 1987.

Gantz, Timothy. *Early Greek Myth: A Guide to Literary and Artistic Sources.* Baltimore, MD: The Johns Hopkins University Press, 1993.

Goethe, Johann Wolfgang. von. *Elective Affinities.* Translated by R. J. Hollingdale. London: Penguin Books, 1971.

Graf, Fritz and Sarah Iles Johnston. *Ritual Texts for the Afterlife.* London: Routledge, 2007.

Hesiod. *Theogony and Works and Days.* Translated by Martin L. West. Oxford: Oxford University Press, 2008.

Homer. *The Iliad.* Translated by Robert Fagles. New York: Penguin Books, 1998.

Kafka, Franz. *The Zürau Aphorisms.* Translated by Michael Hofmann. London: Harvill Secker, 2006.

Kingsley, Peter. *Ancient Philosophy, Mystery, and Magic.* Oxford: Clarendon Press, 1995.

Marcovich, M. *Heraclitus. Greek text with a short commentary.* Mérida: Los Andes University Press, 1967.

Plato. *Meno and Phaedo.* Edited by David Sedley and Alex Long. Cambridge: Cambridge University Press, 2011.

—*The Republic.* Translated by Chris Emlyn-Jones and William Preddy. 2 vols. Cambridge, MA: Harvard University Press, 2013.

Pindar. *The Complete Odes.* Translated by Anthony Verity. Oxford: Oxford University Press, 2007.

Redfield, James. 'The politics of immortality'. *Orphisme et Orphée.* Edited by Philippe Borgeaud. Geneva: Librairie Droz, 1991.

Ross, Alison. 'The distinction between mythic and divine violence: Walter Benjamin's "Critique of violence" from the perspective of "Goethe's *Elective Affinities*"'. *New German Critique* 41.1 (2014): 93–120.

Sourvinou-Inwood, Christiane. 'Crime and punishment: Tityos, Tantalos and Sisyphos in *Odyssey* 11'. *Bulletin of the Institute of Classical Studies* 33.1 (1986): 37–58.

Vernant, Jean-Pierre. 'At man's table: Hesiod's foundation myth of sacrifice'. *The Cuisine of Sacrifice among the Greeks*. Edited by Marcel Detienne and Jean-Pierre Vernant. Chicago, IL: The University of Chicago Press, 1989.

—*Myth and Society in Ancient Greece*. Translated by Janet Lloyd. New York: Zone Books, 1990.

—*Mortals and Immortals: Collected Essays*. Edited by Froma I. Zeitlin. Princeton, NJ: Princeton University Press, 1991.

4

Nature, Decision and Muteness

Brendan Moran

Introduction: Decay and the attitude of decision

In 'Towards the Critique of Violence', Benjamin outlines a dynamic in which law-preserving might be overcome by new law-positing. He stresses, however, that the ensuing 'new law' is itself heading for eventual 'decay' (*Verfall*). Benjamin's proposed critique of violence is at least partly a critique of the attempted closure of history from the force of 'decay'.

He thus writes on behalf of 'a critical, cutting and deciding attitude [*kritische, scheidende und entscheidende Einstellung*] towards' the 'temporal data'. The temporal data are the object of critique. These data are isolated, closed, from the time – the decay – prevailing over them. They are the data of violence, the data that the critique of violence is to critique. If '[t]he critique of violence is the philosophy' of the 'history' of violence, it is the philosophy of the history of data that are produced in denial of their decay. Data isolated from decay are mythic data. The philosophy of the history of violence does not offer, therefore, a grand systematic account. It is rather the critical, cutting and deciding attitude towards allegedly enclosed data. This attitude is the '"philosophy"' that Benjamin proposes can be exerted against the history of mythic violence. That he puts the term 'philosophy' in quotation marks may indicate his admission of how unusual it might seem to define philosophy as an attitude. Philosophy entails an attitude of dissatisfaction with closure. Divine violence – God's violence, pure violence – is unrecognizable as such, but can be recalled in the critique of mythic closure, mythic violence (*GS* 2.1:202–3/*SW* 1:251–2, translation modified).[1] In recognizing mythic violence as mythic, there must be recollection of all that mythic violence could never enclose: divine violence. Although divine violence – pure violence – is thus the permanent basis for critique, critique is also facilitated by the discernible wrongness of, closure by, myth against its own decay. Critique can decide against such recognizable myth.

Given the elusiveness of divine violence for the attempt to recognize it, one of the questions for decision is simply when violence is justifiable. The first paragraph of 'Towards the Critique of Violence' accordingly refers to the need for a 'decision' (*Entscheidung*) about the question of whether 'violence, as a principle, even as means to just ends, is ethical' (*GS* 2.1:179/*SW* 1:236, translation modified). An attempt has already been made elsewhere to outline and criticize aspects of Benjamin's *decision(s)* with regard to this question.[2]

Of concern in the following chapter will simply be that Benjamin associates decision with recognizing and emphasizing the capacity of decay to prevail over the violence of closures about history and its possibilities.

Apart from the passages mentioned above, 'Towards the Critique of Violence' says relatively little about decision, and indeed next to nothing about decay. There is one passage in which Benjamin discusses not the philosophically deciding attitude, but rather the dubiousness of decision within a legal context. The term 'decision' accordingly appears in quotation marks. Benjamin refers to the situation in which 'law [*Recht*]' 'in the "decision [*Entscheidung*]" determined by place and time' 'acknowledges ... a metaphysical category'. The metaphysical category is 'decision'. In contrast with police interventions and police prerogatives that are less clearly determinable, introduction by law of the metaphysical category of decision makes a situation more clearly open to critique; it 'raises a claim to critique' (*GS* 2.1:189/*SW* 1:243, translation modified). This '"decision"' (in quotation marks) is thereby shown to be distinct from the critical decision with regard to it. The critical decision recalls the time that will prevail over the legal decision.

The only further comment (in 'Towards the Critique of Violence') directly on decision is Benjamin's acknowledgement that 'decision' (*Entscheidung*) concerning 'when pure violence really was [*war*] in a particular case' may be neither 'possible' nor 'urgent' for 'humans'. Pure – that is, divine – violence as such remains unrecognizable to humans. Benjamin's usage of the past tense (*war*) might seem to suggest that decision now concerning pure violence is even more unlikely. He does add, however, that 'mythic' violence, the opposite of divine or pure violence, 'can be recognized as such with certainty', unless the effects are 'incomparable' (*GS* 2.1:202–3/*SW* 1:252, translation modified). In suggesting that even myth could have incomparable effects, Benjamin seems to be acknowledging that myth can affect each of us in unique ways and that its effects presumably often remain inaccessible to our resources of comparison. Perhaps he is also trying to convey that comparable effects are mythic effects; they can occasion exceptions to the applied comparison. If this tendency of myth to create exceptions is regarded philosophically, there is recognition of exception to the mythic per se and there is thus a potential unsettling of the dominance of myth. This recognition can emerge as decision recalling permanent exception to myth (although that decision is always confronted with the possibility – indeed the likelihood, or even certainty – of its embroilment in hitherto unnoticed, unaddressed, or simply accepted mythic complicities).

In the association of the critical attitude of decision with decay, an implication is that decision has a distinct relationship with nature – specifically, with nature in its transience. This is also suggested in the so-called 'Theological-Political Fragment' (dated – following Scholem – at 1920-1 in *GS*, and – following Adorno – at 1938 in *SW*): Benjamin says that 'the task of world politics, whose method is to be called nihilism', is a striving for the 'eternal and total passing away [*Vergängnis*]' that is messianic nature.

Benjamin does add, however, that this task will entail such a striving for messianic passing away that it will also be striving for 'even the passing away of those stages of the human that are nature' (*GS* 2.1:204/*SW* 3:306). Benjamin thus considers there to be – or considers there to be the prospect of – *stages of the human that are not nature*. Like the 'Theological-Political Fragment', many of Benjamin's works associate redemption, messianism, or even revelation in some way with transient nature, but also suggest that – at its utmost – this quest will be for the transience of nature itself, for the passing away of nature. In his note of 1918 on 'Sorts of history', he accordingly insists that 'natural history does not extend to the human'; 'the human is neither phenomenon nor effect but creation [*Geschöpf*]' (*GS* 6:93/*SW* 1:115, translation modified).

As will be evident in this chapter, nonetheless, Benjamin conceives of a nature – or a rudiment of nature – that is not simply phenomenon or effect. In the epilogue, moreover, brief but critical consideration will be given to ways in which his notion of the human's uniqueness may entail potentially calamitous assumptions about prerogatives of the human over the putatively less than human.

More than any other text by Benjamin, 'Goethe's *Elective Affinities*' (written 1921–22, published 1924–5) provides elaborations pertaining to the relationship of philosophic decision with nature. It is an essay that is chronologically as well as thematically quite close to 'Towards the Critique of Violence'. Its extensive, and sometimes extraordinarily dense, comments on nature often conflict with one another, and the reader can have difficulty at times not to confuse one ultimately distinct usage of the term 'nature' (or its derivatives, such as 'natural') with another. There do seem to be two natures – or two quite distinct rudiments of nature – for many of Benjamin's writings, and this is perhaps especially the case in the *Elective Affinities*-essay: first, a mythic nature associated with adaptation, resignation to fate, and acquiescent muteness; second, a somewhat less clearly stated, but nonetheless discussed, nature that is destructive but also – in its elusion of mythic containment or escape – redemptive and liberatory. An attempt will be made in this chapter to clarify ways in which the two, quite divergent, notions of nature are pertinent to Benjamin's conception of philosophically impelled decision. In the epilogue, as mentioned, consideration will be given to possible problems with Benjamin's conception of the relationship of human expressivity with a nature that he portrays as comparatively mute.

From mythic nature (mere life) to corporeal decision

In the *Elective Affinities*-essay especially, it could seem that all nature is mythic for Benjamin. This is often alleged in readings of Benjamin's essay, where indeed there is an abundance of references to nature as that which renders humans resignatively mute, adaptive to guilt-inducing notions of fate.[3]

The relevant myth involves enthrallment before the chaos of nature. In this 'idolatry of nature', there is simply fear of nature as that which ultimately gives and takes away. All limits are ultimately those of nature (*GS* 1.1:149/*SW* 1:316). Nature is granted a power that 'could never be entirely clarified by thought' (*GS* 1.1:148/*SW* 1:315).

Benjamin's statement about thought only concerns, however, the possibility of entire clarification of the realm that Goethe calls *ur-phenomena*, which are mythically isolated phenomena much like the temporal data from which the deciding attitude of the violence-essay distinguishes itself. Entire clarification of myth – as myth – is sometimes possible, at least in the sense that myth can every so often be recognized as myth. Not to acknowledge this capacity of thought is to deny any possibility of setting limits that would counter mythic enthrallment. This denial is detected by Benjamin in Goethe, who – according to Benjamin's portrayal – 'deprived himself of the possibility of drawing up limits [*beraubte ... sich der Möglichkeit Grenzen zu ziehen*]. Without distinctions, existence becomes subject to the concept of nature, which grows into monstrosity' (*GS* 1.1:148/*SW* 1:315).

For Goethe, says Benjamin, 'the concept of nature' ... 'designates ... at once the sphere of perceptible phenomena and that of intuitable archetypes [*Urbilder*]' (*GS* 1.1:147/*SW* 1:314). It is this mythic cloaking of perceptible contents by allegedly intuitable *Urbilder* that Benjamin rejects.[4] The abdication of nature to mythic *Urbilder* is an abdication of the capacity of humans to engage expressively with nature. Nature becomes 'mythic' – 'sunk into itself' – 'nature' that 'in speechless rigidity, indwells Goethean artistry'. A correlate of the abdication to myth is the withdrawal from criticism. According to Benjamin, Goethe thus sets himself up 'as Olympian' 'vis-à-vis all criticism' (*GS* 1.1:146–47/*SW* 1:314, translation modified): 'The rejection of criticism and the idolatry of nature are the mythic forms of life in the existence of the artist' (*GS* 1.1:149/*SW* 1:316). For Benjamin, criticism is against any surrender to nature as something requiring idolatrous, enthralled behaviour. This is the context in which he is opposed to reckoning the '"words of reason"' to 'the credit of nature' (*GS* 1.1:148/*SW* 1:315).

In the *Elective Affinities*-essay, however, nature is not just mythic nature. There is nature that is *innocent*. Humans must, though, *become human* in order to appreciate nature in its innocence. They surrender otherwise to the natural power that will make them submissive and resignative. They need to become human if they are to benefit from attention to innocent nature – the nature that will offset rather than instil human closures:

> When they [humans] turn their attention away from the human and succumb to the power of nature [*Naturmacht*], then natural life [*das natürliche Leben*], which in the human preserves its innocence only so long as natural life binds itself to something higher, drags the human down.

Natural life *in the human* drags down the human; nature has this power to which the human can succumb. To become attentive to innocent nature, the human must become *supernatural*:

> With the disappearance of supernatural life [*des übernatürlichen Lebens*] in the human, the human's natural life turns into guilt, even without the human committing an act contrary to ethics. For now it is in league with mere life [*des bloßen Lebens*], which manifests itself in the human as guilt. (*GS* 1.1:139/*SW* 1:308, translation modified)

In the abdication by the human of the human, nature is treated as a source of fated guilt and the human has thereby abandoned itself to *mere life*. In 'Towards the Critique of Violence', Benjamin refers to 'the guilt [*Verschuldung*] of mere natural life' (*GS* 2.1:200/*SW* 1:250, translation modified). In abandoning itself to mere life, however, the human has also disregarded the innocence of nature, the nature independent of idolatry, resignation, and fated guilt. This nature is discussed not only in the *Elective Affinities*-essay but also elsewhere: 'Fate and Character' (1919) opposes a 'natural innocence of the human' to 'the dogma of the natural guilt of human life' (*GS* 2.1:178/ *SW* 1:205–6).

In 'Towards the Critique of Violence', Benjamin is critical of Kurt Hiller's pacifism insofar as Hiller equates the human with the human's mere existence, 'mere life' [*das bloße Leben*], and regards that existence as something sacred (*GS* 2.1:201–2/ *SW* 1:250–1).[5] For Benjamin, Hiller's identification of the human with mere life is identification of the human with a guilt context that requires submission to it. Hiller says: 'We recognize that even higher than happiness and justice is an existence … existence in itself [*eines Daseins … Dasein an sich*]'.[6]

According to Benjamin's critical response to this outlook that turns existence into a fate requiring submission, the human does not 'coincide with the mere life in the human'; the human does not coincide with any specific 'conditions or characteristics', including any 'uniqueness' of one's 'bodily person'. There is simply no fateful existence. If the human is considered sacred, or even if plants and animals are considered sacred, that sacredness could not possibly be based on 'mere life'. Pronouncements about the sacred – be they ancient or modern – risk, however, treating 'mere life' as 'the marked bearer of guilt' (*GS* 2.1:202/*SW* 1:251, translation modified), as something requiring submission. Hiller exemplifies this tendency by invoking existence against priorities of happiness and justice, priorities Hiller worries might lead to killing. In countering, Benjamin claims the Judaic tradition treats the commandment not to kill as a guideline that might in 'dreadful cases' require taking on 'the responsibility of ignoring' the commandment (*GS* 2.1:200–1/*SW* 1:250–1). This might seem to invite recklessness about killing, and Benjamin could at least be critically scrutinized concerning his views – in 'Towards the Critique of Violence' – on the revolutionary killing of oppressors and on true wars.[7] This problem does not detract, however, from his concern that normative invocations of mere life, or of existence in itself, such as those by Hiller against priorities of happiness and justice, could involve or instil surrender to a fated guilt context.

For the *Elective Affinities*-essay too, a principal object of criticism is any invocation of mere life that instils complacency about the conditions of this life. Goethe's *Elective Affinities* is criticized for treating a marriage as a 'fate' [*Schicksal, Geschick*] in relation to which figures in the novel become subordinate (*GS* 1.1:139/*SW* 1:308, translation modified). If there is subordination to an alleged fate, life is from the outset guilty. '[F]ate [*Schicksal*] unfolds inexorably in the culpable life. Fate is the guilt context of the living' (*GS* 1.1:138/*SW* 1:307, translation modified). This fate befalls the principal figures in Goethe's novel: Ottilie, Eduard, Charlotte, and the Captain. With regard to the first two figures, Benjamin claims: not only does the 'death symbolism' in the 'fate [*Geschick*]' of Ottilie fulfil a mythic archetype of sacrifice (*GS* 1.1:140/*SW* 1:309, translation modified) but the 'downfall' of both Eduard and Ottilie – in this respect like

Werther's suicide in *The Sorrows of the Young Werther* – is treated as 'atonement' for the injury done by '"sensuality"' [*Sinnlichkeit*] to ethical order (*GS* 1.1:144/*SW* 1:312).

The reference to '*Sinnlichkeit*' is apparently Goethe's; it is quoted by Benjamin from conversations with Goethe reported by Friedrich Wilhelm Riemer. Benjamin's ensuing reference to sensuality as a violator of mythic order might seem to be contradicted a few pages later in the *Elective Affinities*-essay. Critically outlining Goethe's notion of *ur-phenomena*, Benjamin says: 'If, in this contamination of the pure domain and the empirical domain, sensuous nature [*die sinnliche Natur*] already seems [*(s)cheint*] to claim the highest place, its mythic face triumphs in the total-appearance of its being [*Gesamterscheinung ihres Seins*]' (*GS* 1.1:148/*SW* 1:315, translation modified).[8] The reference to '*die sinnliche Natur*' complementing myth could well seem to contradict the earlier described force of '*Sinnlichkeit*' (sensuality) that is opposed to mythic order. This might be a self-contradiction on Benjamin's part. It seems possible, however, that a different reading of the later sentence could be made. There is indeed the risk that to give sensuous nature the highest place will result in a myth of nature: if sensuous nature 'seems' [*(s)cheint*] to take the highest place, it is really 'its mythic face' that triumphs. It would be myth to grant dominance to sensuous nature. That this assessment is not an equation of all sensuousness with myth is, nonetheless, indicated by Benjamin's follow-up to his quotation of Goethe's reference to '*Sinnlichkeit*': Benjamin refers to Goethe's 'reflections' as 'inadequate in their opposition of the sensual and the ethical [*unzugänglich in ihrem Gegansatz zwischen Sinnlichem und Sittlichem*]' (*GS* 1.1:144/ *SW* 1:312, translation modified). The sensuality not simply opposed to the ethical is the nature that is not just mere life; this sensuality is not just a fate-inducing existence. There could be a sensuality that is opposed to mythic order. In 'Towards the Critique of Violence', Benjamin surmises: 'mythic violence' is 'for the sake of mere life'; 'divine violence' is 'for the sake of the living'. Mythic violence 'demands sacrifice'; divine violence 'accepts' sacrifice (*GS* 2.1:200/*SW* 1:250). To combine this point with terms from the *Elective Affinities*-essay: mythic nature demands sacrifice; innocent nature, the nature of the living as opposed to the nature of mere life, accepts sacrifice if it is offered. The latter sacrifice is not simply dictated by allegedly fated imperatives.

The nature not instilling fateful guilt is God's nature. In the *Elective Affinities*-essay, there is the following remark: 'Incapable of being unveiled is only the nature that keeps safe [*verwahrt*] a secret [*Geheimnis*] as long as God lets this nature exist' (*GS* 1.1:197/ *SW* 1:353, translation modified). God's nature keeps safe a secret. God's nature is the messianic nature that is discussed in the 'Theological-Political Fragment' cited earlier. This nature is a release for and of the body. The importance of the body in Benjamin's *Elective Affinities*-essay is often overlooked.[9] The nature that is God's secret and cannot be entirely unveiled is the nature of the body that is insubordinate to mythic constraint. The insubordination has no solution – hence its elusiveness for myth. Art and criticism are accordingly presentation of an insoluble problem as opposed to a mythically resolved problem: Benjamin refers to the unposeable, insoluble philosophic ideal. If philosophy has an ideal, it is not soluble; it is a problem for which there is not (yet) even the question (*GS* 1.1:172–3, 1:3:834/*SW* 1:333–4, 218).

There is a body abiding mythic solution, but also a body defying such solution. There is the 'living body' (*lebendiger Leib*) – subordinate to 'law' and the 'living' who uphold law. This body is subordinate to an allure of semblance, a beauty of semblance – a *scheinhafte Schönheit* (*GS* 1.1:197/*SW* 1:353). The other body is a 'body' (*Körper*) that rises above what seeks beauty as essential (*GS* 1.1:196/*SW* 1:351–2). This body divested of semblance is the body before God (*GS* 1.1:197/*SW* 1:353). This is the body that can attenuate attachment to semblance. This body can exercise the 'divine will' that can provide a 'new life' on which 'the old rights lose their claim' (*GS* 1.1:188/*SW* 1:345). What is this new life? It is the mystery or secret (*Geheimnis*) that does not rest with any phenomenal reality (*GS* 1.1:169/*SW* 1:331). Nor does it rest with any conceptual reality.

'Mystery' [*das Mysterium*] is 'the "dramatic" ['*Dramatische*'] in the strictest sense'; it can be expressed in no way besides 'presentation [*Darstellung*]' (*GS* 1.1:200–1/*SW* 1:355, translation modified). '*Darstellung*' can mean 'dramatic performance', and – in this case – is dramatic performance, for the dramatic, in the strictest sense, is 'the mystery of hope' (*GS* 1.1:201/*SW* 1:355). There can accordingly be a Dionysian 'tremor' (*Erschütterung*) in which space gives 'resonance' (*Resonanz*) to 'emotion' (*Rührung*) that is itself, in its deepest realization, 'transition' (*Übergang*) executed in the 'downfall (*Untergang*) of semblance' (*GS* 1.1:192–3/*SW* 1:348–9, translation modified). A fragment titled 'World and Time' (1919–20) states: in the 'becoming-obvious' of 'the divine', 'the life of the performer [*Darstellers*]', the life of the one performing, is subject to 'a great process of fulfilment' whereby the 'decline of the world [*Weltuntergang*]' – the decline of the scene of history – is both 'destruction [*Zerstörung*] and liberation [*Befreiung*] of a (dramatic) performance [*einer (dramatischen) Darstellung*]'. Destruction intrinsic to history is a liberation for performance in it (*GS* 6:98–9/ *SW* 1:226, translation modified). Hence the association in 'Towards the Critique of Violence' of critique with decay. In the *Elective Affinities*-essay, such a liberatory approach to decline is presented as different from going under as a result of the 'kind' of semblance that one acquires, the 'declining semblance' to which one binds oneself (*GS* 1.1:193/*SW* 1:349, translation modified). In 'Towards the Critique of Violence', 'a peculiar process of decay' is identified with 'legal violence' (*GS* 2.1:192/*SW* 1:245). To identify with a semblance that is in decline is to suppress and repress decline. To stress decline, in contrast, is to stress liberatory potential that is not bound to any semblance.

The natural innocence of life has, for instance, an antipodal relationship with sexuality only in the sense that phenomena defined by (either abstinent or active) sexuality – 'all purely sexual phenomena' – belong to 'the demonic [*Dämonischen*]', belong to the demonic not by their sexuality but by being defined in terms of sexuality. They are defined in terms of appearances of nature, not in terms of nature. Only thus is sexual life 'an expression of natural guilt', which is guilt *vis-à-vis* 'the natural innocence of life'. Benjamin also characterizes the natural innocence of life as bound with the – 'equally natural' – 'spirit' (*GS* 1.1:174/ *SW* 1:335). His 'Outline of the Psychophysical Problem' (1922–3) suggests that insofar as sexuality is an attempted (or passive) isolation of the 'body' (*Körper*) from nature, it is the counterpart of 'spirit' isolated from nature (*GS* 6:81/*SW* 1:395–6). Neither body nor spirit is ultimately this affected isolation from nature.

Offsetting such isolation from nature, according to the *Elective Affinities*-essay, is inclination. Inclination is the nature that is not absorbed by our passionate attachment to semblance. Passion attached to semblance may well eventually crack, and there could then be the devastating outbreak of something chaotic. Inclination is always already wayward in relation to such attachment to semblance. Inclination (*Neigung*) 'is able to soften [*zu sänftigen*]' semblance (*GS* 1.1:186/*SW* 1:344, translation modified).[10] Critically outlining Goethe's outlook concerning nature as all-powerful fate, Benjamin surmises '[i]n this world view is chaos', and on the basis of this world view there ultimately develops 'myth, which, without ruler or limits, imposes itself as the sole power in the domain of existence' (*GS* 1.1:149/*SW* 1:316, translation modified). Again, the problem seems not nature so much as myth, which then dominates all consideration of nature. 'God's intervention [*Walten*]', Benjamin claims, could indeed elevate above nature (*GS* 1.1:187/*SW* 1:345), as was suggested in the 'Theological-Political Fragment' as quoted earlier. Benjamin even conceives of a love that would correlatively rise above nature. That *Eros* cannot dispense with inclination is not, however, 'a naked failure [*ein naktes Scheitern*]' so much as it is 'the true redemption [*wahrhafte Einlösung*] of the most profound imperfection' in 'the nature of the human' (*GS* 1.1:187/*SW* 1:344–5, translation modified). Inclination cannot complete. It brings semblance to decline. Precisely in ruining semblance, however, it can circumvent attempted subordination to dubiously acclaimed completion (*GS* 1.1:191–2/*SW* 1:348–9). Hence, the importance of addressing the struggle between inclination and 'duty' (such as legal-conventional marital obligation) (*GS* 1.1:144/*SW* 1:312).

In his 'Outline of the Psychophysical Problem', Benjamin accordingly discusses the 'body' (*Körper*) as 'a moral instrument'. In the biblical story of creation, the body was created to fulfil the commandments. Even its 'perceptions', however, draw the 'body' (*Körper*) away from, or towards, its duty (*GS* 6:82/*SW* 1:396). This body is not just duty. This 'body' as '*Körper*', which belongs to God, is within yet also independent of the 'body' as '*Leib*', which belongs to humanity. Humans have, nonetheless, the possibility of 'decision' (*Entscheidung*) about the dynamic of these two natures, these two bodies, these two 'universal contexts' of body as '*Leib*' and body as '*Körper*', which involve – respectively – 'dissolution and resurrection' (*GS* 6:80/*SW* 1:395). In terms closer to those used in the *Elective Affinities*-essay: dissolution happens in the body that has attached itself entirely to its semblance; resurrection happens in the body that is attentive to destructive, and thereby redemptive, nature. A decision can be made to recall '*Körper*'.

Muteness, decision and the acoustics of innocent nature

Benjamin's essay of 1916 'On Language as Such and the Language of the Human' addresses a dynamic of nature, human, and muteness. This may be noteworthy for consideration of his somewhat later views on decision and nature. To give language to nature would, it is stressed, be 'more than to "make able to speak"' (*GS* 2.1:155/ *SW* 1:72). To give language to nature would be, rather, an allowance for necessary silence, for the withdrawal of nature from what humans can entirely perceive or say. There is thus 'a double meaning' (*einen doppelten Sinn*) to the proposition that nature would lament if language were given to it. First, the proposition means that nature would lament about 'language itself', about being left out of language; '[b]eing without language [*Sprachlösigkeit*] ... is the great sorrow [*Leid*] of nature'. The second meaning of the proposition is that nature would simply lament on the basis of the *language* that eludes containment by all extant languages. As 'the most undifferentiated, impotent expression of language', this lament 'contains scarcely more than the sensuous breath [*sinnlichen Hauch*]'. This sensuous lament offsets, nonetheless, disregard of nature. It is the lament that 'always' already 'resonates', 'even where only plants rustle'. Nature mourns '[b]ecause it is mute', but 'the inversion of this proposition' – the second meaning of the proposition (that nature would lament if language is given to it) – 'leads even deeper into the essence of nature: the sadness of nature makes it mute' (*GS* 2.1:154–5/*SW* 1:72–3, translation modified). Maintaining itself against extant languages, nature withholding itself laments indistinctly. Nature laments in a becoming-mute. In doing so, it is a corrective to the naming that is otherwise oblivious to this lament. The latter 'overnaming' is the 'deepest linguistic reason' for all 'sadness [*Traurigkeit*]'; it is 'the linguistic being of the sad [*sprachliches Wesen des Traurigen*]' and it is the linguistic reason for 'all deliberate muteness [*Verstummens*]' of things (*GS* 2.1:155–6/*SW* 1:73, translation modified). If the terminology in this essay of 1916 seems unduly anthropomorphic (nature laments, is sad, is deliberately mute), this takes nothing from the point that there is a realm – here called nature – resistant to human endeavours at entirely expressing or controlling it.

In the *Elective Affinities*-essay, Benjamin does say 'Truth is discovered in the essence of language'. In the correlative exercise of language, however, it is 'the human body [*Körper*]' that 'lays itself bare' and thereby provides 'a sign that the human steps before God'. In stepping before God, the body divests itself of so much that there remains only the nature that 'cannot be unveiled [(*u*)*nenthüllbar ist*]' (*GS* 1.1:197/*SW* 1:353, translation modified). Discovery of truth in the essence of language releases the human body as *Körper*. In standing before God, the body shows that it is not completely cognized by any human. It is, rather, the body where there is no fated form: this body, this interaction with nature, has no fate.

A 'fateful [*schicksalhafte*] sort of existence' may, of course, enclose 'living natures in a particular context of guilt and atonement' (*GS* 1.1:138/*SW* 1:307, translation modified). For Benjamin, however, it is humans that have fate. Fate 'does not concern the life of innocent plants', whereas the human living in a specific guilt context is accountable to this guilt-context (*GS* 1.1:138/*SW* 1:307, translation modified). On the other hand, to become helpless before fate is to become plant-like – according to the vocabulary of the *Elective Affinities*-essay.[11] Ottilie's '[p]lant-like muteness', Benjamin says, seems to recall Daphne seeking to escape Apollo, imploring to be turned into a bay-tree, and thereafter existing as Apollo's shrine with 'pleading upraised hands'. On the basis of this '[p]flanzenhaftes Stummsein', some interpreters formulate Goethe's novel as a tragedy (*GS* 1.1:175–6/*SW* 1:336–7).[12] For Benjamin, Goethe's novel is something less than a tragedy. In the *Trauerspiel*-book, it is contended that even the pathos of the tragic heroic figure includes coming to a self-consciousness in which the 'demonic jurisdiction' of mythic guilt is outgrown (*GS* 1.1: 310/*OT* 131). In the terms of the *Elective Affinities*-essay: momentarily introducing the 'word' that broaches the 'edge of decision' where mythic guilt and innocence are wrenched into a confusing abyss, the tragic figure acquires an independence from such guilt and innocence (*GS* 1.1:176–7/*SW* 1:337, translation modified). Ottilie, 'the hesitating maiden', does not get this far (*GS* 1.1:177/*SW* 1:337, translation modified). She just seems abandoned to her end; without 'resolution', her death wish is a 'drive' (*GS* 1.1:176/*SW* 1:336, translation modified). Ottilie's thoroughly silent suicide – unannounced to those around her but also somehow inconceivable for herself – is simply sacrifice to a 'morality' that is 'questionable' (*GS* 1.1:176/*SW* 1:336). Her end is 'mournful' (*trauervoll*); could not be more untragic (*GS* 1.1:177/*SW* 1:337).

For Benjamin, she abdicates the human. Benjamin's critical review in 1917–18 of Adalbert Stifter's *Bunte Steine* states it would be 'subhuman' (a lowly kind of demonism and ghostliness) to attempt to bind 'the ethical world' and 'destiny' (*Schicksal*) with a nature considered innocent in its simple appearance – its 'innocent appearance of simplicity' (*GS* 2.2:609, 608/*SW* 1:112, translation modified). This critique of Stifter is echoed in Benjamin's critique of Goethe's *Elective Affinities*. Insofar as 'mute diffidence [*Befangenheit*]' in the realm of 'human, indeed bourgeois custom' is supposed to save 'the life of passion' in *Elective Affinities*, Benjamin detects in Goethe a Stifter-like tendency (*GS* 1.1:185/*SW* 1:343, translation modified). The marriage of Charlotte and Eduard seems to turn into a 'fate' (*Geschick*). Ottilie's death is celebrated as a 'sacrifice' necessary to atone for the 'guilty' (*Schuldigen*) who had broached feelings deviating from this fate (*GS* 1.1:139–40, 173, 175/*SW* 1:308–9, 334, 336, translation modified). So 'dangerous' is Ottilie's 'magic of innocence', an innocence that is not 'purity but its semblance [*Schein*]' (*GS* 1.1:175/*SW* 1:335–6). In 'Fate and Character' (1919), Benjamin says: 'Fate is the guilt context of the living. It corresponds to the natural condition of the living'. The natural condition of the human is 'that semblance [*Schein*], not yet wholly dispelled, from which the human is so far removed that, under its rule, the human was never wholly immersed in it'. Under this rule, the human in its 'best part' was 'only invisible'. 'It is not therefore really' the human 'who has a fate; rather, the subject of fate is indeterminable'. A judge might see 'fate' but 'every punishment' proclaimed by the judge involves that the judge 'must blindly dictate fate. It is never the human but only the mere life [*das bloße Leben*] in the human that it strikes – the part involved in natural guilt and misfortune by virtue of semblance' (*GS* 2.1:175/*SW* 1:204, translation modified). The statement from *Elective Affinities*-essay has already been mentioned in which Benjamin claims that there is disregard of 'the human [*Menschliches*]' if there is such a reduction to the 'guilt' of 'mere life' (*GS* 1.1:138–9/ *SW* 1:308). It is disregard of the human to confine it to any particular guilt-context.

Such a confined human is at best a human with choices, not a human able to make a decision. With the title *Die Wahlverwandtschaften* (*Elective Affinities*), Goethe refers – half-unconsciously perhaps – to the dilemma in the novel that 'choice [*Wahl*]' is unable to reach 'the greatness of decision' (*GS* 1.1:188/*SW* 1:346). Choice belongs to natural 'elements' and their sequences of adaptation; in relation to these elements, 'decision is transcendent' (*GS* 1.1:189/*SW* 1:346).[13] The *Trauerspiel*-book highlights adaptation to the elements that is openly vice-ridden, openly Satanic – for example, in the manner of Shakespeare's Richard III. In Shakespeare's dramas, such an elemental tendency is paramount. Yet even here something tends to break through to be juxtaposed with the 'elemental of the world of senses [*Elementare der Sinnenwelt*]'

(*GS* 1.1:402/ *OT* 228–9, translation modified). Such a breakthrough is against tyrants and intriguers but also against the resigned. Goethe's figures under the 'spell of elective affinities [*Wahlverwandtschaften*]' (*GS* 1.1:134/*SW* 1:304) do not rise to more than 'choice [*Wahl*]', which does not strengthen the development of 'affinity' or 'kinship' (*Verwandtschaft*), does not provide any basis for 'the spiritual' (*das Geistige*) in affinity (*GS* 1.1:189/*SW* 1:346 translation modified). Benjamin uses the word 'spiritual' in various ways but its usage here – as on many other occasions – evidently concerns a potential that is beyond adaptive nature. Only 'kinship' or 'affinity' (*Verwandtschaft*) as 'object of a resolution' can proceed over the level of choice to decision (*GS* 1.1:189/ *SW* 1:346).

This object of resolution is, however, mystery. To have mystery as object of resolution is to recall mystery for whatever is silenced by semblance. Hence the importance of mystery in affinity and of the art form least obviously bound to semblance: music. Whereas those in a powerful bond of emotion with semblance are not 'moved in their innermost being by music' (*GS* 1.1:192/*SW* 1:349), those for whom beauty is not decisive (*GS* 1.1:185/*SW* 1:343) are 'in the realm of music', which is even characterized – through a quotation of Goethe – as surpassing the '"senses"' (*GS* 1.1:191/*SW* 1:348, translation modified). It is within the senses, however, that it surpasses the senses. The 'resounding' (*Erklingen*) of music is conceived, moreover, as no fulfilment of the mute world but rather as 'dedicated' (*zugeignet*) to the mute world; it 'promises' the mute world 'the redemption' (*Erlösung*) that is more than 'conciliation' (*Aussöhnung*) (*GS* 1.1:201/*SW* 1:355, translation modified).[14] The mute world is that to which the redemptive hope is dedicated – not to make the muteness speak but to let it convey its silence that is not conciliated. Genius is born, Benjamin says in 'Fate and Character', not in a determinable moral order but in an infantile silence *vis-à-vis* such order. The paradoxical birth of genius in infantile silence may be 'the basis of all sublimity' (*GS* 2.1:175/*SW* 1:203–4). This disruptive acoustics of silence is contrasted by Benjamin with the quiet in Stifter's work. For Benjamin's 1917–18 Stifter-review, the 'world-being' (*Weltwesen*), the 'language' that is the origin of all speaking, is heard only by a 'contact' quite distinct from the 'quiet' (*Ruhe*) in Stifter's writings, which not only tend to exclude 'any acoustic sensation' (*jegliche ... akustische ... Sensation*) and be visually oriented, but also tend to show Stifter to be 'spiritually mute' (*seelisch stumm*) (*GS* 2.2:609–10/*SW* 1:112, translation modified). The figures of *Elective Affinities* also cannot ascend to much, for they have not descended into the mysterious depths of God; they are '[d]eaf to God' and, therefore, 'mute before the world' (*GS* 1.1:134/*SW* 1:305). In order *not* to become mutely acquiescent to conceptions of fate, it is necessary to be effectively attentive to the mystery beyond anything specific conveyed to us by our senses. This attention contrasts with what the *Elective Affinities*-essay refers to as the 'act of choosing' (*Wahlakt*) that cannot reach beyond 'what is seized' (*GS* 1.1:189/*SW* 1:346). The attention is not the muteness surrendering to semblance, but rather the insistence on letting resonate a muteness that leads beyond what can be grasped and defies association with fate.

Although Benjamin's critical letter of 1916 to Buber does invoke the prospect of 'the crystal clear elimination of the unsayable', it adds that;

[m]y concept of objective and, at the same time, highly political style and writing is this: to lead to what is denied to the word. Only where this sphere of the wordless in the unspeakably pure night discloses itself can the magic spark leap between word and moving deed, where the unity of these two is equally real. Only the intensive direction of words into the core of the innermost muteness [*des innersten Verstummens*] attains the true effect'. (*GB* 1:326–7/*C* 80–1, translation modified)

As Benjamin says in the *Elective Affinities*-essay, 'linguistic shape [*sprachliche Gestalt*]' – that is, becoming 'an object of communication' – is indeed necessary for 'ethical resolution [*sittlicher Entschluß*]' to enter life, to enter 'the moral world [*die moralische Welt*]'. This moral world can, however, be 'illuminated by the spirit of language' only in ethical resolution (*GS* 1.1:176/*SW* 1:336, translation modified). Ethical resolution recalls mystery that is insubordinate to myth. It is silence under myth that Benjamin criticizes as he favours freedom over hesitancy, clarity (*Klarheit*) over silence (*Schweigen*), and decision over acquiescent forbearance (*GS* 1.1:131/*SW* 1:302). Myth lacks the *unequivocalness* or *clarity* (*Eindeutigkeit*) with which character simply recognizes the lived-guilt context as erroneous (*GS* 1.1:162, 174/*SW* 1:326, 335). Character thereby shows its awareness, nonetheless, of the muteness that is not subordinate to semblance. Loyalty to innermost muteness is required if there is to be betrayal of subordinate silence under myth.

Decision for hope

The *Elective Affinities*-essay continues: a 'dramatic crowning' of the confrontation of myth with passion and inclination is 'in the mystery of hope' (a formulation mentioned above). This 'moment can never come to expression in words but solely in presentation [*Darstellung*]' (*GS* 1.1:200–1/*SW* 1:355, translation modified). The presentation conveys mystery without being able to expunge it. In an outline for the *Elective Affinities*-essay, the decision in the novella within *Elective Affinities* is characterized as the 'antithesis' to the 'thesis' that is myth, and is followed by the 'synthesis' that is hope ('Zu den Wahlverwandtschaften. Disposition', *GS* 1.3:835–7); in certain manuscripts of the *Elective Affinities*-essay, the divisions – myth as thesis, redemption as antithesis, hope as synthesis – are given as titles of the three respective parts of the essay (*GS* 1.3:846, 851, 858). It is not that the decision in the novella is unrelated to the synthesis of hope. Benjamin even claims that the *law of the novella-form*, the law evident in this novella within *Elective Affinities*, is that 'the secret [*Geheimnis*]' is 'an essential characteristic [*Wesenszug*]' (*GS* 1.1:169/*SW* 1:331, translation modified). The portrayal in the novella of redemptive decision alerts to the persistence of mystery or secret, and thus hope, against myth. Hope maintains mystery against myth.

In depicting the decision that takes place in the novella, Benjamin does indeed refer to a brilliant or bright light that makes everything 'sharply contoured' and, from the outset, somehow pushing towards 'the day of decision', the day that 'shines into the dusk-like Hades of the novel' (*GS* 1.1:169/*SW* 1:331). This day of decision (*Tag der*

Entscheidung), which does happen in the novella, is a cutting – *Scheidung* – from or away from – *Ent* – the conformist conciliation that hazily prevails in the novel. The decision is, moreover, 'beyond' all later happening and comparison, and is thus experienced as 'essentially singular … and unique [*einmalig … und einzig*]' (*GS* 1.1:190/*SW* 1:347).

Even such decision is singular and unique, however, only insofar as it is based on the inability of 'experience' (*Erfahrung*) to be absorbed by humans' presumptions to contain it. Experience constantly takes exception to whatever is regarded or identified as 'lived experience' (*Erlebnis*) (*GS* 1.1:190, 199/*SW* 1:347, 354). The 'decision' indicates a 'readiness for reconciliation' (*Versöhnungsbereitschaft*), but this readiness to become 'reconciled' (*ausgesöhnt*) ensues from what makes it a very distinct *readiness for reconciliation*: 'There is true reconciliation only with God'. In true reconciliation, one becomes 'reconciled [*versöhnt*]' with God and only 'thereby' becomes 'reconciled [*ausgesöhnt*] with human beings'. '[T]rue reconciliation with God' is only possible for one who 'destroys everything' associated with herself or himself in order to find this everything 'resurrected [*wieder erstanden*]'. This may seem terribly demanding or even threatening, but important is indeed the adjective 'true' before the noun 'reconciliation'. Precisely the importance of God assures that human beings will not rest with pseudo-reconciliations. Only 'reconciliation [*Versöhnung*]' that is 'entirely supramundane [*überweltlich*]' 'has its worldly reflection in conciliation of fellow human beings [*Aussöhnung der Mitmenschen*]' (*GS* 1.1:184/*SW* 1:343). One of Benjamin's notes of 1919–20 says divine violence 'breathes destruction' in 'the earthly world' (*GS* 6:99/*SW* 1:226). Divine violence destroys attempts to contain it.

Perhaps not accomplishing the kind of redemption detected by Benjamin in Goethe's novella within *Elective Affinities*, the deciding, cutting, critical attitude mentioned in 'Towards the Critique of Violence' cannot have decision as last judgement, or even as a utopian completeness or perfection. Cutting, critical decisiveness can, however, often reject discernible judgements perpetrated by a mythic context. That is the hope of mystery, and mystery of hope, it offers. In other words, mystery assures that there can be hope against the closures by myth.

Enacted in and on behalf of mystery, the decision will never be certain of its motivations or impulses but will at least raise a priority that might otherwise be neglected. The 'sense' of the 'action [*Handelns*]' in 'the seconds of decision' by the figures in the novella within *Elective Affinities* is 'courageous resolution' that breaks an ostensible 'fate [*Schicksal*]' (*GS* 1.1:170–1/*SW* 1:332). It is not possible, however, to break all the ostensible fates of guilt that make up our mythic lives. We can, nonetheless, engage the attitude of decisiveness that recalls mystery against those fates insofar as we are even aware of them. We can offset our propensity to regard such fates as the last word.

Perhaps the critical, cutting and decisive attitude is – to use the terminology of the *Elective Affinities*-essay – no guarantor of utter 'redemption' but is a guarantor of 'hope' that resurrects mystery against mythic solution or dissolution (*GS* 1.1:201/ *SW* 1:355; *GS* 1.3:835–7). Notes from 1922–3 thus object to a Roman Catholic refusal to recognize 'the situation of decision'. Not to recognize the situation of decision is 'objective mendacity', the kind of lying that takes its lies to be truth. Focusing on the 'practical … Catholic authority' (the practical 'administration of justice in church discipline and confessional judgement'), Benjamin refers to the 'Catholic, bad, deferment [*Verschiebung*] of the last judgement'. He contrasts this deferment, which amounts to an institutional denial of deferment, with the 'Jewish, good, postponement [*Aufschub*] of the last judgement (namely, of the decision)' ('Notizen über "Objektive Verlogenheit" I', *GS* 6:60–2, especially 60). The latter postponement, the postponement of the last judgement, has been discussed above as Benjamin's advocacy of decision that endeavours to recall non-mythic nature. In 'Outline of the Psychophysical Problem', he remarks: the body – '*Körper*' – within, yet also independent of, the body as lived '*Leib*' is the possibility of 'decision' with regard to the 'resurrection' of '*körperliche*' nature (*GS* 6:80/*SW* 1:395). The latter nature is to be resurrected only as destructive mystery, but precisely this is guarantor of hope against myth, which cannot tolerate such mystery.

Epilogue: The vegetative

Apart from using the word *nature* in contradictory ways without always clarifying his terminology, Benjamin – not least in the *Elective Affinities*-essay – could seem to invite various questions that he himself does not pose concerning his accounts of nature. Benjamin's view is not that there is strict separation of nature and humans' redemptive potentials; in many respects, the latter potentials are dependent on attentiveness to nature that withholds itself from expression. Disregard of this nature would itself be mythic. There remains, however, what might seem an ultimately arbitrary elevation of human expressiveness and a correlative vilification of the allegedly less than human nature as resigned muteness.

The supernatural in the human is opposed to a nature that itself supposedly instils in the human a muteness involving guilt-ridden surrender to a presumed fate. On the one hand, the latter guilt-ridden surrender is also something Benjamin considers unique to humans in their abdication of their humanity. Nature – in one nuance of Benjamin's conception of nature – is removed from human criteria of guilt and innocence; nature is innocent of such criteria. Whereas in humans this innocent nature is considered by Benjamin to facilitate redemptive destruction, such redemptiveness is also considered by him to be *relatively* non-existent and mute in all other entities – even if nature resists human's 'overnaming', as can the lament discussed in the 1916– essay 'On language as such'. This relative muteness can lead, according to Benjamin, to surrender to Apollonian orders – hence, his critique of plant-like muteness in Ottilie or in Stifter's works. Benjamin thereby portrays a nature sunk into itself that simply adapts to the pressures of fate-ridden orders. Even Heidegger, who is not without his own assumptions concerning the human as unique conduit of opening to being as such, wonders if we really have access to what constitutes the plant as plant.[15] We do not know, in other words, what plant-like would really be *like*, for we do not entirely know plants or indeed their relationship with us. Insofar as Benjamin disregards this not-knowing, he seems to engage in the very overnaming that he otherwise criticizes.

There are, furthermore, implications of characterizing certain human beings as vegetative – plant-like – in the ways that Benjamin has been shown above to do. There seems a risk of disregard and – here too – of overnaming when some are judged as severely as Benjamin judges concerning their putative vegetativeness. The *Elective Affinities*-essay stresses that figures in an artwork are not to be subject to ethics – Benjamin says 'ethical judgement' is, after all, 'executable only on humans' (*GS* 1.1:133/ *SW* 1:303–4, translation modified). His critical judgements of the figures in Goethe's novel, and his exalting assessments of the two figures in the novella within Goethe's novel, indicate nonetheless that his literary criticism involves drawing ethical implications for human beings.[16] In his assessments of the plant-like figure (Ottilie) in the novel, this figure is somehow removed from further consideration. The characterization of someone as vegetative makes assumptions about what the vegetative is, but also employs this definition to characterize the person as less-than-human.

To criticize Benjamin in this way is not to propose the treatment of 'mere life' as sacred, a proposition Benjamin opposes in 'Towards the Critique of Violence' as well as in the *Elective Affinities*-essay. In this respect, Goethe may well be criticized insofar as he enshrines Ottilie as chaste and mute innocence that must be sacrificed to fulfil the assumed demands of fate.

The question may, nonetheless, be posed: Does not the innocence of nature – the innocence Benjamin says (in the *Elective Affinities*-essay) impels the revolt of 'character' (*GS* 1.1:174/*SW* 1:335) – also require refraining from dismissals of someone as simply an instance of 'mere life'? On the one hand, Benjamin is telling those who turn 'mere life' into a fated condition that it is not a fated condition. In other words, the fate is ostensible and can be questioned, perhaps even opposed. Benjamin even detects 'character' in things, such as plants, as well as in humans: both can – in their indivisible innocence – demonstrate an inability to be completed by moral-legal order (*GS* 1.1:138/*SW* 1:307). On the other hand, his judgement of those he considers to have become fated includes depreciating characterizations of them as simply vegetative. Where this fatedness results in a suicide, as with Ottilie, Benjamin's judgement of a supposedly (at least somewhat) self-inflicted vegetativeness is perhaps all the less compelling. There is an often devastatingly brutal history of treating people, and many aspects of nature, under a depreciating notion of the vegetative, and of regarding that ascribed condition as indicative of an inferiority.

Benjamin's participation in such a tradition is, of course, qualified. For instance, he even implies in 'Towards the Critique of Violence' that perhaps the human, and plants and animals, could be considered sacred, but that such sacredness could not possibly be based on mere life. The reason for this is that mere life as a standard bearer for what is sacred will instil subordination and instil abandonment of concerns with justice or happiness. Mere life thereby instils feelings of obligation to proscribed guilt and fate. A further qualification is the view, expressed particularly clearly in 1916, that nature's withdrawal can be a corrective to attempts at human domination: this withdrawal is the becoming-mute that 'always' already 'resonates'. In other words, the non-compliance of nature registers itself if anyone is inclined to listen.

Notes

1   Also see 'The Significance of Time in the Moral World' [a note of 1921], *GS* 6:97–8/*SW*
    1:286–7). (In *SW*, the title is given as 'The Meaning of Time in the Moral Universe'.)
2   Brendan Moran, 'Exception, decision and philosophic politics: Benjamin and the
    extreme', *Philosophy and Social Criticism* 40.2 (2014): 145–70,
3   For readings emphasizing this nature in the *Elective Affinities*-essay, see: Rodolphe
    Gasché, 'Critique, authentic biographism, and ethical judgement', *The Honor of
    Thinking: Critique, Theory, Philosophy* (Stanford, CA: Stanford University Press,
    2007), especially 75–77; Judith Butler, 'Walter Benjamin and the Critique of
    Violence', *Parting Ways: Jewishness and the Critique of Zionism* (New York: Columbia
    University Press, 2012), 81.
4   Benjamin would eventually develop a critique of the role of *Urbilder* in works by
    Ludwig Klages and the latter's followers. Concerning Ludwig Klages's transformation
    of Johann Jakob Bachofen's views into a 'philosophy' or 'neo-paganism' that invokes
    mythic 'primal images' (*Urbilder*), see Benjamin's Bachofen-essay of the mid-1930s:
    (*GS* 2.1:229–30, 232/*SW* 3:18–19, 21).
5   See Kurt Hiller, 'Anti-Cain', in *Das Ziel. Jahrbücher für geistige Politik*, vol. III.1 ed.
    Kurt Hiller(Leipzig: Kurt Wolff Verlag, 1919): 24–32, especially 25.
6   Hiller, 'Anti-Cain': 25.
7   As mentioned already, this criticism of Benjamin has been considered elsewhere
    (see n. 2 above).
8   This might be one context for Benjamin's depreciating remarks in 'The Task of
    the Translator' (1921) on 'nature', including '*Empfindung*' (feeling, sensation,
    impression), in contrast with history (*GS* 4.1:11/*SW* 1:255). More detailed
    consideration of this passage, and similar ones, in the translation-essay cannot
    unfortunately be undertaken here.
9   One exception is Winfried Menninghaus's account of the *Elective Affinities*-essay
    and related writings by Benjamin. This is an essay that has appeared in slightly
    varying versions over more than two decades; its most recent appearance is 'Walter
    Benjamin's variations of imagelessness', trans. Timothy Bahti and David Hensley,
    Critical Horizons 14.3 (2013): 407–28, especially 422–4. An attempt to discuss the
    'ethical body' in early works by Benjamin may also be found in Monad Rrenban,
    Wild, Unforgettable Philosophy in Early Works of Walter Benjamin (Lanham, MD:
    Lexington Books, 2005), 233–59.
10 In a note of 1918, Benjamin identifies 'inclination' as an ethical force. He makes this
    point against Kant ('Zur Kantischen Ethik', *GS* 6:55).
11 Benjamin's *Elective Affinities*-essay is dedicated (*GS* 1.1:123/*SW* 1:297) to Jula Cohn,
    who belonged to the wider circle of Stefan George's followers and was friendly with
    Friedrich Gundolf, whose work on Goethe Benjamin's essay criticizes severely.
    (The dedication did not appear with the publication of the essay in *Neue Deutsche
    Beiträge* [April 1924, January 1925].) Benjamin visited Cohn in July 1921, while
    she was studying in Heidelberg with Gundolf (Scholem, *GB* 2:167, 170/*C* 181,
    182; also see: *GB* 2:156, 164). In 1921–2, Benjamin developed an overwhelming
    romantic attachment to this young sculptor and sister of his former schoolmate,
    Alfred Cohn. In 'A Berlin Chronicle', Benjamin says Jula Cohn 'never really was the
    centre [*Mittelpunkt*] of people but, in the strictest sense, really that of the fates'. It
    was 'as if her plantlike passivity and inertia had assigned her to these fates – which

indeed, of all human things, seem the most subject to vegetative laws' (*GS* 6:493/ *SW* 2:616). Scholem claims that 'the "plantlike muteness" and beauty of that "Ottilie" [Jula Cohn]', who so consequentially entered Benjamin's life at the time, inspired Benjamin's views on the beautiful and on 'the Luciferian depth' of beautiful semblance (Gershom Scholem, *Walter Benjamin und sein Engel: Vierzehn Aufsätze und kleine Beiträge* [Frankfurt a.M.: Suhrkamp Verlag, 1983], 38 / 'Walter Benjamin and his Angel', in *On Jews and Judaism in Crisis. Selected Essays* [New York: Schocken Books, 1976], 202).

12   A variation of this Daphne-motif seems to be the description in 'Towards the Critique of Violence' of Niobe being turned into stone (*GS* 2.1:197/*SW* 1:248).

13   In the novel, there is discussion of the concept of 'elective affinities' as a concept with fairly recent currency among those interested in relations between chemical substances (*Die Wahlverwandtschaften*, in *Sämtliche Werke*, vol. 19 [Munich: Deutscher Taschenbuch Verlag, 1963], 29–35 / *Elective Affinities* [Harmondsworth: Penguin Books, 1971], 50–7).

14   For an attempt to outline Benjamin's early views of the relations between visual, literary and musical arts, see Rrenban, *Wild, Unforgettable Philosophy,* 121–37.

15   Martin Heidegger, *Die Grundbegriffe der Metaphysik* (Frankfurt a.M.: Vittorio Klostermann, 1983), 266 / *The Fundamental Concepts of Metaphysics* (Bloomington, IN: Indiana University Press, 1995), 179. Derrida critically discusses this passage in *La bête et le souverain (2002–2003)* (Paris: Éditions Galilée, 2010), 171 / *The Beast and the Sovereign*, vol. 2 (Chicago, IL: University of Chicago Press, 2011), 113–14.

16   For brief remarks on the relationship of aesthetics and ethics in Benjamin's early works, see Rrenban, *Wild, Unforgettable Philosophy,* 77–9, 224–5.

Works cited

Butler, Judith. 'Walter Benjamin and the Critique of Violence'. In *Parting Ways: Jewishness and the Critique of Zionism*. New York: Columbia University Press, 2012, 69–98.

Derrida, Jacques. *La bête et le souverain (2002–2003)*. Edited by Michel Lisse, Marie-Louise Mallet, and Ginette Michaud. Paris: Éditions Galilée, 2010.

—*The Beast and the Sovereign*, vol. 2. Translated by Geoffrey Bennington. Chicago, IL: University of Chicago Press, 2011.

Gasché, Rodolphe. 'Critique, authentic biographism, and ethical judgement'. In *The Honor of Thinking: Critique, Theory, Philosophy*. Stanford, CA: Stanford University Press, 2007, 60–102.

Goethe, Johann Wolfgang von. *Die Wahlverwandtschaften*. In *Sämtliche Werke*, vol. 19. Munich: Deutscher Taschenbuch Verlag, 1963.

—*Elective Affinities*. Translated by R. J. Hollingdale. Harmondsworth, Middlesex: Penguin Books, 1971.

Heidegger, Martin. *Die Grundbegriffe der Metaphysik. Welt – Endlichkeit – Einsamkeit.* Frankfurt a.M.: Vittorio Klostermann, 1983.

—*The Fundamental Concepts of Metaphysics. World, Finitude, Solitude.* Translated by William McNeill and Nicholas Walker. Bloomington, IN: Indiana University Press, 1995.

Hiller, Kurt. 'Anti-Cain'. In Kurt Hiller (ed.), *Das Ziel. Jahrbücher für geistige Politik*, vol. III.1. Edited by Kurt Hiller. Leipzig: Kurt Wolff Verlag, 1919, 24–32.

Menninghaus, Winfried. 'Walter Benjamin's variations of imagelessness'. Translated by Timothy Bahti and David Hensley. *Critical Horizons* 14.3 (2013): 407–28. Special issue on *The Image*. Edited by Andrew Benjamin and Alison Ross.

Moran, Brendan. 'Exception, decision and philosophic politics: Benjamin and the extreme'. *Philosophy and Social Criticism* 40.2 (2014): 145–70.

Rrenban, Monad. *Wild, Unforgettable Philosophy in Early Works of Walter Benjamin*. Lanham, MD: Lexington Books, 2005.

Scholem, Gershom. *On Jews and Judaism in Crisis. Selected Essays*. Edited by W. J. Dannhauser. New York: Schocken Books, 1976.

—*Walter Benjamin und sein Engel: Vierzehn Aufsätze und kleine Beiträge*. Edited by Rolf Tiedemann. Frankfurt a.M.: Suhrkamp Verlag, 1983.

5

Variations of Fate

Antonia Birnbaum
(trans. Carlo Salzani and Brendan Moran)[1]

Bad artists throughout history have always tried to make their art like life. Only an artist who is close to his life gives us an art that is like death.

(Morton Feldman)

In Walter Benjamin's work, the concept of fate is associated with that of guilt. The guilt specific to fate never relates to a moral lapse, but rather names a life condemned to misfortune, a life chained to its own loss. This is why, in fate, guilt and misfortune are almost identical. And this is also why the sphere of fate is strictly alien to justice. In humans, the sphere of fate does not reach their ethical or religious existence. Either it designates the simple fact that they are alive, according to a natural life delivered to the exactions of the gods – this is the ancient reign of myth – or it designates the status of the creature, marked by original sin – this is the life lived in what Benjamin calls the 'language of the human', a language expelled from the paradisiacal coincidence of being and name, a language imprisoned in the communicative logic.

The variation of fate is discontinuous in a radical sense: it engages divergent streams within Benjamin's thought. One of them concerns struggle, or conflict; the other examines the breaks, the decline of history – its relation to death – as a vector of philosophical lucidity. Each time, fate is conceived in relation to the possibility of its interruption. This can result in a political, ethical affirmation of our existence, which rests on means of contestation intrinsically bound to justice. It can be read directly from the temporality that ties history to its ruin, and in which philosophical critique deciphers its incompletion. These two caesuras of fate – contestation of the arbitrary, on the one hand, and the incompletion of history on the other – are permeable; indeed, they involve each other. For all that, their contact is not direct. Benjamin elaborates the concept of fate and thinks of the interruption of fate from the standpoint of the difference that occurs to it. Demonic fate, fate of ruin: the divergence of the two emerges first between ancient tragedy and baroque drama, whereas the combination of the two inscribes itself in the law, the reign of commodity, and melancholy.

The following exploration will not claim to render the difference of demonic fate and fate of ruin coherent in one overriding fate. Far from aiming at connecting these moments, the task is rather to cast light on their discontinuity. The variations of the concept of fate to be considered here configure a highly unstable 'prehistory' of Benjamin's philosophy of history. How does 'fate' designate the annihilation proper to the mythic reign of vengeance? How does the latter extend into the modern juridical order? How does the break with the divine cast the existence of humans and things into the orbit of their own decline? How does this attraction of death work? These are the two poles – demonic fate and fate of ruin – around which the presentation of fate crystalizes, in 'Fate and Character' and 'Critique of Violence' on the one hand, and in *The Origin of German Tragic Drama* on the other, in particular in the section devoted to 'The concept of fate in the fate-drama'.

Demonic fate, the drama of fate

As we have seen, Benjamin first defines the variation of the concept of fate with regard to aesthetic forms. Let us briefly outline them.

There is first demonic fate, drawn from Greek tragedy. Connected to the ancient order of the gods, to their myths, demonic fate imprisons all life within the unending cycle of a community devoted to uniting with the divine outbursts of vengeance. Since the limits imposed on human life were those of natural hostility, this hostility was the only thing humans had in common. According to myth, which is the content of the tragic form, misfortune has force of law, given that all human conditions are beset by guilt. If it was for an instant granted to humans to be happy, the human would have already been guilty for having wanted to escape its misfortune; but in misfortune, too, the human is again guilty for wanting out of it: human existence, reduced to an opaque continuity, doubles culpability. 'Not to be born is best / when all is reckoned in, but once a man has seen the light / the next best thing, by far, is to go back / where he came from, quickly as he can'.[2]

Benjamin identifies this demonic quality in another fate, that associated with baroque drama. Linked above all to the Spanish 'drama of fate', this concept designates a world where the guilt of original sin – the guilt of the creature – rules, when any link to redemption has been lost. This strained, antinomic combination of immanence and transcendence produces an uneasy hybrid in which history, severed from its progression towards a divine end, enters a continuum with nature. This continuum becomes the scene of a profane space torn by political violence, permeated by passions that have been dissociated from their Christian stability and abandoned to their erratic impulses. Like these ravages, the significations, dissociated from a transcendent meaning, only amplify the gap between language and things; they settle directly in the amorphous exteriority of a soulless physis by shattering it, breaking it, saturating it with arbitrary and uncertain signs. Thus the baroque profusion responds both to the mourning caused by the absence of eternity and to the play provoked by the endless and incomplete repetition of profane time.

Benjamin also conceives this variation of fate between ancient and baroque tragedy from a different perspective, now considering its content. Ancient demonic fate already possesses its content in the meaning and unity of myth. With regard to this meaning, the tragic representation shows the tragic hero in his rejection of the guilt that strikes him. At issue, therefore, is a challenging of fate, even though, as we will see, this is a mute challenge. Baroque fate poses a different, much more thorny problem. It deals with a history deprived of divine meaning that arises from an infinite course. The task of the baroque work will thus be that of dramatizing this privation, of arranging its dynamics and coordinates, of producing its scene and fulfilment – in a word, of presenting a piece of history become nature. The issue is consequently in fact to render fate perceptible, to represent it. Or, to put it in Benjamin's words: 'In classical tragedy, the emphasis lies on the conflict with fate; in historical drama, on its representation' (*GS* 2.1:250/*SW* 1:365).[3] We will see that to this variation of the object corresponds a variation of the effects of fate in modernity. Benjamin discerns the persistence of demonic violence within the modern juridical order, beyond the historical victory over myths. The baroque inextricability of natural and historical temporalities is revived in order to illustrate the aporias of 'progress'.

If Benjamin first locates the concept of fate in aesthetic forms, this in no way means, however, that fate is confined within this field. On the contrary, Benjamin's elucidation shows how fate is at work in the law, in economic poverty, and in the spiritual poverty of life during the Weimar Republic. The two major variations of fate mentioned above lead Benjamin to reformulate the problem of class struggle, to give a new resolve to critical asceticism, to create the idea of 'history-nature'. In short, they lead him to invent new ways out of the influence of fate in the world surrounding him.

Demonic fate: Critique of law and class struggle

In 'Fate and Character' (published in 1921), Benjamin outlines the demonic fate that is doomed to unhappiness by identifying fate with the sphere of law. He examines both its power and the tragic act which has overcome and shattered it:

> It was not in law but in tragedy that the head of genius lifted itself for the first time from the mist of guilt, for in tragedy demonic fate is breached … in tragedy pagan man becomes aware that he is better than his god, but the realization robs him of speech, remains unspoken. Without declaring itself, it seeks secretly to gather its forces. Guilt and atonement it does not measure justly in the balance, but mixes indiscriminately. There is no question of the 'moral world order' being restored; instead, the moral hero, still dumb, not yet of age – as such he is called a hero – wishes to raise himself by shaking that tormented world. The paradox of the birth of genius in moral speechlessness, moral infantility, is the sublimity of tragedy. (*GS* 2.1:175/*SW* 1:203)

Benjamin does not cease to insist on this point: the tragic refusal of the hero cannot express itself in the language of the demonic order that condemns him, for the latter names in one and only way: it names him as guilty. The language of fate installs the reign of a misfortune with no outside. This means that the hero joins up with the revolt precisely where he cannot express it anymore. The mortal exposition of an obtuse, speechless body, which refuses to justify itself, takes the place and stead of an impossible declaration. Its mute entrenchment entails the presentiment of a life without misfortune, even though the hero knows only misfortune. According to Benjamin, the heroic act thus proves to be incommensurable with the order that pushes it outside language. Its lack of expression emerges at the same time as the revolt. By introducing a hiatus in the cycle of fate, the heroic decision opens the way for another language, foreign to that of ancient vengeance. The construction of that language of conflict, heterogeneous to the continuous order of fate, is the procedure that Benjamin deciphers in the ancient tragic representation. This is also the scheme of intelligibility that innervates his critique of the violence of fate proper to modern law.

Nothing is less self-evident than to define positive law as a renewal of the demonic vengeance in ancient myth. Yet this is precisely what Benjamin undertakes in 'Critique of Violence' (published in 1921). 'Fate and Character' clearly names the problematic core of his critical account of law: 'Mistakenly, through confusing itself with the realm of justice, the order of law – which is merely a residue of the demonic stage of human existence [...] has preserved itself long past the time of the victory over the demons' (*GS* 2.1:174/*SW* 1:203).

'Lawmaking is powermaking, assumption of power, and to that extent an immediate manifestation of violence' (*GS* 2.1:198/*SW* 1:248). In this remark of 'Critique of Violence', Benjamin merely restates what all serious thinkers affirm about the state monopoly of violence. However, what distinguishes him is the fact that he proposes to show that this violence of the power inherent in law ineluctably pursues a colonizing expansion, which encloses more and more acts and facts within the system of guilt.

When it conceives its own terms according to their legitimacy, the law claims to guarantee a relation between a perpetrated act and the liable punishment by substituting a predictable juridical consequence for all possible reactions to an unjust act (natural violence, but also the arbitrary violence of the state). Law thus presupposes a causal connection between crime and punishment, conceived according to a commensurability, an equivalence established between the degree of punishment and that of guilt. Against the claim inherent to this conception, Benjamin shows that these terms only make sense if we invert their temporality. The law can only capture those acts that it grasps as guilty: this means, on the one hand, that the juridical constitution of guilt is an integral moment of the rule of law, and, on the other, that this constitution logically precedes any act. It is not first the acts of human life, Benjamin maintains, but rather the law that establishes itself by defining what constitutes or does not constitute guilt.

There is guilt because there is law; there is not first guilt followed by punishment: 'The judge can perceive fate wherever he pleases; with every judgement he must blindly dictate fate' ('Fate and Character', *GS* 2.1:175/*SW* 1:204). Naturally, according to law, society and indeed the perpetrator himself are protected by the law. But this statement is in many respects false. It is undeniably false in that the punishment cannot in any sense undo the act it condemns, since it claims precisely to rest on an *a posteriori* causal connection: it is the guilty act that is supposed to summon the punishment. Against the liberal error, Benjamin notes that laws are not dissuasive, but threatening. But more importantly, this 'protection' excludes, *de facto* and violently, all other possible ways of articulating the 'before' and 'after' of the unjust act and of its consequences; it excludes the indetermination of time as well as the different configurations of before and after that temporality allows for.

Benjamin clarifies this rather obscure point through a comparison with the demonic order. We have seen above that, confronting a vengeance without an outside, the tragic hero's revolt has no language to express his refusal of misfortune. The modern legal order perpetuates this demonic ubiquity, but under the sign of an inverted temporal logic. What was the departure point in tragedy – the stifling and the muteness of the hero – turns into the goal: in order to impose its successive and causal connection, the law tends to suppress all free and uncertain means of articulation, which mediate the relations among humans. The argument which justifies this narrowing is always the same: this incertitude, this instability cannot be tolerated, for it entails the risk of natural violence. Here again Benjamin identifies a distorted perspective: he shows that, under the pretext of guaranteeing the exclusion of natural violence, the temporal continuity of the juridical really excludes all that eludes it, all means other than those founded on the definition of an infraction or of a violation – in short, on the definition of a guilt.

This means that the monopoly of violence proper to the law does suppress natural violence only to the extent that it expands legal violence, and this at the expense of all other non-violent procedures of agreement or conflict. The law tends to colonize all other possible means of referring to the acts of life, even those that appeared at first alien to the order of guilt. We must emphasize that in this colonization, the issue is no longer that of simply prohibiting an act, but also of imposing a conduct. In other words, the determination of law as guilt introduces a continuity that embraces both the laws linked to social norms and the laws founded on a prohibition. In the conceptual frame established by Benjamin, this difference is one of degree. Needless to say, the diagnosis of the expansion of the legal sphere is prophetic: the colonization of life by the law is a dominant trait of our world. Under different forms in rich and poor societies, it has experienced an exponential acceleration in recent years.[4]

Another effect arises: by extending more and more its causality to all spheres of life, the domain of law more and more also excludes happiness, since the latter can never result from the constraint of law. In this respect, Benjamin refers to civil contractuality: no matter what will to agreement is here expressed, it immediately becomes dependent on violence as soon as it 'guarantees' itself legally. The recourse to trust is undermined in favour of the latent threat inherent in conservative violence. Since legality inevitably proceeds through homogenization, i.e., by erasing all divergent voices, the penetration of society by the causal connection of its temporality increasingly 'produces' a lack of expression. For Benjamin, the issue is thus to break up this causal temporal connection proper to law, which remains marked by the reign of vengeance. We have to add that this connection is also one of commensurability, of an exchange between punishment and guilt. Benjamin does not need, therefore, to refer to the infrastructure of the relations of production in order to identify the continuity between law and the reign of equivalence. In 'Critique of Violence', it is rather the opposite: it is the juridical superstructure that is the direct polemical object of Benjamin's critique.[5]

But what about the moral sphere? By aiming at breaking off the causality of law, at opening temporal hiatuses between the acts and their consequences, is not Benjamin quite simply bound to annul guilt, and thus also any moral commandment? On this point, Benjamin is adamant, since his text quotes the divine commandment:

> For the question 'May I kill?' meets its irreducible answer in the commandment 'Thou shalt not kill' … the injunction becomes inapplicable, incommensurable, once the deed is accomplished. No judgement of the deed can be derived from the commandment. And so neither the divine judgement nor the grounds for this judgement can be known in advance. Those who base a condemnation of all violent killing of one person by another on the commandment are therefore mistaken. It exists not as a criterion of judgement, but as a guideline for the actions of persons or communities. (*GS* 2.1:200–1/*SW* 1:250)

The interpretation of law from the perspective of its continuity with fate allows Benjamin to produce a new division between violent and non-violent means. Or, more precisely, he traces a division between violence as a means subjected to an end – this holds for all legal violence, either law-preserving or law-making – and violence and non-violence as 'pure means'. Among the non-violent means and those of pure violence Benjamin counts the discussion (*Unterredung*) as technique of civil agreement, trust and the 'courteousness of the heart', beside which he places politics as deployed in the proletarian general strike. All these techniques pass through a relation between people and things, and all keep in reserve a potential natural violence (that which deceit or treason could provoke as a reaction) without ever resting on anything but their own mediation. It is striking that Benjamin conceives politics as a means of justice among others, and not as the central means capable of subsuming all non-violent means and those of pure violence. It is not only that pure means are mediation, but they are so by mediating each other.

Let us consider politics. From his division between legal means and pure means Benjamin draws a new differentiation within class struggle. In order to do this, he relies on the distinction made by Georges Sorel between proletarian general strike and political general strike. The former refers to a pure violence in that its rejection of arbitrariness disconnects the struggle from any power struggle. Such a means immediately carries out the destruction of the division of work and undoes all social roles. Without regard for the logic of interests and its corollary, the calculation of consequences, the proletarian general strike takes as its only task the destruction of state violence, which coincides with its own disorder. In short, by being itself the sought process of transformation, the proletarian general strike has no goal external to itself. The proletarian general strike is opposed to the political general strike, which is a means for taking over state power, and is thus a founding violence.

We have to keep in mind that this text was written after the bankruptcy of German Social Democracy, which in 1914 voted in favour of the war bonds, and shortly after the failure of the Spartacist revolution. The issue is thus above all to glean a critical lucidity from the defeat, and not to propose a political programme. Likewise, the reference to pure means does not resolve the problem of the relations between law and politics, but rather it reveals their content. At least it has the merit of forcing us to name the gap between the struggle for a cause and the struggle for a right. It remains to be asked, however, what is the efficacy of a pure means, how does it relate to the heterogeneity intrinsic to the rights gained through struggles – the right to strike, the establishing of a limit to working time, compulsory schooling, etc.? Indeed, in this respect the proletarian strike is not so much opposed to the political general strike (we cannot imagine the one taking place without the other), as it names an inner difference within all strikes, even those polarized by interests or by power struggles.

The proletarian general strike does not exclude physical violence; it rather names that which in politics renounces all power: the manifestation of the human aspiration to justice. Benjamin discerns here a profane disorder that does not tolerate any hierarchy within itself. This disorder is anarchy, not in the sense of a position simply opposed to the state, but rather in the sense of a dissolution of the founding and preserving laws from which its monopoly proceeds. Irrespective of the consequences, the proletarian strike never lowers its means to the rank of an end. Its violence is entirely a mediation, and not an order. Relying on this distinction, Benjamin argues that a position of the revolutionary class is not above all relative to its intention to overthrow the economic order; what is decisive in it is rather the will to destroy the juridical order. His critique of the complicity between law and fate thus transforms the notion of class struggle. The destruction at issue corresponds to a peculiar criss-crossing: the *less* of mastery, through which the hold of law comes undone, becomes a *more* on the side of mediation.

Permeability of bodies, affects and words, intensification and multiplication of their connections – all become suddenly depositaries of what occurs to them in common; the common is delivered to an unexpected, conflictual and unstable web of its configurations. In as much as it names the communicability of the extremes, the proletarian general strike marks the range extending from 'the division of opinions [to] bloody confrontation':[6] it releases the uncertain articulation of bodies to the symbolic as remit of politics. However, this modification in no way erases the economic question; rather, it gives it a different nuance. Concerning the mythic ambiguity of laws, Benjamin quotes Anatole France: 'Poor and rich are equally forbidden to spend the night under the bridges' (*GS* 2.1:198/*SW* 1:249). Marxist critique denounces the abstraction of a law supposedly equal for all, rich and poor. More radically, Benjamin's critique shows that modern law incessantly transforms poverty into guilt. In addition to being poor, the poor person is guilty of his poverty. To reduce life to the simple fact of being alive – to the exhausting constraint of being a commodity – and simultaneously to stigmatize this condition as offense delivered to the violence of law: this is the form the persistence of fate takes in the modern world, as mythic violence inherent to capitalism.

The poverty considered here is the poverty that pushes life to its natural condition.[7] This is the poverty that will strike the working class collectively with all its arbitrariness during the crisis of the 1920s, which is described by Benjamin in 'A Tour through the German Inflation' (in *One-Way Street*, published in 1928):

> When there was work that fed a man, there was also poverty that did not disgrace him, if it arose from deformity or other misfortune. But this deprivation, into which millions are born and hundreds of thousands are dragged by impoverishment, does indeed bring disgrace … But no one may ever make peace with poverty when it falls like a gigantic shadow upon his countrymen and his house.

> Then he must be alert to every humiliation done to him, and so discipline himself
> that his suffering becomes no longer the downhill road of grief but the rising path
> of revolt. (*GS* 4.1:96–7/*SW* 1:452)

'It is not therefore really man who has a fate; rather, the subject of fate is indeterminable' ('Fate and Character', *GS* 2.1:175/*SW* 1:204). In Weimar capitalism, this impossibility takes form in the analyses that tirelessly dissect causes and effects of the economic crisis. For these analyses, humanity does not exist; there only exist the parameters of accumulation, loss, inflation, etc. This means that humanity returns to the masses hit by unemployment and inflation when they refuse the objectification of these economic explanations, when they directly consider the intolerable character of market arbitrariness. Only then will they be able to break out of the mythic circle of capital, to speak a language other than that of its naturalization: the language of justice, which opens the path of revolt.

Dramatization of fate, reflexivity and mortification of critique

To bump into the walls, there is no need to know the plan of a house. All who venture into the conception of German baroque drama deployed by Benjamin immediately find themselves in this situation evoked by Lacan. Baroque drama is seized by Benjamin from numerous points of impact; the effects, indirect, are not easy to grasp: back and forth between a theory of sovereignty, a theory of play, a theory of allegory. The difficulty of circulating between these different moments is all the more evident if one considers a lateral facet of *The Origin of German Tragic Drama* (published in 1928): the concept of fate in the fatality-drama, which corresponds with the Spanish baroque drama, and in particular to the oeuvre of Calderón.[8]

The reading of Calderón exemplifies one of the paradoxes of the whole study: Benjamin presents us with the 'drama of fate' as one of the significant, brilliant versions of Spanish baroque and simultaneously states that precisely that which prevents its revival in Germany is what reveals the truth of the baroque. The dramatization proper to the 'drama of fate' will thus provide one of the keys to understanding the move carried out by Benjamin, that from the accomplished, Spanish form of the baroque to the form – decisive precisely because of its imperfection – of the German baroque *Trauerspiel*. Moreover, it is from this flaw in the German drama that Benjamin develops a critical procedure that is no longer reflexive, but mortifying.

What is it that art imitates? Never simply a series of facts, but rather the meaning or the idea that constitutes its remit. This holds also for the historical drama of the baroque and thus raises a particular question for the playwright, since he first finds his material in such a series. How to transform a historic sequence with an infinite course into a 'little complex of life' subordinated to one action? More precisely, given that this is the baroque, how to show history in its separation from the paradisiacal state, history as subordinate to the effect of original sin in it? This transformation of historical sources into pieces of nature (into fate) is the function of baroque dramatization. This is clearly exemplified in the happy version, the Spanish one, of this drama, which emphasizes fate as play.[9]

Benjamin differentiates the concept of fate associated with the Spanish dramas of fate from the demonic fate proper to ancient tragedy. The latter's content is a myth whose meaning is already given from the start, whereas the content of baroque drama is history in which the creature's guilt actualizes itself. The role of the oracle in both confirms this difference. In Sophocles, Tiresias tells Oedipus about his past; when he was a child, he was abandoned to savage nature with his feet pierced. To the contrary, baroque drama talks about the present world on which there weighs the threat of guilt. In *La vida es sueño* (*Life Is a Dream*), Basilio confines his son to the tower in order to dodge the portents he deciphered in his horoscope. *El mayor mónstruo del mundo* begins with the tale of an unhappy prophecy: Marianne will be the victim of a monster and Herod will kill the one whom he loves the most. This prophecy magnetizes the play; it constitutes its virtual kernel which fulfils itself in the unfurling of the plot.

In the drama of fate, the creature's guilt can be read in the unfolding of the action. This guilt, we must remember, does not belong to the register of the ethical act, but arises from original sin. This is why fate is neither a purely historical nor a purely natural category: 'It is the elemental force of nature in historical events, which are not themselves entirely nature, because the light of grace is still reflected from the state of creation. But it is mirrored in the swamp of Adam's guilt' (*GS* 1.1:308/*OT* 129). This remark outlines the peculiar technique of the Spanish baroque, which preserves a relation with grace, even though this is present only in a reflexive way. In fact, the Counter Reformation knows a profane equivalent of theological grace: grace miniaturizes itself in order to appear in a scene of play, the play of the court which surrounds the absolute monarch. Appearing as a secularized redemptive instance, the sovereign represents a force capable of subduing the force of guilt: in particular, the polarization between the action of guilt and the sovereign's action constitutes the drama itself as an unstable and mobile play of forces. While it is deserted by the earnestness proper to the absolute of the religious, life turns to the play of that profane and highly unstable space that is the cosmos of honour. By this detour, it appropriates a reflection of transcendence.

In the German space of the Reformation we cannot find any part of this dialectic. Here, the drama sinks ever more into an irrational flight towards a nature excluded from all grace; its landscape of ruin and death merges with immanence to the point that it also ruins the distance enjoyed by play: the German *Trauerspiel* appears as rigid, sinking completely into a despair with no outcome. Its sadness has no recourse; it is a melancholy taking in its ruination even the coherence of the form which is supposed to represent it.

It is thus only by means of the pretension of the powerful Counter Reformation – the pretension of coming close to grace, even indirectly – that fate can develop its logic as play. In it we find the will of restoration carried by absolutist power as well as the pagan cosmological science that informs Catholic Christendom. Play is carried out according to a polarity stretched between this sovereign majesty and astrological or magical fate. Pointing out the asymmetry between the two, Benjamin writes: 'Fate is the entelechy of events within the field of guilt' (*GS* 1.1:308/*OT* 129). The astral pole is the determining force, which acts in relation to the aim towards which the piece tends; it constitutes both the dynamics and the finality of the drama.

We have seen that fate seizes history by transforming it into pieces of nature. This means that the dramatization does not restrict itself to the plot in the strict sense of the sequence of acts, but it dynamically spreads itself among all elements of the play – the characters, but also the props, the set, nature. This is what constitutes the so amazing and modern trait of Calderón's theatre. Fate indifferently seizes human passions (Herod's jealousy) and inanimate things (the dagger and the portrait, the stars, the flowers and the landscape) in order to produce the premonitory signs of misfortune and misfortune itself. This means that fate always occurs by means of an alien element, through intermediary relations, through chance and passion. Guilt does not produce a necessary development of the drama; to the contrary, it is the dramatization of the fortuitous character of things that makes legible the action of guilt.

According to such a dramatization, virtuality and actuality of guilt correspond to each other, but without being alike, with no direct path taken from the one to the other. This holds even for the most contaminated elements of the drama. So Marianne, Herod's wife, dies because of his jealousy, but Herod does not kill his wife out of jealousy; he kills her by accident, in the course of an imbroglio concerning the dagger and the presence of Octave in his wife's chambers. Calderón has done all he could in order to avoid this conclusion: Herod killing out of jealousy. According to Benjamin, the Spaniard is the only playwright who succeeded with this historical material. Having from beginning to end linked Herod's jealousy to love, without letting it slip into hatred, he is the only one who succeeded in dramatizing a fate, in locating the cause of the murderous act outside of the character who commits it, and yet within the constellation of the piece.

In relation to this dramatic logic, the absolute monarch has a double status. The sovereign is the highest creature; close to the divine, he reigns over history and can infuse in it an order that reflects the hereafter: projecting the illusory dimension of the here-below, turning the totality of waking life towards the logic of dream. *Life Is a Dream* marvellously exemplifies this resolution of the drama. But in spite of his power, the sovereign is and remains a creature, himself subordinated to the immanence of guilt; his decision is spoiled, ruined by the passions that imprint his will with opposite impulses. In one moment, he restores order and we are presented with a romantic drama; in another moment, he founders, and one of the figures of this loss is the drama of fate.

And yet, the issue is always to stage fate as machination, or play; and Calderón accomplishes this by means of reducing the action, by means of one of those reflections that the heroes keep at hand to make turn in reflections the whole order of fate the way one turns a ball in one's hand to see now one side, now the other.

For Benjamin, the virtuosity of the Spanish playwright consists in his capacity to harmonize sadness and play. To all the dissociations, to all the effects of misfortune bound to passion and chance, there corresponds a renewal of these effects in the shimmering reflexivity of an illusion that extends to the totality of life: the theatre of the world. Such a dramatization only represents the closure of the sublunar world upon itself, 'where again and again the rules of fate to which every creature is subject were to confirm their validity in an astonishing and virtuosic way, *ad maiorem dei gloriam* and for the enjoyment of the spectators' (*GS* 2.1:267–8/*SW* 1:378),[10] but the dramatization represents the closure according to the infinite relations produced by appearance.

Even while he emphasizes the brilliance of the Spanish dramatization (Calderón's virtuosity), Benjamin sees in this very success a blockage. Certainly no one is better than the Spanish playwright in arranging the discontinuities of chance and passion by means of which the creature's guilt takes effect. But he underlines them only in order to annul them better. Calderón connects the misfortunes of the profane world with a dream in order to dissolve, within this dream, the separation of the finite world from the absolute. So every little complex of dramatic life is illuminated as a totality. This trait is common to Romanticism and to Calderón's baroque; the instance of salvation and redemption lies in the paradoxical reflection of play, where fiction disputes reality. Through the fulfilment of its form, the Spanish baroque reintegrates the separation in the absolute, and takes it to the level of an aesthetic absolutization. And yet it is precisely this brilliant capacity for form that blocks the access to the truth of profane separation.

In contrast, German baroque drama never succeeds in giving a formal life to the separation which would transcend its finitude. It can but expose the aggravation of this formal life. A nocturnal plunge, the fate proper to German drama no longer contains any glimmer from the sun of grace. Its stiffness does not produce new developments, but rather progresses by digging 'most deeply the jagged line of demarcation between physical nature and significance' (*GS* 1.1:343/*OT* 166). Exponentially bringing history closer to what divides it from infinity, the drama inscribes humans and things into the decline proper to physis. Settling within the soulless – amorphous – continuum of nature, significations shatter nature by fragmenting it, by saturating it with arbitrary signs, by taking the content to its ruin, in turn ruining themselves in the decline they reveal. Bringing it close to 'history-nature', fate takes history to its devastation, or, in Benjamin's vocabulary, it exposes the 'mortification' of history. Seized by the dynamics of this mortification, the *Trauerspiel* never succeeds in giving itself life as a form. By this very flaw, it accesses the truth of profane separation, that of a temporality struggling with death.

The paradox of baroque is that only its unaccomplished, failed, minor version – its German rigidity – truly produces its intelligibility, including that of its major, successful, Spanish version. Because it perfectly dramatizes chance and passion, the latter certainly succeeds in revealing the creature's guilt as remit of profane life. But because it captures this guilt in the form of an appearance, in and through the infinity of appearance, Spanish baroque annuls the effects of this guilt, the effects of disassemblage, of fragmentation, of mortification. For these effects no longer adhere to aesthetic form, but adhere to the destruction of reality. It is thus up to the form that fails as form – to the German baroque drama, itself corroded by the decline it reveals – to expose the reality of this mortification. Here, *in nuce*, is what forces Benjamin to shift his attention from Spanish brilliance to the ruptures in German baroque drama.

This shift also marks a change in Benjamin's critical-philosophical praxis, which breaks for good with some of its romantic traits. In fact, relying on Romanticism,

Benjamin does reject critique as measure or source, in order instead to find its starting point in the immanence of works. Such a critique approaches the work as close as possible to its processuality, analysing the relations and connections between elements that produce together two things. These two things are the form proper to the singular existence of the work, and the dissolution of its relative contingency into its relation with infinity: with the idea of art. This reflexivity implies as well a compenetration of philosophy and art, since each singular work encounters the question of the idea of art at the very core of its own procedure.

Yet in the dramas of Gryphius, Lohenstein and Haugwitz Benjamin is faced with an obstacle to this compenetration: in these dramas, the fracturing of the elements ruins the coherence of the work as well, it breaks off all synthesis. Far from the inclusion of everything into the logic of the form, here it is the very form that shatters and scatters itself when confronted by the dissociations which break it apart. The allegorical fragments of these dramas are no longer little totalities in relation with the absolute, curled up like a hedgehog. They are opaque fragments, in rapport with death, that can be indifferently charged with a host of significations. Nothing connects these fragments any more to art. They are aesthetic elements merely because they are elements of finitude: splinters of reality to be deciphered. This also means that a critique capable of grasping the truth of this fragmentation can no longer merely call itself aesthetics, for it finds itself up against a reality that exceeds the artwork, the reality of history. Such a critique does not reduce, but rather amplifies this fragmentation of coherence; in Benjamin's words, it becomes 'mortification'.

What does this mean? By exacerbating the dissociations characteristic of a world severed from the divine, by destroying the synthetic principle of the form, by shattering the reconciling unification of reflection, mortifying critique apprehends the separation with the absolute no longer as a fall from truth, but as the truth of the profane as such. If in the baroque work mortification is melancholy, mortifying critique performs a lucid conversion of this melancholy. Benjamin recovers all the moments of ruin, of loss, of downfall that occurs to the rigidity of these dramas, but in order to reverse their potential. Instead of discrediting the profane world, the degradation in the profane world degrades the value of symbolic closure in the works. It is not that the ambiguity of allegorical significations annuls their certainty; far from it. Rather, this ambiguity affirms that each concrete element can signify any other, according to an immanent cross-referencing carried out *ad infinitum*. Likewise, the relation to death no longer denotes our removal from the absolute; it denotes instead the incompletion in which history proceeds.

In a certain way, this critical inversion does but seize the instability of the allegorical system of signification, in which the profane world is simultaneously devalued and elevated; but this inversion seizes it according to a peculiar inclination, which imparts a sober twist to its melancholic disposition. Thus Benjamin: 'Criticism means the mortifications of the works. By their very essence these works [the baroque *Trauerspiele*] confirm this more readily than any others. Mortification of the works: not then – as the romantics have it – awakening of the consciousness in living works, but the settlement of knowledge in dead ones' (*GS* 1.1:357/*OT* 182).

On the relevance of the concept of fate

This brief outline underlines the amplitude of the variations entailed by the concept of fate in Benjamin's oeuvre, the capacity of the philosopher to let the concept of fate enter his own work according to the sphere of its manifestations, the nature of guilt, etc. What remains to be examined is the task Benjamin assigns to the concept of fate, the questions it raises.

As we have seen, the analysis of the continuity between fate and modern law leads Benjamin to radically separate all real practice of justice – be it ethical or political – from that of the law. This gesture only makes sense, though, if we situate it in its context. At the conclusion of the First World War and of its defeat, Germany becomes a republic by means of a revolutionary movement that is immediately suppressed by the republic. This reversal leads Benjamin and many others to rethink the terms of class struggle. As we have seen, he makes the antinomy between law and justice a central category of class struggle. His main example is the strike, which is divided according to whether or not it participates in the founding violence of power or participates in a real manifestation of justice, in a conflictual mediation with no end beyond itself. We can interpret this division in several ways. Either the political manifestations of justice – its pure violence – coincide with the immediate extinction of the state, and thus they only find their effective truth in a revolutionary situation, or the antinomy between justice and law finds its truth in an effective utopian capacity, which bursts into innumerable 'points of intervention'. In the latter case, therefore, Benjamin's critique of the colonization by the law underlines what in every conflict is heterogeneous to the sphere of the law, starting with the strike itself.[11]

In this second case of the figure, which for us is the most relevant, the tipping-point is not easy to grasp. For example, Benjamin emphasizes that it is the reality of the strike which forces the state to grant rights. It remains to be seen whether this point of intervention refers to an original dissociation between law and justice, whether it proceeds from a heterogeneous constraint applied by the political sphere on the sphere of power, or again whether it merely designates the assimilation of the strike to a founding violence of this power.

No doubt the historical situation pushes Benjamin towards the latter interpretation. But what he bequeaths to us is the difficulty we encounter in this question. We find it again in Foucault's philosophy, for which power incessantly produces a continuity precisely where the act is supposed to produce a rupture. We also find it, in a different guise, in Agamben's philosophy, for which there can be an infinite mediation only because there already exists an original caesura between bare life and the sovereign power over this life.[12] More simply, we find this difficulty in all attempts to think political subjectification that is not identical with a legal subject. What happens to the gap between the struggle for a cause and that for a right? Is the difference between them to be ascribed to a heteronomy or to a heterogeneity? In any case, Benjamin forces us to problematize the fetishization of parliamentarianism as well as the dream of the seizure of power, and he does that from 1921 onwards.

We have seen that Benjamin decentres the baroque from reflexive dramatization towards fragmentation, towards the ruin of the profane, and in doing this, he singles out a 'mortifying' critical procedure. He has explored a 'detour'; he has severed the Spanish drama of fate from its appropriation by Romanticism in order to compare it with the long-unheeded German works. Rather than inscribing itself in the opposition of reality and art, this critique troubles the opposition of reality and art; in Benjamin, the critique becomes a writing critical of present history. Yet this development produces a new difficulty. For if the analysis of baroque allegory astoundingly clarifies the dissociations at work in the latter, if it deciphers the incompleteness within the ruin of the profane, it is by no means evident how one can make use of this incompleteness for a critique of capitalism.

For the continuity that must be broken is precisely that of the frightening multiplicity of commodities, where everything incessantly doubles up into its signification, where signs inscribe themselves into the vertigo of commensurable circulation proper to equivalence, where devastation presents itself as objectivity. It is as a response to this devastation that the concept of mortification proves its destructive range. Freezing of the circulation in a precise and heterogeneous configuration, actualization of a risk which divides the present, short-circuiting of reality and dream: these are the parameters in and through which Benjamin dramatizes his own philosophical work; to put it in a brief formula: 'Take incompleteness seriously'.

Notes

1   The French version of this essay appeared as 'Variations du destin', preface to Walter Benjamin, *Critique de la violence et autres essais*, trans. Nicole Casanova (Paris: Payot, 2012), 7–51. The translators thank Antonia Birnbaum for her helpful responses to their inquiries.

2   Sophocles, *Oedipus at Colonus*, in Sophocles, *The Three Theban Plays*, trans. Robert Fagles, introduction and notes by Bernard Knox (London: Penguin Books, 1984), 1388–91.

3   'Calderón's *El Mayor Monstruo, Los Celos* and Hebbel's *Herodes und Marianne*. Comments on the problem of historical dramas' (1923).

4   In rich societies, this colonization leads to an extension of control and of right to property (for example, the right to an image); in poor societies, it leads to despoiling by the same law (for example, the patents on seeds).

5   This is why the interpretations of 'Critique of Violence' that proceed along strictly Marxist lines are not very convincing.

6   According to Nicole Loraux, the passage from the one to the other is what the Greeks keep doing under the name of democracy. Cf. Nicole Loraux, *The Divided City: On Memory and Forgetting in Ancient Athens*, trans. Corinne Pache and Jeff Fort (New York: Zone Books, 2006), 24.

7   In Benjamin's works, there may, of course, be found the virtues and an independence in an impoverished response to the spiritual overbidding by Nazism. See Benjamin, 'Erfahrung und Armut', *GS* 2:1, 213–19 / 'Experience and Poverty', *SW* 1:731–6.

8   This detour has scarcely been surveyed: even though there is no passage of *The Origin of German Tragic Drama* more frequently quoted and commented upon than that on history allegorized in nature, presenting itself to the spectator's gaze as

a 'petrified, primordial landscape' and inscribing itself in a death's head, much less attention has been paid to the problem of dramatization.

9   For his reflections, Benjamin relies mainly on Calderón's drama, *El mayor mónstruo del mundo* (*The Greatest Monster in the World*). (The second, modified edition of this play, published in 1637, carries a new title, *El mayor mónstruo, los celos* [*Jealousy, the Greatest Monster*], and it is to this edition and this title that Benjamin refers. Trans.)

10   Benjamin, 'Calderón's *El Mayor Monstruo*'.

11   This is the difference drawn by Benjamin between a generally valid violence and a violence of generalization. The former is a pure, 'generally valid' (*allgemeingültig*) violence – otherwise it would no longer be justice – but which is not for all that 'capable of generalization' (*verallgemeinerungsfähig*) or generally applicable, that is, one cannot take away its singularity. For all generalization would remove from violence precisely its nature of means with no other justification than the real proof of its existence. Captured in the structure of a form, violence would again be subjected to a finalization, and thus to the law.

12   Agamben's position tends perhaps more to find the effective truth of pure violence in the immediate extinction of the state, and he thereby tends rather to reduce the whole question of politics to ethics. But on this point he takes many diverse positions.

Works cited

Calderón de la Barca, Pedro. *Life's a Dream*. Translated and with an introduction by Michael Kidd. Oxford: Aris & Phillips, 2011.

—*Jealousy The Greatest Monster*. Edited with an introduction and commentary by Ann L. Mackenzie and José María Ruano de la Haza. Translated by Kenneth Muir. Oxford: Aris & Phillips, 2012.

Loraux, Nicole. *The Divided City: On Memory and Forgetting in Ancient Athens*. Translated by Corinne Pache and Jeff Fort. New York: Zone Books, 2006.

Sophocles. *Oedipus at Colonus*. In Sophocles, *The Three Theban Plays*. Translated by Robert Fagles. Introduction and notes by Bernard Knox. London: Penguin Books, 1984.

Part Two

Agamben's Readings of Benjamin

6

From Benjamin's *bloßes Leben* to Agamben's *Nuda Vita*: A Genealogy

Carlo Salzani

La nuda vita, 'bare life', is certainly the most popular and popularized notion of Agamben's philosophical vocabulary. Its derivation from Benjamin's phrase *das bloße Leben* in 'Critique of Violence' is explicit but problematic: Agamben uses the expression as if he merely adopted it in its full significance, as if *la nuda vita* were in fact nothing but the Italian translation of *das bloße Leben*.[1] The two notions, to the contrary, not only belong to two different historical, cultural and philosophical contexts, but are also literally 'construed' in very different ways, so that, in the end, they cannot be said to coincide. The decision of Hubert Thüring, the German translator of *Homo Sacer*, not to re-translate *la nuda vita* as *das bloße Leben* but to render it instead as *das nackte Leben*, appears therefore fully justified.[2]

The enormous influence of Agamben's work in the past two decades has produced a renewed critical interest and re-evaluation of Benjamin's essay, but has also resulted in a sort of 'Agambenization' of many of its theses and concepts, first and foremost of *das bloße Leben*, which more often than not takes on, today, the biopolitical features of *la nuda vita*. Agamben's readings of Benjamin are philologically very insightful, acute, and extremely original, to the point of becoming 'creative'; they pursue, however, as they should, their own 'philosophical' agenda, which goes beyond the scope and limits of philology. It seems important, therefore, to situate the two notions in their respective contexts in order to appreciate their differences and significance, not least because Agamben himself endorses, and calls for, such philological attention.

From *bloßes Leben* to *Kreatur*

In a quite dismissive footnote, Andrew Norris remarks that it is Benjamin who, in the 'often cited but incredibly opaque and inconclusive 1921 "On the Critique of Violence" introduces the concept of mere life that Agamben's work develops'. Norris continues: 'Unfortunately, it is almost impossible to say what Benjamin means by this phrase'.[3] If, however, we situate 'this phrase' within the historical, cultural and intellectual context of Benjamin's writings, it ceases to be that mysterious and esoteric notion that appears to Norris. It might not become a 'clear and distinct' idea, but we certainly can say something about 'what Benjamin means' by it.

The first point to note is that *das bloße Leben* is not a Benjaminian coinage, but, in German, it is a quite common and recurrent syntagm, still present in today's parlance in expressions such as '*das bloße* [or, more often, *naktes*] *Leben retten*', which can be translated as 'to escape with one's life' or 'to escape with nothing but the clothes on one's back'. A few literary usages can be found in classical works certainly known to Benjamin: for example, in Friedrich Schiller's *On the Aesthetic Education of Man in a series of Letters* (1794), where the syntagm is frequently used, as in the sentence '*das Schöne soll nicht bloßes Leben und nicht bloße Gestalt, sondern lebende Gestalt, d. i. Schönheit sein*';[4] or in Friedrich Schlegel's *Idee* no. 48 of the *Athenäum* fragments (1800): '*Einen gemeinen Standpunkt, eine nur im Gegensatz der Kunst und Bildung natürliche Denkart, ein bloßes Leben soll es gar nicht geben*'.[5] It might be pointless, however, to look for a 'source', or to ask where Benjamin found the phrase, since the expression is, not only current, but in his work, too, it means precisely what it means in the common usage: mere life, nothing but life. It is certain, though, that Benjamin endows the common usage with a complex and articulated philosophical meaning. More interesting is therefore to analyse (however briefly) Benjamin's use of this syntagm and to do so against the philosophical background of his early writings up to 1925: on the one hand, the Neo-Kantian schools of Hermann Cohen and Heinrich Rickert, on the other, the *Lebensphilosophie(s)* that, in various forms, would have constituted the unavoidable terrain of any philosophical inquiry since the second half of the nineteenth century.

The Neo-Kantian context of Benjamin's early writings and his debt to Cohen, founder of the Marburg School of Neo-Kantianism, have been thoroughly explored and analysed.[6] For the present argument, it is important to emphasize, as others have, Benjamin's indebtedness to Cohen for his interpretation of myth, fate and guilt, and to pay particular attention to the relation of myth, fate and guilt to life. Myth is, for Cohen, the closure of the orders of life and emanates directly from fate (*Schicksal*), which, in turn, is grounded on the notion of guilt (*Schuld*). In the chapter of *Ethik des reinen Willens* (1904) quoted by Benjamin in 'Critique of Violence' (*GS* 2.1:199/ *SW* 1:249) (and one page right after the passage Benjamin quotes),[7] Cohen elaborates the relation between myth and life: myth, he writes, 'sees no difference between the individual and its stirps [*Geschlecht*]'; in myth, 'the context of blood – [*Der Zusammenhang des Blutes*] is perceived as nature and as natural necessity', and it is 'this natural context [*natürlichen Zusammenhang*] [that] precisely is represented by the guilt of fate'. Fate and guilt, therefore, are not so much perceived in the individual, but rather in the stirps, or more precisely in what Cohen calls *natürliches Wesen*, natural being: it is the *Geschlecht* as *natürliches Wesen*, as natural necessity, that, in myth, represents the human.[8] Though Cohen never uses the syntagm *bloßes Leben*, Benjamin construes it along the lines of Cohen's *natürliches Wesen* and *Naturwesen*. It is in 'Fate and Character' (written in September 1919 but published in *Die Argonauten* in December 1921), that *das bloße Leben* is used for the first time in connection with fate and 'the guilt context of the living' (*der Schuldzusammenhang des Lebendigen*), and coupled to the expressions *natürliches Leben im Menschen* (natural life in humans) and *natürlichen Menschen/die Natur im Menschen* (natural human beings/nature in human beings) (*GS* 2.1:175–6/*SW* 1:204).

Cohen, like Benjamin after him, employs this definition of myth in order to refute many of the social theories of the time: in a later chapter of *Ethik des reinen Willen*, he attacks what he calls the 'materialist view of history' (in which he includes Darwin and Hobbes) because it reduces the peoples and the nations of history to a mere *Naturwesen*, because it flattens history into nature. To this reduction, he counterpoises the notion of human being as an 'individual of history'.[9] Some of the same terminology appears in 'The Task of the Translator' (also written in Autumn 1921 and published in 1923), where Benjamin, contrasting the reduction of life to 'organic corporeality', writes:

> The concept of life is given its due only if everything that has a history of its own, and is not merely the setting for history, is credited with life. In the final analysis, the range of life must be determined by the standpoint of history rather than of nature, least of all by such tenuous factors as sensation and soul. The philosopher's task consists in comprehending all of natural life through the more encompassing life of history. (*GS* 4.1:11/*SW* 1:255)

From the 'standpoint of history', '[a]ll purposeful manifestations of life, including their very purposiveness, in the final analysis have their end not in life but in the expression of its nature, in the representation of its significance', that is, in a 'special and high form of life' (*eigentümlichen und hohen Lebens*) (*GS* 4.1:11/*SW* 1:255). This 'high form of life' takes the name, in 'Goethe's *Elective Affinities*' (written between 1919–22 and published in 1924–5), of 'supernatural life' (*übernatürliches Leben*), of a life that goes 'over' or 'beyond' (*über-*) mere natural life:

> When they turn their attention away from the human and succumb to the power of nature (*Naturmacht*), then natural life (*das natürliche Leben*), which in man preserves its innocence only so long as natural life binds itself to something higher, drags the human down. With the disappearance of supernatural life in man, his natural life turns into guilt, even without his committing an act contrary to ethics. For now it is in league with mere life (*dem bloßen Leben*), which manifests itself in man as guilt. (*GS* 1.1:139/*SW* 1:308)

These are precisely the terms in which *das bloße Leben* also first appears in 'Critique of Violence', in the site of the contraposition between the pagan myth of Niobe and the biblical story of Korah: as in Cohen, *das bloße Leben* or *das bloße natürliche Leben* is here symbolized by 'blood', characterized by 'guilt' and opposed to 'the living' (*der Lebendige*, which can be therefore read as *übernatürliches Leben*) (*GS* 2.1:199–200/ *SW* 1:250).

Cohen, and Benjamin after him, construe the opposition between *Naturwesen/ bloßes Leben* and a higher, historical life that goes over/beyond the mere fact of living, on the basis of the opposition between pagan myth and Jewish tradition. The true target of their philosophical constructions are, however, the various forms of vitalism, biologism or social Darwinism that were in fashion at the time. In order to understand the wider context of Benjamin's use of *bloßes Leben*, his relation to Heinrich Rickert,

leading thinker of the Baden or Southwest School of Neo-Kantianism, is therefore
as important as his relation to Cohen. Benjamin had attended Rickert's lectures in
Freiburg in 1913 and as late as 1940 he described himself (though perhaps ironically) as 'a pupil of Rickert' in a letter to Adorno (*GB* 6:455). Uwe Steiner notes that
of particular importance for Benjamin was Rickert's course 'Exercises in metaphysics
in conjunction with the writings of Henri Bergson', in which Rickert began to outline
the contours of his own philosophy of value in relation to the *Lebensphilosophie*.[10]
This confrontation coagulated into a slim volume published in 1920 under the title
Die Philosophie des Lebens and with the significant subtitle 'Presentation and critique
of the philosophical fashions of our time'.[11] This volume does not appear in the list of
books read by Benjamin, but Steiner notes that Benjamin's announcement of his own
dissertation was published in 1921 in the same issue of the *Kant-Studien* in which
Rickert's book was discussed at length in an article, so we can safely assume that
Benjamin knew about it.[12]

The target of Rickert's critique is the 'biologism' he identifies in most philosophies of
his time and which he locates within the influence of Nietzsche's thought. Importantly,
in the preface he emphasizes the necessity for philosophy to think about life, but
argues that this task must go beyond a 'philosophy of *mere* life [*des bloßen Leben*]':
'in philosophizing about life, life itself is not sufficient material'.[13] Contemporary
philosophy of life is instead governed by the principle of the 'immanence of life'
(*Lebensimmanenz*), which does not know anything beyond life and attempts to explain
everything within life.[14] The book concludes by emphasizing that philosophy demands
a distance from 'mere lived life' (*vom bloß gelebten Leben*), and only from this distance
it is possible to philosophize about life.[15] Steiner places Benjamin's project about
politics, of which 'Critique of Violence' is supposed to be a part, in the context of the
Nietzsche-reception in the milieu of early Expressionism, thus *grosso modo* within the
philosophical milieu analysed and criticized by Rickert. In particular, he mentions the
prominent socialist writer Kurt Hiller, to whom he ascribes a 'thoroughly Nietzschean
vitalism',[16] and it is thus against this background that we must read the second usage
of *bloßes Leben* in 'Critique of Violence': it is against this Nietzschean vitalism and
biologism that Benjamin refutes Hiller's version of pacifism in 'Anti-Cain'. When
Hiller, against Bolshevik and Spartacist ideologies of class warfare, writes that 'we
profess that higher even than happiness and justice of existence stands … existence
in itself (*Dasein an sich*)',[17] Benjamin counters that: 'Man cannot, at any price, be said
to coincide with the mere life (*mit dem bloßen Leben*) in him, any more than it can
be said to coincide with any other of his conditions and qualities, including even the
uniqueness of his bodily person' (*GS* 2.1:201/*SW* 1:251). Against the Nietzschean
vitalism and biologism of the various currents of the *Lebensphilosophie* Benjamin
upholds the notion of a just, *über-natürliches* life issuing from the Jewish legacy.

The vocabulary of *bloßes Leben* must therefore be placed in the context of the
'philosophical fashions' of the time. For our purpose, it can be said to cover the
semantic field to which Agamben refers with the term *zoē* – and thus *not* that of
nuda vita. In the 'Epistemo-Critical Prologue' of *The Origin of German Tragic Drama*,
Benjamin will use again the expression *natürliches Leben* in a similar context, with an
endnote that refers back to the passage of 'The Task of the Translator' quoted above

(*GS* 1.1:227/*OT* 47). The *Trauerspiel*-book marks, however, Benjamin's distancing from the Neo-Kantian paradigm of his previous writings, and, importantly, also from the 'organic', *lebensphilosophisch* vocabulary clustered around the term 'life'.[18] The central term of this work is in fact *Kreatur*, which presents a slightly – but important – different connotation: *Kreatur* is a theological concept and signifies a being *created* and permanently marked by a relation to a *creator*, by an exposure to a superior (we might say, from an Agambenian perspective, 'sovereign') power. It is not only the mere, natural, biological fact of living – it is not *bloßes Leben* – but is already a life determined by, and subjected to, a divine/sovereign *law*. The context of the *Trauerspiel*-book is no longer that of the *Lebensphilosophie* and of its Neo-Kantian critique, but the theologico-political one established by Schmitt. And the 'Critique of Violence' – or at least the vocabulary of *bloßes Leben* – belongs ultimately more to the context of *Lebensphilosophie* and its Neo-Kantian critique than to the context established by Schmitt. It is true that *die Kreatur* takes on, in the *Trauerspiel*-book, the Cohenian traits that characterized *das bloße Leben* (guilt and submission to fate), and that, *vice versa*, in 'Fate and Character' and 'Critique of Violence', *das bloße Leben* is construed in a relation to law and legal violence. The emphasis, however, is (again, slightly, but importantly) different: the *Kreatur* emerges *always* and *only* in the relation to a creating/sovereign power; *das bloße Leben*, as for the *Lebensphilosophie*, is just and simply 'mere life'.

From *creatura* to *nuda vita*

The Agambenization of the notion of *bloßes Leben* has led to its transposition into the theologico-political semantic field of the *Kreatur*; Eric Santner, who in a sense exemplifies this move, has named this 'creaturely life'.[19] Agamben does not appreciate the (at least terminological) difference between the early, Neo-Kantian phase of Benjamin's writings and his later phase; in fact, he collapses *das bloße Leben* into *die Kreatur*, and does so from the very beginning of his career.

The origins of the *Homo Sacer*-project can certainly be dated back to the mid-1970s. In the 'Preface' to *The End of the Poem*, while recounting the origins of the essays on literature eventually collected in the 1996 book, Agamben writes that between 1974 and 1976 he was working on the project of a journal with Italo Calvino and Claudio Rugafiori; a section of the journal was to be devoted to the definition of 'Italian categories' (which is the title of the book in Italian), organized along opposed pairs of concepts. One of the oppositions Agamben intended to explore was *diritto/creatura*, 'law/creature' (*EP* vii/xi). The journal never materialized, but the idea of this opposition continued to flow, as it were, as a subterranean current in Agamben's thoughts, until it re-surfaced, in the 1990s, as the founding category of the *Homo Sacer*-project. The opposition (*diritto/creatura*, 'law/creature') re-emerged, however, in a different form, whereby *creatura* was replaced by *nuda vita*.

Agamben had already used the syntagm *nuda vita* in the previous decade, namely in 1982 in the final paragraph of *Language and Death* (though with the addition of the adjective *naturale*, 'natural'; *LD* 133/106) and twice in 1990 in *The Coming*

Community (*CC* 52/64–5, 68/86),[20] leaving it ambiguously unexplained. In the 1993 essay 'Beyond Human Rights' (originally published in French and later collected in *Means Without End*, 1996), he seems to propose an explanation by relating, through a parenthesis, *nuda vita* to *creatura*: '*la nuda vita (la creatura umana)* [naked life (the human creature)]' (*ME* 24/20, translation modified).[21] It is only in the first 'Threshold' of *Homo Sacer* that we are told (again, through a simple parenthesis) that *nuda vita* is the translation of Benjamin's *bloßes Leben* (*HS* 75/65). This translation is problematic, however, since in Italian the adjective *nudo* usually refers to the nakedness of the human body and suggests (intuitively) exposure, vulnerability and powerlessness – which is of course Agamben's point, but this overstretches the more neutral German *bloß*, and also Benjamin's use of it.[22] It must be noted, however, that this translation is not Agamben's own: he merely found it in the first Italian translation of 'Critique of Violence', in the collection of Benjamin's essays and fragments *Angelus Novus*, translated and edited by Renato Solmi and first published in 1962, which introduced Benjamin to the Italian public (only 'The work of art' essay had been previously translated). Agamben avidly read this collection in the 1960s.[23]

Though it is presented, in the 'Introduction' to *Homo Sacer*, as the 'protagonist' of the book (*HS* 11/8), *la nuda vita*, as Norris has aptly noted, is never precisely defined by Agamben, but it is rather presented through examples of the structure of the 'inclusive exclusion'.[24] Perhaps, the only definition of a sort is to be found at the end, in the third 'Threshold' that concludes *Homo Sacer*:

> In the syntagm 'bare life', 'bare' corresponds to the Greek *haplōs*, the term by which first philosophy defines pure Being. The isolation of the sphere of pure Being, which constitutes the fundamental activity of Western metaphysics, is not without analogies with the isolation of bare life in the realm of Western politics. What constitutes man as a thinking animal has its exact counterpart in what constitutes him as a political animal. In the first case, the problem is to isolate pure Being (*on haplōs*) from the many meanings of the term 'Being' (which, according to Aristotle, 'is said in many ways'); in the second, what is at stake is the separation of bare life from the many forms of concrete life. Pure Being, bare life – what is contained in these two concepts, such that both the metaphysics and the politics of the West find their foundation and sense in them and in them alone? What is the link between the two constitutive processes by which metaphysics and politics seem, in isolating their proper element, simultaneously to run up against an unthinkable limit? For bare life is certainly as indeterminate and impenetrable as *haplōs* Being, and one could say that reason cannot think bare life except as it thinks pure being, in stupor and astonishment. (*HS* 203/182)

Here Agamben refers to book VI (Epsilon) of the *Metaphysics*, where Aristotle defines 'first philosophy' as that science that is 'theoretical' but, unlike physics and mathematics (the other two theoretical sciences), is also 'universal', insofar as its object is the supersensible substance, separated and immobile, Being *qua* Being (*on hē on*), Being as 'simple' (*on haplōs*) (1026a 31–3).[25] Unlike Aristotle, however, Agamben construes pure Being (and *la nuda vita*) as an 'unthinkable limit', as 'indeterminate and impenetrable', as 'empty' (*HS* 203/182), and again, in the very last paragraph of the book, as 'both the task and the enigma of Western metaphysics' (*HS* 210–11/188).[26]

Mathew Abbott reads this passage as an indication that 'the crucial Agambenian concept of bare life has to be understood as beginning from a transposition of Heidegger's ontological difference onto classical biological categories, where *zoē* (the fact of life) is equated with the fact of being *as such*, and *bios* (politically qualified life) with the ontic level of particular beings':[27] as for Heidegger there is within metaphysics nothing to being as such, so for Agamben there is within politics nothing to life as such; the Heideggerian 'forgetting of being' is transposed into politics as a fundamental (and metaphysical) forgetting of life, but what is forgotten, Abbott proceeds, returns as a repressed metaphysical problem to haunt our politics. This Heideggerian reading seems to be validated by later refinements of Agamben's quasi-definition of *nuda vita*. In the 1996 essay 'Absolute immanence' (in a section later transposed almost word for word in *The Open*, 2002), Agamben identifies the 'decisive moment' in which *la nuda vita* is classified in the history of Western philosophy, not in the *on haplōs* of the *Metaphysics*, but rather in Aristotle's *De anima*. In a passage that Agamben quotes at length (413a 20–b 10),[28] Aristotle observes that it is the fact of living (*zēn*) that distinguishes the animal from the inanimate, but, since life 'is said in many ways' (just as is *on haplōs* in the *Metaphysics*; cf. 1026a 33), he narrows down the difference between animal and inanimate to the 'nutritive faculty'. Agamben notes that Aristotle does not define what life his, but merely divides it up in isolating the nutritive function and then ordering it into a series of distinct faculties. At work here, according to Agamben, is the metaphysical principle of isolating an 'indifferentiated foundation' (*fondo indifferenziato*) which must 'founder' (*andare a fondo*) in order to become the principle upon which all attributions are construed (*PO* 392–3/230–1, *O* 21–2/13–14, translation modified).

This is precisely the Heideggerian logic of the *Ab-Grund*,[29] of Being as the absent (or, for Agamben, negative) foundation, which structures many a figure throughout Agamben's works: from the Voice in *Language and Death* (1982), which is '*ground* (fondamento), but in the sense that it goes *to the ground* (*va a fondo*) and disappears in order for being and language to take place' (*LD* 49/35, emphases in the original), to testimony in *Remnants of Auschwitz* (1998), in which 'to speak, to bear witness, is thus to enter into a vertiginous movement in which something sinks to the bottom (*va a fondo*), wholly desubjectified and silenced, and something subjectified speaks without truly having anything to say of its own' (*RA* 112/120). The reference to the Voice is important, because it returns in the 'Introduction' to *Homo Sacer* as indication that politics is the 'truly fundamental structure of Western metaphysics'. Here, too, Agamben refers to Aristotle, this time to the passage of the *Politics* in which the proper place of the *polis* is situated in the transition from voice (*phōnē*) to language (*logos*): if voice belongs also to the other living beings, since it is the sign of pain and pleasure, language belongs only to man and is 'designed to indicate the advantageous and the harmful, and therefore also the right and the wrong' (1253a 10–18).[30] Agamben glosses: 'the living being has *logos* by taking away and conserving its own voice in it, even as it dwells in the *polis* by letting its own bare life be excluded, as an exception, within it' (*HS* 11/8).[31] Here an imperceptible but fundamental shift occurs:

to the Heideggerian logic of the *Ab-Grund* that structures his reading of the voice, Agamben superimposes the Schmittian structure of the exception. Unlike Heidegger's, and certainly unlike Aristotle's, Schmitt's logic, as Norris has noted, presents a *spatial* structure: 'it conceives of concepts in terms of groups in space with borders that need to be defined and patrolled'.[32] It is true that Agamben's reading of Aristotle's *Politics* in *Homo Sacer*, and specifically of the separation between *oikos* and *polis*, is based on Arendt's *The Human Condition*; Agamben stretches, however, the Arendtian 'opposition' between the two to a Schmittian 'inclusionary exclusion'.[33] If Abbott is right in underlying Agamben's ontological debt to Heidegger, he underestimates though his 'structural' debt to Schmitt: unlike Heidegger's logic and Aristotle's logic, the logic of the exception implies a *decision* about the inside and about the outside, about the inclusion and about the exclusion, and it is according to this logic that, ultimately, Agamben construes *la nuda vita*.

The 'examples' of *nuda vita* mentioned by Norris (*Versuchspersonen*, Karen Quinlan, people in 'overcoma', refugees) are located in the third part of *Homo Sacer*, the properly 'biopolitical' one. What they 'exemplify', however, is the structure of the *homo sacer*, that of an 'inclusive exclusion' which is construed, in the first two parts, as a 'topology' and explained with spatial metaphors. Agamben construes the relation between life and politics along the lines of Schmitt's sovereign *nomos*, by characterizing the latter's 'ordering of space' – defined, in *The Nomos of the Earth* (1950), as 'the determination of a juridical and territorial ordering (of an *Ordnung* and an *Ortung*)' (qtd. in *HS* 23/19)[34] – as a 'taking of the outside', as ex-ception (*Aus-nahme*) (*HS* 23/19). The *sacratio*, the curse that renders life 'sacred', even takes the form of a 'double exception', whereby life is ex-cepted both from the sphere of the profane and from that of the religious, and as such cannot be sacrificed and yet may be killed (*HS* 91/83). This double ex-ception is for Agamben structurally analogous to the sovereign exception and as such it names 'the originary form of the inclusion of bare life in the juridical order' (*HS* 94/85). This inclusion 'produces' *la nuda vita*, which is therefore not simply 'mere' life, not the simple fact of living, but rather a product, a result: '*Not simple natural life, but life exposed to death (bare life or sacred life) is the originary political element*'; 'Neither political *bios* nor natural *zoē*, sacred life is the zone of indistinction in which *zoē* and *bios* constitute each other in including and excluding each other' (*HS* 98/88, 101/90, emphasis in the original). The second part of the book tellingly concludes in wrapping up the analysis with the following Schmittian sentence: 'The banishment of sacred life is the sovereign *nomos* that conditions every rule, the originary *spatialization* that governs and makes possible every *localization* and every *territorialization*' (*HS* 123/111, emphases added).

From *bloßes Leben* to *nuda vita*

The spatial – Schmittian – topology of *la nuda vita* is extraneous to Benjamin's *bloßes Leben*. It is true that Benjamin shares with Schmitt a 'methodological' interest in the extreme/exception – central, for example, in the *Trauerspiel*-book – but this cannot be merely attributed to a Schmittian 'influence' (which would be posterior to the reading of *Political Theology* and *On Dictatorship*). The emphasis on the extreme is in fact already essential to the essay on Hölderlin (1914–15), where Benjamin defined his central notion, the 'poetized', as a 'limit-concept' (*GS* 2.1:107/*SW* 1:19) and, as Astrid Deuber-Mankowsky has noted, is rather to be ascribed to the influence of Cohen.[35] Moreover – and this is the fundamental point – Benjamin and Schmitt envision the relation between exception and life (or bare life) in opposed fashions. At the conclusion of the first essay of *Political Theology*, Schmitt writes: 'In the exception the power of real life [*des wirklichen Lebens*] breaks through the crust of a mechanism that has become torpid by repetition', and that is why, for him, '[t]he exception is more interesting than the rule'.[36] For Schmitt, this 'real' (or, a few lines before, 'concrete') life is the exception, a vivifying, life-bringing instance against the background of the mechanical repetition of the rule. Agamben refers to these lines at the end of the first 'Threshold' of *Homo Sacer*, stating that '[b]oth Benjamin and Schmitt, if differently, point to life ("bare life" in Benjamin and, in Schmitt, the "real life" that "breaks the crust of a mechanism rigidified through repetition") as the element that, in the exception, finds itself in the most intimate relation with sovereignty' (*HS* 76/67). Here Agamben ultimately conflates Benjamin's *bloßes Leben* and Schmitt's *wirkliches Leben* into 'life' as exception; however, for Benjamin *das bloße Leben* does not constitute the exception, but rather the mythic rule of biologico-mechanical repetition. If it is possible to describe, as Brendan Moran does, Benjamin's politics as a 'politics of taking exception to, becoming extreme in relation to, myth',[37] then this exception is precisely set *against* the mythical closure of *das bloße Leben*; *das bloße Leben* means blood, guilt, fate, in a word, myth, and myth is the 'attempted elimination of the exception'.[38] And Agamben's *nuda vita*, though inverting its terms, finally replicates Schmitt's structure and is therefore more indebted to the latter than to Benjamin's notion.

Agamben extracts the syntagm *bloßes Leben* from its context (the turn-of-the-century, Nietzsche-influenced *Lebensphilosophie* and its Neo-Kantian critique) and transposes it into a different context, that of a Foucault-inspired critique of biopolitics structured, however, along the (spatial) lines of Schmitt's *nomos* and theory of sovereignty. The two notions – 'mere life' in Benjamin and 'bare life' in Agamben – ultimately differ to such a point that they must be considered independent from one other. These philological remarks, however, can merely underline the differences; in philosophical inquiry, Agamben often remarks, philological attention is paramount, but necessarily bumps into a limit: 'The philologist who really got to the bottom of her practice', he says in an interview, 'needs philosophy, she must at some point … become a philosopher'.[39] And one of the methodological tenets on which he insists time and again is that, as he states in *The Signature of All Things*:

> the genuine philosophical element in every work, whether it be a work of art, of science, or of thought, is its capacity for elaboration, which Ludwig Feuerbach defined as *Entwicklungsfähigkeit*. It is precisely when one follows such a principle that the difference between what belongs to the author of a work and what is attributable to the interpreter becomes as essential as it is difficult to grasp. (*ST* 8/7–8)

Agamben has *entwickelt*, developed, and not merely adopted, Benjamin's notion into something which has become fully his own. It is up to the philological attention of the reader to discern and not confuse *das bloße Leben* and *la nuda vita*.

Notes

1   Benjamin's expression is usually translated into English as 'mere life'. Agamben's phrase has however entered the international politico-philosophical vocabulary as 'bare life', the form given to it by Daniel Heller-Roazen in his translations of Agamben's works (*Homo Sacer, The End of the Poem, Remnants of Auschwitz, Potentialities*). Before Heller-Roazen's norm-establishing translations, the syntagm was rendered differently: in their 1991 translation of *Language and Death*, Karen Pinkus and Michael Hardt had rendered it as 'naked life'; in his 1993 translation of *The Coming Community*, Michael Hardt had rendered it as 'life in all its nakedness'; even after Heller-Roazen's translations, Vincenzo Binetti and Cesare Casarino opted, in their translation of *Means Without End* (2000), for the form 'naked life'; David Kishik and Stefan Pradella, in their translation of *Nudities* (2011), were in a sense forced to adopt 'naked life' because of the book's references to corporeal nudity. I will hereby maintain, when possible, the original Italian and German forms in order to preserve and underline the specificity of, and differences between, the two notions.

2   In the translator's note, Thüring writes: 'Despite the explicit reference to Walter Benjamin's *bloßes Leben*, after consideration of the semantic fields, and in order to underscore the author's autonomous development and characterization of the concept, *la nuda vita* was here translated as *das nackte Leben*' ('Anmerkungen zur Übersetzung und zur Zitierweise', in Giorgio Agamben, *Homo sacer. Die souveräne Macht und das nackte Leben*, trans. Hubert Thüring [Frankfurt a.M.: Suhrkamp, 2002], 199).

3   Andrew Norris, 'The exemplary exception: philosophical and political decisions in Giorgio Agamben's *Homo Sacer*', in *Politics, Metaphysics, and Death: Essays on Giorgio Agamben's Homo Sacer*, ed. Andrew Norris (Durham, NC: Duke University Press, 2005), 281 n.33.

4   'The beautiful shall be not mere life and not mere form, but living form, i.e. beauty', Friedrich Schiller, *Über die ästhetische Erziehung des Menschen in einer Reihe von Briefen*, in *Sämtliche Werke*, vol. 5, *Erzälungen/Theoretische Schriften*, eds. Gerhard Fricke and Herbert G. Göpfert (Munich: Carl Hanser Verlag, 1962), letter 15, 617. This work is not mentioned in Benjamin's 'Verzeichnis der gelesenen Schriften' (*GS* 7.1:437–76), although part of this list of writings he read is lost. The list does not begin until the end of 1916 or the beginning of 1917 (see editorial comments, *GS* 7:2, 724).

5   'There should be no common standpoint, no natural mindset only opposed to art and culture, no mere life', Friedrich Schlegel, *Ideen*, in *Kritische Friedrich-Schlegel-Ausgabe*, vol. 2, *Charakteristiken und Kritiken I (1796–1801)*, ed. Hans Eichner (Paderborn: Ferdinand Schöning, 1967), 261. This 'idea' is not quoted by Benjamin in *The Concept of Criticism in German Romanticism* (1919).

6   The most extensive study is Astrid Deuber-Mankowsky's *Der frühe Walter Benjamin und Hermann Cohen. Jüdische Werte, kritische Philosophie und vergängliche Erfahrung* (Berlin: Vorwerk 8 Verlag, 2000).

7   Incidentally, it is interesting to note that Benjamin refers to Cohen – though not to the relevant passages – in all, and only in, the three essays in which the expression *bloßes Leben* appears, 'Fate and Character', 'Critique of Violence' and 'Goethe's *Elective Affinities*'.

8   Hermann Cohen, *Ethik des reinen Willen*, in *Werke*, ed. Helmut Holzhey, Vol.7. (Hildesheim: Olms, 1981), 363–4. The pagination is the same as the second edition (1907) quoted by Benjamin.

9   Cohen, *Ethik des reinen Willen*, 426.

10 Uwe Steiner, 'The true politician: Walter Benjamin's concept of the political', trans. Colin Sample, *New German Critique* 83 (2001): 54.

11 Heinrich Rickert, *Die Philosophie des Lebens. Darstellung und Kritik der philosophischen Modeströmungen unserer Zeit* (Tübingen: Mohr/Paul Siebeck, 1920).

12 Steiner, 'The true politician', 54. Cf. Benjamin, 'Der Begriff der Kunstkritik in der deutschen Romantik' [Selbstanzeige], *Kant-Studien* 26 (1921): 219 (*GS* 1.2:707–8), and Max Frischeisen-Kohler, 'Philosophie und Leben. Bemerkungen zu Heinrich Rickerts Buch: *Die Philosophie des Lebens*', *Kant-Studien* 26 (1921): 112–38.

13 Rickert, *Die Philosophie des Lebens*, iii, emphasis in the original.

14 Rickert, *Die Philosophie des Lebens*, 5.

15 Rickert, *Die Philosophie des Lebens*, 194. As Nitzan Lebovic notes (*The Philosophy of Life and Death: Ludwig Klages and the Rise of a Nazi Biopolitics* [New York: Palgrave-Macmillan, 2013], 185), the term *bloßes Leben* was actually popularized by Georg Simmel in his *Lebensanschauung. Vier metaphysische Kapitel* (Munich: Duncker & Humblot, 1918), one of the main targets of Rickert's criticism. Lebovic's book constitutes an excellent introduction to the milieu and terminology of the *Lebensphilosophie* in the 1910s and 1920s, and thus to the wider context and background of Benjamin's critique of *bloßes Leben*.

16 Steiner, 'The true politician', 62.

17 Kurt Hiller, 'Anti-Cain', in *Das Ziel. Jahrbücher für geistige Politik* 3.1 ed. Kurt Hiller (1919), 25. Quoted in *GS* 2.1:201/*SW* 1:251.

18 Beatrice Hanssen adds that Benjamin's 'willingness to entertain the organic term "life" remained very much informed by the disclosure of romanticism and by what he then still regarded to be the early romantics' profound insight in "the life of literary works"' (Beatrice Hanssen, *Walter Benjamin's Other History: Of Stones, Animals, Human Beings, and Angels* [Berkeley, CA: University of California Press, 1998], 33).

19 See Eric L. Santner, *On Creaturely Life: Rilke – Benjamin – Sebald* (Chicago, IL: University of Chicago Press, 2006); for another, telling example of this Agambenization in recent criticism, see Mathew Abbott, 'The creature before the law: notes on Walter Benjamin's *Critique of Violence*', in *Colloquy: text theory critique* 16 (2008): 80–96.

20 The English translator opted here to render *la nuda vita*, in the first case, as 'life in all its nakedness' and, in the second, simply as 'human life'.

21 The English translators drop the term *creatura* and render *la creatura umana* as 'the human being'.

22 And in fact, in most Italian translations of Benjamin's works, *bloßes Leben* is rendered as *mera vita*, 'mere life'.

23 See Walter Benjamin, *Angelus Novus. Saggi e frammenti* (1962), trans. and ed. Renato Solmi (Turin: Einaudi, 1995), 26–8. In a 1985 interview with Adriano Sofri

Agamben states that 'I read him [Benjamin] for the first time in the 1960s in the Italian edition of *Angelus Novus*, edited by Renato Solmi. He immediately made the strongest impression on me: for no other author have I felt such an unsettling affinity', Adriano Sofri, 'Un'idea di Giorgio Agamben', in *Reporter* (November 9–10, 1985): 32.

24　Norris, 'The exemplary exception', 270.

25　The passage reads: 'but if there is a substance which is immutable, the science which studies this will be prior to physics, and will be primary philosophy, and universal in this sense, that it is primary. And it will be the province of this science to study Being *qua* Being; what it is, and what the attributes are which belong to it *qua* Being. But since the single term "being" (*to on to haplōs*) is used in various senses ...' etc. (Aristotle, *The Metaphysics*, Vol. 1, Books I–IX, trans. Hugh Tredennick, The Loeb Classical Library [London: William Heinemann/Cambridge, MA: Harvard University Press, 1933], 297–9). As a cursory remark, we can note that in German translations *on haplōs* is usually rendered as '*das einfache Sein*' or '*das Seiende schlechthin*', and never as '*das bloße Sein*', and in Italian translations as '*l'essere, inteso in generale*'.

26　Agamben had already used the reference to Aristotle's 'first philosophy' and '*on hē on, on haplōs*' in the book review 'Philosophy and linguistics' (1990, *PO* 64/67), and in *The Signature of All Things* (2008) he will call *on haplōs* a 'signature' (*ST* 67/66).

27　Mathew Abbott, 'No life is bare, the ordinary is exceptional: Giorgio Agamben and the question of political ontology', in *Parrhesia* 14 (2012): 27.

28　The passage quoted by Agamben reads: 'We say then ... that that which has soul is distinguished from that which has not by living. But the word living is used in many senses, and we say that a thing lives if any one of the following is present in it – mind, sensation, movement or rest in space, besides the movement implied in nutrition and decay or growth. Consequently all plants are considered to live, for they evidently have in themselves a capacity and first principle by means of which they exhibit both growth and decay in opposite directions ... This capacity to absorb food may exist apart from this in mortal beings. This is evident in the case of plants; for they have no other capacity of the soul. This, then, is the principle through which all living things have life ... By "nutritive faculty" [*threptikon*] I mean that part of the soul which even the plants share' (Aristotle, *On the Soul, Parva Naturalia, On Breath*, trans. W. S. Hett, The Loeb Classical Library [London: William Heinemann/Cambridge, MA: Harvard University Press, 1957], 75).

29　This becomes progressively central in Heidegger's thought, from 'Vom Wesen des Grundes' (1929) up to *Beträge zur Philosophie (vom Ereignis)* (1936–8) and *Der Satz vom Grund* (1955–6).

30　The entire passage quoted by Agamben reads: 'man alone of the animals possesses speech. The mere voice, it is true, can indicate pain and pleasure, and therefore is possessed by the other animals as well (for their nature has been developed so far as to have sensations of what is painful and pleasant and to signify those sensations to one another), but speech is designed to indicate the advantageous and the harmful, and therefore also the right and the wrong; for it is the special property of man in distinction from the other animals that he alone has perception of good and bad and right and wrong and the other moral qualities, and it is partnership in these things that makes a household and a city-state' (Aristotle, *Politics*, trans. H. Rackham, The Loeb Classical Library [London: William Heinemann/Cambridge, MA: Harvard University Press, 1950], 11). The same passage is already quoted in full and commented on in *LD* 108–9/87.

31 Agamben's readings of Aristotle (and in particular of the *Politics*) have become the object of harsh criticisms, which however go beyond the scope of this essay. For some examples see Laurent Dubreuil, 'Leaving politics: bios, zōē, life', *Diacritics* 36.2 (2006): 83–98; Jacques Derrida, *The Beast and the Sovereign*, vol. 1, trans. Geoffrey Bennington and Peggy Kamuf (Chicago, IL: University of Chicago Press, 2009), 314–16 and 325–33; James Gordon Finlayson, '"Bare life" and politics in Agamben's reading of Aristotle', *The Review of Politics* 72 (2010): 97–126.

32 Norris, 'The exemplary exception', 270.

33 Arendt writes, for example: 'According to Greek thought, the human capacity for political organization is not only different from but stands in direct opposition to that natural association whose centre is the home (*oikia*) and the family. ... It was not just an opinion or theory of Aristotle but a simple historical fact that the foundation of the *polis* was preceded by the destruction of all organized units resting on kinship, such as the *phratria* and the *phylē*' (Hannah Arendt, *The Human Condition*, 2nd edn. [Chicago, IL: University of Chicago Press, 1998], 24). Incidentally, also the distinction between *zoē* and *bios* is derived from Arendt: 'The chief characteristic of this specifically human life, whose appearance and disappearance constitute worldly events, is that it is itself always full of events which ultimately can be told as a story, establish a biography; it is of this life, *bios* as distinguished from mere *zoē*, that Aristotle said that it "somehow is a kind of *praxis*"' (*The Human Condition*, 97). Criticisms of Agamben's distinction are usually addressed also at Arendt.

34 The spatial topology of Schmitt's construction – which Agamben fully adopts – is all contained in the term *nomos*: '*Nomos* comes from *nemein* – a [Greek] word that means both "to divide" and "to pasture". Thus, *nomos* is the immediate form in which the political and social order of a people becomes spatially visible – the initial measure and division of pasture-land, i.e., the land-appropriation as well as the concrete order contained in it and following from it' (Carl Schmitt, *The* Nomos *of the Earth in the International Law of the* Jus Publicum Europaeum, trans. G. L. Ulmen [New York: Telos, 2003], 70). *The Nomos of the Earth* was published 28 years after *Political Theology*, but the latter presents, in the notion of exception, the spatial topology of the former: the *ex-cepere* of the exception already contains the *nemein* of the *nomos*.

35 Deuber-Mankowsky, *Der frühe Walter Benjamin und Hermann Cohen*, 89.

36 Carl Schmitt, *Political Theology: Four Chapters on the Concept of Sovereignty*, trans. George Schwab (Chicago, IL: University of Chicago Press, 2005), 15.

37 Brendan Moran, 'Exception, decision, and philosophic politics: Benjamin and the extreme', *Philosophy and Social Criticism* 40.2 (2014): 146.

38 Moran, 'Exception, decision, and philosophic politics', 149.

39 Sofri, 'Un'idea di Giorgio Agamben', 33.

Works cited

Abbott, Mathew. 'The creature before the law: notes on Walter Benjamin's *Critique of Violence*'. In *Colloquy: text theory critique* 16 (2008): 80–96.

—'No life is bare, the ordinary is exceptional: Giorgio Agamben and the question of political ontology'. In *Parrhesia* 14 (2012): 23–36.

Agamben, Giorgio. *Homo Sacer. Die souveräne Macht und das nackte Leben*. Translated by Hubert Thüring. Frankfurt a.M.: Suhrkamp, 2002.

Arendt, Hannah. *The Human Condition*, 2nd edn. Chicago, IL: The University of Chicago Press, 1998.

Aristotle. *The Metaphysics*, Vol. 1, Books I–IX. Translated by Hugh Tredennick. The Loeb Classical Library. London: William Heinemann/Cambridge, MA: Harvard University Press, 1933.

—*Politics*. Translated by H. Rackham. The Loeb Classical Library. London: William Heinemann/Cambridge, MA: Harvard University Press, 1950.

—*On the Soul, Parva Naturalia, On Breath*. Translated by W. S. Hett. The Loeb Classical Library. London: William Heinemann/Cambridge, MA: Harvard University Press, 1957.

Benjamin, Walter. *Angelus Novus. Saggi e frammenti* (1962). Translated and edited by Renato Solmi. Turin: Einaudi, 1995.

Cohen, Hermann. *Ethik des reinen Willen*. In *Werke*. Edited by Helmut Holzhey. Vol. 7. Hildesheim: Olms, 1981.

Derrida, Jacques. *The Beast and the Sovereign*. Vol. 1. Translated by Geoffrey Bennington and Peggy Kamuf. Chicago, IL: University of Chicago Press, 2009.

Deuber-Mankowsky, Astrid. *Der frühe Walter Benjamin und Hermann Cohen. Jüdische Werte, kritische Philosophie und vergängliche Erfahrung*. Berlin: Vorwerk 8 Verlag, 2000.

Dubreuil, Laurent. 'Leaving politics: bios, zōē, life'. *Diacritics* 36.2 (2006): 83–98.

Finlayson, James Gordon. '"Bare life" and politics in Agamben's reading of Aristotle'. *The Review of Politics* 72 (2010): 97–126.

Frischeisen-Kohler, Max. 'Philosophie und Leben. Bemerkungen zu Heinrich Rickerts Buch: *Die Philosophie des Lebens*'. *Kant-Studien* 26 (1921): 112–38.

Hanssen, Beatrice. *Walter Benjamin's Other History: Of Stones, Animals, Human Beings, and Angels*. Berkeley, CA: University of California Press, 1998.

Hiller, Kurt. 'Anti-Cain'. In *Das Ziel. Jahrbücher für geistige Politik* 3.1. Edited by Kurt Hiller (1919): 24–32.

Lebovic, Nitzan. *The Philosophy of Life and Death: Ludwig Klages and the Rise of a Nazi Biopolitics*. New York: Palgrave-Macmillan, 2013.

Moran, Brendan. 'Exception, decision, and philosophic politics: Benjamin and the extreme'. *Philosophy and Social Criticism* 40.2 (2014): 145–70.

Norris, Andrew. 'The exemplary exception: philosophical and political decisions in Giorgio Agamben's *Homo Sacer*'. In *Politics, Metaphysics, and Death: Essays on Giorgio Agamben's Homo Sacer*. Edited by Andrew Norris. Durham, NC: Duke University Press, 2005. 262–83.

Rickert, Heinrich. *Die Philosophie des Lebens. Darstellung und Kritik der philosophischen Modeströmungen unserer Zeit*. Tübingen: Mohr/Paul Siebeck, 1920.

Santner, Eric L. *On Creaturely Life: Rilke – Benjamin – Sebald*. Chicago, IL: University of Chicago Press, 2006.

Schiller, Friedrich. *Über die ästhetische Erziehung des Menschen in einer Reihe von Briefen*. In *Sämtliche Werke*, vol. 5, *Erzälungen/Theoretische Schriften*, edited by Gerhard Fricke and Herbert G. Göpfert. Munich: Carl Hanser Verlag, 1962, 570–669.

Schlegel, Friedrich. *Ideen*. In *Kritische Friedrich-Schlegel-Ausgabe*, vol. 2, *Charakteristiken und Kritiken I (1796–1801)*. Edited by Hans Eichner. Paderborn: Ferdinand Schöning, 1967. 256–72.

Schmitt, Carl. *The Nomos of the Earth in the International Law of the Jus Publicum Europaeum*. Translated by G. L. Ulmen. New York: Telos, 2003.

—*Political Theology: Four Chapters on the Concept of Sovereignty.* Translated by George Schwab. Chicago, IL: University of Chicago Press, 2005.

Simmel. Georg. *Lebensanschauung. Vier metaphysische Kapitel.* Munich: Duncker & Humblot, 1918.

Sofri, Adriano. 'Un'idea di Giorgio Agamben', interview with Giorgio Agamben, *Reporter* (November 9–10 1985): 32–3.

Steiner, Uwe. 'The true politician: Walter Benjamin's concept of the political'. Translated by Colin Sample. *New German Critique* 83 (Spring–Summer 2001): 43–88.

7

Agamben's Critique of Sacrificial Violence

J. Colin McQuillan

Introduction

Sacrifice has played a significant role in Giorgio Agamben's thought since the early 1980s, when he concluded the seminars documented in *Language and Death* with a meditation on the relationship between sacrifice and the law. Sacrifice became an even more central theme for Agamben during the 1990s, when he devoted his most famous work, *Homo Sacer*, to the political function of sacrifice. Agamben's preoccupation with sacrifice may be less evident in the larger system that he has constructed on the basis of *Homo Sacer* in the 2000s and 2010s than it was in his earlier works, but it continues to play a role in the genealogy of government he undertakes in *The Kingdom and the Glory* (*Homo Sacer II.2*) and the genealogy of the moral concept of duty that he presents in *Opus Dei* (*Homo Sacer II.5*). The consistency with which Agamben returns to the concept of sacrifice suggests that it lies close to the heart of his thought about morality, politics, and the law.

In what follows, I will argue that sacrifice plays such an important role in Agamben's thought because it allows him to address the problem of violence. The connection between sacrifice and violence is most evident in early works like *Language and Death*, where Agamben treats sacrifice as a form of violence that founds human communities and their laws. Yet it is also present in *Homo Sacer*, where Agamben argues that sacred life is defined by exclusion from the political order, leaving *homo sacer* exposed to lawless violence. Taken together, these works show that Agamben identifies violence with exclusion. He treats sacrifice as the paradigmatic form of exclusion, though he will also say that every human action is an act of exclusion and, therefore, a sacrifice. He reduces this conclusion to a formula in *Language and Death*: 'every *facere* is *sacrum facere*' (*LD* 105; *PO* 135).

Instead of regarding Agamben's work as the diagnosis of the violence of our times or a catalogue of the forms in which it has appeared, I would like to suggest that it is best understood as a genealogical critique that aims to expose the violence of sacrifice and explore different ways of being and acting. His discussions of government, *désoeuvrement*, profanation, and form-of-life show that Agamben is searching for a way of being and acting that is not reducible to exclusion and breaks with the sacrificial violence that lies at the foundation of our laws and our politics. And though it is sometimes difficult to see how all the different elements of Agamben's critique fit together, I will argue at the end of this chapter that his account of sacrificial violence, as well as the alternatives he has proposed, are best understood as an elaboration of the distinction between mythic and divine violence that Walter Benjamin introduces in his 'Critique of Violence'.

Violence and sacrifice

Before we can assess Agamben's critique of sacrificial violence and its relation to Benjamin's critique of violence, we must consider Agamben's comments on sacrifice and violence in greater depth and more detail. The first and arguably most important of these comments are to be found at the end of *Language and Death*, a work devoted to the negative foundation of language and human existence. After summarizing the conclusions of the discussions of Hegel and Heidegger earlier in the book, Agamben turns to a more general anthropological reflection on 'the fact that man, the animal possessing language, is, as such, ungrounded' and 'the fact that he has no foundation except in his own action,' which Agamben regards as 'an ancient truth' that constitutes 'the basis for the oldest religious practice of humanity: sacrifice' (*LD* 105).[1]

Agamben goes on to define sacrifice as 'a determinate action that, as such, is separated and marked by exclusion' (*LD* 105). While this definition is unremarkable in itself, the consequences that Agamben draws from it are both extensive and severe. According to Agamben, the object of sacrifice becomes sacred through its separation and exclusion, which means it is 'invested with a series of prohibitions and ritual prescriptives' (*LD* 105). Prohibitions and prescriptions concerning the sacred serve two purposes: they remove the object of sacrifice from the profane world of ordinary use and also from the relations that define it under normal circumstances; at the same time, the prohibitions and prescriptions of sacrifice make the sacred available 'for certain people and according to determinate rules' (*LD* 105). Access to the sacred and knowledge of the rules governing its use grant special powers to those engaged in sacrifice, but Agamben does not attribute the violence of sacrifice to the power it authorizes. On the contrary, he attributes the violent character of sacrifice to 'the very ungroundedness of human action' that leads to the separation of the sacred and the profane (*LD* 105). It is because the separation of people, things, places and times associated with the sacred are arbitrary, grounded in nothing other than 'determinate action', that Agamben regards sacrifice as violent. 'All human action, inasmuch as it is not naturally grounded but must construct its own foundation is', according to Agamben, 'violent' (*LD* 105). Sacrifice fits this description, because the separation of the sacred from the profane is arbitrary. It is nothing more than a 'determinate action', undertaken by human beings, that imposes a distinction where no distinction is to be found in nature.

Although the separation achieved through sacrifice is arbitrary, the distinctions it creates can be normalized and systematized. Sacrifice distinguishes the people for whom, the things which, the places where, and times when the sacred is available from those which are excluded from the sacred, because they are profane or ordinary. These distinctions make it possible to regulate and codify what it is permissible, for whom, and under which conditions, which is why Agamben regards sacrifice as the origin of law. Law is, for Agamben, nothing more than the systematic elaboration of a set of arbitrary distinctions that are established by sacrificial violence. No matter how formal legal systems may become, they cannot deny the violence of their foundation, which is based on nothing more than the 'determinate action' of those who saw fit to distinguish between one set of people, places, things and times and another. In time, the distinctions established by sacrificial violence may come to be regarded as both normal and normative. They may also be regarded as entirely natural, though they will never be more than second nature, because it will never be demonstrated that they are actually found in nature, much to the chagrin of natural law theorists. The distinctions upon which the law is founded are ultimately 'a historical product of man', meaning that they are derived from human action, which can be traced back to a particular place and time (*LD* 106). The groundlessness of that action is simply obscured by the systematization of the distinctions it imposes, the separation it effects, and the exclusions we come to take for granted.

Agamben maintains that sacrifice continues to play a role after the foundation of human communities and their legal orders, because it 'furnishes society and its ungrounded legislation with the fiction of a beginning: that which is excluded from the community is, in reality, that on which the entire life of the community is founded, and it is assumed by the society as an immemorial, and yet memorable, past' (*LD* 106). And though Agamben wrote *Homo Sacer* more than ten years after this passage from the end of *Language and Death* was published, a better summary would be difficult to find. In *Homo Sacer*, Agamben argues that politics is founded on the politicization of bare life, which is achieved through the separation of *bios* and *zoē* in the Greek *polis*. He maintains that the Greek word *bios* refers to 'the form or way of living proper to an individual or group', while *zoē* stands for 'the simple fact of living common to all living beings (animals, men, or gods)' (*HS* 1).[2] *Zoē* may be remembered or imagined as a pre-historical state of nature preceding the foundation of the political order, but politics really begins with the creation of a political form of life. This form of life gives the members of the community a definite political or legal status, but it is also predicated on a life that has no place in the political order. The laws that govern the political order, as well as the rights and privileges they bestow on subjects and citizens, apply only to those who have assumed the form of life established by that order, so bare life – life that is deprived of political form – is necessarily excluded. The exclusion of bare life and the creation of political forms of life have no more ground in nature than any other acts of sacrificial violence, but Agamben is convinced that they serve as the condition of any and all political life.

Agamben devotes most of *Homo Sacer* to an examination of two figures of exclusion, which follow from the sacrifice of bare life, and which constitute the political order. The first is the paradoxical figure of the sovereign, who is 'at the same time, outside and inside the juridical order' (*HS* 15). Because the sovereign is 'the one to whom the juridical order grants the power of proclaiming a state of exception' (Schmitt), the sovereign has the power to distinguish those cases in which the law applies (the norm) from those in which it does not (the exception) (*HS* 15). The distinction between the norm and the exception cannot be derived from the law, since that would presuppose the law was already in force. Consequently, the sovereign must stand outside the law in order to determine when the law applies, even though the decision of the sovereign is the only grounds for the application of the law. The violence of this decision is the same as the sacrificial violence that founds the law, because it is without foundation in nature or the law. Agamben explores the consequences of this violence when he discusses the second figure of exception, which is the figure of *homo sacer*. According to 'the oldest punishment of Roman criminal law', *homo sacer* is the one who may be killed but not sacrificed (*HS* 71).[3] What interests Agamben in this figure is the coincidence of violence and the sacred. *Homo sacer* is *sacer*, which means it is set apart from profane order of the secular world; at the same time, *homo sacer* is considered *impune occidi*, which means that striking or killing *homo sacer* is not punishable by law (*HS* 72). While something that is both sacred and which may be freely violated may appear nonsensical or contradictory, Agamben explains that the act that makes *homo sacer* sacred excludes *homo sacer* from both human and divine law. To be excluded from the law is to be denied the rights and privileges the law offers, including the protection it offers against certain forms of violence. The violence to which *homo sacer* is exposed by its exclusion from the legal order is not the normalized violence that is achieved through the systematic articulation of the law, but the arbitrary violence of sovereign decision, which decides when the law does and does not apply. That violence cannot be sanctioned, because it takes place in an anomic space outside the law (*SE* 32–40).

The most shocking chapters in *Homo Sacer* and in the project which bears that name explore the kinds of violence that take place at the point where sovereign decision and bare life coincide. At the end of *Homo Sacer*, in the section titled 'The camp as the *Nomos* of the modern', Agamben contends that the 'constitutive nexus between the state of exception and the concentration camp cannot be overstated', because the camp is 'the space that is opened when the state of exception begins to become the rule' (*HS* 168–9). The state of exception becomes the rule in the camp through the suspension of the normal functions of the law. While the suspension of the law is typically exceptional, it is the norm in the camps, leading to a condition in which 'bare life and juridical rule enter into a threshold of indistinction' (*HS* 174). Because it is through a political act and by means of law that life in the camps is excluded from the legal and political order, the violence to which that life is subject is indistinguishably arbitrary and legal. Nor can the object of that violence be identified as *bios* or *zoē*, since it is a life that is excluded from the political order, while also being subject to sovereign decision. Life in the camps is that of *homo sacer*, since it is a political life that is excluded from the community, denied the protection of the law, and abandoned to the most extreme forms of violence. Agamben explores the consequences of this violence in *Remnants of Auschwitz* (1998), where he suggests that the end of the sacrificial violence that founds the human community, grounds its laws, and authorizes its politics is the dehumanization experienced by inmates in the camps (*RA* 41–86).[4]

It would be difficult to extend an account of sacrificial violence beyond the horrors Agamben describes in *Remnants of Auschwitz*, but sacrifice has continued to play a role – for various reasons – in the genealogies of government and morality that Agamben has undertaken in later parts of the *Homo Sacer* project. The most important of these reasons is the privilege Agamben affords to Christian theology. When he discusses sacrifice in *The Kingdom and the Glory* and *Opus Dei*, for example, Agamben mentions the sacrifice in the Jewish temple, the sacrifice of Christ at Golgotha, the sacrificial dimensions of the Eucharist, and other kinds of liturgical sacrifice (*KG* 74, 172, 173, 176, 208, 218, 226, 232–4, 266; see also *OD* 6–8, 12–16, 37–40, 65–6). The function of these forms of sacrifice is irreducible to the violence that founds the legal and political order, since the sacrifices that took place in the Jewish temple were intended to maintain the law and preserve the covenant between God and his people. The sacrifice of Christ is understood as a substitute for sacrifice in the Jewish temple in Christian theology, but it has a different function, because it is supposed to bring about the end of the law, at least according to the Pauline interpretation Agamben prefers (see, for example, *TR* 91–112). The role sacrifice plays in the Eucharist, in prayers, and in Christian liturgical acclamations have still different functions, though it should already be clear that they are very different from the sacrificial violence Agamben describes in *Language and Death* and *Homo Sacer*. Does this mean that Agamben thinks Judaism and Christianity have brought about the end of sacrificial violence, as some theologians have claimed?[5]

While Agamben would agree that the form, content, and function of sacrifice have been changed by Judaism and Christianity, he does not think they have brought an end to sacrificial violence. When one considers the broad definition of violence that Agamben employs, it becomes clear that the Jewish and Christian conceptions of sacrifice are no less violent than any other form of sacrifice, because they have no more ground in nature. That they are no less exclusive is evident from the liturgical reforms recently enacted by Benedict XVI. While the Catholic Church holds it as a 'dogma of faith' that Christ died for all men and women, it now prefers translations of the Eucharistic prayer that say his blood was shed 'for you and for many' instead of 'for you and for all'. 'For you and for all' has been accepted as a legitimate translation of the Latin *'pro vobis et pro multis'* for many years and is even acknowledged as 'the correct interpretation of the Lord's intention', but the Catholic Church wishes to clarify through the translation 'for you and for many' that while all people are invited to share in the salvation offered by Christ's sacrifice, they cannot do so unless they are also 'willing to be numbered among the "many" to whom the text refers'.[6] The separation of the willing and the unwilling, presupposed by the Catholic Church as justification for its translation, also makes possible a distinction between those who count and those who belong to the innumerable multitude, which is among the most ancient functions of sacrifice.

Genealogy and critique

The account of sacrifice that Agamben presents in works like *Language and Death*, *Homo Sacer*, and *The Kingdom and the Glory* could be regarded as an archaeology or a genealogy tracing the concepts of law, politics and government back to their origins in sacrificial violence.[7] It is clear, however, that Agamben has much grander ambitions than that. In the last paragraph of *Language and Death*, he writes that 'a completed foundation of humanity in itself should ... signify the definitive elimination of the sacrificial mythogeme and of the ideas of nature and culture, of the unspeakable and the speakable, which are grounded in it' (*LD* 106). Agamben even calls for the abandonment of 'the sacralization of life', which, he says, 'derives from sacrifice' (*LD* 106). The fact that he combines his genealogy of sacrificial violence with calls for its elimination suggests that his works are not neutral from a moral or political point of view. In fact, they are part of a critique of sacrificial violence, modelled on Benjamin's critique of violence, which extends from Agamben's earliest works to his most recent publications.

If *Homo Sacer* is to be regarded as an extension of the account of sacrifice that Agamben presents at the end of *Language and Death*, it can also be seen as an extension of his call for the abandonment of the doctrine of the sacredness of life. *Homo Sacer* makes it clear that this doctrine is the product of sacrifice. It does not cherish and protect life, as those who assert the sacredness of life often claim, but separates life from the things and relations that constitute the order of the profane world. This separation exposes life to the arbitrary violence of the same sovereign decision that made life an object of sacrifice in the first place. As we have seen in the figure of *homo sacer* and in the camps, life that is exposed to sovereign decision is not inviolable; on the contrary, it is abandoned to indiscriminate violence and exposed to killing without sanction. That is why Agamben contends that 'the sacredness of life, which is invoked today as an absolutely fundamental right in opposition to sovereign power, in fact originally expresses precisely both life's subjection to a power over death and life's irreparable exposure in the relation of abandonment' (*HS* 83). However, his objections to the doctrine of the sacredness of life do not stop with the revelation of its 'secret complicity' with sacrificial violence. At the end of *Homo Sacer*, Agamben outlines the programme for what he calls 'a new politics', which would no longer be governed by sacrificial violence. Many of the works he has published in the years since the publication of *Homo Sacer* are meant to bring this new politics to life.

One alternative to the violence of sacrifice is to be found in the theological genealogy of government that Agamben undertakes in *The Kingdom and the Glory*. What is most important about government is its attempt to contain the violence of sovereign power. In several places, Agamben notes that government 'is not a despotic power that does violence to the freedom of creatures' (*KG* 141). On the contrary, he finds that government is 'a very particular form of activity, which is necessarily not violent (in the sense of "against nature", which the term assumes in medieval thought – as opposed to *spontaneous*, *qui sponte fit*) and articulates itself by means of the very nature of governed things', so that 'divine government and the self-government of the creatures coincides', and government becomes (in the eighteenth century) nothing other than 'knowing the nature of things and letting it act' (*KG* 132). Government is best understood as the attempt to administer creation and manage the effects of sacrificial violence, so that there is order in the economy of the world. And while this is certainly an improvement over the arbitrary violence of the camps, it is not to be mistaken for Agamben's new politics.

Instead of managing the effects of sacrificial violence through government, Agamben calls for the *désœuvrement* of the distinctions instituted through sacrifice. The term *désœuvrement,* which Agamben derives from the works of Alexandre Kojève, Georges Bataille and Jean-Luc Nancy, is often translated as 'inoperativeness' and 'inactivity' in Agamben's works, in order to preserve the etymological connection with the French *œuvre* ('work') and the Italian *opera* ('work,' 'action,' 'deed'), though a more conventional translation would be 'idleness'.[8] At the end of the first part of *Homo Sacer*, Agamben writes that 'everything depends on what is meant by inoperativeness', and rejects the view that it could be 'the simple absence of work' or 'a sovereign and useless form of negativity', before concluding that 'the only coherent way to understand inoperativeness is to think of it as a generic mode of potentiality that is not exhausted (like individual action or collective action understood as the sum of individual actions) in a *transitus de potential ad actum*' (*HS* 61–2). Agamben does not discuss this 'generic mode of potentiality' in any great detail in *Homo Sacer*, but he describes the *désœuvrement* of the distinction between animal life and human life in *The Open* (2002) and the *désœuvrement* of the law in *State of Exception* (*Homo Sacer* II.1, 2003). The *désœuvrement* of the distinction between animal life and human life 'renders inoperative the machine that governs our conception of man', revealing its 'central emptiness, the hiatus that – within man – separates man and animal' (*O* 85–7, 92). The *désœuvrement* of the law renders it an object of study and play, rather than an instrument of sovereign power, and brings about a kind of 'justice' that 'absolutely cannot be appropriated or made juridical' (*SE* 64).[9] Applied to the problem of sacrificial violence, Agamben's call for *désœuvrement* amounts to the undoing of distinctions that have their origins in sacrifice. Undoing these distinctions does not return humanity to a primal unity or to a state of nature, but to a free and open potentiality that remains undetermined by sacrificial prohibitions and prescriptions.

Agamben's attempt to found a new politics on *désœuvrement* has led him to be criticized as a messianic thinker, waiting in expectation for the end of the world, but unwilling to commit to political action. There may be some truth to this criticism, but it cannot be denied that Agamben has tried to identify a practical means with which to undo the violence of sacrifice. The prohibitions and prescriptions established by sacrificial violence are deactivated by profanation, which returns their objects to ordinary use. This is the programme Agamben has proposed in *Profanations* (2005), where he elaborates on the concept of play that he had introduced in *State of Exception* (see *PR* 75–6, 85–6). Play profanes the sacred 'by means of an entirely inappropriate use', which negates the prohibitions and prescriptions that distinguish the sacred from other objects by transgressing them (*PR* 75). It can also be extended beyond the sacred. Agamben notes that 'children, who play with whatever old thing falls into their hands, make toys out of things that also belong to the spheres of economics, war, law, and other activities that we are used to thinking of as serious' (*PR* 76). By treating these objects as if they were no different from anything else, play makes what is regarded as separate and different available for 'a new dimension of use' (*PR* 76). This 'new dimension of use' is free, because it is no longer encumbered by the arbitrary determinations of sacrifice. It does not abide what is proper for certain kinds of objects or consider the ends and purposes of things, because these are functions of sacrifice. What is proper to an object can only be established by distinguishing it from what is improper, just as the purpose of a thing can only be determined by differentiating between uses that are appropriate and inappropriate. Ignoring these distinctions allows for a different kind of use, which could become 'the gateway to a new happiness' (*PR* 86).

Désœuvrement and profanation make possible what Agamben calls form-of-life, which is perhaps the closest approximation of the new politics he proposes in *Homo Sacer* and the new form of happiness he suggests in *Profanations*. The term form-of-life first appears in Agamben's works as the title of an essay published in the journal *Futur Antérieur* (1993), which was subsequently incorporated into *Homo Sacer* and reprinted in *Means without End* (1996). The essay proposes several definitions of form-of-life, including 'a life that can never be separated from its form, a life in which it is never possible to isolate something such as naked life' and 'a life – human life – in which the single ways, acts, and processes of living are never simply facts, but always and above all possibilities of life, always and above all power' (*ME* 3–4). Both of these definitions play an important role in *Homo Sacer*, where Agamben considers the possibility of a life in which the distinction between bare life and political life has been rendered inoperative, as well as a life that is no longer subject to sovereign power. As an example of such a life, he offers Heidegger's *Dasein*, which he regards as an 'inseparable unity of Being and ways of Being, of subject and qualities, life and world', in which 'the life of *homo sacer*, which was the correlate of sovereign power, turns into an existence over which power no longer seems to have any hold' (*HS* 153). More recently, in *The Highest Poverty*, Agamben has developed his concept of form-of-life in the context of the Franciscan 'abdication of every right' ('*abdicatio omnis iuris*'), in which he sees '*the attempt to realize a human life and practice absolutely outside the determinations of the law*' (*HP* 110, emphasis in the original). The account of Franciscanism that Agamben presents in *The Highest Poverty* is closely related to his account in *Profanations* of the inappropriate use children make of objects in play, because it focuses on the use that Friars make of things after denouncing any right to property and even the rightful use of things in usufruct. For the Franciscans, Agamben argues, the simple *de facto* use of things is a way of relinquishing any claim to dominion, which has as its consequence a different form-of-life and a different way of being in the world.[10] Agamben criticizes the Franciscans for defining this new form-of-life negatively, in opposition to the law, and for failing to articulate a positive and integral conception of form-of-life, but he credits them with having achieved the 'maximum disjunction' between law and life and presents their 'vital practice' as an exemplary form-of-life (*HP* 119, 141).

Agamben's account of form-of-life remains obscure and is probably still incomplete. Yet the attempt to define a way of being and acting in the world that is not only free from the law, but which escapes the violence of sacrifice, is crucial for understanding all of his work. As we have seen, Agamben defines sacrifice as an arbitrary action that establishes a set of prohibitions and prescriptions. He elaborates on the idea that sacrifice is arbitrary action in his account of sovereign decision in *Homo Sacer*, but Agamben already identifies the prohibitions and prescriptions of sacrifice as the foundation of the legal order in *Language and Death*. Undoing that action and rendering sacrificial prohibitions inoperative cannot be achieved by declaring that the law no longer applies, because the negation of the law reproduces and reaffirms the arbitrariness of the act that instituted the law in the first place. It is the sovereign who decides where the law applies and where it does not, so there is very little difference between law and the suspension of the law in the state of exception – both are expressions of sovereign power. The mutual dependence of law, the state of exception and sovereign power ultimately leads Agamben to seek an alternative to sacrificial violence in form-of-life, which is not only an exception to the rule, but a life which is not subject to the sovereign decision that institutes the rule and escapes the distinctions that follow from it. For this reason, form-of-life could be described as a singular potentiality, in contrast with the conception of 'integral actuality' that Alexander Garcia Düttmann has used to describe Agamben's conception of language (see *IP* 6).[11] Form-of-life is singular, not integral, because it is not composed of a number of elements that can be united or divided; and it is a potentiality, not an actuality, because it is not determined with respect to what it is and what it is not. It is a way of being, 'whatever it is' and 'such as it is', which does not deny the possibility that it could be otherwise, that will ultimately render sacrificial violence obsolete.[12]

Agamben's critique and Benjamin's critique

Before concluding, a few words about the relationship between Agamben's critique of sacrificial violence and Walter Benjamin's 'Critique of Violence' are in order. Readers familiar with Agamben's works know that he returns to Benjamin's critique as frequently as he does to the problem of sacrifice. The use Agamben makes of Benjamin's critique also suggests that it has served as a model for Agamben's critique of sacrificial violence. One could even say that Agamben's critique is an extended meditation on, and a systematic elaboration of, Benjamin's critique.

The similarities between Agamben's critique and Benjamin's critique are many. The first and perhaps most important of these similarities is the relationship between the law-making and law-preserving functions of mythic violence in Benjamin's essay and Agamben's account of sacrifice. In *Homo Sacer*, Agamben praises Benjamin's account of mythic violence for 'laying bare the irreducible link uniting violence and law' (*HS* 63). He does not mention that he had identified a similar link in sacrifice in *Language and Death*, but Agamben's analysis of the logic of sovereignty and the figure of *homo sacer* makes the connection between mythic violence and sacrifice quite clear. Like mythic violence, sacrifice is a manifestation of power – an act, a sovereign decision – that gives rise to a set of distinctions. These distinctions may at first be informal or unwritten, but they are later given a more systematic articulation in the law, which contains provisions for its own maintenance (*SW* 1:248–9). The conception of divine violence that Benjamin opposes to mythic violence is also very similar to Agamben's conceptions of *désœuvrement* and profanation, since it seeks to depose the law-making and law-preserving violence of myth. Nor can there be any doubt that the objections Benjamin raises to the doctrine of the sacredness of life in his essay are the source for Agamben's own objections. Agamben even goes so far as to characterize his discussion of *homo sacer* as an investigation of the origin of the complicity between the sacredness of life and the power of law that Benjamin identifies in his critique (*HS* 67).

Still, there are at least two significant differences between Benjamin's critique and Agamben's critique. The first concerns the dichotomy between mythic violence and divine violence in Benjamin's critique, which seems to trade one form of violence for another. There are some places where Agamben accepts the possibility that the alternative to sacrificial violence is simply a different kind of violence. When he discusses the 'debate' between Benjamin and Schmitt over Benjamin's essay, for example, Agamben says the purpose of Benjamin's critique is 'to ensure the possibility of a violence that lies absolutely outside and beyond the law and that, as such, could shatter the dialectic between law-making and law-preserving violence' (*SE* 53).[13] Agamben calls this kind of violence 'pure violence', and uses 'pure violence' and 'wholly anomic human action' interchangeably, suggesting that human action remains a kind of violence, even when it has severed its connection to sacrifice (*SE* 54–5). And though he is critical of Schmitt's attempt to capture Benjamin's 'pure violence' and re inscribe it within the matrix of politics and law in his theory of sovereignty, Agamben does not criticize the 'pure violence' that Benjamin defends, first because its antipathy to law-making and law-preserving violence distinguishes it from violence of sovereign power; and second, because it represents the possibility of 'mere existence outside the law', which is associated with both justice and happiness in Benjamin's works (*SE* 53, 64; *HS* 64–5).[14] When he describes the deactivation of the law through study and play at the end of his discussion of the 'debate' between Benjamin and Schmitt, however, Agamben does not say the activities that follow the deactivation of the law are forms of violence (*SE* 64). Nor does he call *désœuvrement* and profanation forms of violence in his other works. It is certainly true that any and every action that does not follow directly from nature could be considered violent, given the breadth of the definition Agamben employs in *Language and Death*; yet it is noteworthy that he refrains from calling his alternative to sacrificial violence a different kind of violence. Instead of trading one form of violence for another, it may be that Agamben seeks an end to violence as such. This non-violence would not be the managerial administration of government (*KG* 132, 141), nor the peace that 'comes from war and will end in war' that he denounces in *Idea of Prose* (*IP* 81–2), but it might very well be the non-juridical sense of 'justice' that he mentions in *State of Exception* (*SE* 64) or the 'new happiness' to which he refers in *Profanations* (*PR* 76).[15]

A second difference between Benjamin's critique and Agamben's critique concerns sacrifice. In his essay, Benjamin says mythic violence 'demands sacrifice' (*fordert Opfer*) while divine violence 'accepts sacrifice' (*nimmt Opfer an*). It is not entirely clear what Benjamin means, though his claim comes at the end of a powerful paragraph in which he lists a series of distinctions between mythic violence and divine violence and then contrasts the legend of Niobe with the biblical tale of the rebellion of Korah and the destruction of his band. Through these distinctions and contrasts, Benjamin emphasizes the 'bloodless and expiatory character' of divine violence, which 'purifies the guilty, not of guilt, however, but of law' (*GS* 2.1:200/*SW* 1:250, translation modified). If divine violence 'receives' sacrifice, it is perhaps because it accepts what mythic violence does not: the possibility of life without law. Agamben is concerned with demonstrating the same possibility, but he does not say that *désœuvrement,* profanation, or form-of-life 'receive' or 'accept' sacrifice. The fact that he calls for the elimination of 'the sacrificial mythogeme' in *Language and Death* suggests that he is less interested in an alternative relation to sacrifice than its abolition (see *GS* 2.1:200/*SW* 1:250; and *LD* 106). The 'new politics' Agamben proposes at the end of *Homo Sacer* would have to be a politics in which the prohibitions and prescriptions that are established through sacrifice are no longer in force. This is only possible when sacrificial violence no longer serves as the 'negative foundation' of politics and law, which is why Agamben is compelled to seek a different way of being and acting, rather than a different relation to sacrifice. Instead of receiving the victims of sacrifice, an act that presupposes what Benjamin calls 'pure power over all life', Agamben has tried to think 'an existence over which power no longer seems to have any hold' (*HS* 153).[16] In recent years, he has identified the means for achieving this existence – *désœuvrement* and profanation – and explored the form he thinks such an existence would have to take – form-of-life.

Even if Agamben's accounts of *désœuvrement,* profanation, and form-of-life differ from Benjamin's conception of divine violence, it can hardly be denied that Agamben's critique of sacrificial violence has its origins in Benjamin's critique of mythic violence. And though Agamben's critique may range far beyond Benjamin's critique, by suggesting the possibility of non-violence and describing a form-of-life over which power has no hold, it can still be regarded as an extension and elaboration of Benjamin's critique. Understanding Agamben's work in these terms makes us better able to appreciate the origins of Agamben's critique of sacrificial violence, the breadth of his claims, and the alternative he has proposed.

Notes

1   Agamben repeats these claims at the end of '*Se: Hegel's Absolute and Heidegger's Ereignis*', which can be read as a summary of *Language and Death*. See *PO* 135–7.

2   Jacques Derrida, Laurent Dubreuil, and Gordon Finlayson have argued that the distinction Agamben draws between *bios* and *zoē* is without foundation in the language or the texts in which he claims to find the distinction at work. This objection seems to be well-founded, though I do not think Agamben's argument rests on philological authenticity of his distinction. See Jacques Derrida, *The Beast and the Sovereign,* trans. Geoffrey Bennington and Peggy Kamuf (Chicago, IL: University of Chicago Press, 2009), vol. 1, 109; Laurent Dubreuil, 'Leaving politics: bios, zōē, life', *Diacritics* 36.2 (2006): 84–7; James Gordon Finlayson, '"Bare life" and politics in Agamben's reading of Aristotle', *The Review of Politics* 72.1 (2010): 105–16; and J. Colin McQuillan, 'Agamben's fictions', *Philosophy Compass* 7.6 (2012): 381.

3   Even before *Homo Sacer*, Agamben writes that 'Sacer was the one who had been excluded from the human world and who, even though she or he could not be sacrificed, could be killed without committing homicide' in *The Coming Community* (*CC* 86–7).

4   It is true Agamben objects to calling what happened in the camps a Holocaust for many reasons, but not because he denies that those who were sent to the camps were

homines sacri. It is to the idea that the killing of those in the camps constituted a sacrifice that Agamben objects, in part because *homo sacer* cannot be sacrificed, and also because Agamben thinks the term 'Holocaust' has 'a semantic heredity that is from its inception anti-Semitic' (see *RA* 28–31).

5 Against those who credit rabbinic Judaism and Christianity with bringing about the end of religious sacrifice, Guy Stroumsa has insisted that they are 'sacrificial religions without blood sacrifices', because they both devised alternative forms of sacrifice (prayer, the study and interpretation of scripture, liturgy, etc.) after the destruction of the Temple of Jerusalem in 70 CE. See Guy G. Stroumsa, *The End of Sacrifice: Religious Transformations in Late Antiquity*, trans. Susan Emanuel (Chicago, IL: University of Chicago Press, 2009), 62–83. Agamben discusses Stroumsa's work in *OD* 13–16.

6 Quotations are from the letter by Cardinal Francis Arinze to the Presidents of the Conferences of Bishops on the Translation of *Pro Multis* (17 October 2006). See also the letter Benedict XVI sent to the President of the Episcopal Conference of Germany (14 April 2012) after some German Bishops objected to the revised translations and suggested they would continue using 'for all' (*für alle*). Although Agamben has not, to my knowledge, publicly commented on this controversy, it is worth noting that he identifies the multitude as an 'infinite mass' in *The Kingdom and the Glory*, which was written during the time when Benedict XVI enacted his liturgical reform. See *KG* 152.

7 Agamben often uses the terms 'archaeology' and 'genealogy' interchangeably. The subtitle of *The Kingdom and the Glory* indicates that the work is 'A Theological Genealogy of Economy and Government', but it contains, in §8, an 'Archaeology of Glory', and Agamben also seems to refer to the work as a whole as an archaeology in several places (see *KG* 112–13, 168, 247, 255). The opposite is true of *Opus Dei*, whose subtitle is 'An Archaeology of Duty', but which Agamben also describes as a genealogy (see *OD* 110–11). Agamben even uses archaeology and genealogy interchangeably to describe Foucault's work in *The Signature of All Things* (see *ST* 79–80).

8 See the helpful discussion of Agamben's use of this term in Leland de la Durantaye, *Giorgio Agamben: A Critical Introduction* (Stanford, CA: Stanford University Press, 2009), 18–20.

9 Agamben paraphrases this definition of justice from Walter Benjamin's 'Notes toward a work on the category of justice'. An English translation of Benjamin's text is included in Peter Fenves, *The Messianic Reduction: Walter Benjamin and the Shape of Time* (Stanford, CA: Stanford University Press, 2011), 257–8.

10 Michael Hardt and Antonio Negri also use St Francis of Assisi to illuminate 'the future life of communist militancy' at the end of *Empire*. See Michael Hardt and Antonio Negri, *Empire* (Cambridge, MA: Harvard University Press, 2000), 413.

11 See also Alexander Garcia Düttmann, 'Integral actuality: on Giorgio Agamben's *Idea of Prose*', in *The Work of Giorgio Agamben: Law, Literature, Life*, eds. Justin Clemens, Nicholas Heron, and Alex Murray (Edinburgh: Edinburgh University Press, 2008), 30.

12 For Agamben's discussion of being 'whatever' and being 'such as it is', see *CC* 1–3.

13 On Agamben's account of the 'debate' between Benjamin and Schmitt, see J. Colin McQuillan, 'The real state of emergency: Agamben on Benjamin and Schmitt', *Studies in Social and Political Thought* 18 (2011): 96–108.

14 It should be noted that while Edmund Jephcott's translation of the 'Critique of Violence' ends by saying that 'divine violence, which is the sign and seal but never

the means of sacred dispatch, may be called "sovereign" violence', Benjamin writes that divine violence may be called '*die waltende*' ('prevailing', 'presiding'). Benjamin's conclusion plays on its etymological connection of *walten* ('to prevail', 'to preside over') and *Ge-walt* ('violence', 'authority', 'power') in order to suggest that divine violence prevails over mythic violence, not that it is synonymous with sovereign power. See *GS* 2.1:203/*SW* 1:252.

15   See also Arne De Boever, 'Politics and poetics of divine violence: on a figure in Giorgio Agamben and Walter Benjamin', in *The Work of Giorgio Agamben*, eds. Justin Clemens, Nicholas Heron, and Alex Murray, 82–96.

16   To be sure, Benjamin says this 'pure power [*Gewalt*] over life' is exercised 'for the sake of the living', but there is still a sharp difference between 'a power [*Gewalt*] over life for the sake of the living' (Benjamin, *GS* 2.1:200/*SW* 1:250) and 'an existence over which power no longer seems to have any hold' (Agamben, *HS* 153).

Works cited

Arinza, Cardinal Francis. 'Letter to the Presidents of the Conferences of Bishops on the Translation of *Pro Multis*' (2006). http://usccb.org/prayer-and-worship/the-mass/ order-of-mass/liturgy-of-the-eucharist/letter-from-cardinal-arinze-on-the-translation-of-pro-multis.cfm (accessed February 2014).

Benedict XVI. 'Letter of his Holiness Pope Benedict XVI *Pro Multis* to H. E. Msgr. Robert Zollitsch, Archbishop of Freiburg, President of the Episcopal Conference of Germany' (2012), http://www.vatica.va/holy_father/benedict_xvi/letters/2012/documents/ hf_benxvi_let_201 20414_zollitsch_en.html (accessed February 2014).

De Boever, Arne. 'Politics and poetics of divine violence: on a figure in Giorgio Agamben and Walter Benjamin'. *The Work of Giorgio Agamben: Law, Literature, Life*. Edited by Justin Clemens, Nicholas Heron, and Alex Murray. Edinburgh: Edinburgh University Press, 82–96.

de la Durantaye, Leland. *Giorgio Agamben: A Critical Introduction*. Stanford, CA: Stanford University Press, 2009.

Derrida, Jacques. *The Beast and the Sovereign*. Vol. 1. Translated by Geoffrey Bennington and Peggy Kamuf. Chicago, IL: University of Chicago Press, 2009.

Dubreuil, Laurent. 'Leaving politics: bios, zōē, life'. *Diacritics* 36.2 (2006): 83–98.

Düttmann, Alexander Garcia. 'Integral actuality: on Giorgio Agamben's *Idea of Prose*'. In *The Work of Giorgio Agamben: Law, Literature, Life*. Edited by Justin Clemens, Nicholas Heron, and Alex Murray. Edinburgh: Edinburgh University Press, 2008, 28–42.

Fenves, Peter. *The Messianic Reduction: Walter Benjamin and the Shape of Time*. Stanford, CA: Stanford University Press, 2011.

Finlayson, James Gordon. '"Bare life" and politics in Agamben's reading of Aristotle'. *The Review of Politics* 72.1 (2010): 97–126.

Hardt, Michael and Negri, Antonio. *Empire*. Cambridge, MA: Harvard University Press, 2000.

McQuillan, J. Colin. 'The real state of emergency: Agamben on Benjamin and Schmitt'. *Studies in Social and Political Thought* 18 (2011): 96–108.

—'Agamben's fictions'. *Philosophy Compass* 7.6 (2012): 376–87.

Stroumsa, Guy G. *The End of Sacrifice: Religious Transformations in Late Antiquity*. Translated by Susan Emanuel. Chicago, IL: University of Chicago Press, 2009.

8

Agamben, Benjamin and the Indifference of Violence

William Watkin

In a manner that owes a lot to Foucault's conception of discursive intelligibility, Giorgio Agamben's philosophical method consists of tracing the origins of large-scale concepts, which he calls 'signatures' (*ST* 33–80), back to the moment when they first became operative as modes of organizing, legitimizing and disseminating discourse (cf. *KG* 4).[1] By intelligibility, or what Agamben also calls communicability,[2] it is not *what* is said that is primarily meaningful, but that such and such is allowed to be said by the sanctions of power and our complicity with these. These moments of arising, as Agamben calls them (*ST* 87–9), are not origins founded on historical data in the usual sense but, inspired by Benjaminian now-time, they actually say as much about us as contemporaries as they do about historical origins. Every contemporary moment is founded on an origin or *archē*, yet every *archē* is constructed by our contemporary discourse as the *found* origin.[3] The past, Agamben argues, only lives in the present, yet the present is constantly a construct of the past as Benjamin contends. In this way, time is marked by an essential double anachronism, of past things projected forward into the present and the present as a construct of the past. One can feel the beatific breath of Benjamin's angel of history at one's back in these remarks (*ST* 99).

Revealing this historical paradox as the basis of large-scale concepts such as power, being, secularization, language and so on, is Agamben's aim, so as to show them as logically unworkable. In all his studies, one common economy persists wherever he looks. The past, or temporal common, is founded on the present or temporal proper, yet the present founds the past through its attempts to access it as legitimating origin. Take any large-scale signature-concept and you reveal the paradox between a past found, even created, by the present and a present founded on the past, allowing you to suspend or make indifferent a clear separation between origins and current examples (what Agamben calls paradigms, *ST* 9–32), subsequently freeing yourself of the discursive control of said signature distributed across time through stable sets of operative paradigms. This is what philosophical archaeology consists of, a radical violence committed to the idea of history as sequence, which is also of course in accord with Benjamin's own ideas as regards the effect of the dialectical image on standard historiography, as can be found in the notes for the *Arcades Project* (for example N2a,3).

As everything is, ostensibly, discursive for Agamben, this form of radical historiography reveals itself to be a powerful political tool for change. In particular because power is one of the most prevalent signatures there is in the West and also one of the most susceptible to the paradox of the logic of a foundation founded by that which it is presumed to found. This is the relation between a signature, say life, and its paradigmatic instances at any one time, such as camps, coma patients and scientific testing (*HS* 136–80). Render indifferent the opposition between signatory origin (the common foundation of all) and the paradigmatic present (the proper actualization of our common foundation) through philosophical archaeology, and you kill the power of signatures to sanction and thus control what we think, what we say and also what we do through sets of paradigms. At which point, as Benjamin says, the dialectic of historical sequence is brought to a standstill (N10a,3). Fail to render indifferent such signatures and whatever political action you take will still occur within the sanctioned confines of discursive intelligibility, especially the essential political act of the modern age: revolutionary difference through acts of violence.

Operative violence

From his earliest statements on violence Agamben has been interested to define it not in terms of the use of violence as a means, as we find in Arendt's famous consideration of the topic,[4] but what violence is in itself (*LOV* 231). So it seems legitimate to ask: What is violence? The World Health Organization has an operative definition of violence, for example, fit for their named purpose of 'social service intervention':

> the intentional use of physical force or power, threatened or actual, against oneself, another person, or against a group or community, that either results in or has a high likelihood of resulting in injury, death, psychological harm, maldevelopment, or deprivation.[5]

The WHO openly subscribes to a tripartite typology of violence here. Self-directed violence: self-abuse and suicide. Interpersonal violence: violence between individuals. And collective violence, committed by larger groups of individuals including states. Yet at the same time they believe that it is all but impossible to define violence in itself. First because it depends on what you need the definition for. Second because any definition exists within a set of cultural and temporal norms that are changing, so that violence here and today was not necessarily seen as violence over there fifty years ago. All of which means finally one needs a broad-based definition of violence that all 61 UN signatories will subscribe to, yet not so broad as it is meaningless or 'describes the natural vicissitudes of everyday living in terms of pathology'.[6] This way of defining violence then is what I am calling operative violence: violence defined by what it allows you to do as a collective or, after Badiou, a state.[7]

Putting aside the issue of self-directed violence, the relation between the interpersonal and the collective modes of violence is particularly revealing in this regard. Our specific concern is the role of violence as it pertains to the perpetuation and founding of states, in that precise order. In other words, it is not so much the definition of violence and its relation to inter-subjective violence *and* its relation to collective violence that we are engaging with, but rather the nature of violence as a means of articulating and perpetuating states, specifically but not exclusively nation-states, through the economy of the need for collective violence to limit that of the inter-subjective: a need hinted at darkly by the WHO's own phrase 'the vicissitudes of everyday living', suggesting we are all perpetually in a state of potential or constant violence. Make no mistake, this articulation is all that state violence in actual fact is: a mode of legitimating actions through differential articulation. Or, to put it another way, there is no violence as such as an act of one subject against another, only violence as a signatory means of making things happen. Specifically through the operation of a conception of violence which, based on the presumption of inter-subjective violence if the state is not allowed to found and perpetuate itself through occasional and necessary acts of violence, is able to regulate behaviour precisely through the mode of its articulation between assumed differential positions.[8] In this context the WHO would count as a state whose mission is as follows:

> WHO is the directing and coordinating authority for health within the United Nations system. It is responsible for providing leadership on global health matters, shaping the health research agenda, setting norms and standards, articulating evidence-based policy options, providing technical support to countries and monitoring and assessing health trends.[9]

We are speaking here of violence making operative not sovereign, foundational power, but governing, perpetuating power. It is this state-operative violence, not violence of the state but use of violence to articulate an effective economy of the state, that concerns Agamben in his reading of Benjamin's essay.

Divine violence

Walter Benjamin's 1921 essay 'Critique of Violence' considers the two traditional forms of justified, state-sanctioned acts of violence: law-positing and law-preserving. He famously conflates these differing meanings of violence together under a single heading, 'mythic violence', and opposes this compound or articulated violence to a third 'pure' or 'divine' violence. Pure violence, he explains, is a violence that takes place outside of juridical structures. It is in a sense violence without justification, which he defines in contradistinction to legal and justified mythic violence: 'If mythical violence is lawmaking, divine violence is law-destroying; if the former sets boundaries, the latter boundlessly destroys them; ... if the former threatens, the latter strikes; if the former is bloody, the latter is lethal without spilling blood' (*SW* 1:249–50).

The specific question of blood then permits Benjamin to relate violence to the fact of pure existence or, as he calls it, mere life. If blood is, as he says, the symbol of mere life then:

> The dissolution of legal violence stems ... from the guilt of mere natural life, which consigns the living ... to a retribution that 'expiates' the guilt of mere life – and

doubtless also purifies the guilty, not of guilt, however, but of law. For with mere life the rule of law over the living ceases. Mythical violence is a bloody power over mere life for its own sake; divine violence is pure power over all life for the sake of the living. (*SW* 1:250).

To clarify, mythic and pure violence are placed in opposition over the issue of the relation of violence to mere, or as Agamben famously calls it, bare, life. Pure violence does not spill blood; therefore it does violence to something other than living bodies. In a phrase I will borrow from Zartaloudis, Benjaminian pure violence does violence to violence.[10] It is not another form of violence, but the possibility of acting violently towards the oppositional structure of legally sanctioned state violence. So we see that pure violence purifies the living not of their very guilt at being alive and thus by definition in a state of potential violence, but rather from the law.

At the end of the essay Benjamin turns to how one can do violence to violence through a form of radical philology: '[t]he critique of violence is the philosophy of its history', he says, going on to add:

A gaze directed only at what is close at hand can at most perceive a dialectical rising and falling in the lawmaking and law-preserving formations of violence. The law governing their oscillation rests on the circumstance that all law-preserving violence, in its duration, indirectly weakens the lawmaking violence it represents, by suppressing hostile counterviolence … On the breaking of this cycle maintained by mythic forms of law, on the suspension of law with all the forces on which it depends as they depend on it, finally therefore on the abolition of state power, a new historical epoch is founded. (*SW* 1:251–2)

On this reading pure violence is a philological mode of hermeneutics applied to the history of mythic violence, revealing its cyclical nature, and suspending the law from within the law itself. It is not *stricto sensu* an act of violence itself. This being the case, the new historical epoch of which Benjamin speaks and of which Agamben is somewhat critical in his early work (*LOV* 235), would not be a new epoch in history. That would simply perpetuate mythic violence's combination of state plus event. Rather, it would be a new epoch in what we take to be history through a radical revision of the signature 'violence' and its usage to perpetuate states. This radical hermeneutics due to philological 'violence' is the basis of what Agamben now calls philosophical archaeology, speaking of his own related project of 'indifferentiating' the term violence as a basis for political action. At this juncture it may be worth saying, after Zartaloudis, that Agambenian pure violence does not in actual fact do violence to violence, if we take violence here to be decisionist, evental or an act in some sense, as this would not escape the discourse of mythic violence.[11] Instead, it indifferentiates the two elements of the signature of violence so as to suspend them. For Agamben, divine violence suspends violence rather than violently deciding on violence.

The history of violence then is the cycle of interchange between law-making and law-preserving violence permanently under threat from an external form of violence; this is not divine violence by the way, but violence from another state, which law-preserving violence protects us from through acts of violence against the other state, until the external threat is either nullified, or violently takes over through law-making violence, and the whole cycle commences once more. Please note this other state could be a 'state' within the state. The only way to suspend this cycle, therefore, is through an act of divine violence that attacks the logic of the dialectic, resulting in the dissolution of law, state and even what we have taken to be human life. What Benjamin's essay presents, therefore, is an alternative typology of violence to juxtapose to that of the WHO. First, there are two types of violence: law-making and law-preserving. These are modes of justifiable violence due to a double threat to the state. The first threat is that of our mere (animalistic) life. Left to our own devices Jane will eventually take up a stick and brain John. As we saw, the WHO document also suggests that, in the vicissitudes of everyday life, how we actually live as human beings is effectively violent.

The second threat is violence to the state from another state. We need law-making violence to protect human beings from their own violently competitive nature, and we need law-preserving violence to protect states from violently competitive other states. Benjamin then opposes mythic violence to pure violence or violence outside these juridical structures. He suggests that pure violence is a means of suspending the endless dialectic of law-making and law-preserving violence, justified for millennia based on two elements outside the state: humans in a position of natural violence before the state was founded, and other violent states who would destroy this one. Benjamin's pure violence is a mode of critical reading that first shows us the nature of the dialectic of violence, and then a means of suspending it, or at least that is Agamben's reading/use of this mysterious text.[12] It is not, therefore, an act of violence committed by subjects on the bodies of other subjects, nor sanctioned acts of decision designed to found-perpetuate states through the activity of law. In this sense the term divine or pure violence is bound to be misunderstood. Benjaminian violence is not divine or pure in actual fact, but negates such divisionist signatures. Nor is it actually violent in any traditional sense of physical or psychological attack resulting in trauma.

Agamben's indifferent violence

At the heart of Giorgio Agamben's 2003 *State of Exception* is a chapter entitled, 'Gigantomachy concerning a void', a sustained consideration of violence, law and the state through a close critical reading of Benjaminian pure violence. Towards the end of the chapter Agamben explains his title comes from the Greek '*gigantomachia peri tes ousias*, the "battle of giants concerning being", that defines Western metaphysics' (*SE* 59). The two giants in question represent philosophers of the one or, as Agamben tends to call it, the common, and the thinkers of the many or the proper. As regards the actual chapter under consideration, however, the giants at war are the fascist political theorist Carl Schmitt, and Walter Benjamin. What they bicker over is the status of a violence that exceeds the law. Specifically, Agamben explains, as regards states of exception where the law is suspended, Schmitt wants to recuperate Benjamin's pure violence and prove that there is no violence outside of the law. Violence as *anomie* or lawlessness is, therefore, the void in question.

The thesis of Agamben's *State of Exception* as a whole is as follows. The state of exception or emergency is when, due to an exceptional fact, a fact that exceeds the norm, a necessity occurs, which means that sovereignty in whatever form suspends the law and becomes the direct agency of legal decision. This act results in a double exclusion, a fact excluded from the very norm which defines fact, and the arbiter of the norm becoming abnormal by stepping outside of the law in its entirety. As is seen in Agamben's most famous work, *Homo Sacer*, this leads to a complex zone of indistinction where the most debased and most elevated members of any society are bound together by being subject to the impossible logic of included exclusion (*HS* 15–29). The *homo sacer* or subject of bare life is included in the state by being legally excluded from the law (they can be killed without it being defined as murder). The sovereign founds the legal norms of the state only because it can stand outside the state becoming ab-normal so as to prove the state's normative metaphysical foundation: pure decision as definition of sovereign power.

The second part of this lethal syllogism is Agamben's belief that we are all held in a world-wide *de facto* state of exception, or that the state of exception is now the norm. This leads to a simple concluding deduction on his part: the logic of the state of exception is the logic of all our legal and political situations, so if we pay attention to this logic, first we will see the reality of our situation and second we will also perceive a possible way forward from our current political catastrophe (*SE* 85–8). This is because, as we said, the *gigantomachia* in question always concerns a void, here violence as a form of *anomie* (lawlessness). If we can make it intelligible that state violence is hollow at its core, then we may no longer feel the need to be complicit with or bullied by it.

Taking these comments on board, *the* law is the founding common of the state, but there is in actual fact no law as such. Law as the norm is only in force as regards the fact of specific cases, so, as we can see, it is founded by what it is taken to found: facts. Mostly this difficult economy between the law and an actual instance of the law goes relatively unremarked upon because, although illogical, it works, it is operative, it sanctions intelligible common-sense and apparently consensual situations we are complicit in our sanction of. In states of emergency or exception, however, where the norms of law have to be suspended due to an exceptional necessity seen to threaten them, a specific fact of law means that the law as such has to be invoked.

We now enter into a profound zone of indistinction as regards fact and norm or proper and common. We have a fact so factical that it is an exception, an ontico-singularity that undermines ontology. And we have a norm so abnormal that sovereigns are the only ones who can speak for the law when a fact occurs which the norms of law have no jurisdiction over. All Agamben argues is that this exceptional state is, when we look at the day-to-day logic of the economy of the interchange between fact and norm in every legal system, *in* fact *the* norm. Everything included in the legal system of the West is based on a logically impossible doubly included exclusion. Our entire *nomos* is, in fact, in a state of *anomie* because we cannot distinguish between fact and norm, and yet by definition our states must be able to distinguish between them to continue to exist.

In *Homo Sacer* Agamben states unequivocally that in 'laying bare the irreducible link uniting violence and law', Benjamin's 'Critique of Violence' … 'proves the necessary and, even today, indispensable premise of every enquiry into sovereignty' (*HS* 63). This link, he confirms, is 'a dialectical oscillation between the violence that posits law and the violence that preserves it', leading to the necessity of a 'third figure to break the circular dialectic' (HS 63). That figure is of course divine or pure violence as a mode of indifferential suspension. Such a form of violence neither posits nor preserves law, but de-poses it (in German, *entsetzt*). Deposing here should be taken in all its potential meanings. Divine violence is then a process by which the articulation of law and violence – as it pertains to one half of the double question of the signature of power, sovereignty (the other half being governance of course; cf. *The Kingdom and the Glory*) – is re-presented. In so doing the mode of oscillation is replaced by something very different, something that dethrones and de-questions, through an act of relocating the issue due to the legal process of the oath. That something is indifference.

Agamben goes on to note that divine violence, though not reducible in any way to sovereign violence, specifically as defined by Schmitt, shares with sovereign violence the key characteristic of not being reducible to either of the two elements it articulates. As regards sovereign violence, which is the main concern of *Homo Sacer*, he says of these two elements:

> Sovereign violence opens a zone of indistinction between law and nature, outside and inside, violence and law. And yet the sovereign is precisely the one who maintains the possibility of deciding on the two to the very degree that he renders them indistinguishable from each other. As long as the state of exception is distinguished from the normal case, the dialectic between the violence that posits law and the violence that preserves it is not truly broken, and the sovereign decision even appears simply as the medium in which the passage from one to the other takes place ... [T]he link between violence and law is maintained, even at the point of their indistinction. (*HS* 64–5)

We are now better placed to decide ourselves on this complex logic. What we can conclude is that sovereign decision is content neutral (indifferent). It is not what the sovereign decides upon that matters, but that they decide. In the state of exception, the sovereign's word is law to such a degree that the violence of pure decisionism versus the communicable nature of law becomes indistinguishable. Yet at those precise moments the sovereign insists on the fiction that there is a difference between violence (*anomie*) and law (*nomos*). In other words, speaking of Schmitt here, at the moment when decisionism insists there must be an outside the law to justify a sovereign's power to decide when this zone of *anomie* threatens the state represented by the rule of law, the sovereign actually renders such a clear distinction indistinct. Yet they still insist that there is such a distinction.

In contrast, Agamben explains:

> [t]he violence that Benjamin defines as divine is instead situated in a zone in which it is no longer possible to distinguish between exception and rule. ... [D]ivine violence neither posits nor conserves violence, but deposes it. Divine violence shows the connection between the two violences – and, even more, between violence and law – to be the single real content of law. (*HS* 65)

Agamben is clear in this engagement with 'Critique of Violence' that Benjamin had almost certainly not read Schmitt's work on sovereign violence when he was composing his essay, so the clarity of the distinction is all the more stark. In actual fact, in Agamben's system there are not different orders of violence, so there is no marked difference between sovereign and divine violence *per se*. Rather, divine violence is what happens to the distinction of violence and law, or *anomie* and *nomos*, or decision and conservation, at moments when the clear distinction between violence and law are subject to the kinds of pressures we see in Schmitt's decisionist states of exception. In these moments it is logically apparent that decision and law cannot be differentiated, yet the sovereign not only insists that they are distinguishable, but can only insist on said distinction in such exceptional circumstances. This is because Schmitt has to accept that juridically the large majority of all legal decisions are not in fact decisionist but emanate from the communicable systems of jurisprudence approved generally by groups. To prove that all these local agreements or norms of behaviour (rather than decisions as such) are only possible due to the implied sanction of sovereign decision, Schmitt has to push the state to a point where a fact exceeds the norm. As no one can predict what this fact will be, then only a sovereign gifted with the power of decision will be able to respond to such events. Or, because sovereign power is pure event, it is the only agency capable of tackling the imminent threat of unseen events. So that when a zone of indistinction due to an exception occurs, the sovereign reveals the necessity of distinction at the moment of indistinction. In contrast divine violence, when faced with the insistence of distinction when indistinction is so apparent, has no other choice than to commit an act of 'violence' to the articulation of violence and law. One cannot do this by deciding. Divine violence is denied decisionism because decision is intrinsic to the system it wishes to destroy, so instead it points out that law is defined not in contradistinction to violence (*anomie* but also pure decision), but actually is nothing other than the process of their articulation via distinction.

Žižek: Violence as event

Moving away from issues of included exclusion and indistinction in relation to the law, we may now pose the question: How does the indifference of violence pertain to bare life (*bloßes Leben*)? This is after all the topic that this engagement with Benjamin is strategically placed to develop. Agamben admits himself the transition in Benjamin's essay is abrupt (*HS* 65), but also essential in helping to clarify Agamben's own main thesis, that the link between sovereignty and life, what Foucault calls biopolitics, is the founding political topos of the West. Specific to this project is the relation between the sacred and the act of separation. Girard's foundational study *Violence and the Sacred* stresses that the act of separation performed through acts of excluding violence in troubled communities is unconscious.[13] For Agamben, in contrast, something becomes sacred in traditional and ancient societies through the *deliberate* act of its being removed from ordinary use. This then is the crucial link between bare life and sovereignty. If the sovereign is the one who can decide, then they can remove from legal norms elements that otherwise require no decision from them. Benjamin,

Agamben, Arendt and others all join in explaining that Greek culture had no sense of life as sacred, and indeed had no sense of politics as violence. The concepts life and the sacred, in other words, are historically linked, meaning sacred life is a discursive construct. A politics of decision is a politics of violence and it is such a politics that makes it possible to have a sacred life because it is such a political situation that results in *homines sacri*. At the moment when human life became a sacred right, what happened was a biopolitical decisionism revealing, as Agamben states, that *homo sacer* is the original *nomos* of the political in the West. Agamben concludes:

> Sacredness is … the originary form of the inclusion of bare life in the juridical order, and the syntagm *homo sacer* names something like the 'original' political relation, which is to say, bare life insofar as it operates in an inclusive exclusion as the referent of sovereign decision. Life is sacred only insofar as it is taken into sovereign exception. (*HS* 85)

Adding that it is because the state took a religious phenomenon to stand for what is in fact a simple juridico-political relation that we have become confused enough to assume, say in relation to Benjamin's divine violence, that it has anything to do with gods. I mention these issues because they relate directly to perhaps the most powerfully competitive reading of Benjaminian divine violence in our age, Žižek's reading of the 'Critique of Violence' in his recent study, *Violence*.

Žižek's reading of Benjamin's text is revelatory in terms of how the same essay can result in widely divergent positions. More than this, it perhaps gives a sense in which both Agamben and Žižek present operative definitions of Benjamin's divine violence, designed to make their own political ideas more widely communicable. Agamben concentrates on pure violence as a mode of radical philology designed to suspend the *gigantomachia* of Western politics over the void of violence as *anomie*, so that through a consideration of violence the signature 'violence' can be suspended and politics suspended. Žižek's concerns are of a different order. Although his text is engaged with what he calls symbolic violence, his term for discourse,[14] Žižek seems to miss entirely this 'symbolic' aspect of Benjamin's work and instead reads it as a treatise on revolutionary violence. So that, while for Agamben pure violence suspends the law from within the discourse of juridical power, for Žižek it stands for '[b]rutal intrusions of justice beyond the law'.[15] In other words, violent explosions of illegal action covering the spectrum of 'mob lynchings to organized revolutionary terror'.[16]

Agamben himself concedes that Benjamin is not concerned with sovereign violence and its difference from divine violence in the text in question, and much more engaged with the issues of revolutionary violence. Yet when Žižek says that divine and sovereign violence are the same, going on to cite the *homo sacer*, he surely must be in open disagreement with Agamben's own insistence that the two forms of violence share structural similarities in being concerned with *anomie* or that which is outside the law, but are otherwise fundamentally at odds. As we saw, divine violence does violence, philologically speaking, to sovereign violence.

Žižek goes further by suggesting that divine violence, which on his reading signifies unprecedented and thus illegal explosions of violence, shares with sovereign violence the fact that those who are killed are not sacrificed. This is doubly incorrect. The defining characteristic of sacredness in Agamben is presenting something as included in a state as separate. Thus in a sense every *homo sacer* is always-already sacrificed and their death is irrelevant to this fact. Death is just a means of brutally designating separation, but being included as excluded is just as brutal and in this sense just as violent. So while it is true to say the *homo sacer* can be killed and it not be a crime, the only reason their death is not a sacrifice is that they are pre-approved for sacrifice. Žižek says that the victims of divine violence are not sacrificed either: 'Those annihilated by divine violence are fully and completely guilty: they are not sacrificed, since they are not worthy of being sacrificed to and accepted by God'.[17] Again, on our reading of divine violence this is wrong. Without either mounting the argument as to whether the victims of divine violence are sacrificed or not and quibbling with Žižek's misunderstanding of what sacrifice amounts to (sacrifice is defined as included exclusion with God as just an epi-phenomenon), the simple fact is that divine violence has no victims because it is not violence to the body at all.

This confusion is compounded by Žižek's messy presentation of the relation of (bare) life to the act of violence. Speaking of the inexistent victims of divine violence he asks: 'Of what are they guilty? Of leading a mere (natural) life. Divine violence purifies the guilty not of guilt but of law, because law is limited to the living: it cannot reach beyond life to touch what is in excess of life, what is more than mere life'.[18] It is true that divine violence gives Agamben access to the term bare life, but bare life is not mere (natural) life but a constructed idea of mere life. When Žižek says divine violence purifies us of the law, this is correct, but when he says this is because the law is limited to the living, this is way off and truly violent on his part in relation to Agamben at least. The law is not limited to the living as the law itself determines what life is. In one way yes, it is limited to life as a category, but the dead do not escape the law, as life and death are category positions within a juridical state, not pure states of existence and inexistence as Žižek presents them. Taking all this into consideration, in fact, overall, Žižek's conclusion that divine violence is non-sacrificial is correct, as are his comments on the reach of law as regards life. So if Žižek can grasp the essence of the Benjaminian text and, by implication here, Agamben's reading of it, why does he present it in terms which are clearly, forcibly incorrect?

The answer comes in the following section, where he considers Benjamin's assertion that divine violence is invisible and can be taken for sovereign violence, but only as the sign and seal of sacred violence, never its means. This is a crucial section, as the idea of divine violence as a sign without a meaning is central to Agamben's reading of Benjamin (a sign without meaning is a signature), and Žižek's reading which, it transpires, is effectively Badiou's reading by proxy. Žižek says of divine justice as a sign without meaning:

> What this entails is that, to put it in Badiou's terms, mythic violence belongs to the order of Being, while divine violence belongs to the order of the event: there are no 'objective' criteria enabling us to identify an act of violence as divine; the same act that, to an external observer, is merely an outburst of violence can be divine for those engaged in it – there is no big Other guaranteeing its divine nature, the risk of reading and assuming it as divine is fully the subject's own.[19]

This position leads to a dramatic divergence from Agamben in the reflections which follow, where Žižek concludes that divine violence is pure decisionism in the form of death: 'the heroic assumption of the solitude of sovereign decision. It is a decision (to kill, to risk or lose one's own life) made in absolute solitude'.[20] While Žižek tries to strong-arm Agamben into the equation by terming such violence a 'means without end', Agamben's phrase for a politics to come – which ironically is also the basis for Arendt's attack on the relation of violence and power[21] – in the end Žižek is clear when he says: 'violence belongs to the order of the Event'.[22]

This passage is a rather crucial moment for the future direction of philosophy as well as being exemplary of how Benjamin continues to be used violently by contemporary theory. The whole debate centres on what it means to have a sign without meaning and how this can be sovereign. For Badiou-Žižek, naturally this pertains to the manner in which an event is an outburst of truth that is – by definition – initially meaningless and whose 'meaning' is defined retroactively through the militant, subjective point-by-point delineation of how the event comes to be a truth, the subject's naming of the event, and their adherence to its new effects. On this reading, divine violence is meaningless because it is truthful. Brilliant though this is, it cannot be accepted as accurate either in terms of Žižek's coercion of Benjamin or Agamben to the cause. Agamben is adamant and with strong evidential support that Benjamin is absolutely opposed to political decisionism especially as it is represented by his adversary Schmitt.

Having said that, Badiou has renovated decisionism for our age, and freed it from the statist, theological jurists to a large degree. In that decisionism is not about the content of the decision but the fact of being able to decide, yes certainly the indifferent neutrality of the event is a radical form of decisionism. A fact made clear by Badiou's insistence that when it comes to the real of the void, one must decide. And again Agamben is clear that divine violence is not a form of subjective violence at all, so there are no victims. On Agamben's reading, divine violence is a mode of symbolic violence that does violence to the signature 'violence'. This is precisely what Agamben means by a sign that has no meaning. A signature, like the event, is indifferently neutral as regards content. But in contrast to the event, a signature is not a one-off but a persistent structure, and so what divine violence reveals about sovereign violence is that it is a mere signature. Like decisionism, the signature is determined not by what it means but that it means. And, unlike in Badiou, this decisionist maxim can be suspended without succumbing to the logic of decisionism. This is, ultimately, what Agamben has Benjamin make divine violence do, put an end to the signature of violence as *anomie* as the basis of Western political systems.

Inoperative violence

Agamben, like many before him, is ineluctably drawn to the possibility of a pure violence which Benjamin seems to simultaneously praise and present as terrifying. For Agamben the issue is the possibility of a discourse or conception of violence that exists outside the law, outside the state, and yet cannot exist either as an original founding violence or an exceptional and singular violence, as both possibilities are entirely within the legal compound of mythic violence as law-positing and law-preserving. Agamben's gloss on the essay is as follows:

> The aim of this essay is to ensure the possibility of a violence … that lies absolutely 'outside' and 'beyond' the law and that, as such, could shatter the dialectic between lawmaking violence and lawpreserving violence. Benjamin calls this other figure of violence 'pure' or 'divine' … What the law can never tolerate … is the existence of a violence outside the law; and this is not because the ends of such a violence are incompatible with the law, but because of its 'mere existence outside the law' … The proper characteristic of this [pure] violence is that it neither makes nor preserves the law, but deposes it … and thus inaugurates a new historical epoch. (*SE* 53)

What this citation makes clear is that every state founds its legal system on the myth of a founding act of violence that was justified and necessary to found the state and revert its regress back into violence, and then applies actual violence to preserve this initial, violently-founded state. When in fact the necessity of the founding act of violence, violence to end all violence, is not proven, so that the justification of this specific act of violence – we need to be violent now to prevent our returning to the mythical violence of then – is inexistent. As Benjamin contends, what bothers any state in terms of an act of violence outside the state, is the raw possibility that it shows there could be an outside of the state or a pure violence. More than this, one can argue, in fact the very violence of the state is outside the state. There was no necessary founding act of violence, so there can be no justified specific and contemporary act of violence. This being the case, every justified act of mythic violence is in actual fact a non-justifiable moment of pure or divine violence because it is, by definition, outside of the control of the foundational or founded nature of the state.

After founding and preserving violence, this third form of lawless or divine violence is the violence of evisceration. First, such violence shows there can be an outside of law or act of non-justified violence. Second it reveals that this *anomie* or lawless violence is the basis of law. Law is created to negate pure violence. Third it demonstrates that in fact law as such *is* the outside of law, or *nomos* is *anomie*. Violence outside the law forces the actual law to accept that the inside/outside structure it is based on means, by definition, that all *nomos* is foundationally and eventually anomic, all the insides of the law are outside, every fact is in fact an exception and every norm is founded on a profound abnormality.

It is immediately apparent that Benjamin's conception of pure violence is not in accordance with the WHO's operative definition. There is no space therein to define the relation of inter-subjective and collective violence as 'mythic'. One cannot act, legislate or intervene on the basis of a mythic violence. Further, there is certainly no sense of a 'pure' violence, and yet it is the articulation and complex interaction of mythic and pure violence that helps us to fully understand, after Benjamin and Agamben, how states are formed, perpetuated and maintained under the auspices of certain acts of legitimate and illegitimate acts of violence.

The problem with pure violence is that it does not exist as such. For example, we have already seen that the logic of pure violence is illogical, based on the necessity to differentiate norm and fact, then the need to place norm and fact in the causal series in which the norm founds the state, the fact preserves it. This causal chain then reveals that the clear difference between norm and fact is impossible due to the complex of an included exclusion, and so the causal link is placed in a kind of impossible chiasmus: the norm founds the fact only in as much as the fact constructs its norm. More than this, violence, as a signature, contains no stable semantic content and so it makes no sense to present a systematic definition of it as the WHO and its 160 experts tried to do a decade ago.

As was the case for the WHO, clearly we have three orders of violence in play here, although our typology differs dramatically from theirs. The first violence is actually law-preserving. Law-preserving violence however needs a mythologeme of law-making violence to justify its own recourse to violence and also to show that said violence is not groundless. According to Agamben, these two forms of violence are actually one single signatory element called 'violence' that, like all signatures, operates via a dialectical economy of common and proper. What it tells us is that, in effect, left to their own devices, beings will resort to violence due to indifference: the natural indifference of one animal to another when it comes to their own concerns. The result would be chaos and cruelty.

Contrasting with mythical violence is so-called pure violence. The argument is that we need the economy of violence, law-making then law-preserving, to save us from our guilt of pure violence: to be alive simply means to be violent and subject to violence. The reality is that bare life is a construct of our politics and in no way precedes the foundation of a state. Bare life threatens the state, not through the potential for violence, but through its impotentiality. What bothers law-makers is not violence outside the state, menacing from the margins, that is what they tell us we are all *de facto* guilty of (people and states just naturally kill), but the state of *anomie* itself as the foundation of every *nomos*. Thus we are guilty for something that has not been committed and the concept of innocence, as Zartaloudis notes, is based on this presupposition.[23] Not innocent until proven guilty but provably innocent because we are initially and inevitably guilty. Our job is not to expiate for this guilt, but to occupy it and show that in fact to be guilty means simply to be in a state of pure violence. Bare life, pure violence, guilt: none of these actually exist. The whole glorious and epic story of Western states is a *gigantomachia* over a void. The economy of a dialectical argument between law as common and law as proper is composed, sanctioned and inserted into our collective past to distract from what, ironically, precisely that which the argument creates: the indifference of pure, inoperative violence as bare, human, life.

Notes

1   See also Michel Foucault, *The Archaeology of Knowledge*, trans. A. M. Sheridan Smith (London: Routledge, 1972).

2   See William Watkin, *Agamben and Indifference* (London: Rowman & Littlefield International, 2014), 245–70.

3   Watkin, *Agamben and Indifference*, 30–1.
4   Hannah Arendt, *On Violence* (New York: Harcourt Brace & Company, 1970), 4 and 51.
5   World Health Organization, *World Report on Violence and Health: Summary* (Geneva: WHO, 2002), 4.
6   *World Report on Violence and Health*, 4.
7   Alain Badiou, *Being and Event*, trans. Oliver Feltham (London: Continuum, 2005), 93–103.
8   I must make it clear that I do not deny the 'existence' of violent acts. I am talking of violence as a signature determined by its state-sanctioned usage both in terms of acts that we might term violence, but also how a state uses violence as a signature to secure said state.
9   WHO, *About WHO*, http://www.who.int/about/en/ (accessed February 2014).
10   Thanos Zartaloudis, *Giorgio Agamben: Power, Law and the Uses of Criticism* (London: Routledge, 2010), 130.
11   When I speak of 'decisionism' in this essay I refer to the widely accepted term within political philosophy which stems from Schmitt's work and covers any political theory based on a sovereign act of deciding.
12   Note that we are presenting Agamben's presentation of Benjamin's position, not simply a reading based on Benjamin's writings alone.
13   René Girard, *Violence and the Sacred*, trans. Patrick Gregory (London: Bloomsbury, 2013).
14   Slavoj Žižek, *Violence* (London: Polity, 2009), 1.
15   Žižek, *Violence*, 151.
16   Žižek, *Violence*, 157.
17   Žižek, *Violence*, 168.
18   Žižek, *Violence*, 168.
19   Žižek, *Violence*, 169.
20   Žižek, *Violence*, 171.
21   Cf. Arendt, *On Violence*.
22   Žižek, *Violence*, 172.
23   Zartaloudis, *Giorgio Agamben*, 161.

Works cited

Arendt, Hannah. *On Violence*. New York: Harcourt Brace & Company, 1970.
Badiou, Alain. *Being and Event*. Translated by Oliver Feltham. London: Continuum, 2005.
Foucault, Michel. *The Archaeology of Knowledge*. Translated by A. M. Sheridan Smith. London: Routledge, 1972.
Girard, René. *Violence and the Sacred*. Translated by Patrick Gregory. London: Bloomsbury, 2013.
Watkin, William. *Agamben and Indifference*. London: Rowman & Littlefield International, 2014.
World Health Organization. *World Report on Violence and Health: Summary*. Geneva: WHO, 2002.
WHO. *About WHO*. http://www.who.int/about/en/ (accessed February 2014).
Zartaloudis, Thanos. *Giorgio Agamben: Power, Law and the Uses of Criticism*. London: Routledge, 2010.
Žižek, Slavoj. *Violence*. London: Polity, 2009.

9

Suchness and the Threshold between Possession and Violence

Paolo Bartoloni

Suchness, purity, irreparability

'Suchness' is an ontological category that occurs time and again in the philosophical discourse of Giorgio Agamben and that connects with aspects of Walter Benjamin's philosophy in ways that are germane to the theme of this volume. As I will argue in the course of this essay, Agamben's suchness is philosophically contiguous to Benjamin's notion of purity, as they are mobilized by the two thinkers to articulate an alternative ontology predicated on forms of life that run contrary to established norms of competition, antagonism, possession and privatization. The revolutionary proletarian strike characterized by pure means, which Benjamin illustrates in his essay on the critique of violence, is equated with religious violence by Agamben in the 1970s and employed to offer examples of an experience the ultimate purpose of which is to alter time and renew life. What would this new form of life look like? According to Agamben's later elaboration, it might be analogous to the life of the Franciscan friars, who elected to live along and with things rather than in pursuit of their possession. But contrary to the Franciscan experience, this new life should not seek to be justified legally but lived instead according to the irreparability of life as such or pure life.

In Agamben, 'suchness' (*talità*) makes one of its first appearances in the book *The Coming Community* (1990), where it is articulated as pure presence; a presence, in other words, not yet qualified by representational traits such as identity, belonging, religion and ethnicity.[1] Life as such is comparable to a life that is given in its pure form, to 'existence as exposure' (*CC* 97). In time, 'suchness' has come to indicate in Agamben a variety of modes of being that are impermeable to forms of employability, be they aesthetic, political or economic. Agamben often compares 'suchness' with potentiality in that 'suchness', as opposed to the potential, cannot develop into an agency defined by cultural markers (linguistic, religious, ethnic), but remains in its potentiality of-not-to-be.[2] It is 'thus' and not otherwise, and it resides in a space the only ascertainable element of which is its being, and its presencing.

Agamben's articulation of 'suchness' is indebted to Benjamin's discussion of language in his famous essays 'The Task of the Translator' (1921) and 'On Language as Such and on the Language of Man' (1916). Here, although with different intentions, Benjamin investigates the modality of language per se, that is a language that differs from the conventional understanding of language as instrument of communication – he also describes the latter as the bourgeois conception of language (*SW* 1:65). In 'On Language as Such and on the Language of Man', Benjamin thinks of a modality of speech that transcends everyday employability, and becomes its own thing in its own right.[3] Language is no longer to be understood, therefore, as referring to something outside of itself. It becomes instead language as such, whose presence, borrowing Agamben's terminology, is an 'irreparable' and pure given. In the essay on Goethe's *Elective Affinities*, Benjamin applies his notion of language as such to argue for the inherent 'expressionlessness' of Goethe's language in which, to him, resides the greatness of the German author, who achieved the creation of a language that lives according to moments of 'interruption', 'fragmentation', 'objection'.[4] In 'The Task of the Translator', Benjamin speaks of pure language, which he employs to interrogate translation as the medium in-between pure language and historical languages.

The term 'irreparable', which was mobilized a few lines above, plays a strategic role in the context of this discussion. In fact, it is my contention that the idea of 'irreparability' provides the essential link through which Agamben's suchness and Benjamin's purity can be reconnected and investigated comparatively. 'Irreparable' is the essential condition which can, according to Agamben in *The Coming Community*, instil and trigger hope.[5] He writes: 'we can have hope only in what is without remedy' (*CC* 101). The 'without remedy' is precisely that which cannot be changed: the 'irreparable'. And yet, the 'irreparable' is nothing other than life as presencing or life as such. It is 'suchness', therefore, that, according to Agamben, affords hope. This is not without analogies to Benjamin's articulation of 'purity' or things as such – as in the case of language – and especially to his somewhat optimistic view that violence can be suspended when placed in a context of pure means, an example of which is provided by the non-violent proletarian strike, to which Benjamin refers in 'Critique of Violence' (*SW* 1:245–6). It is highly significant that the proletarian strike can be also interpreted as 'the manifestation of the political as such',[6] a kind of given irreparable, whose effects might very well be that of suspending the cyclical occurrence of violence determined by historical, social and political processes. Is Benjamin's optimism cognate to Agamben's notion of the coming community, and to the hope that a future common life could be founded on something approaching the ontological category of 'suchness'?

Agamben's suchness and Benjamin's purity

The last section of *The Coming Community* is titled 'The Irreparable'. Agamben defines the 'Irreparable' thus:

> The Irreparable is that things are just as they are, in this or that mode, consigned without remedy to their way of being. States of things are irreparable, whatever they may be: sad or happy, atrocious or blessed. How you are, how the world is – this is the irreparable. (*CC* 89)

What we witness here are the crystallization of life and an image of a world fixed and suspended, deprived of the ability to change, modify and transform. Or better, the irreparability of things appears to be a mode of being that, although plunging things into the transformative effect of history, preserves them from change. As such things transcend the dynamic movement characteristic of social and cultural developments. The 'irreparable' renders things static and passive. The articulation of this philosophical idea is insidiously complex given its obvious simplicity but also its obdurate reluctance to be conceived as an integral part of everyday life. It comes as no surprise that Agamben himself struggles with the 'irreparable'. For instance, after having said that the 'irreparable' is a given mode of being, Agamben varies his perspective by claiming that:

> the Irreparable is neither an essence nor an existence, neither a substance nor a quality, neither a possibility nor a necessity. It is not properly a modality of being, but it is the being that is always already given in modality, that *is* its modalities. It is not *thus*, but rather it is *its* thus. (*CC* 91, emphases in the original)

There is a further element that might be helpful to shed light on the meaning of the 'irreparable'. Agamben often employs the notion of purity to describe states which might be analogous to the experience of the 'irreparable'. He writes:

> The root of all pure joy and sadness is that the world is as it is. Joy or sadness that arises because the world is not what it seems or what we want it to be is impure or provisional. But in the highest degree of their purity, in the *so be it* said to the world when every legitimate cause of doubt and hope has been removed, sadness and joy refer not to negative or positive qualities, but to pure *being-thus* without any attributes. (*CC* 90, emphases in the original)

In Agamben, purity and suchness – the condition of things as they enter the mode of irreparability – share a degree of semantic similarity in that the pure thing is presented without attributes apart from that of being as such. 'Suchness' and purity are not tainted or qualified by religion, ethnicity or language, and as a result they are not implicated in the process of identity-making and belonging. While attributes are employed to enter a process of representation and configuration, the ends of which is to construct categories for drawing distinction, 'suchness' and purity are devoid of employability and instrumentality. It is precisely here, in the zone of unemployability, that the idea of purity as described by Agamben in his articulation of 'suchness' intersects with the notion of purity as it is investigated by Benjamin.

In Benjamin, purity is often paired with language. As we have already seen when introducing 'Language as Such and the Language of Man' and 'The Task of the Translator', Benjamin interrogates the idea of 'pure language', as opposed to historical languages, in the attempt to describe an ontological state of being prior to the entrance into history, grammar and culture. Benjamin conceives a prelapsarian language whose characteristic separates it from historical languages on the basis of its meaning. This is not a language that signifies, but rather a language that demonstrates. It is made of nouns instead of propositions, and its indicating is the pure act of connecting sounds to things. Its being as such does not induce division or interpretation and thus precludes the possibility of persuasion and ultimately linguistic violence. The pure language that Benjamin thinks of in his two essays of 1916 and 1921, and the implications of which, as we shall see, echo in other essays, including the 'Critique of Violence', is a kind of Platonic archetype.[7] It is by employing this idea of language that Benjamin initiates an investigation of historical, ethical and aesthetic issues and concerns. Pure language is thus employed to broaden the understanding of historical languages and to dig deep into the mystery of a mode of expression that transcends and goes beyond the conventionality and intentionality of everyday usage. Language is not only the mirror of the new bourgeois society marked by individualism, self-interest, consumption and profit (the conventional use of language); it is also the language of poetry, of literature – in a word, of work of arts the secrecy of which emerges more potently when subjected to the act of translation. It is when different historical languages encounter and meet in the middle ground of translation that, according to Benjamin, the pure essence of language can be momentarily glimpsed as a flash.[8]

Agamben appears to catch the messianic thread running through Benjamin's work when he deliberately emphasizes the central connection between language and history. According to Agamben's reading of Benjamin, the beginning of history is also the beginning of the passage from the state of nature to the world of culture (see especially *PO* 48–51). This passage is also determined by the creation of historical languages whose differences introduce not only language barriers, but also different levels of language competence, which gradually determine and reinforce class separation, distinction, marginalization and inequality.

The transition (*il tramandamento*)[9] of language according to class and status, and historical events marked by the cyclical interchange of subversion and preservation, are emblematic examples of a power struggle between the retention of the *status quo* and its upending. The power of language and the power over language equate with political power, and the preservation or destruction of political power must pass perforce via language as well. The cyclical progression of history marked by revolutionary and counter-revolutionary events is also the history of language and the language of history. It is because of this that in thinking of pure language Benjamin, according to Agamben, proposes a reflection on the end of history, which is also the advent of the classless society:

> Just as the classless society becomes what founds and guides all historical development without ever being attained in experience, so hermeneutics transforms ideal language into the unsayable foundation that, without ever itself coming to speech, destines the infinite movement of all language. For Benjamin, on the other hand, 'the classless society is not the final end of historical progress, but rather its often failed and finally accomplished interruption'. (*PO* 56)

As opposed to traditional Marxist beliefs, according to which the just revolution is the transformation of capitalism into communism, in Agamben's reading of Benjamin a revolution is just when it is without ends. But for this to happen we must pass from historical languages to pure language and from an ontology of instrumentality to an ontology of purity and 'suchness'.[10]

Violence as self-denial

In the early essay 'On the Limits of Violence' (1970), Agamben attempts a re-elaboration of Benjamin's 'Critique of Violence' by shifting the attention from the relation between violence, law and justice to the relation between violence and politics.[11] He claims that Benjamin's messianic idea of pure violence as opposed to mythical violence, the latter instituting a system of binding legislations, could be better understood in a context of self-sacrifice and denial. By following this line of thought, Agamben draws a parallel between pure violence and religious violence. According to Agamben, religious violence as practised by people such as the Babylonians, Egyptians, Hebrews, Iranians and Romans, is marked by a kind of palingenesis, the aim of which was to regenerate time and thus life.[12] The intention of these peoples was certainly not that of initiating a political transformation, which would amount to the end of a political dynasty and the advent of a new one with attendant new laws. Religious violence was instead dictated by the will to follow and submit to the cyclical nature of life in which death is the essential passage to life. It is in this sense that, according to Agamben, sacrifice, self-denial, and annihilation were seen as the inevitable steps towards renewal (*LOV* 235–6). By following this line of thought, Agamben seeks to look for affinities between religious violence and proletarian violence as articulated by Benjamin in 'Critique of Violence'.

Agamben interprets Benjamin's pure and proletarian violence as an event of renewal, whose task is not so much that of gaining power over another class as that of interrupting and starting history over again: 'The ability to open a new historical age', writes Agamben, 'belongs solely to a revolutionary class that experiences its own negation in the negation of the ruling class' (*LOV* 236). Agamben links this idea directly to Benjamin's investigation of violence when he writes that:

> Benjamin expands upon the Sorelian theory of a general proletarian strike, finding his model of revolutionary violence in the distinction between mythic violence, which imposes law and may thus be called dominant, and 'pure and immediate' violence, which seeks to impose no law, not even in the form of *ius condendum*. Instead, pure and immediate violence ousts both law and the force that upholds it, the State, thereby inaugurating a new historical age. (*LOV* 235).

Purity, 'suchness', the 'irreparable', are all concepts that link Benjamin's and Agamben's thought, characterizing their philosophical discussions of language, history, law, politics, life and violence. They both indicate a zone or space of political engagement in which historicity and evolution influenced by Darwinian theories are halted and perhaps even discarded. In their place they provide a set of ideas that, despite Benjamin's and Agamben's genuine wishes, appear to remain in the domain of pure archetypes or potential possibilities alluded to in concepts such as the 'coming community'. But has this coming community any actual grounds on which it can progress and eventually arise? In other words, have purity, 'suchness' and the 'irreparable' any relevance and currency in the actuality of life; are they applicable, and if so in which ways?

The immediate answer to these questions is that philosophical investigations are not there to provide workable answers to the political dilemma confronting humanity.

They are useful though, but in order to be so they have to be subjected to scrutiny and a further level of inquiry to tease out some of the implications that, not uncommonly, remain hidden in-between the lines of the text or in the interstices that open up as one crosses the work of one philosopher to meet that of another one. And it is precisely in these interstices and thresholds between the work of Benjamin and Agamben that I wish to dwell more in order to provide further answers to the questions posed above.

The circularity of violence

In 'Critique of Violence', Benjamin investigates violence by linking it to law and justice and, further, by dividing law into positive and natural law. He argues that while law is concerned with the adjudication of the validity of means, justice's interest rests with the purpose of the ends (*SW* 1:237). This means that if law validates just means, justice recognizes just ends. From the very outset Benjamin puts the question of the relation between justice and violence to one side ('the realm of ends, and therefore also the question of a criterion of justness, are excluded for the time being from this study', *SW* 1:237), and focuses instead on the pair law/violence.

The distinction that Benjamin draws between natural and positive law is rooted in the historical grounding of the latter and on the assumed righteousness of humans in the case of the former. It is in this sense that for natural law violence is justified according to the natural right accorded to humans to reach just ends. For natural law 'violence is a product of nature, as it were a raw material, the use of which is in no way problematical unless force is misused for unjust ends' (*SW* 1:236–7). Benjamin ascribes this type of violence and the ensuing law to events such as the terrorism of the French Revolution, and more subtly, but with a great degree of chilling foresight, to branches of Darwinian biology and evolution which 'in a thoroughly dogmatic manner, regard … violence as the only original means, besides natural selection, appropriate to all the vital ends of nature' (*SW* 1:237).

Benjamin recognizes here the potential dangers implicit in the ability of humans to arrogate to themselves the right to decide what is naturally right and just predicated on a 'raw' sense of superiority in relation to things, nature, and eventually other human beings. It is this type of potential predisposition to a violence that is not concerned with the means at its disposal, and its moral implications, that is at the basis of late nineteenth-century and early twentieth-century forms of eugenics, racial purity and ethnic cleansing.

Positive law, on the other end, must find its origin in history as a set of legislations or juridical norms that have been approved by a constituted power. In this instance, law may justify violence ('sanctioned' and 'legitimate' violence) as the necessary means to the preservation of State power against internal or external acts of subversion ('illegitimate' and 'unsanctioned' violence) (*SW* 1:237–8). And yet by justifying legitimate violence as a means to counterbalance and repel illegitimate violence, positive law ignores or feigns to forget that the constituted power that it purports to protect is very likely the result of violent and unsanctioned actions. It appears, therefore, as if violence is the inherent propulsive engine of historical developments even when inscribed and administered by positive law, and that the moral imperative that Benjamin stressed at the beginning of his essay ('For a cause, however effective, becomes violent, in the precise sense of the word, only when it enters into moral relations', *SW* 1:236) is always already suspended and negated by the continuous and self-preserving nature of violence.

The moral impasse, which is also the result of the legal anomaly of law-making and law-preserving violence, to which we will return in a moment, had the potential to be addressed six years after the death of Benjamin with the advent of Western democracies in the aftermath of the Second World War. The democracy that emerged then over totalitarianism and dictatorship provided perhaps an ephemeral and temporary hope in a future in which State violence could be reined in. And yet this hope has been far too rapidly questioned by continuous upheavals which have taken and are taking different forms and shapes (from religious to sectarian to colonial and political armed struggles, to the war against terrorism to the more recent economic crisis and austerity measures in Europe). The problem is, as Benjamin intimated in his essay on violence, that whatever angle or perspective is applied to interpret violence, be it the angle of natural or positive law, violence resurfaces invariably as a theoretical anomaly and an act of dispossession:

> If natural law can judge all existing law only in criticizing its ends, then positive law can judge all evolving law only in criticizing its means. ... Notwithstanding this antithesis, however, both schools meet in their common basic dogma: just ends can be attained by justified means, justified means used for just ends. Natural law attempts, by the justness of the ends, to 'justify' the means, positive law to 'guarantee' the justness of the ends through the justification of the means. This antinomy would prove insoluble if the common dogmatic assumption were false, if justified means on the one hand and just ends on the other were in irreconcilable conflict. (*SW* 1:237)

Violence seems commensurate to life, available *de facto* to humans either to claim their natural desire and will or *de iure* to institute laws that, although emancipating individuals from a primeval condition, resort nevertheless to violence as an indispensable law-preserving measure. And yet, according to Benjamin there are instances in which violence is suspended. Non-violent means are those, claims Benjamin, dealing with indirect solutions, which 'never apply directly to the resolution of conflict between man and man, but apply only to matters concerning objects' (*SW* 1:244). Benjamin is here thinking of transactions where the parties arrive at agreements based on 'trust', 'civility' and 'courtesy' prepared and consolidated by the use of language. The proper sphere of understanding, that is language, is according to Benjamin 'inaccessible to violence' (*SW* 1:245).

Agamben, as he states in his article on the limits of violence (*LOV* 231–2), does not agree with this view. Agamben accepts that language in ancient Greece was seen as the vehicle of peaceful resolution and persuasion, and the essential binding element that kept society together and that ensured the harmonious life of the *polis* (*LOV* 232). And yet he points out that even in this allegedly peaceful conduct of the city's business, language was already containing clear signs of potential violence, discrimination and exclusion. Those who did not belong to the *polis* were in fact called *aneu logou*, without language, a label that automatically excluded them 'from the only way of life in which language alone had meaning' (*LOV* 231).

The development of language into a form of political power, distinction, and ferocious propaganda and violence against the enemies of the State, which is a common trope in modern and nationalistic societies, has its roots in the Greek *polis*. The employment of language to draw a divide between the inside and the outside has provided the modern and colonial State with the opportunity to erect visible as well as invisible barriers in the form of borders, and in the development of citizenship laws and attendant regulations impacting on education, health, employment and security. In doing so, the modern and colonial State introduced a subtle notion of property, not without analogy to private property, instilling a sense of entitlement which its citizens would feel compelled to protect and preserve, even by resorting to violence.[13]

State and property are two of the knots around which revolve Benjamin's and Agamben's discussion of violence, and to which it is now time to turn. While Benjamin does not develop his articulation of non-violent means 'concerning objects', and limits his investigation of language to a few lines of text, he spends more time on another form of resolution which is equally significant in the context of this essay, and which, as we shall see later with Agamben, reconnects and interacts with the idea of indirect solutions.

Means without ends

It is through the distinction between the political and proletarian strike that Benjamin contributes to a further clarification of our discussion of violence. He elaborates Sorel's deliberation according to which the political is distinguished from the proletarian on the basis of the intended outcome of the strike, and argues that the premeditated organization of a strike called to cause 'external modification of labor conditions' (better pay, better hours, etc.) is violent. By contrast, Benjamin claims that a strike whose purpose is indifferent to 'material gain', and which focuses instead on the abolition of the State, is non-violent since its means are pure (*SW* 1:246). It is in this sense that while the political strike is integral and organic to the Capitalistic State, conferring on the State the role of necessary and indispensable interlocutor and agent of potential intervention for the betterment of the life of the workers, the proletarian strike is the negation of the State, not simply as a form of insubordination but, more significantly, as a form of life *tout court*. It is this act of annihilation, which is also a self-annihilation and sacrifice through which the working class renounces its status and its labour by annulling its contractual responsibilities and obligations as well as its rights, that Agamben in the essay 'On the Limits of Violence' could see a link and an affinity with religious violence. In both instances – religious and revolutionary violence – the price to pay to achieve the goal of renewal predicated on the basis of a new time is self-renunciation. The abolition and the negation of the State is, therefore, the necessary passage towards a time devoid of law-making and law-preserving violence. But would this time not re-instate the state of natural violence?

Officium and *habitus*

In two books in the series *Homo Sacer*, *The Highest Poverty* (2011), and *Opus Dei* (2012), Agamben discusses monastic rules and liturgy in ways that both reconnect and expand his interrogation of suchness, violence, and life. In *Opus Dei*, the focus of his argument is on the relation between law and duty, obedience to and respect for the law, and the *officium* (office) and *habitus* (practice) connected with the dutiful discharging of a service. Referring to Thomistic principles, Agamben distinguishes a good from an evil action on the premises that a good action is always in harmony with the nature of the agent of the action (*OD* 100). An action, any action, can be potentially good or evil, but its ethical merit is measured according to the virtue of the person who performs it. What is striking here is the co-implication of action and agent in which the goodness and the virtue of both action and person are embedded in a relation of mutual correspondence. The virtue and the virtuous practice of the agent make the action good as does the action in relation to the agent. It is in this context that Agamben, paraphrasing Aristotle, can write:

> Virtue is that by means of which being is indetermined into praxis and action is substantialized into being (or in the words of Aristotle, that thanks to which a human being 'becomes good' and, at the same time, that thanks to which 'he does his work well'). (*OD* 101)

As an example of this ethical co-implication and circularity, Agamben discusses the liturgic service, as well as the office and practice of the priest. The agent of the Eucharistic service is impersonating, and thus acting through, Christ, and yet this practice, which is inherently good, can only translate into good practice and service if the person officiating it is in complete harmony with it (*OD* 101). Being in complete harmony does not only mean to dutifully conduct the office in accordance with the pre-established norms and conditions, but to perform the duties with virtue and belief informed by respect for the law. Is it on the basis of virtue and respect as transmitted and handed down by theology that a new consideration of the interconnections between violence and morality, political power and individual could be renegotiated? Before attempting some preliminary answers to this question, we must turn to the distinction between respect for and obedience to the law, and how this distinction informs duty related to the discharging of office and practice. Not only this, we also need to bring into focus the discriminating manners in which duty is carried out and officiated, whether they be voluntary or imposed.

As we have seen, Agamben's discussion of *officium* and *habitus* is primarily concerned with the religious office and the Eucharistic service, and the relation between the priest and his *habitus*, and Christ. The effective and virtuous practice of the priest depends on his symbiotic relation to Christ, to the extent that his actions are a direct emanation of Christ's volition and office (*ex opere operato*). The priest obeys and respects the faith and laws of the Church, and by conducting the office in harmony with his person he fulfils his duty.

The circularity of the binding theological principle between individual and the law, which is actuated through duty, is according to Agamben the model upon which Kant articulates the relation between the individual and the law of the State. Little changes in the passage from theology to the State of Law, to the extent that for Kant duty is an action determined and ordained by pure respect for the law (*OD* 113). 'Respect' in Kant is defined by Agamben as an *a priori* feeling, which in reality is more akin to a conscious awareness than an emotion (*OD* 113).

Respect for the law has the power and effect of neutralizing the natural inclination of the individual by repositioning her/him within the fold of legality. But for the law of the State to prevail over the law of nature, the individual must fully and consciously embrace the former and discard the latter. It is not a simple matter of merely obeying the law, but is rather a process based on a deep and conscious co-implication between the individual and the law by way of which both the virtue of the law and the individual upholding it are celebrated. Mere obedience to the law devoid of respect can result in acts of brutal, blind and gratuitous violence, opportunism, conformism, self-interest and advancement. This equates with the barbarization of the law practised by individuals, whose *habitus* is not in harmony with the law, but itself outside of the law and ultimately against it.

Is the literal translation from faith to legality the ultimate and necessary passage to guarantee the indissoluble connection between morality and the law, and to preserve law from the perpetration of amoral acts? Is the distinction between respect and obedience the defining factor, discriminating between a dutifully good actuation of the law as opposed to a potentially evil performance of the law? From whichever angle one wishes to look at these questions, one cannot avoid being reminded of Benjamin's argument that law-making and law-preserving are the products of violent acts, and that the state of legality is far from being a harmonious idea predicated on universal justice and principles.

Law is by its own definition violent first because it must subject other laws to its binding norms, and second because it must preserve itself from emerging and opposing laws. It is in this context that duty, practice and office are in their own turn always already implicated in violence.

Examples of violence and their relation to law

Among several literary texts that deal with law, justice and violence,[14] two seem to me particularly apt to exemplify issues of duty, *officium* and *habitus* in ways that are germane to Agamben's discussion: Herman Melville's *Billy Budd* and Alberto Moravia's *Il conformista* (*The Conformist*). They present instances that directly address preoccupations relating to respect for and obedience to the law, and practices of duty; but more instructively they both link these preoccupations with acts of violence that are simultaneously events against and for the law.

Billy Budd was written by Melville between 1888 and 1891, and was published in 1924 after Melville's death in 1891. It tells the story of a handsome sailor by the name of Billy Budd, whose almost unnaturally good personality and demeanour is paired with the inability to speak under strongly charged emotional and psychological circumstances. Billy is unjustly accused by a superior, John Claggart, of conspiring against the law. As Billy is summoned by the Captain of the ship, Captain Vere, to defend himself against the accuser, Billy is seized by aphasia. The only possible means left to him to demonstrate his innocence is to strike at the injustice perpetrated against him by physically hitting and involuntarily killing Claggart.

In *Billy Budd* violence is produced to neutralize an evil act committed by an officer (John Claggart) in the discharge of his duties before the law of the navy; and this very violence is condemned by the dutiful application of the martial law by Captain Vere who, after a trial, and in compliance with his duties as chief in command of the ship, condemns Billy Budd to death. The *officium* in deference of the law (military law) is in the case of *Billy Budd* double as it is represented by both Claggart and Vere. While Claggart is the emblem of the severance between the law and the individual who applies the law in the service of personal revenge and self-motivated hatred, Vere is the upholder of the full, voluntary and respectful adherence to the law against his own emotions and inclinations to compassion.

Double is also the representation of violence, in that if Billy's blow is the 'act of an angel of God', and the natural and just reaction to lies and injustice, the death penalty is the law by which the 'angel of God must hang'.[15] Billy's action and punishment is also the testimony to the passage from natural to positive law, and in turn to the transition from pure inclination and *de facto* violence to duty and *de iure* violence.

There is no escaping from the law; and not even justice, be it natural or divine, can alter the course of law and the *officium* of its duty. In *Billy Budd* Melville caught the conflict, the tensions and the ambiguities innate in law-making and law-preserving. He also emphasized the co-implication of law and individual, and the potential morality and a-morality of any law as it is by necessity carried out through the undecidibility of obedience, respect, will and inclinations. It is this continuous circularity that ties law and violence inseparably, for better or for worse.

In Alberto Moravia's *The Conformist* (1951), the main character, Marcello Clerici, joins the fascist regime and the fascist secret police because of an obsessive drive to normality and conformity. Since an early age Clerici has experienced a strong attraction to violence. He is only thirteen years old when, in self-defence, he believes in having committed a murder. The rest of the book is the story of the adult Marcello Clerici who finds in the fascist regime the perfect context in which not only to blend perfectly with the rest of the population, but also to redeem his early crime by committing other violent acts, which however, in this context, are considered acts of patriotism, fidelity and obedience to the State. In a crucial passage of the book we read:

> What was needed, for him, was the complete success of that government, that social system, that nation: and not merely an external success but an intimate, essential success as well. Only in that way could what was normally considered an ordinary crime become, instead, a positive step in a necessary direction. In other words, there must be brought about, thanks to the forces which did not depend on him, a complete transformation of values: injustice must become justice; treachery, heroism; death, life.[16]

As opposed to Captain Vere, in whom law, duty and *officium* converge to produce a verdict, which however unjust in the face of nature, is the result of a process based on a complete adherence between law and individual, in Marcello Clerici's case the co-implication between the individual and the laws of a dictatorial state is simply acted out and artificial, paradoxically serving simultaneously the treacherous schemes of the individual and that of the State.

Are not the issues of duty and *officium* in the end a question of conformism or total belief in the law? And what would the difference be between a State whose laws are followed by conviction and a State the laws of which are carried out through conformism or fear or indifference? The difference is certainly not that between a democratic and a totalitarian state, since conviction is not the result of consensus. But even in the case of democratic consensus the resulting law will inevitably be followed and adhered to through a mixture of conviction, conformism and indifference, and the violence which will inevitably erupt to preserve the law will be by consequence a mixture of belief, compliance, apathy, justice and injustice, and morality and a-morality.

It is not by accident, then, if Agamben ends *Opus Dei* by positing the problem facing the future philosophy, which is that of thinking an ontology beyond the performativity of the command, and an ethics and a politics freed from the concepts of duty and will (*OD* 129).[17]

Pure forms of life

Is it possible to find traces of this ethics and politics of the future, signs that could provide some, however tenuous, examples of what this life would or could be like? Agamben looks for it in the monastic life of the Franciscan order.

As he writes in *The Highest Poverty*, it was 1269 when Bonaventure distinguished four different relations to material things in his treatise *Apologia pauperum*: ownership, possession, usufruct and simple use (*simplicem usum*) (*HP* 124). The Franciscans based their practice and *habitus* on the renunciation of all forms of ownership, possession and even usufruct. Their relation to things was to be entirely predicated on the simple use, necessary and indispensable for life-nurturing and survival and yet removed from legal claims and demands. They only asked to use the things that were made available to them (buildings, food, books) but declined the ownership and property of such things. Buildings remained, therefore, the property of the Church, as well as all the other things that made life possible.

It is instructive, insists Agamben in the illustration of the Franciscans' attempt to establish a new ontology of relation to things, that the Franciscan order and their mode of life encountered the resistance of the Church and other religious orders. The validity if not altogether the possibility of conducting such a life was questioned through legalistic points and arguments, including challenging the assumption that simple use is irreducible to ownership and property. The example made was that of food, the argument being that there is no difference between use and possession since at the moment in which food is ingested it becomes the intrinsic property of the subject. The Franciscans responded by applying legalistic argumentations of their own, thus tacitly accepting and confirming the inextricable link between life and law, and the principle that life is marked and ordered by legal requirements that must either be obeyed and respected or otherwise challenged and replaced by other sets of legal requirements.

As Agamben claims, the novelty and the potentially revolutionary choice of a life that renounces any forms of property and possession and embraces simple use was partly compromised by the Franciscans' insistence on winning their argument via the law rather than asserting life as such and outside the law (*HP* 137–38). Contrary to the Franciscans' strategy, Agamben insists that a new time – and a new ontology of life outside the law, duty and obedience – must be instead arrived at through a transformation of modalities of relation that are predicated upon pure forms of life. If the Franciscans were ultimately defeated through legal arguments, and if their simple use has been reformulated and granted the right of uncontrolled consumption based on individual possession, there seems to remain a sign of a modality of life which might still be current and valid. This form of life as such, an example of which is the Franciscan order, reconnects with Agamben's essay on the limits of violence, and with Benjamin's suggestion to think a revolutionary strike not so much as the bearer of better conditions as that of a new time. It is in this sense that the Franciscans' simple use could be seen not only as a refutation of the order of the law, but also as self-sacrifice and self-denial, and as an act that reconstitutes anew the rapport between individual and things that is no longer based on materiality, possession, consumption and ultimately violence.

As it comes to be described by Agamben, simple use equates with a life lived as such. Life as such is also pure in so far as the conditions of law-making and law-preserving violence are suspended. The necessity of instituting a legal system whose role is that of safeguarding rights predicated on private property as well as social and economic privileges is removed. Suchness and purity, and their binding principle of irreparability, introduce an ontological revolution that must pass through a process of self-denial, that is the renunciation to operate within a system in which identity is predicated on legislating differences based on attributes, such as language, religion, citizenship and status, that automatically decree a disparity of treatment in the face of the law. Life as such or pure life cannot be handed down and transmitted according to preconfigured rules and traditions; it can only be lived in the now of the present and its irreparable happening. The impositions of past and history are not recognized simply because they have been made irrelevant and unemployable in the community of pure forms of life. The messianisms of Benjamin and Agamben meet and converge at the intersection of purity, suchness and the end of history, and from there keep on challenging modes of living, be they democratic or totalitarian, which cannot escape the spiral of violence and its circularity.

Notes

1   See especially the discussion of singularity and 'the Whatever' and their relation to *being such as it is* (*CC* 2), which is reinforced and emphasized later when Agamben writes: 'Assuming my being-such, my manner of being, is not assuming this or that

quality, this or that character, virtue or vice, wealth or poverty. My qualities and my being-thus are not qualifications of a substance (of a subject) that remains behind them and that I would truly be. I am never *this or that*, but always *such, thus*' (*CC* 96, emphases in the original).

2 Agamben's discussion of potentiality occurs on several occasions and in several publications, commonly as an articulation of Aristotle's distinction between *energia* and *dynamis*; see for instance the section 'Bartleby' in *The Coming Community* (*CC* 34); 'On potentiality' (*PO* 177–84); and 'Pardes: The writing of potentiality' (*PO* 205–19).

3 For a discussion of Benjamin, language and translation, see also my *On the Cultures of Exile, Translation and Writing* (West Lafayette, IN: Purdue University Press, 2008).

4 See Werner Hamacher, 'Afformative, strike: Benjamin's "Critique of Violence"', in *Walter Benjamin's Philosophy: Destruction and Experience*, eds. Andrew Benjamin and Peter Osborne (Manchester: Clinamen Press, 2000), especially 121.

5 For a general discussion of the irreparable and hope in Agamben, see also my 'The threshold and the topos of the remnant: Giorgio Agamben', *Angelaki*, 13.1 (2008): 51–63.

6 'Like language, the strike as pure means would be non-violent, neither coercion nor extortion, neither instrument nor the anticipation of transformed power relations, but, in its sheer mediacy, the overthrow itself: "an overthrow that this kind of strike not so much causes as accomplishes". Not as a particular form of politics, *but as a manifestation of the political as such*, and of the only contemporary political force recognized by Benjamin, the proletariat' (Hamacher, 'Afformative, strike', 119, emphasis added).

7 In 'Language and history: Linguistic and historical categories in Benjamin's thought' (1983), Agamben writes: 'With an intuition whose audacity and coherence must be considered, Benjamin thus holds that the universal language at issue here can only be the idea of language, that is, not an *Ideal* (in the neo-Kantian sense) but the very *Platonic idea* that saves and in itself fulfills all languages, and that an enigmatic Aristotelian fragment describes as "a kind of mean between prose and poetry"' (*PO* 59–60, emphases in the original).

8 'In the individual, unsupplemented languages, what is meant is never found in relative independence, as in individual words or sentences; rather, it is in a constant state of flux – until it is able to emerge as the pure language from the harmony of all the various ways of meaning. For a long time it remains hidden in the languages. If, however, these languages continue to grow in this way until the messianic end of their history, it is translation that catches fire from the eternal life of the works and the perpetually renewed life of language' (*SW* 1:257).

9 'Since humans can receive names – which always precede them – only through transmission, the access to this fundamental dimension of language is mediated and conditioned by history. Speaking beings do not invent names, and names do not emerge from speaking beings as from animal voices. Instead, Varro says, names reach humans *in descending*, that is, through historical transmission' (*PO* 49–50).

10 Two recent studies of Agamben's philosophy have significantly shifted the critical attention of their inquiry from the political to the ontological, reorienting the investigation of Agamben's thought according to the paradigm of political ontology. I refer to Mathew Abbott, *The Figure of This World: Agamben and the Question of Political Ontology* (Edinburgh: Edinburgh University Press, 2014), and Carlo Salzani, *Introduzione a Giorgio Agamben* (Genoa: Il Melangolo, 2013).

11 'this critique diverges from Benjamin's exposition of violence's relation to law and justice, seeking instead to determine its relation to politics …' (*LOV* 231).

12 'Curiously, these rites of regeneration were often celebrated among peoples commonly considered to be the creators of history: Babylonians, Egyptians, Hebrews, Iranians, Romans. It is almost as though these peoples, no longer bound to a way of life determined by purely cyclical and biological temporality, felt more keenly the need to periodically regenerate time, ritually reaffirming the violence at the origin of their history' (*LOV* 235).

13 On these issues see, for instance, the work of Abdelmalek Sayad, and especially 'Colonialismo e migrações. Entevista concedida a Federigo Neiburg', *Mana: Estudos de Antropologia Social* 2.1 (1996): 155–70, and 'État, nation et immigration: l'ordre national à l'épreuve de l'immigration', *Peuples méditerranéens*, 27–8 (1983): 187–205. For a general overview of Sayad's work, see the recent book *Abdelmalek Sayad: per una teoria postcoloniale delle migrazioni*, eds. Gennaro Avallone and Salvo Torre (Catania: Il Carrubo, 2013).

14 One could mention the classical genre of tragedy from Aeschylus to Euripides or Dante or Shakespeare or, closer to our times, the works of Dostoyevsky, Büchner, Celan and Kafka, to name only a few authors who have dealt with the relationship between law, violence, religion and politics. On the issue of violence in literature, see also the recent article by Barnaba Maj, 'Georg Büchner e la moderna costellazione del tragico. Ontologia della storia e nichilismo', *Studi Germanici* 3.4 (2103): 13–40.

15 Herman Melville, 'Billy Budd, sailor', in Herman Melville, *Billy Budd and Other Stories* (London: Everyman, 1993), 51.

16 Alberto Moravia, *The Conformist*, trans. Angus Davidson (London: Secker & Warburg, 1952), 269.

17 On the relation between law and violence in Agamben, see also Connal Parsley, 'Law', in *The Agamben Dictionary*, eds. Alex Murray and Jessica White (Edinburgh: Edinburgh University Press, 2011), especially 122: 'This confrontation [with juridico-normative categories], part of the broader relationship between the messianic and thought, entails that the law itself is not to be destroyed – and still less replaced with another, "better" law. Rather, it is to be rendered inoperative …'.

Works cited

Abbott, Mathew. *The Figure of This World: Agamben and the Question of Political Ontology*. Edinburgh: Edinburgh University Press, 2014.

Avallone, Gennaro, and Salvo Torre, eds. *Abdelmalek Sayad: per una teoria postcoloniale delle migrazioni*. Catania: Il Carrubo, 2013.

Bartoloni, Paolo. *On the Cultures of Exile, Translation and Writing*. West Lafayette, IN: Purdue University Press, 2008.

—'The threshold and the topos of the remnant: Giorgio Agamben'. *Angelaki* 13.1 (2008): 51–63.

Hamacher, Werner. 'Afformative, strike: Benjamin's "Critique of Violence"'. In *Walter Benjamin's Philosophy: Destruction and Experience*. Edited by Andrew Benjamin and Peter Osborne. Manchester: Clinamen Press, 2000, 108–36.

Maj, Barnaba. 'Georg Büchner e la moderna costellazione del tragico. Ontologia della storia e nichilismo'. *Studi Germanici* 3.4 (2013): 13–40.

Melville, Herman. 'Billy Budd, sailor'. In Herman Melville, *Billy Budd and Other Stories*. London: Everyman, 1993, 1–77.

Moravia, Alberto. *The Conformist*. Translated by Angus Davidson. London: Secker & Warburg, 1952.

Parsley, Connal. 'Law'. In *The Agamben Dictionary*. Edited by Alex Murray and Jessica White. Edinburgh: Edinburgh University Press, 2011. 119–22.

Salzani, Carlo. *Introduzione a Giorgio Agamben*. Genoa: Il Melangolo, 2013.

Sayad, Abdelmalek. État, nation et immigration: l'ordre national à l'épreuve de l'immigration'. In *Peuples méditerranéens* 27–28 (1983): 187–205.

—'Colonialismo e migrações. Entevista concedida a Federigo Neiburg'. *Mana: Estudos de Antropologia Social* 2.1 (1996): 155–70.

10

Violence Without Law? On Pure Violence as a Destituent Power

Thanos Zartaloudis

A juridical system of powers

The positing of a relation or passage between transcendence (law, justification, ground, origin, nature, essence) and immanence (casus, situation, position, culture, existence) has often been placed at the point where theological, philosophical and legal 'fundamental' questioning of positing and of power find their fragile point of intersection. It is archetypically instructive, in this regard, that in the decisive clash during the thirteenth century between the 'pagan' philosophy of Aristotle and the evangelic faith of the Christian monastic orders (and in particular the Franciscans) a doctrine of two powers comes to characterize God's power.[1] God's power is formed on a relation between *potentia absoluta* and *potentia ordinata*. *Potentia absoluta* is God's creative power as a perfectly absolute and indifferent (excepted) power to the created world and to the needs and being of creatures (God could replace his creation with another). His absolute power transcends the created world. *Potentia ordinata* is God's ordered power as immanent to creation, adapting itself to the prevailing conditions and situations of the created. These powers and their relation form the dogma of a functional ontology between a conditioning and a conditioned power, a state of exception and one of normalcy, or, in the terms of constitutionalism, between constitutive and constituted power.

God's absolute power has, perhaps, been a key model for the transcendent causes (beyond human experience). Transcendent causes typically locate the origin, or first cause, of a certain situation as external to the situation. Such an external cause assumes the arch-position or dignity of an absolute master or sovereign ruler. This kind of transcendence enables the absoluteness of the ruler's power, while at the same time necessitating a problem. Transcendence necessarily leads to the distinction from, and vicarious support of, a second power. At the very point of a limitless and indifferent power the question arises of *the positing* of limits as a fictive passage between two powers. Power is related somehow with its created situation or world. The second (ordered) power appears as necessarily immanent to the created world.

In other words, immanent causes are located within the effects to which they give rise. The power of the absolute master must be distinguished from the particularity of his action or position, but at the same time he has ordered his indifferent power in a particular direction that must be reckoned with in relation to absolute power. Otherwise God's rule could be subject to the embarrassing indifference of the created towards its creator. The enactment of absolute mastery is coupled with the threat of the demolition of the absoluteness of mastery, the demolition of its transcendent causality.

In late modernity when God 'dies', the world must continue to be commanded and ruled and the relation between the two powers must survive its crisis. The indifference of absolute power towards its creation must confront the indifference of the created towards its master. In order for the imperative power that supposedly commands this world to survive the consequences of its creation or commands-in-action, it must continuously be confronted with its duality, its scission: between law and fact, cause and action, state of exception and norm. Nihilistic immanence is turned into itself, into a zero degree of self-reference, yet appearing as still commanded by a transcendent phantasmagoria. In the time of a still prevalent nihilism, it is the *Nothing* that assumes the place of an absolute power; but more than ever the threatening neutralization of its own zero-degree power could itself at any moment be exposed as a Nothing that cannot command, a pure void: the nothing as primary cause could be exposed as a no-*thingness*. For the campaigners of transcendental causes the void must continue to be filled even if only by the negative relation to it.

Consider Carl Schmitt who, with some proximity to Descartes or Kant, will discover a compromising relation between law and its exception, through the sovereign's capturing of its outside *in advance*. The power of the sovereign must remain unlimited, for he must be able to command the resetting (transcending) of his limits. Alternatively consider Spinoza, who proposed a singularly uncompromising absolute immanence. God's absolute mastery becomes perfectly immanent in the world (nature) and ceases to be a mastery *of* the world. In Spinoza, however, while God is stripped of his sovereign rule, whereby his power is immanent in the world and not immanent to another cause, the effect may be said to be comparable to its opposition. The difference between Schmitt and Spinoza could be said to be that while Schmitt collapses transcendence into the sovereign's zero degree of power so to continue to render it operative, Spinoza contracts immanence to God's own zero degree of power to render it inoperative. Yet the result remains at least comparable, despite the differences, in that in either way God can remain enabled and powerful (intentionally so in Schmitt, and indirectly so in Spinoza).[2]

The situation of modern law may be particularly instructive of the problem at hand. The modern state has not only the right but also the duty to go against the supposedly transcendental will of its subjects in the name of its immanent order. This purported immanence of the law *to* itself (as we are to be governed by law rather than absolute masters) reposts a transcendent relation to itself 'as' a semi-external cause (a Law of law). This is the type of immanence that Deleuze and Guattari criticized as pseudo-immanence.[3] If human actions in relation to legal actions were once separable (as events that could, on occasion, give rise to procedural situations – *actiones* – to which the law could relate and decide upon), today legal positions are said to relate, in contrast, to every event in society. Juridification (*Verrechtlichung*), probably a modern condition, universalizes the categorizations of law to the whole world. The earlier form of a posited law would once ask the question of whether an act falls within the jurisdiction of the law (one jurisdiction, then, among others). In addition, the law, today, cannot but answer self-referentially the question of whether the application of the distinction between right and wrong in respect to all human actions, is juridically right itself. In order for the law to juridify the world it must become immanent to it in the most absolute manner possible. To do so, however, it has to posit itself as immanent to its self-transcendent Law (of law). For the juridical system's maintenance of the distinction between life (world) and law, the law must turn, bereft of another absolute master, to its self-mastery: a paradox that the mythologeme of law must find a way to render ever smooth.

By raising its *quaestio juris* the law cuts through the world with its binary code of (legally) right and wrong, in order to place itself in a self-commanding world that it, however, rules. Yet in the age of nihilism and functional differentiation of 'society', the law cannot assess itself in order to decide whether it itself is true or untrue, just or unjust, without being confronted with the abyss of its creative as well as now disruptive self-referentiality. The law will set its limits at the same time as it purports to delimit itself and be pseudo-immanent to the world. The law must create another juridical world (a *fictio*) in order to maintain its indifference with the so-called real world, and at the same time it must collapse the world to its *fictio*. It must capture above all the relation between the two worlds and collapse it in an ever spectacular *relation*, whereby fact and right, exception and norm, can only be located in a zone of indistinction. The juridical description of the world is a life-falsification, an impoverishment, yet while this remains an Achilles heel for the law, the law must presuppose a masterless plane of normativity in the name of its self-imposed necessity of mastering.

Legal order in its inevitable orthodoxy must appear as a state of peace. Its own form of immanence to the world must hide the fact that its second fictional world has no guarantee of being 'the best of all possible worlds'. Hence the law cannot avoid placing itself in a position of guilt towards the world as such, at the same time as it places all events and all human actions as subject to the law's suspicion. It must capture the void that threatens its power and claim it as its own void, its own juridical state of exception, an infinitely displaceable and replenished void. To do so, an absolute ('secular') sovereign will need to pre-empt the world and presuppose the outside of its rule, as if it is existent *in* the (juridified) world. No fact or act shall remain unturned (non-juridified). Every action shall remain potentially guilty through the fate-giving law that can co-exist with its outside (exception). For instance, Gunther Teubner's 'self-deconstructing' law: the relation of the law to the world shall forever acknowledge its undecidability, its fragility and self-suspicion, in order to continue to command the world in the name of the law's own outside (justice or self-transcendence).[4] Teubner's law is a kind of autoimmune law (not dissimilar, in one sense, to Schmitt's sovereign law). Apologist and critic meet at the structuring and re-structuring of a relation to a juridical impoverishment of the world.

If modern law 'has to' situate a point of self-emergence or power, it is in this manner not dissimilar to philosophy. Philosophy takes as its starting point the non-denial of such self-situating, yet participates in the problem of its own power (turned juridical since, at least, Kant). If in philosophy the positing is always a positing of a limit-thesis, which must however at the same time acknowledge its limits, then every positing contains within itself a destructive violence (a fragility or self-suspicion) that threatens it with another positing. The positing must hold excess within a limit and at the same time expose itself without limit to an excess.[5] If, in turn, the law can maintain its efficiency against its own transcendence or destruction, then it can only do so by maintaining at least a minimal zero-degree relation between two worlds (the world of real effects, actions, situations or events and the world of its *office* [*ufficium*]), its being-at-work 'in the name' of Law.[6] Life as a juridical institution (where life and law are collapsed into a zone of indistinction) becomes the enabling device through which the law can exceed itself and maintain its office intact.

In opposed philosophical terms such necessity out of a contingency emerges today as yet another form of vertigo before a void – a meta-physics (what lies beside a situation) that can be expressed (shown), but not proven, as the peculiar 'taking place' of situational life. Lacking an essential primary cause, its cause cannot be an absent condition (still a predisposed hidden condition to which only the privileged can have access), or a mere non-conditionality (still a condition), but the exposition of any condition as a contingent necessity and a necessary contingency: the situation of a para-transcendent life of immanence. It is asserted, for instance by Agamben, that human beings have no essential substance, destiny or vocation, but simply contingency as the only peculiar self-effacing immanent necessity of their power (*potentia*) to act. Inessential, yet necessary, contingency has no cause outside itself. Human power in its ability to be *and* not be confronts constantly its own unconditionality. Human acts must be made, acted (when they are made or acted) without a necessary claim to operativity, by posing the affirmation of their inoperativity as a plane of immanence and their only consistency.[7]

For Agamben, perhaps, no meta-act determines an act, other than the affirmative synchronous potentiality of each contingent power of action, expression and existence. Contingency as a pure potentiality, in the exposure of every form, signs no contracts and yet consists, for itself, in the zero degree of another unbreakable *nomos* (a *nomos*, however, that does not command a – distributive – justice, but remains an apportionment without shares). The law in its originary form is a non-ordered array of letters. Limits, distinctions, will be drawn, but they will be met by the synchronous contingency and potentiality of their exposure as limits drawn and positions held in their *potentia*. The crucial strategy, in Agamben, to exit what could be awkwardly termed the still negative structure of transimmanence, is that coming to being (*genesis*) is not an operation in the name of some sanctified cause, thing or essence, for which and through which it is actualized. Being can be admitted to no tribunal for it has committed no wrong (or right, for that matter, which could then be opposed to another right). In this sense, coming to being is, paradoxically, a truly transcendental experience (an existential *nomos*) only when it is understood as properly immanent in its power (pure potentiality), and no passage. Our continuous genesis in a scission, a continuous syntagm of syncopes (privations, passions), means that no absolute order or community pre-exists our common immanent plane of potentiality.

This is not a theodicy but a *kosmodicy*, not a Law but a properly *human* law, a form-of-life, a way of life (*ethos*). If human beings are born out of a continuous passage or scission between what is variably called nature (*physis*) and culture (*logos*), (f)acts can only exist, within their counter(f)actual dynamism. If the relation *to* a transcendent, though, becomes a plateau and is affirmed as immanent *in* human life, its existence remains within its factical dynamism. To the separation of a life that can be hollowed out (as mere or bare life) in order to be juridified, Agamben opposes a life that cannot be separated from its form and vice versa (a form-of-life). To the fictional state of exception, Agamben (via Benjamin) opposes a real state of exception that ceases to claim to produce the real from the outside of dynamic existence.

The systematization of juridical violence

It is useful to appreciate Benjamin's 'Critique of Violence' as a confrontation with a problem. The problem is that of how to show a plane of possibility for what Benjamin calls divine, or pure violence: the possibility of a violence that is absolutely outside or beyond the law. This is a peculiarly phrased problem in that it claims for the proving of a 'right' to non-juridical violence, a non-justification displacing all justifications. Benjamin wishes to break the dialectic of 'law-founding and law-preserving violence' or the state's systematization of violence, by decomposing the foundational (Kantian) juridical structure of a *juris-dictio* (a saying of right that is *at the same time* a right to say; a *potentia ordinata* that is at the same time related to a *potentia absoluta*). Benjamin, in this sense, rejects the so-called *juridical* monopoly of law/right, as much as the *juridical* monopoly of violence. In Benjamin's case, a saying of right, a situation of violent action, does not claim to find its cause outside of itself (in some Right of rights). The right of revolutionary violence or pure violence, in this sense, points not to the juridical framing of rights/Right, but to the ethical category of a situated right.

Benjamin writes that pure (divine) non-juridical violence cannot be recognized as such in particular cases as to whether it has been realized or not (*SW* 1:252). Benjamin could be said to stage his own type of absolute immanence at this point, by investing in the divine such indifference to the world that any claim to be working 'in the name' of the divine would become redundant. Does this not increase, in fact, the power of the divine to an exponential degree? Agamben has compared Benjamin's statement to Schmitt's: 'it is impossible to ascertain with complete clarity when a situation of necessity exists.'[8] If, indeed, as Agamben shows, the necessity of sovereign violence, for Schmitt, is founded on this very impossibility (or undecidability), then pure or divine violence appears to be founded, in turn, on a somehow identical structure of negativity.

If sovereignty is recognized as based on a structure of a presupposed and repro-duced state of exception, then pure violence is structured like an exception too, only its exception is a once-and-for-all without a claim to reproducibility. Benjamin counter-poses a *real* state of exception to a fictional or pseudo-exception. The *fictio juris* of Schmitt attempts to enclose outside in advance the case of the opposite of the rule of law, whereas Benjamin wishes to show that what lies outside the law is pure violence without recourse to the law. Benjamin is not interested in maintaining the continuum of the dialectic of violence within a juridical systematization of human action. For Benjamin, as well as Agamben, an over-juridification of life has taken place, which must be responded to by a de-juridification of the ethical plane of existence. Breaking this continuum of juridification would be, to the existing systematization of the *duration* of violence, a once-and-for-all rupture. Is such violence, however, available to us?

Will the new situation that ruptures the continuum of violence and depositions the old law, not always impose or require a new law? The proposition in question could perhaps be reconstructed to suggest that to the pseudo-dialectic of violence and law, Agamben and Benjamin counter-pose a *human* law (a law that does not claim to find its cause and justification outside of its immanent existence). Truly human law would be an ethics, a way of life that fulfils itself. What may then be the plane of immanence of the conception of violence outside and beyond the schema of the 'Law of law'? Is it a hollow space, a void? This would remain a peculiar claim to immanence unless perhaps this void was understood as absolutely immanent in itself in turn. By affirming this indifferent void (to human power), human life would turn all negative relation to a plane of immanence, into a positive ontology without a relation outside itself. In this sense, human life lacking any principle, *archē* (not even the empty but still powerful *archē* of an empty command to command) would affirm its ungovernability. As ungovernable human power is conceived as truly *epekeina*, *beyond being*, in an absolute sense: without a possible relation to an identity or difference. This is not, however, a naïve nihilistic life of 'anything goes' (that would still be a relation to a principle, a *panomie*, *a plenitude out of nothing*).

There could be no differential relation of powers between life and institutions (forms). Only the self-negation (affirmation) of a life de-void of essential determination that is not structured by the necessity of having to be its own law-giver, *auto-nomos*, or receive its law from outside, a *hetero-nomos*. This would be a life that does not accuse itself; nor can it be accused from outside of its *ethos*. Human law, as much as life, after the destruction of the systematization of juridical violence and its pseudo-dialectics, is, however, anything but simple. Pure violence is not another claim to the purity of Being or the absoluteness of Law. It is pure only in the sense of being immanent in itself, modest, that is, existential, and fully responsible for its powers and actions. Only a kind of responsibility that is an affirmation rather than an accusation. It does not act in the name of a principle that exceeds its case, position and contingency. It can only be transcendent in its immanence.

It is worth revisiting then the systematization of juridical violence that Benjamin counter-poses in the 'Critique of Violence'. *Gewalt* contains in German an ambiguity that forms its problem. As a word that refers to both *potestas* (power) and *violentia*, it is a term that entails a dual sense: both the negation of the law and its realization.[9] Any transcendent ends to the law are neutralized in the state's systematization of *Gewalt*, while the authority of such neutralization remains intact and is over-valorized as the surplus value of the law's violence. The origin of what Benjamin terms mythical violence or law is a situated 'violence crowned by fate' (*SW* 1:242), crowned as in justified, grounded. Legal dogmatism or mythology asserts a fated law through the impure mixture of ideality and nature. To the dogmatic pseudo-dialectic between positive law and natural law must be counter-posed a pure violence that undoes this negative bond.

Natural law asserts that the rightful foundations of law are exclusively accessible to (natural) reason, while the scepticism of positive law asserts that the rightful foundations of law are exclusively accessible to the State's norms. The presupposition of both is a relation to a general rule or command. The illusion that unites the two, for Benjamin, becomes clear through their employment of the means-ends dialectic: 'just ends can be attained by justified means, justified means used for just ends' (*SW* 1:237). Whether through an established norm of the State or a universal natural principle, coercive force leads to justice and leaves the law's claim to act in the name of a higher cause intact. Principles are turned either way to permissory justifications for the means or ends that claim to glorify a power in its general (absolute) form. Each time, the relation to such an absolute power or ground, is the covering or transposition of the arbitrariness of violence/force. Violence, either way, will be situated (as to its justification) outside the act of violence itself. Violence is structured as a means to an end and it is stamped by a relation to transcendence (to an end outside of itself). Otherwise the duration of violence would be breakable and its positing in a particular time, space and situation would be exposed. In this sense, for Benjamin, law-positing violence and law-preserving violence are bound up with the maintenance (*Ver-waltung*, *GS* 2.1: 203/*SW* 1:252) or continuum of violence.

The logic (justificatory and foundational) of *Gewalt* does not come, for Benjamin, to exhibit itself historically; it does not manifest in historical terms but under the cloak of mythic outer sanctification (SW 1:251). What is at stake for such juridical violence is the coincidence of *anomie* with *panomie* (legal plenitude), so that the law can maintain its hold on history by appearing to coincide with all possible reality. The reality of an individual's pursuit of 'natural ends' through violent means is denied through the systematic rationalization of *Gewalt* as the exclusive means of the juridical power inherent in the state. The reduction of *Gewalt* to juridical means, means that the use of violence can only be justified as this kind of means: either as state violence that preserves law [*rechtserhaltende Gewalt*] and protects it from violation, or as a violence (revolutionary or reformist) that leads to the creation of a new law [*rechtsetzende Gewalt*]. As Franz Rosenzweig notes: 'The meaning of every violence is that it founds new law. It is not the negation of law, as is believed by those attracted to its subversive act, but on the contrary is its foundation'.[10] Even when the law is confronted with its decay (it is programmed to do so by suppressing its own self-founding violence), the law can re-assert itself in an evolutionary continuum of its mythic status. In this sense, too, the extra-statist violent exercise of power by the individual can momentarily appear subversive, but then actually constitutes the confirmation of the juridical framing of a continuum of violence. Such counter-violence claims the throne of power, while leaving the dogma of the enthronement intact.

For Benjamin, the truly revolutionary escalation must necessarily pass through the practice of another kind of *Gewalt* that can break the dual nature of the state's violence. This wholly other *Gewalt* is founded on the assumption that not every kind of violence will found a new law within the continuum between the 'constitutional state' and the 'repressive state'. It is a rupture primarily with the atemporal and essential continuum of this dual power, that Benjamin's other type of violence must achieve. In this regard, Furio Jesi writes:

> That which primarily distinguishes revolt from revolution is a different sense of time. ... one can say that revolt suspends historic time and unexpectedly replaces it with a time in which everything is valued for itself, independently of its consequences and of the complex of transitoriness and perenniality of which history consists. The revolution instead falls completely and deliberately in historic time.[11]

For Benjamin, in the 'Critique of Violence', the genuine proletarian strike forms such a rupture (Benjamin refers to the question of other kinds of violence, '*die Frage nach andern Arten der Gewalt*', GS 2.1:196/*SW* 1:247) under certain conditions. The destruction of state power and violence is not an end but the lived praxis of the proletariat. To end, the violent continuum of the law becomes then not a conquest of power or a reforming progression, but a break of the *Zweck-Mittel-Relation*. It is a whole transformation (the '*gänzlich veränderte*') of the ethical relations (*sittliche Verhältnisse*), of the way of life as such so that in such action, as Benjamin wrote much earlier, 'justice is the ethical side of the struggle [*Gerechtigkeit ist die ethische Seite des Kampfes*]'.[12]

Yet the strategies of radical reformation of the law and that of militarized revolt against the law find their mutual limitation, if seen through the guise in which the function of the police in democratic states is not merely the enforcement of the law, but the essential *operation* of the violence continuum (cf. *SW* 1:242–3). In the function of the police the indistinction of law and *Gewalt* is exposed as the greatest possible degeneration of *Gewalt*. The police who are to guarantee the conforming to the law show that such conformity is not direct, but must be enacted, policed. In the exposition of the absoluteness of the law, in the continuum between its enactment and enforcement, the purported indistinction with represented reality in the fusion of the dual power of the State/police is ex-posed.

The greatest effort of juridical *Gewalt* was perhaps directed at rendering its representation infinite (and therefore, ironically for its ordered model, orgiastic). It is a question of extending representation as far as the too large and too small of individual situated difference. Adding in this sense a hitherto unsuspected dimension to representation – in other words, inventing juridical techniques (state of exception; natural law; *Grundnorm*), which allow it to integrate the depth of difference in itself – allows representation to conquer the obscure and threatening outside. It allows the juridical continuum, henceforth, to include the difference which is too small, and to dismember the difference which is too large (revolution). This effort has always permeated the world of the juridical representation (*fictio*) of the world.[13]

Pure or divine violence

There is justice, but not for us. It is crucial to appreciate that for Benjamin justice is not a political or juridical category, but an existential or ethical one. Benjamin's aim, as expressed in 'On the Program of the Coming Philosophy' (1918), is to transform 'the entire context of ethics' (*SW* 1:105) and in doing so transform all social, legal and political vocations. It is this understanding that forms his reference to a pure violence or divine violence. Mythical violence is essentially tragic in the sense that the tragic hero is a guilty-innocent hero, who in his quest for justice and truth cannot but expose his guilt at the same time as his innocence, arriving at a point of undecidability between the two. Mythical tragedy, however, is a partial understanding of the tragic in that it is presented as immanent (a natural form of justice) in its transcendence (rupture). It is not a genuine bipolarity between tragedy and comedy, but a pseudo-bipolarity, akin to the juridical pseudo-dialectic between law-founding and law-preserving violence. This partial understanding of tragedy, and of the pseudo-dialectic of juridical or mythical violence, shares in the institution of a permanent state of exception as the primary cause of fate.

For Benjamin, the essence of pure violence is not to decide a conflict between two supposedly equal positions (or rights), but rather to interrupt this continuum (to provide an *Ausnahmezustand*, as it is named in 'On the Concept of History'). The Kantian 'divine command' serves as a counter-example. The task to obey the law is ultimately derived from a divine command authorizing bloodshed in the name of justice.[14] In contrast, for Benjamin all authority is of God's creation, but this serves to demystify state power, rather than sanctify it. For Kant: 'A people should not inquire with any practical aim in view into the origin of the supreme authority [*obersten Gewalt*] to which it is subject'.[15] For Benjamin, the heterogeneity of the divine means that one cannot ground one's right or power in it. Human authority is essentially groundless and all that remains is a non-essential life, a way of living itself. Hence, 'Mythic *Gewalt* is bloody *Gewalt* over mere life for its own sake; divine *Gewalt* is pure *Gewalt* over all life for the sake of the living' (*SW* 1:250). Given the non-availability of divine authority as a ground for human power, the separation of a sphere of life (mere or bare life), on the basis of which we may treat each other as means in the name of a direct or vicarious absolute authority, is rendered impossible. Hence, Benjamin's end is not the heroic perfection of human power but the liquidation of juridical *Gewalt*.

If (divine) justice/violence is not accessible to us, then what remains is the understanding of (human) justice/power as, in Benjamin's earlier formulation, the ethical side of the struggle (*Gerechtigkeit ist die ethische Seite des Kampfes*).[16] Agamben's early analysis, in *Language and Death: The Place of Negativity*, of the ungroundedness of human action is helpful in understanding what could be understood as ethical in this regard. A functional relation of every *conditum* to an *absconditum* presupposes that, given the ungroundedness of human being, violence is the originary (and therefore rendered naturalized, sacred) fact (a 'having-been') of politics and law. In turn, this necessitates the assumption of power by a sanctified sovereign through a sacrificial institution (systematization) of violence. Agamben explains that, instead:

> Violence is not something like an originary biological fact that man is forced to assume and regulate in his own praxis through sacrificial institution; rather it is the very ungroundedness of human action (which the sacrificial mythologeme hopes to cure) that constitutes the violent character (that is contra naturam,

according to the Latin meaning of the word) of sacrifice. All human action, inasmuch as it is not naturally grounded but must construct its own foundation, is, according to the sacrificial mythologeme, violent. And it is this sacred violence that sacrifice presupposes in order to repeat it and regulate it within its own structure. (*LD* 105–6)

With Schmitt, in the so-called secular political-theologization of sovereign (absolute) power, the ungroundedness of human action necessitates the sacrificial mythologeme of sovereignty, of a supreme ruler aiming to fill anew such ungroundedness by procuring a sanctified foundation or ground (that may remain in force, without significance). God and nature as foundations of human power may be 'dead', but the structure of presupposition that authorizes a sacred act of foundation remains intact. Things are, however, still more complicated. Agamben writes:

> The unnaturalness of human violence – without common measure with respect to natural violence – is a historical product of man, and as such it is implicit in the very conception of the relation between nature and culture, between living being and *logos*, where man grounds his own humanity. The foundation of violence is the violence of the foundation. (*LD* 106)

Action, violent action, must, in the sacrificial mythologeme's construction of foundational power, remain always a causative action (otherwise there would be no guarantee of a direct relation to both the ground and the things that form its subjects as such). A causative action aims to reconcile freedom and necessity in the guise of a sacrificial mythologeme, so that action will be each time the midwife of history and power. Only violence that serves the end of history's necessary laws (natural, historical, evolutionary, political) will be 'just violence'. The justification of violence is each time posited outside of the act itself under the cloak of a sacred violence that forms the passage from potentiality to action. Agamben, in his early text 'On the Limits of Violence', writes:

> It simply places violence within a broader theory of means that justify a superior end; the end is the sole criterion to determine the justice of the means. Benjamin correctly noted that, while such a framework can justify the application of violence, it fails to justify the principle of violence itself. Ultimately, any theory that defines the legitimacy of revolutionary means through the justice of their end is as contradictory as legalistic theories that guarantee a just end by legitimizing repressive means. (*LOV* 234)

You must believe in some kind of cosmic, natural or divine providence (a founding force of law or revolution) for this kind of violence to be proclaimed pre-emptively just. Consequently: 'A theory of revolutionary violence is meaningless within historical theodicy, which paradoxically renders the revolutionary into a kind of Pangloss, convinced that everything is happening for the best, in this best of all possible worlds' (*LOV* 234). It is in this sense that for Benjamin, divine or pure violence must not seek to identify a pre-emptive justification of violence, but rather propose an understanding of a violence that requires no justification from anywhere else than within itself.

A destituent power

Agamben could be said to have developed Benjamin's theory of divine violence further in his conception of a *destituent* power. It is a destituent power, not a constituent power, which Benjamin perhaps has in mind when he opposes a power that destroys the law (only to recreate it in a new form) and a pure violence that deposes all positing of law (in order to open a new historical era; *SW* 1:251–2). Benjamin was aware of the key problem for any conception of such a destituent power, in that bourgeois power is in its essence an-archical and all its efforts lie in sanctifying such anarchy (ground-lessness) under the cloak of yet another mythologeme of justification between means and ends. This is the problem that Agamben expresses:

> It is precisely because power constitutes itself through the inclusion and the capture of anarchy and anomy, that it is so difficult to have an immediate access to these dimensions, it is so hard to think today something as a true anarchy or a true anomy ... A really new political dimension becomes possible only when we grasp and depose the anarchy and the anomy of power. But this is not only a theoretical task: it means first of all the rediscovery of a form-of-life, the access to a new figure of that political life whose memory the Security State tries at any price to cancel.[17]

To the sacrificial system of juridical violence and power, Agamben, in his early piece 'On the Limits of Violence', opposed an understanding of sacrifice in primitive rituals, which aimed through sacrifice to resurrect primordial chaos: 'making humans contemporaries of the gods and granting them access to the original dimension of creation' (*LOV* 235). Agamben, at that moment in time, writes:

> Whenever the life of the community was threatened, whenever the cosmos seemed empty and vacant, primitive peoples would turn to this regeneration of time; only then could a new era (a new revolution of time) begin ... It is almost as though these peoples, no longer bound to a way of life determined by purely cyclical and biological temporality, felt more keenly the need to periodically regenerate time, ritually reaffirming the violence at the origin of their history. (*LOV* 235)

Such violence, which through the spilling of one's own blood offered the regaining of the authority to participate in the creation of a new historical world by rupturing the continuity of time, is in this early text seen by Agamben as an affirmation of life. This may indeed be paradoxical, given the problem of the sacrificial mythologeme that Benjamin and Agamben criticize. This understanding of the destituent sacrificial ritual must be understood in a manner that differentiates it from the mythologeme that aims to perform sacrifice in order to merely resume *itself*. The difference lies between the type of sacrificial action that aims to teleologically re-establish itself anew and the one that, as pure violence, aims at a new historical era, at an affirmation of continuous infancy.

The pseudo-sacrificial paradigm will depose the old law in order to re-affirm its own self (and its authority or power). Repressive violence (what enforces law) and delinquent violence (which defies law) are negations of the other without becoming negations of the self. The genuine paradigm of sacrifice or violence is one that does not depose the old law without paradoxically also deposing itself. In the 1970s text, Agamben had already sketched such an understanding:

> Revolutionary violence is not a violence of means, aimed at the just end of negating the existing system. Rather, *it is a violence that negates the self as it negates the other; it awakens a consciousness of the death of the self, even as it visits death on the other.* Only the revolutionary class can know that enacting violence against the other inevitably kills the self; only the revolutionary class can have the right (or perhaps, the terrible imperative) to violence. Like sacred violence before it, revolutionary violence can be described as passion, in its etymological sense: self-negation and self-sacrifice. (*LOV* 236)

Revolutionary violence is an extreme act of self-negation: a willing that paradoxically abdicates its own willing. In this manner the genuine revolutionary, for Agamben, casts himself into the absolute which breaks apart the bond between words and deeds, will and action, cause and effect, and in this manner violence becomes self-negation in which violence belongs neither to its agent nor its victim. This is evidently the power and the limit of revolutionary violence. Is it not that the sacrifice of the *homines sacrii* forms the paradigmatic practice of a kind of pseudo-sacrifice, which aims not at negating the (sovereign) self but reaffirming its power? At the same time is it not that such self-negation can appear identical to the kind of self-negation of responsibility that characterizes the *anomie* of bourgeois power, that negates its *anomie* in order to found its *nomos* through establishing a sacrificial pseudo-dialectic? A kind of self-negation can be seen, further, in the negation of responsibility that marks the late modern *oikonomia* or government in neo-liberal capitalism, whereby the managerial administration of human affairs means that no person as such can be responsible, but a performative process (which as it is not an agent, no person can usually be held accountable, but only through exceptional procedures). In the secular and functional democratic law of late-modernity, the law determines its own guilt, but by acting 'in the name of the Law', the functionaries of the Law cannot usually be found to be responsible, but only responsive.

For Agamben, self-negation becomes genuine when it is elation and dispossession of the self, akin to a divine delirium. Perhaps self-negation could be understood not as non-accountability, but as a fully assumed responsibility without recourse to a justification outside the self (or self-accusation). It is this that politics is not capable of. Genuine revolutionary violence does not only depose power (the old law) but also renders power (including its own) inoperative as such; in order to neutralize it as a long-held paradigm of an operation, passage or initiation. In such neutralization, revolutionary violence inaugurates a new reality, but only as the irreparable manner of present reality. A reality that can be studied rather than rendered sacred or equally be accused. But what is violence that imposes no operative law? To rupture the homogeneous flux of time through the passion of revolutionary violence (self-negation) means to consciously confront the self's own negation. It means to become able to contemplate salvation only to the extent of losing one's self in what cannot be saved, one's own ungroundedness.

Revolutionary violence does not aim to teleologically change the world, but instead, leaving life to its own eternal irreparability, to abandon all active attempts 'to mend the world' in the name of a new essence or operativity. It does not aim at a sacrificial religion of violence or a tragic religion, but at the rendering of negation (death) as ordinary and meaningless in affirming the renewal of life for the sake of the living in their infancy. In such affirmation our own-most (death) becomes affirmed at the same time as our indifferent heterogeneity. If divine justice as the principle of all end-making is not a means to an end but a manifestation of the existence of the gods, human justice is not a means to an end but a manifestation of the irreparable existence of the living.

Pure violence or revolutionary *Gewalt* is non-derivable: it arises where the sphere of life (the living body) is immediately threatened in a real state of exception. Natural law, it could be noted, offers a comparable device, at least to an extent. Natural necessity requires no authorization from posited law; nor does it establish a new law – *quia necessitas non habet legem*. What juridical violence (posited violence, positive law) suppresses above all is the violence that is exercised by such natural necessity, because it was once the case that while positive law could be renounced, such natural necessity was held as irrenounceable and formed a real exception to the posited law. In a modern reversal when posited law attempts to assume the form of an *atemporal* law, a law without limits that attempts to capture its outside in advance, a revolutionary or pure violence stands opposed as a *temporalized* situation, without any limits that would be determined from outside the truly exceptional situation that has arisen. Who can determine what would be a truly exceptional situation? No one can and not without negligence and modesty at the same time, in any case.

Such violence is not limitless, but situational: its limits are determined from within its situation and ultimately by its own self-negation, its affirmative singularity rather than a claim to universal or uniform identity: ends that are just in one situation are singular ends. There can be no principle of human justice. Benjamin's and Agamben's strategies are in this sense proximate to the ever-lasting battle between natural and positive law. They perhaps point to an absolute reversal of the natural in the posited, only a nature that is no longer sacred, excepted and related to negatively. It is perhaps in this manner that their position is intensified when it is seen as one where the subject of the right to revolutionary violence in a state of real necessity is not the person but the situation itself. And as such it can never be a right. It is, in one sense, the paradoxical (natural) 'right' of the situation to be a situation (a tautology) that self-negates its rightness.

Hence pure or natural violence (in this particular human sense) cannot be possessed. There is no *direct* natural *right* to things since human beings are essentially inoperative; what remains direct is the *use* of things in a universalized state of necessity.[18] The 'source' of a self-negating revolutionary power is located in the fact that pure power or violence cannot be stored up, but only exercised, negligently as much as modestly, in a singular situation as a contraction or rupture. This is why Benjamin will insist that it is impossible to know whether there is such a thing as pure *Gewalt* generally: 'it does not come to light for human beings' (*GS* 2.1:203/*SW* 1:252; translation modified). This is also why Benjamin can say that divine violence can only be destructive in this world. Only in the coming world can it be anything but destructive.

In this reading, divine or pure justice is heterogeneous to positive law, yet it experiences its own singular *nomos*: it is not identical with a pre-posited essence of existence. Pure justice as an ethical category is, in this sense, not identical with a having to be, with a categorical imperative (not even with a void imperative). Instead it finds itself in the paradoxical formation of a singular *nomos*: *the not having to be of a having to be*, where nomos is just a life. Pure violence as deforming violence turns formation itself to its potency because for it 'the messianic kingdom is always present', but all that it ever experiences is a life.[19]

Human life can turn to its own inoperativity to affirm a plane of immanence after the deposition of the metaphysics of a Law of law. For its powers to remain entirely its own after the neutralization or rendering-inoperative of the law, the act of human beings is conceived as other than a having to be, a norm that must be adhered to and actualized. Agamben writes:

> Since power (*archē*) constitutes itself through the inclusive exclusion (the *exceptio*) of anarchy, the only possibility of thinking a true anarchy coincides with the exhibition of the anarchy internal to power. Anarchy is that which becomes possible only in the moment that we grasp and destitute the anarchy of power. The same goes for every attempt to think anomy.[20]

The first step is to release the form of power, law and life that the *dispositif* of the pseudo-exception (as the fundamental structure of the *archē*) has captured and deformed. Agamben writes:

> Something is 'excepted' in the state and, in this way, 'politicized': but, for that to happen, it is necessary that it be reduced to the state of 'nudity' (bare life, anarchy as war of all against all, anomy as being-in-force [*vigenza*] without application). We know of life only bare life …, of anarchy we understand only the war of all against all, of anomy we see only chaos and the state of exception, etc.[21]

Agamben has emphasized the arduous task of such revolutionary or destituent power in that this can only become sufficient if it becomes the form-of-life adequate to the new historical era, not a what, but a how: an ontology of modality. Agamben writes:

> The decisive problem is no longer 'what' I am, but 'how' I am what I am. It is necessary, in this sense, to radicalize the Spinozan thesis according to which there is only being (substance) and its modes or modifications. Substance is not something that precedes the modes and exists independently from them. Being is not other than its modes, substance is only its modifications, its own 'how' (its own *quomodo*). Modal ontology makes it possible to go beyond the ontological difference that has dominated the Western conception of being. Between being and modes the relation is neither of identity nor of difference because the mode is at once identical and different – or, rather, it implies the coincidence – that is, the falling together [*cadere insieme*] – of the two terms. In this sense, the problem of the pantheist risk is badly put: the Spinozist syntagma *Deus sive* (or) *natura* does not mean 'God = nature': the *sive* (whether *sive* derives from the conditional and concessive *si* or the anaphoric *sic*) expresses

the modalization, that is, the neutralizing and the failure as much of identity as of difference. What is divine is not being in itself, but its own *sive*, its own always already modifying and 'naturing' – being born – in the modes. Modal ontology means rethinking from the start the problem of the relation between potentiality and act.[22]

In this way, a form-of-life encounters its immanent inoperativity in its power. Pure *Gewalt* in this sense is a living that immanently coincides completely and constitutively with its destitution, so that living can remain continuously within what it can do. But what it can do, nobody indeed knows. To perceive potentiality as a lack that requires a cure or salvation would mean to remain subjected to a fated law, a law that still condemns human beings to the guilt-nexus of the living, a destinal debt. The juridical command must still command, even in its state of impotence, because it remains the demonic structure according to which potentiality is a fault that must be repressed through its actualization.

The coincidence of the law's command with the real is not possible (in the form of mythical violence) unless a functionary actualizes what it has to be through the oracle or spell of the command that commands nothing but an absolute imperative. Command! Actualize! Work! Be someone! In *Opus Dei: An Archaeology of Duty*, Agamben locates in sacramental liturgy (the unceasing re-actualization of the sacrifice by Christ as *leitourgos*, the high priest) the central mystery of Christianity as one of ministry/*praxis*. In this liturgical ontology the always-pure *opus operatum* (the effective reality of the sacramental act) and the *opus operantis* (or *opus operans*) – the carrying out of the action by the agent (who can be pure or impure) establishes the institutional separation of an individual from his functional act. Agamben writes: 'As it happens in every institution, it is a matter of distinguishing the individual from the function he exercises, so as to secure the validity of the acts that he carries out, in the name of the institution' (*OD* 21). There is no ethical connection between the subject and his action, instead a functional relation where the subject is subsumed in it. This is the mystery of operativity/*praxis* – 'in effectiveness being is inseparable from its effects' (*OD* 25). You are what you must become.

In modernity, effectiveness coincides with being itself: *effectus* is 'the operation that actualizes a potential *from the outside* and in this sense renders it effective' (*OD* 43, emphasis added). Thus this is the ontological model of constitutive vicariousness: there is no originary place of liturgical *praxis*, it is always already an 'alteration' (function). Being is, here, something that must be realized (Plotinus), a hypostatic process of putting-to-work (*energheia*) (*OD* 57–8). In this manner, the official is a being of command, a juridical functionary, rendering (or erasing) his being under the command of a *debitum* that commands the execution of a duty without remainder (without impotence). The zero degree of the original modality of law dissolves being into a being commanded by an infinite guilt/debt, to which the law can only as a result respond with the necessity of a coercive act. If you do not actualize, you must be actualized. In this manner the systematized continuum of violence, grounded now in the zero-degree of a command that commands nothing, attempts once more to flee from its impotence and adopt it as its ultimate necessity of commandment. In a time of generalized anxiety as the internalized command of everyday life, the need, as well as the difficulty, of deposing this ontology, for Agamben, goes through the abdication of the commanding of one's free but functionary self.

Notes

1   See the special issue of *Divus Thomas* – 115 (2012/2) – on *The theology of 'potentia Dei' and the history of European normativity*.

2   On this see Anton Schütz, 'A quandary concerning immanence', *Law and Critique* 22.2 (2011): 189–203.

3   See Gilles Deleuze and Félix Guattari, *What is philosophy?*, trans. Graham Burchell and Hugh Tomlinson (London: Verso, 1994). As to whether they escape the problem will remain the question of another work.

4   See Gunther Teubner, 'Self-subversive justice: contingency or transcendence formula of law?', *Modern Law Review* 72 (2009): 1–23.

5   Alexander García Düttmann, 'The violence of destruction', in *Walter Benjamin: Theoretical Questions*, ed. David S. Ferris (Stanford, CA: Stanford University Press, 1996), 166.

6   See Agamben's *Opus Dei* (2013).

7   See generally the first part of Agamben's *Potentialities* (1999).

8   Carl Schmitt, *Political Theology: Four Chapters on the Concept of Sovereignty*, trans. George Schwab (Chicago, IL: University of Chicago Press, 2005), 6, translation modified as in *SE* 55.

9   See Alfred Hirsch, *Recht auf Gewalt? Spuren philosophischer Gewaltrechtfertigung nach Hobbes* (Munich: Wilhelm Fink Verlag, 2004), 26, and generally Massimiliano Tomba, *La vera politica. Kant e Benjamin: la possibilità della giustizia* (Macerata: Quodlibet, 2006).

10 Franz Rosenzweig, *Der Stern der Erlösung* (The Hague: Martinus Nijhoff, 1981), III, 1.

11 Furio Jesi, *Spartakus. Simbologia della rivolta* (Turin: Boringhieri, 2000), 19.

12 Walter Benjamin, 'Notizen zu einer Arbeit über die Kategorie der Gerechtigkeit', *Frankfurter Adorno Blätter* VI (1995): 42. These notes can be located in Geschom Scholem's transcription as an entry in his diary in 1916; they were then published in 1995 in the *Frankfurter Adorno Blätter* with a commentary by Hermann Schweppenhäuser, but are not included in the *Gesammelte Schriften*. An English translation of Benjamin's text is included and extensively discussed in Eric Jacobson, *Metaphysics of the Profane: The Political Theology of Walter Benjamin and Gershom Scholem* (New York: Columbia University Press, 2003), 166–9.

13 This is an adaptation of Deleuze's description of philosophy's effort at rendering representation infinite. See Gilles Deleuze, *Différence et répétition* (Paris: Presses Universitaires de France, 1968), 262.

14 Immanuel Kant, *Religion within the Bounds of Bare Reason* (1793), trans. Theodore M. Greene and Hoyt H. Hudson (New York: Harper and Brothers, 1960), 90.

15 Immanuel Kant, *The Metaphysics of Morals* (1797), ed. and trans. Mary Gregor (Cambridge: Cambridge University Press, 1996), 95.

16 Benjamin, 'Notizen zu einer Arbeit über die Kategorie der Gerechtigkeit', 42.

17 Giorgio Agamben, 'For a theory of destituent power', Public lecture in Athens,

transcript, 16 November 2013. Published by the online magazine *Chronos*: http://www.
chronosmag.eu/index.php/g-agamben-for-a-theory-of-destituent-power.html
18 See Giorgio Agamben, *The Highest Poverty* (2013).
19 Gershom Scholem, *Lamentations of Youth: The Diaries of Gershom Scholem,
    1913–1919*, ed. and trans. Anthony David Skinner (Cambridge, MA: Belknap Press
    of Harvard University Press, 2008), 192. Scholem introduces the sentence with
    'Walter once said that …'.
20 Giorgio Agamben, 'What is a destituent power?' trans. Stephanie Wakefield,
    Environment and Planning D: Society and Space 32.1 (2014): 72.
21 Agamben, 'What is a destituent power?', 72.
22 Agamben, 'What is a destituent power?', 74.

Works cited

Agamben, Giorgio. 'For a theory of destituent power'. Public lecture in Athens,
    transcript, 16 November 2013. Published by the online magazine *Chronos*: http://
    www.chronosmag.eu/index.php/g-agamben-for-a-theory-of-destituent-power.html
    (accessed November 20, 2014).
—'What is a destituent power?'. Translated by Stephanie Wakefield. *Environment and
    Planning D: Society and Space* 32.1 (2014): 65–74.
Benjamin, Walter. 'Notizen zu einer Arbeit über die Kategorie der Gerechtigkeit'.
    Frankfurter Adorno Blätter IV (1995): 41–2.
Deleuze, Gilles. *Différence et répétition*. Paris: Presses Universitaires de France, 1968.
Deleuze, Gilles, and Félix Guattari. *What is Philosophy?* Translated by Graham Burchell
    and Hugh Tomlinson. London: Verso, 1994.
Düttmann, Alexander García. 'The violence of destruction'. In *Walter Benjamin:
    Theoretical Questions*. Edited by David S. Ferris. Stanford, CA: Stanford University
    Press, 1996. 165–84.
Hirsch, Alfred. *Recht auf Gewalt? Spuren philosophischer Gewaltrechtfertigung nach
    Hobbes*. Munich: Wilhelm Fink Verlag, 2004.
Jacobson, Eric. *Metaphysics of the Profane: The Political Theology of Walter Benjamin and
    Gershom Scholem*. New York: Columbia University Press, 2003.
Jesi, Furio. *Spartakus. Simbologia della rivolta*. Turin: Boringhieri, 2000.
Kant, Immanuel. *Religion within the Bounds of Bare Reason* (1793). Translated by
    Theodore M. Greene and Hoyt H. Hudson. New York: Harper and Brothers, 1960.
—*The Metaphysics of Morals* (1797). Edited and translated by Mary Gregor. Cambridge:
    Cambridge University Press, 1996.
Rosenzweig, Franz. *Der Stern der Erlösung* (1921). The Hague: Martinus Nijhoff, 1981.
Schmitt, Carl. *Political Theology: Four Chapters on the Concept of Sovereignty*. Translated
    by George Schwab. Chicago, IL: University of Chicago Press, 2005.
Scholem, Gershom. *Lamentations of Youth: The Diaries of Gershom Scholem, 1913–1919*.
    Edited and translated by Anthony David Skinner. Cambridge, MA: Belknap Press of
    Harvard University Press, 2008.
Schütz, Anton. 'A quandary concerning immanence'. *Law and Critique* 22. 2 (2011):
    189–203.
Teubner, Gunther. 'Self-subversive justice: contingency or transcendence formula of law?'
    Modern Law Review 72 (2009): 1–23.

Tomba, Massimiliano. *La vera politica. Kant e Benjamin: la possibilità della giustizia*, Macerata: Quodlibet, 2006.

Various authors. *The Theology of 'Potentia Dei' and the History of European Normativity* – Alle origini dell'idea di normativismo. Il problema della 'potentia Dei' tra teologia e diritto pubblico europeo. *Divus Thomas* 115 (2012/2).

11

The Anarchist Life we are Already Living: Benjamin and Agamben on Bare Life and the Resistance to Sovereignty

James R. Martel

Introduction

In *The Conquest of Bread*, Peter Kropotkin offers us a vision of anarchism as a set of practices that persists amidst even the most centralizing and authoritarian of states. Kropotkin writes: 'with our eyes shut we pass by thousands and thousands of human groupings which form themselves freely, without any intervention of the law, and attain results infinitely superior to those achieved under governmental tutelage'.[1] If the state has never been able to kill off or utterly supersede these anarchist practices, it still does not seem as though anarchism – with some exceptions such as anarchist Spain in the 1930s or, more recently, Occupy Wall Street, Tahrir Square and Gezi Park – comes out to be much more than a sideline, a space of non-determination. Such spaces exist episodically and in a patchwork, if at all, amidst political systems that are otherwise thoroughly dominated by what might be (and sometimes is) called 'archism', the political processes of states, of capitalism and other forms of domination.

Thinking of anarchism as the inevitable loser in this situation may reflect the fact that even our judgements and values reflect the archist tendencies we are immersed in. In this view, anarchism must be a failure if it only appears now and then, here and there, if it does not replace or destroy archism once and for all. Insofar as archism itself is a model of total domination (so that sovereignty insists on controlling and 'owning' not a patchwork but a totality of territory, so that not having this totalization seems to be a weakness or failing), such a model of success or failure gets projected onto anarchism too and the latter comes up all the weaker for the comparison.

Responding to the possible traps that such views suggest, rather than arguing that anarchists must accept their secondary status as a set of phenomena that are just passing through an archist world, making occasional (sometimes spectacular) trouble, I would like to argue something different. In this essay, I wish to argue that by looking at anarchism on its own terms, and by its own standards, we have the possibility of understanding these anarchist practices as already being a deep threat to, and a subversion of, archism. Rather than seeing the anarchist movement as impoverished and precarious, I would turn the lens around and show how these anarchist practices are in fact far more robust, more anchored in materiality than any form of archism that we currently experience. In fact, I will argue, it is archism – and, in particular, sovereign forms of archism, however in charge and confident they may appear to be – that is actually the ephemeral and perhaps even endangered set of practices. It is anarchism, I will argue, that demonstrates its own resilience and persistence as a form of human political agency. Anarchism, I will claim, is more ontologically suited to a universe that is itself episodic and contingent. In this view, it is archism and not anarchism that is weird, mythic, out of time and place.

To make these arguments, I will turn to the work of two thinkers, Walter Benjamin and Giorgio Agamben, in terms of their respective understandings of the anarchist practices which are generally superseded and overshadowed by archism but which in fact remain central, even basic, to political life.[2] Benjamin definitely is the thinker who fits most easily into this formulation. Benjamin's work, and especially his 'Critique of Violence', highlights and recuperates these anarchist practices (sometimes, but not always, by that name). Benjamin shows us the private relations between citizens, the non-violent relations that for him are the hallmark of anarchist practices which persist amidst larger practices of archism. For Benjamin, the very fact of the presence of non-violent alternatives to archism (which in his view is inherently always violent) indicates archism's failure to achieve totality. For Benjamin, however dispersed or seemingly powerless they may seem, the fact that non-violent alternative forms of politics exist at all suggests that fate, the overarching archist eschatology that binds us into what Benjamin will later call the 'phantasmagoria', is not inevitable, is not, in fact, truly sovereign.

Agamben, on the other hand, seems at first blush to be a thinker that consigns us to suffer from state power. Despite his own desire to combat that power, in his evocation of 'bare life', Agamben often depicts the life that is cast off from sovereignty as miserable, wretched and weak, even as it remains intimately entangled with state power. His emblematic figure of bare life is the *Muselmann*, someone reduced to mere survival. This character has not chosen resistance; the *Muselmänner* become resistant by being reduced to a pith of humanity (hence 'bare' life). It seems that our options from an Agambenian position are to choose between our slow and steady defeat under sovereign life or a life of desperate misery at the margins of politics – the subject of bare life.

Yet, Agamben's work is more nuanced than this initial survey suggests. When we read him in conjunction with Benjamin – that is, when we read him, not according to his own reading of Benjamin but rather in conversation with Benjamin's own thought in and of itself – what emerges is more complicated than what we get with either figure alone. To the grand theoretical picture that Benjamin supplies us with, Agamben adds a more fleshed-out vision of what can be done; he elucidates how Benjaminian theory could be applied in actual practices.

As I will argue further, a big part of the difference between these thinkers comes in terms of their orientation towards the spatial dimensions of sovereignty. For Benjamin, a separate life – a life that is not determined by archism and hence 'bare'

– exists simultaneously and amidst archism. For Agamben, on the other hand, bare life can only be seen at the excluded margins of politics (although in his view, it exists in every one of us; ultimately we are only our own bodies). Thus Benjamin largely describes resistance within the realm of sovereign authority – what he calls 'mythic violence'. Much of Agamben's focus, as I will show, lies just beyond the boundaries of sovereignty, not truly outside sovereignty but formally beyond its limits. This is the area he explores, perhaps most famously in his *Homo Sacer* as well as many other related books that he has written since. In these books, describing life beyond the boundaries, Agamben finds sources of resistance, flight, subterfuge and so forth, but he also describes conditions that are truly desperate; his sites of resistance often take place in the camps, in hospital beds and other areas that do not seem suited to causing much damage to archic systems. However, as I will show further too, there are points where Agamben does consider resistance from deep 'inside' the boundary of sovereign authority, sources that threaten much more damage to the edifice of sovereignty.

One such source of resistance is described in his book *The Highest Poverty*, Agamben's study of life within the monastic orders of the fourth and fifth centuries CE. Here, we come closer to Benjamin's own considerations of resistance, practices that amount to a recognition of those anarchist acts that not only coexist with archism but pose an existential threat to it from within its own boundaries. This is what I am calling 'the anarchist life that we are already living'.

Walter Benjamin and a politics of 'pure means'

To begin this enquiry, let me turn first to Benjamin, to show the basis of his analysis (which, by extension, becomes the base of Agamben's as well, at least to some extent). In 'Critique of Violence', Benjamin describes the ways that violence permeates every aspect of our world. He famously distinguishes between what he calls 'mythic violence' (or force; in German the term *Gewalt* can mean both 'violence' and 'force') and 'divine violence'. For Benjamin, insofar as there is no genuine and legitimate basis for human law or sovereign power, it must stake its claim by projecting false sources of authority onto screens like God, nature and reason. All of these projections add up to a widespread fetishistic practice that he later comes to call 'the phantasmagoria'. The force that is produced in such a context is mythic because it is based on a false ontology, a false association with a universe that it is actually disconnected from; anxious about its existence, mythic violence must ceaselessly re-establish itself. Thus Benjamin writes:

> [I]f violence, violence crowned by fate, is the origin of law, then it may be readily supposed that where the highest violence, that over life and death, occurs in the legal system, the origins of law jut manifestly and fearsomely into existence. ... [The purpose of capital punishment] is not to punish the infringement of law but to establish new law. (*SW* 1:242)

Law is violent, Benjamin tells us, to overcompensate for its lack of real origins. This produces a kind of feedback loop wherein means and ends do not have a causal but rather a circular relationship.

In this economy of false ends, mythic violence is opposed by divine violence, a violence (if it can be said to be a violence at all) that is delivered by God, that is, by the true end of things. Benjamin writes:

> This very task of destruction poses again, ultimately, the question of a pure immediate violence that might be able to call a halt to mythic violence. Just as in all spheres God opposes myth, mythic violence is confronted by the divine ... If mythic violence is lawmaking, divine violence is law-destroying; if the former sets boundaries, the latter boundlessly destroys them; if mythic violence brings at once guilt and retribution, divine power only expiates; if the former threatens, the latter strikes; if the former is bloody, the latter is lethal without spilling blood. (*SW* 1:249–50)

For Benjamin, divine violence serves to break the cycle of means and ends that otherwise trap us in a kind of pernicious instrumentality. He writes: 'it is never reason that decides on the justification of means and the justness of ends: fate-imposed violence decides on the former, and God on the latter' (*SW* 1:247). As a true end, God's violence does not inaugurate new truths into the world. It merely removes false projections done in its name. Fate, that sense of doom and necessity that comes along with mythic law, is broken by God's acts of divine violence and in its brokenness, an opportunity arises for human decision and acting in ways that are not predetermined.

Benjamin's name for that opportunity is 'pure means', that is, means that have had their (necessarily false) ends broken off. He mentions this concept several times in the essay. He writes:

> To induce men to reconcile their interests peacefully without involving the legal system, there is, in the end, apart from all virtues, one effective motive that often enough puts into the most reluctant hands pure instead of violent means: it is the fear of mutual disadvantage that threatens to arise from violent confrontation, whatever the outcome might be. Such motives are clearly visible in countless cases of conflict of interest between private persons. (*SW* 1:245)

In this case, although the subjects Benjamin is referring to here are reflecting the endemic violence of our legal and political system (seeking only to avoid bringing more violence onto themselves), their pursuit of non-violent or pure means nonetheless announces the possibility that the cycle of violence can be broken. Benjamin also says: 'we can therefore point only to pure means in politics as analogous to those which govern peaceful intercourse between private persons' (*SW* 1:245).

Benjamin's turn to private persons as a source of non-violent and peaceful inter-course shows that, without needing the recourse to false projections of God and truth as states and legal systems do, private persons can work out their conflicts just between themselves. In the space that is, not so much free of, but relatively unburdened by such false ends as law and the state, decisions are made, violence is averted. If we recall that, for Benjamin, 'violence', while it certainly includes physical acts such as stabbing and hurting people, is more specifically a matter of falsely asserting truths and using those truths as a justification for domination, we can see that the private sphere is not so much apolitical as it is a space for a different – and non-violent – form of politics.

Benjamin makes clear what kind of politics he believes these private individuals are practising when he turns to the question of class struggle. He writes: 'As regards class struggles, in them strikes must under certain conditions be seen as a pure means' (*SW* 1:244). He makes a well known distinction (one that he takes from Georges Sorel) between the political strike, which is itself a kind of violence, meeting the violence of the state with its own extortionary demands, and the proletarian general strike, which is a demand for a cessation of both state and capital. The latter is not a form of extortion – or even of violence – at all. The general strike is a way of turning the power that is always inherent between private parties into a more generalized practice. Benjamin writes of the contrast between the two kinds of strike:

> Whereas the first form of interruption of work [the political strike] is violent, since it causes only an external modification of labor conditions, the second [the proletarian general strike], as a pure means, is nonviolent. For it takes place not in readiness to resume work following external concessions and this or that modification to working conditions, but in the determination to resume only a wholly transformed work, no longer enforced by the state, an upheaval that this kind of strike not so much causes as consummates. (*SW* 1:246)

When he tells us that the proletarian general strike 'not so much causes as consummates' the shutdown of the state, we see that a politics of 'pure means' does not serve in the usual chain of causality that comes from the endless loop of means and ends that we see under conditions of mythic violence. Because the general strike breaks with myths of state and capitalism once and for all, the workers find that their instrumentalism no longer serves those ends. Accordingly, their actions take on a new ontological dimension. Rather than struggle against the overwhelming power of capitalism when taken on its own terms, the general strike is, as Benjamin suggests, in tune with divine violence, that is, in tune with the larger universe that does not reflect such myths. From this perspective, rather than asserting their own non-violence in the face of a violent system (in a face off that they seem doomed to lose), we can say that the general strike allows the workers to deny the forces that prevent their own non-violent actions from taking on a larger political significance. In a sense, the general strike restores to the strikers an attunement to the pervasive non-violence that marks the material world and which cannot be denied by mythic violence (more on this ontological question in the conclusion of the chapter).[3]

Speaking of the general strike, Benjamin tells us further: '[f]or this reason, the first of these undertakings [the political strike] is lawmaking but the second anarchistic' (*SW* 1:246). Such a statement indicates that political practices that are non-violent are also anarchist. Anarchism, then, is the name that we can give to a politics of pure means. This presumably includes, not only the politics of large-scale attempts at overthrowing or stopping capitalism, like the general strike, but also, and perhaps more pertinently for those of us who continue to live under conditions of capitalism and mythic violence, the private local and ordinary anarchisms, the non-violent resolution of conflicts that occur at all times even in the midst of phantasm.

Benjamin even extends his view of non-violent (and therefore anarchist) politics to the realm of international relations. Insofar as there is no overarching law, no state and no structure to constrain the behavior of states towards one another, this realm too could be said to be a place where a kind of anarchist polity is possible. Benjamin writes:

> Fundamentally [diplomats] must, entirely on the analogy of the agreement between private persons, resolve conflict case by case, in the name of their states, peacefully and without contracts. A delicate task that is more robustly performed by referees, but a method of solution that in principle is above that of the referee because it is beyond all legal systems and therefore beyond violence. Accordingly, like the intercourse of private persons, that of diplomats has engendered its own forms and virtues, which were not always mere formalities, even though they have become so. (*SW* 1:247)

Thus, there are various spheres of life in which non-violent, and hence anarchist politics, a politics of pure means, can be and is practised. When Benjamin writes that these kinds of practices occur 'peacefully and without contracts', we see a contrast between this model of politics and liberal social contract theory. To see the contract as the binding arbiter of all human forms of agreement is to remain bound by some system of ends, whether it be reason or nature or some other projection. To make agreements without contract, means to make agreements on their own terms. Such agreements are neither binding nor based on fundamental principles. They simply relate the fact that an agreement was made and is being held to for as long as it is held to.

This shows too that the private forms of agreement that Benjamin is referring to take place in an entirely different temporality and with an entirely different set of referents than we usually understand. If social contract theory is a way to bind individuals together into a state that they may not afterwards escape, the practices of pure means that Benjamin describes serve to show us what agreement can look like when it is not overladen with myth.

Although it is true that Benjamin's discussion of pure means extends, as we have seen, beyond the ordinary and daily life to the general strike, to revolution and radical alternations of the political landscape, we can see just as clearly that we do not need those things to happen in order to be able to have some form of anarchist practices. As much as Benjamin suggests a direction in which we may go, he shows us just as much that, in the meantime, before we have revolution, we already have this practice of the anarchism of daily life. Sovereignty and law, rather than seeming omnipresent and totalizing, appear to be more like a kind of Swiss cheese with lots of lacunae, lots of moments that have nothing to do with law or state and its phantasms of authority. These enduring lacunae represent what life both is like and would be like when sovereign principles are not dominant. Insofar as sovereignty and law's main power is the concept of their own inevitability, their association with what we have already seen Benjamin call 'fate', we are already doing enormous damage to sovereign conceits when we recognize its lack of reach. Such a view both establishes how and why revolution is possible and shows further how the kind of practices with which we already engage under conditions of mythic violence, can be the basis for whatever order we might find ourselves in should that order be successfully disrupted or destroyed. Far from being a quiet and minor aspect of our contemporary political life then, Benjamin shows us why the anarchism of everyday life is already a powerful force, partaking perhaps in what he will later call the 'weak messianic power' that he attributes to each generation (*SW* 4:390).

Giorgio Agamben and the form of life

For his own part, Giorgio Agamben offers a more complex model of resistance that operates both within and beyond the boundaries of sovereign authority. As already noted, Agamben at first glance seems to be less helpful in terms of thinking about an anarchism of everyday life simply because, in his view, sovereign power is so absolute that resistance to it tends to come (again at first glance) not from within the boundaries of sovereignty but without.

For Agamben, as is well known, the signature of modern sovereign power is the ban, the sovereign's ability to determine its own limits and, in the process, produce a subject who is abandoned beyond those limits. The limit of modern sovereignty is the exception, the line or gap between law and violence, between what is permitted and what is not. In *Homo Sacer*, Agamben writes:

> If the exception is the structure of sovereignty, then sovereignty is not an exclusively political concept, an exclusively juridical character, a power external to law (Schmitt), or the supreme rule of the judicial order (Hans Kelsen): it is the originary structure in which law refers to life and includes it in itself by suspending it ... The relation of exception is the relation of ban. He who has been banned is not, in fact, simply outside the law and made indifferent to it but rather *abandoned* by it, that is, exposed and threatened on the threshold in which life and law, outside and inside, become indistinguishable. It is literally not possible to say whether the one who has been banned is outside or inside the juridical order. (*HS* 28–9)[4]

In this way, for Agamben, sovereignty has deep (and theological) tendrils in Western practice. It is not only a power over life (which we already knew), but in some sense it produces that life. More accurately, for Agamben, sovereignty engages with our animal life (*zoē*) in such a way that blurs the boundaries between what is 'ours' and what belongs to law. Towards the end of *Homo Sacer*, Agamben describes the situation of this subject in more detail:

> Let us now observe the life of *homo sacer* ... [H]is entire existence is reduced to a bare life stripped of every right by virtue of the fact that anyone can kill him without committing homicide; he can save himself only in perpetual flight or a foreign land. And yet he is in a continuous relationship with the power that banished precisely insofar as he is at every instance exposed to an unconditioned threat of death. He is pure *zoē*, but his *zoē* is as such caught in the sovereign ban and must reckon with it at every moment, finding the best way to elude or deceive it. In this sense, no life, as exiles and bandits know well, is more 'political' than his. (*HS* 183–4)

Agamben takes the term 'bare life' from Benjamin himself. He speaks of Benjamin's point in the 'Critique' about the 'bearer of the link between violence and law which he calls "bare life" (*bloßes Leben*)' (*HS* 65). Agamben goes on to say of this (in part citing Benjamin directly):

> The analysis of this figure ... establishes an essential link between bare life and juridical violence. Not only does the rule of law over the living exist and cease to exist alongside bare life, but even the dissolution of juridical violence ... 'stems ... from the guilt of bare natural life, which consigns the living, innocent and unhappy, to the punishment that "expiates" the guilt of bare life – and doubtless also purifies [*entsühnt*] the guilty, not of guilt, however, but of law'. (*HS* 65)

The punishment that Benjamin is referring to here (*SW* 1:250) is the punishment of divine violence, wherein God moves to unmake the fetishes and other evils that human beings commit, often in God's name. Benjamin's notion that divine violence expiates law allows Agamben to think of those who suffer most from law – that is, the *homo sacer*, the one who is banned and who may be killed without the perpetrator committing homicide – as retaining their 'bare' life, thus subject to a different and messianic form of law.

Taking up this possibility about bare life, in *Homo Sacer*, Agamben supplies a few examples of life at the margin, at the limit of sovereignty (but not, very importantly, of the political). A critical example is the figure that he calls, citing Primo Levi, 'the Muslim' or *der Muselmann*. Agamben tells us that:

> [this is] a being from whom humiliation, horror, and fear had so taken away all consciousness and all personality as to make him absolutely apathetic (hence the ironical nickname given to him) ... He no longer belongs to the world of men in any way; he does not even belong to the threatened and precarious world of the camp inhabitants who have forgotten him from the very beginning. Mute and absolutely alone, he has passed into another world without memory and without grief. (*HS* 185)

For Agamben, this character is a physical being who has been reduced to just that, a hulk with nothing resembling 'the human' left within. This figure embodies the resistance to violence and the state; having already had the worst done to him (in this case, forbearing to kill him is no mercy), the *Muselmann* is impervious to anything further:

> We can say that [the *Muselmann*] moves in an absolute indistinction of fact and law, of life and juridical rule, and of nature and politics. Because of this, the guard suddenly seems powerless before him as if struck by the thought that the *Muselmann*'s behavior – which does not register any difference between an order and the cold [that is, between something done to him by human beings and the material world around him] – might perhaps be a silent form of resistance. (*HS* 185)

Here, then, is an assertion of the kind of resistance that can ultimately come out of exclusion, the ban, the super-politicization of the *homo sacer*. This kind of resistance is purely bodily; the muteness of the body itself to answer or to care effectively takes the *Muselmann* out of the political realm; he has become immune to the threats and violence of the state.

Thinking through this concept further, Agamben ends *Homo Sacer* by famously speaking of a '*bios* that is only its own *zoē*' (*HS* 188). Perhaps it can be said that this effort does not entirely abandon *bios* so much as draw it into the body. This view has further promise for a politics of resistance from within the Western narrative. Agamben speaks of the 'interlacement of *zoē* and *bios* that seems to define the political destiny of the West' (*HS* 188). This interlacement, the tensions between our animal body and our necessarily failed aspirations to human perfection are, for Agamben, the root of our contemporary crisis, one where the Greek *polis* has given way to the camps as the exemplary political space of our time. Returning to the passage cited above, in its larger context, Agamben writes:

> This biopolitical body that is bare life must itself instead be transformed into the site for the constitution and installation of a form of life that is wholly exhausted in bare life and a *bios* that is only its own *zoē* … If we give the name form-of-life to this being that is only its own bare existence and to this life that, being its own form, remains inseparable from it, we will witness the emergence of a field of research beyond the terrain defined by the intersection of politics and philosophy, medico-biological sciences and jurisprudence. (*HS* 188)

This view of the body as such is in keeping with Agamben's idea of 'whatever being', the notion of language, for example, that does not mean anything (or whose meaning is unimportant) but whose mere existence matters (see for example *CC* 1). Our *zoē*, our animal life is itself a kind of 'whatever being', a presentation of subjectivity that requires no content (*bios*) or which overrides that content with its basic assertion of its own existence. In this way, it could be said that Agamben's appreciation for animal existence is a counterweight to the fact that mythic violence is always asserting an existence that is not real. Against the non-existent force that asserts itself, Agamben, adapting Benjamin, would counter with the implicitly non-violent assertion of actual existence, bare life.

Yet, if the *Muselmann* is the model for this move (another example Agamben offers is Karen Quinlan), we see a pretty grim set of options for our resistance. If resistance must come down to mere existence, it could be said that we resist all the time (and we do, but so what?). Our bodies do not stop existing but the state, capitalism, phantasms of all variety keep doing what they can to control that existence. If Agamben offers us the 'good news' that at core we are resistant beings (even killing us does not remove the fact of our being), we also get the 'bad news' that the *homo sacer* is in no position to do much more than he or she already does.

The highest poverty

Yet, for Agamben there are other readings that suggest a more nuanced and complicated form of resistance to sovereignty. The principal example I will examine here is his discussion of Franciscan friars in the Middle Ages. This community, as I will explain, manages for Agamben to resist many of the ways that they are acted upon by Church and state. Their position is, however, critically different from the ones that Agamben describes in *Homo Sacer*. These friars are not *homini sacri*. They are not at the other end of a ban. Although Agamben cautions us not to read the *homo sacer* as being actually outside of sovereignty, we can surely say that the friars he describes in *The Highest Poverty* are *more* inside than the *homo sacer*. From this context, and in parallel to what we have seen Benjamin describing from a perspective that is also firmly inside the apparatus of mythic violence, these friars are operating from within the confines of the power that they are resisting (and thus critically different from either the *homo sacer* or the *Muselmann*). Although, in some sense, Agamben's point is that we are all akin to the *homo sacer*, all banned and all vulnerable to the state of exception, it is still instructive to see the different forms that resistance may take in his view when they have not been formally banned, when they remain fully 'inside'.

The first thing to say here is that the monastic practices in question fall somewhere between the ancient *polis* and the modern camp, although they are much closer to the former than the latter. Agamben tells us that 'the monastery, like the *polis,* is a community that intends to realize "the perfection of the cenobial life"' (*HP* 11). Cenoby is a practice of living together for the purposes of 'living well'. Agamben tells us further that '[c]enoby does not name only a place, but first of all a form of life' (*HP* 11).

Agamben's discussion here of 'form of life' is critical for his project in *The Highest Poverty*, as well as for his work more generally. It is the friars' form of life that renders them, if not immune to sovereign authority, then at least able to resist it in ways that are not recognized as threatening, not seen as a usurpation of sovereign authority. In this way, these friars were able to 'hide in plain sight' from a political and theological order that was busily gathering itself together for the sake of its own power and authority. For Agamben, the form of life itself is the source of resistance. This is not unlike his point about the *Muselmann*. Even though the latter cannot be said to have any 'form of life' at all, both the Franciscans and the Muselmann practise a kind of embodied resistance.

Describing the Franciscan form of life, Agamben writes that these friars do not concern themselves with 'theological or dogmatic questions, articles of faith, or problems of scriptural interpretation' (*HP* 92). Agamben goes on to write that:

> Instead, what is at stake is life and the way of living … The claim of poverty, which is present in all the [monastic] movements and which in itself is clearly not new, is only one aspect of this way or form of life, which strikes observers in a special way. … '[T]they [i.e. the Franciscan friars] walked barefoot, they did not accept money, nor did they carry a wallet or shoes or two tunics' … Moreover, it does not represent an ascetic or mortifying practice to obtain salvation as it did in the monastic tradition, but it is now an inseparable and constitutive part of the 'apostolic' or 'holy' life, which they profess to practice in perfect joy. (*HP* 92)

In other words, Agamben reads this movement as constituting, not a formal ideological opposition to mainstream monastic tradition; such moves would have been recognized as heretical and dealt with accordingly. Instead it consisted of a set of practices that themselves defined what these friars were up to. The actual actions they did became their form of resistance, an embodiment, not of a counter-ideology but an alternative practice that flew under the radar of a vigilant Church that was ever alert to threats.

Or rather, there were clashes with the Church, but the clashes came in novel ways that did not bring down the same kind of response that, for example, the Cathars in Southern France received in their own forms of resistance. In the latter case, an entire crusade – the only one enacted against fellow Europeans – was brought down upon their heads. For the Franciscans, on the other hand, Agamben tells us:

> It is … obvious that a form of life practiced with rigor by a group of individuals will necessarily have consequences on the doctrinal level, which can bring forth – as they in fact did bring forth – clashes and disagreements with the Church hierarchy. But it is precisely on these disagreements that the attention of historians has mainly been focused, leaving in shadows the fact that for the first time, what was in question in the movements was not the *rule*, but the *life*, not the ability to profess this or that article of faith, but the ability to live in a certain way, to practice joyfully and openly a certain form of life. (*HP* 93)

For Agamben, the resistance embodied by these practices comes in the form of having such practices fail to be legible as rules (and hence open challenges to Church practices).

He gives a specific example to this, discussing how one commentary dealt with the question of whether there could be any exceptions to the rule of having the friars always walk barefoot. As he notes, in their response to this question, the author wrote: 'Wearing shoes depends on a dispensation from the rule in case of necessity; not wearing shoes is the form of life [*non calciari est foma vitae*]' (*HP* 107–8).

In this way, the rule as such only appears occasionally, as a momentary exception to the way of life. Thus, Agamben tells us: 'walking barefoot does not involve the observance of a rule (in which case the text would had [sic] to say: *non calciari est regula*) but realizes a *forma vitae*' (*HP* 108). Agamben also says a few pages later:

> Necessity, which gives the Friars Minor a dispensation from the rule, restores (natural) law to them; outside the state of necessity [in this case those moments when they have to wear shoes], they have no relationship with the law. What for others is normal thus becomes the exception for them; what for others is the exception becomes for them a form of life. (*HP* 115)

As we see here, the monastic practice of the Franciscans is precisely the opposite of the way Agamben, via Schmitt, characterizes our contemporary experience wherein the exception – and hence the rule – is ubiquitous. Although it precedes the fullest expression of modern sovereignty, this moment nonetheless happens in the face of a busily organizing Church hegemony so it remains a challenge to that usurpation of life. Yet, Agamben tells us that '[l]ife according to the form of the holy Gospel is situated on a level that is so distinct from that of life according to the form of the holy Roman Church that it cannot enter into conflict with it' (*HP* 122).

In this way, there is a kind of exception to the exception, a state of resistance that exists amidst sovereign forms of authority. The challenge to sovereignty promoted here is not of a kind that is commensurate to sovereignty itself. It is not violent. It is not political in the way that we usually understand that term (but then again, our terminology tends to reflect our ensconcement in sovereign forms of authority). Yet the challenge that this alternative model poses to sovereignty is, in some sense, an existential one. The very fact that alternatives can and do exist (another version of the 'anarchist life we are already living') challenges one of the central conceits of sovereign authority, the fact that it is ubiquitous and without alternatives, the fact that its rule extends to all things, all places and all times (even beyond its borders, as Agamben's discussion of the *homo sacer* suggests). The notion that in the midst of a busily self-making sovereign agency, a group of Franciscan friars were living an alternative form of life, shows us that we have recourse to political forms that go far beyond the limitations set by Carl Schmitt. If sovereignty's true power lies in the adage that 'there is no alternative', the very fact of these friars and their way of life suggests otherwise.

This is not necessarily the conclusion that Agamben himself draws. Although he brings this radical alternative to our attention, Agamben himself does not go so far as to suggest that this is a true break with dominant Western practices. At the very end of *The Highest Poverty,* Agamben offers that although the Franciscan order represents a radically different model, a 'life outside the law' which 'makes use of things without ever appropriating them', it has not fully broken with larger Western practices and does not itself constitute a true and existential threat to sovereign authority (*HP* 144). Agamben also tells us that 'the Franciscans tried, certainly in an insufficient way, to break [the mould of Western domination] and confront that paradigm', but that in fact it may be that the 'paradigm of operativity demands that the decisive confrontation be shifted to another terrain' (*HP* 145). Here, we see a move that is very frequently found in Agamben: to suggest something quite radical, quite compatible with Benjaminian readings, but to then defer the implications of this radicality to another plane. Yet, to read Agamben in a more Benjaminian light, it can be argued that the presence of the Franciscan experiment within the heart of the sovereign entity is already a form of resistance, a threat and an alternative that is happening here, and not in 'another terrain'. We do not need to look elsewhere to see the threat that such an order poses. It is not merely a sideline to archism but, as already noted, an existential threat, an anarchist ferment that exists and survives in the midst of archist phantasms of authority and power.

Conclusion: Pure means and the 'ontologies' of anarchism

Agamben's description of the Franciscan challenge to Church authority can be applied many centuries later to our time (clearly this is Agamben's intention in writing this book and other books that are related to it). This seems to be one example of what 'a *bios* that is only its own *zoē*' might look like. Agamben tells us that the goal of *bios* is a perfect life but that does not seem to be exactly what is going on with the Franciscans. Rather than reaching for perfection, for ends, the Franciscan friars seem to have, in their own way, severed with ends, with the goal of perfection, for a focus on means. It is almost as if Francis's message is to say 'forget what you think and believe; live this life and you will discover an entirely different dimension of salvation'. Rather than the salvation of the soul, his followers perhaps discover the salvation of the body, freeing it from being condemned as the source of guilt and making it instead the site upon which specific practices can be enacted. These practices elude law and rule (at least to some extent; I am not sure we can truly say that they are 'outside law' as Agamben suggests). They are not forced upon the friars as norms but are rather lived as a form in its own right.

In this way, these friars could be said to be living a life of 'pure means', another form of non-violent action that is akin to what Benjamin describes with his analysis of everyday non-violence and anarchism. Stripped of its idolatrous ends, *bios* does indeed become 'its own *zoē*', perhaps the one becomes indistinguishable from the other. Is it therefore also accurate to say that these monks are practising a form of anarchism? I'm not sure that Agamben himself would embrace the term but, as already noted, for all his hedging, I think that he offers us a useful insight into how a form of life can become a form of resistance as well, how once again, what Benjamin will later in his life call a 'weak messianic force' can be manifest in a variety of human practices at all points of the temporal order.

Finally, this engagement with Agamben helps further a notion that I already explored with Benjamin, namely the notion of anarchism's own ontology. Insofar as for Benjamin, and to some extent Agamben as well, what passes for reality is merely a series of phantasms, we can see that an anarchist set of practices, of forms of life, can be said to be engaged in life as such rather than life as a goal or destiny (a *bios* oriented towards such ends). 'Ontology' is probably too strong a word to use here insofar as the anarchist practices I have been looking at are not necessarily any 'truer' or more authentic than the ones that they oppose. For Benjamin in particular, any claim to being true is instantly suspect as ultimately constituting a claim for mythic violence and phantasm. Yet the term ontology is still helpful in that it brings our focus towards what a politics of pure means looks like; if we are not oriented towards ends, then our means reflect only what we do, our local decision and practice and nothing more (so an ontology, but a partial and halting one, an ontology of the local and the subjective). Such practices reflect a basis in materiality, in habit and in life patterns that are rarely deemed political. As such, they do have one major advantage over those creations of mythic law that otherwise tend to dominate and overwrite them. These anarchist practices do not share the metaphysical anxiety of their own existence that their archist cousins possess. They are non-violent because they do not need to assert their own reality; that reality is based on the ordinary and the everyday; its own existence is manifest to itself precisely through its own banality, its repetition and connection to life practices.

In the case of more spectacular forms of anarchist politics, such as the general strike, the fact that such practices remain rooted in everyday politics, remaining a matter of 'pure means', allows even the general strike to avoid the anxiety that produces violence in the archist order (at least in terms of the violence of fetishism). The general strike does not negotiate with phantasm, it simply turns its back on it.

Turning away from ends, the general strike would have us turn towards what we are all already doing in the shadows of archism; it returns us to our anarchist practices of everyday life and, in so doing, shows that the true dreamer is not the anarchist but rather those remaining embedded in archist patterns of violence and self-assertion. In this view, it is the archists who are swimming against the tide of the universe. They must assert what does not exist; their power lies in projections, lies and fetishism. The anarchist, on the other hand, merely has to cease making such assertions, to inure herself to the assertions that are being made all around her. Being more contingent and unstructured by definition, working with pure means, the non-violent cooperative methods of the anarchist are, as already noted, more in tune with a universe in which contingency and unstructuredness are the rule; the archists, in this case do not set the exception, they comprise it.

Notes

1   Peter Kropotkin, *The Conquest of Bread* (Mineola, NY: Dover Publications, 2011), 156.
2   For more consideration of these thinkers and anarchism, see for example, Lorenzo Fabbri, 'From inoperativeness to action: on Giorgio Agamben's anarchism', *Radical Philosophy Review* 14:1 (2011): 85–100; Andrew Benjamin, *Working with Walter Benjamin: Recovering a Political Philosophy* (Edinburgh: Edinburgh University Press, 2013).
3   For more on the ontological status of anarchism, how it is the norm rather than the exception, see James C. Scott, *The Art of Not Being Governed: An Anarchist History of Upland Southeast Asia* (New Haven, CT: Yale University Press, 2010). In Scott's analysis, states only come into being through intense efforts. Initially, they are unable to retain citizens. Rather than be subjected to their taxing and military interests, subjects tend to leave and form new communities in inaccessible places. The fight over retaining citizens is one of the primary struggles that nascent states must face.
4   On the notion of exception, see also his *State of Exception* (2003).

Works cited

Benjamin, Andrew. *Working with Walter Benjamin: Recovering a Political Philosophy.* Edinburgh: Edinburgh University Press, 2013.
Fabbri, Lorenzo. 'From inoperativeness to action: on Giorgio Agamben's anarchism'. *Radical Philosophy Review* 14.1 (2011): 85–100.
Kropotkin, Peter. *The Conquest of Bread.* Mineola, NY: Dover Publications, 2011.
Scott, James C. *The Art of Not Being Governed: An Anarchist History of Upland Southeast Asia.* New Haven, CT: Yale University Press, 2010.

12

Benjamin and Agamben on Kafka, Judaism and the Law*

Vivian Liska

Despite innumerable interpretations of Kafka's law-related texts – especially 'Before the law', but also his novels *The Trial*, of which the parable is a part, and, to a somewhat lesser extent, *The Castle* as well as stories such as 'In the penal colony', 'The new advocate', 'The question of our laws' – it remains uncertain whether the law in his work is to be understood in primarily juridical, social and political, or in metaphysical, theological, and religious terms. This uncertainty has elicited numerous, sometimes contradictory interpretations and has inspired often opposing notions of justice and the relationship between law and violence.

The two systems most often identified with Kafka's concern with the law are the juridical apparatus of the modern state, on the one hand, and the Jewish tradition, on the other. Most interpretations of Kafka's stories involving the law opt for one of these perspectives. In the first case, where the law in Kafka is regarded solely in secular terms – the common practice in recent readings by 'law and literature' scholars – Kafka is depicted either as a critic of the juridical systems of his time[1] or as an author who prefigures the present situation and can provide insights into the shortcomings of contemporary jurisprudential procedures.[2] In contrast, readings of Kafka's legal narratives that invoke the Jewish tradition generally equate the law with divine judgement and its inaccessibility, that is with the Jewish idea of God as an all-powerful but remote Other of man. In both cases, these approaches disregard the possibility that Kafka deliberately left open the question of whether the law is to be understood in secular or religious terms. Occasionally, these two realms have been brought together, sometimes to the point of identifying them, as in Carl Schmitt's idea that all juridical and political instances are transpositions of religious ones.[3] In such cases, the common denominator underlying both state law and Jewish law is the idea of an all-powerful, almighty sovereign. Kafka's narrative writings confirm the plight of the human condition of being ruled by an unattainable and powerful sovereign who is the author of the law. When the law – whether state law or theological imperative – is thus seen as oppressive, Kafka's narratives are regarded as the ultimate description of a terrifying law-ruled world and have come to embody the potential of literature to unmask the possibility of reaching justice through the law as an illusion and to condemn the inaccessible sovereign power ruling over man.

Walter Benjamin succinctly writes that it cannot be decided whether Kafka's work 'is … devoted to raising the law up high, or to burying it'. He contends that 'Kafka has no answer to these questions' ('*Ist es der Hebung oder dem Verscharren des Gesetzes gewidmet? Auf diese Fragen hat Kafka, so meine ich, keine Antwort gehabt*', BS 160/CS 128, translation modified). It is indeed difficult to make out whether in Kafka's world the obstacle to justice is that the law is omnipresent or that it is distorted (*entstellt*), compromised and crippled to a point that makes it indistinguishable from lawlessness. It is even more difficult to derive a possible alternative to the dismal state of the world depicted in Kafka's stories. It could indeed be said that Kafka's parable 'Before the law' and his other writings dealing primarily with the law depict a world in which the law is both inaccessible and omnipresent, boundless and without limitations, entering the most minute and private levels of human existence, and at the same time, paradoxically, lacking its primary function: the marking of distinctions and divisions that would instate a moral and just social order in the world. Kafka's world order is one that muddles all borders and limits. In his novel *The Castle* the law is everywhere and nowhere, everyone belongs to the system of the rulers, yet everyone is also terrorized by it: the magistrates receive their plaintiffs in bars and bedrooms and the protagonist K. becomes entangled in an inscrutable network spun by the rulers of this world that exhausts him to death. Similarly, in *The Trial*, the law is inscrutable, the actual court cannot be found or is located in dark attics, the law books turn out to be pornographic booklets, the judges and lawyers are either invisible or fake, yet the effect of their authority is lethal. That the law is 'out of joint' in the world of Kafka's narratives is beyond question. The consequences of this state of affairs, however, have been interpreted in different and often contradictory ways. In what follows I shall contrast two important interpretations of Kafka's relation to the law, one by the contemporary Italian philosopher Giorgio Agamben in dialogue with the French philosopher Jacques Derrida, and the other by the German-Jewish thinker Walter Benjamin in dialogue with his friend, the historian of Kabbalah Gershom Scholem. Both Agamben and Benjamin consider the law in Kafka's writings in religious as well as in secular terms, but they come to radically different conclusions concerning Judaism, Kafka, and the law. While Agamben combines a political perspective with a theological one, Benjamin is concerned with the political dimension, but rejects theological interpretations of the kind that refer to a transcendental realm and instead invokes the Jewish *juridical* tradition. While Agamben equates state law and Jewish law, Benjamin distinguishes between them. These differences are particularly significant in the context of the topic of Jews and justice.

Giorgio Agamben and the fulfilment of the law

Giorgio Agamben is one of the most radical critics of the legal and political state of our times. He proclaims more forcefully than any other thinker today that sovereign tyranny holds the world in the thrall of an all-pervasive domination. With his concepts such as the '*homo sacer*' (the individual exposed to arbitrary exertions of power) and 'naked life' (which is life subjected to bio-political violence) and an oppressive 'state of exception' that 'has become the rule' he configures a diagnosis of today's world that could not be bleaker. He lets the wretchedness of the present swell before our eyes to the point where only an all-redeeming interruption of the course of events could come to the rescue of our planet. Attempting to thwart the perpetuation of the dismal state of the world, Agamben invokes Walter Benjamin's messianism and, in this context, his readings of Kafka. Yet there are major differences between Agamben's and Benjamin's respective interpretations of Kafka's approach to the law.

In his letter to Gershom Scholem dated September 15, 1934, Walter Benjamin calls his writings about Kafka the 'crossroad of the paths of my thinking' ('*Kreuzweg der Wege meines Denkens*', BS 172/CS 139, translation modified). The same can be said about Kafka's place in Agamben's work, though in his case 'crossroad' would not only signify the point where roads leading in opposite directions intersect, but also, literally, the last road taken by the Christian redeemer on his way to the cross. In his interpretations of Kafka's stories Agamben sets himself apart from – and often explicitly argues against – the readings of several of his precursors, foremost among them Jacques Derrida, and claims to adopt Benjamin's exegeses of the Prague author's work. In the process, however, Agamben, shifts Benjamin's stance in a Christian direction, and turns both Benjamin and Kafka into devotees of the apostle Paul.

In his book *State of Exception* Agamben delineates two aspects of Kafka's work that he deems most important: on the one hand, a critical diagnosis of the dismal state of the world in which an oppressive law has become ubiquitous and, on the other, a revelation of a suggestion of hidden possibilities leading to a reversal of these conditions. Agamben finds in Kafka's work the most precise account of life subjected to an oppressive law; simultaneously, he derives the significance of Kafka's figures in their respective strategies of deactivating 'the spectral forms the law takes' in what, quoting Benjamin, he calls the negative 'state of exception' (*SE* 64). The 'state of exception' is a situation in which a powerful sovereign has suspended the existing laws, and instead extends his own power and dominion to every aspect of the life of his subjects by arbitrarily imposing his own rule. In his interpretations of Kafka's parable 'Before the law', but also in his reading of 'In the penal colony' and in numerous other references to Kafka's stories, Agamben illustrates his idea of the oppressive 'state of exception' as well as the messianic reversal of this state. While the state of exception proclaimed by the sovereign spills over into every domain of life and subjugates the entire planet under an arbitrary and oppressive law, the messianic reversal of this situation would abolish the law and release life into a new freedom. Only when life has absorbed the law to the point of annihilating it – an absorption that corresponds to the law's final fulfilment – instead of letting the law rule over life, will humanity be redeemed.

Agamben's anarchist and antinomian reading recognizes an idiosyncrasy in the endings of Kafka's parables, which, as he maintains in *Homo Sacer*, 'offer the possibility of an about-face that completely upsets their meaning' (*HS* 58). Agamben's readings focus on these disturbing endings. It is, in his view, the place where the suspension of the Law succeeds in undoing the power of the ban. For Agamben, again quoting Benjamin, the state of exception is paradigmatically exemplified in 'the life that is lived in the village at the foot of the hill' described in Kafka's novel *The Castle* (*HS* 53). Redemption, for Agamben, is the reversal of this situation as it fulfils and thereby definitively dissolves the laws of the invisible, powerful rulers. The most compelling example of such a reversal in which the force of the law is abolished, occurs in Agamben's reading of Kafka's parable 'Before the law'.[4]

He perceives in Kafka's parable a perfect representation of the structure of the sovereign action of an oppressive, omnipresent law. The situation of the man from the country, who is kept from entering through the door of the law by a doorkeeper, embodies for Agamben the purest form of the law's tyrannical power that has 'lost its significance but continues to be in force' (*PO* 169; cf. also *HS* 50–1, translation modified). In his reading, the open door that cannot be entered points to the world in a state of exception. No decree forbids the man's access to the law, but he is literally held in a ban, which simultaneously includes and excludes him: neither does it accord him access to the law, nor can he turn away from it. In contrast to traditional interpretations that see the situation of the man from the country as a failure because he waits in vain before the door of the law until the doorkeeper pronounces 'Now I will go and close it' ('*Ich gehe jetzt und schliesse ihn*', qtd in *PO* 174; cf. also *HS* 55), Agamben sees the closing of the door as a positive event and understands the country man's 'entire behavior' as nothing but a 'complicated and patient strategy to have the door closed in order to interrupt the Law's being in force' (*PO* 174; cf. also *HS* 55).

With this surprising reading of Kafka's parable, Agamben explicitly counters Derrida's interpretation of the parable as an endless, but positive waiting, and an ongoing negotiation with the representatives of the law. Agamben rejects this vision, which he considers to be inspired by the Jewish tradition of a 'life lived in deferral and delay' (*PO* 166). In Derrida's interpretation, the confrontation between narrative and the law leads to a mutual intermingling between the two that creates an undecidability concerning their respective status. This impossibility to decide is embodied by the man from the country who, in waiting before the entrance to the law, in Derrida's words, 'decides to put off deciding'.[5] In the constitutive inability to reach closure, which stands at the core of Derrida's reading and his understanding of the impact of literature and narration, Agamben recognizes a stance that partakes of our prevailing condition 'of a petrified or paralyzed messianism' (*PO* 171). Derrida's stance contrasts with the provocation of Agamben's man from the country that leads to the closing of the door: for Agamben, Kafka's man from the country is a Christ figure who, as it is said in the gospels, fulfils the law in what is called *pleroma*, fullness, and thereby ends its oppressive effects, bringing about the inversion of the negative state of exception into a state of freedom.

Agamben speaks explicitly of a strategy – a calculated goal – with regard to the man from the country, a strategy aimed at closing the door and suspending the law. Agamben's statement of allegiance to Benjamin notwithstanding, such a calculated design must be contrasted with the latter's idea of eliciting a positive reversal of the world's present state. The figure in Benjamin's most explicitly messianic text, the 'Theological-Political Fragment', in which 'messianic intensity' (*messianische Intensität*) and the 'dynamis of the profane' (*Dynamis des Profanen*) (*GS* 2.1:203/ *SW* 3:305, translation modified) take on the guise of two parallel arrows pointing in opposite directions while propelling one another forward, does not envision such a directed deactivation of the law. No profaning abrogation of the law is required to bring about the divine kingdom, but rather the profane and earthly pursuit of human happiness and justice. Instead, in his interpretation, Agamben emphasizes the destructive impulse and approves of the heretical Messiah Shabbetai Zevi, for whom 'overstepping the torah [is] its fulfillment' and 'fulfilling the torah its banishment from memory' (*PO* 167–8). Turning Kafka's narrative into a modern gospel – and assigning to the narrative aspect of Kafka's parable nothing but the function of illustrating a theological-political doctrine – Agamben conflates state law with Jewish law and Paul's proclamation of the demise of the Jewish law with his own anarchist therapeutic concept for our planet.

How exactly the man from the country succeeds in getting the doorkeeper to shut the door to the law remains a question. It cannot be ascertained what – and whether anything – has occurred 'before the law' at all. Agamben's final sentence in his reading of Kafka's story provides a possible answer, when he claims that in Kafka's parable 'something has really happened in seeming not to happen'; with these words he directly and explicitly contradicts Derrida's conclusion that Kafka's parable is 'an event that succeeds in not happening ... an event that happens not to happen' (*PO* 174; cf. also *HS* 56).[6] For Derrida, the 'success' lies in the man's staying before the law, in not actually entering it. For him, entering the law rather than, say, commenting on it or studying it from some distance, would presuppose that there is such a thing as an actual *fulfilment* of the law. Indeed, Agamben's notion of the messianic task of fulfilling the law by abrogating it, assumes the possibility – and task – carried out by Christ who was said to have enacted the fulfilment of the law once and for all, a notion that is omnipresent in Christian theology and absent from the Jewish idea of justice. Furthermore, in contradistinction to the Jewish concept of messianic time as a change that would be a public event apparent to all, Agamben seems to point to Paul's gesture of revelation of something that has already happened but is not yet visible. Finally, the shimmer of light, however faint, that in Kafka's story shines through the door of the law before the man's death and has repeatedly been interpreted as the rays of the Shekhinah, the divine glory emanating from the Torah,[7] remains unmentioned in Agamben's interpretation and does not seem to play a part in this task. As we shall see, Benjamin has a very different idea of Jews and justice in mind when he reads the relation of Kafka's narrative to the law.

Walter Benjamin: Halachah and Haggadah

Agamben introduces his reading of Kafka's 'Before the law' with a claim that he is interpreting the parable 'from the perspective ... of Benjamin's conception of messianic law' (*PO* 172). Benjamin himself does not give an elaborate interpretation of the parable and merely speaks of 'the cloudy spot' (*wolkige Stelle*) at its core that lends itself to infinite reflections (*GS* 2.2:420/*SW* 2:802). In his notes for a letter to Gershom Scholem, Benjamin even calls the law the 'blind spot' (*toter Punkt*) in Kafka's oeuvre (*GS* 2.3:1245). However, Benjamin's elaborations on Kafka in his important essay 'Franz Kafka. For the Tenth Anniversary of his Death' as well as in his exchange about the Prague author in his correspondence with Scholem, deal extensively with questions of the law. In these writings, Benjamin holds very different views on Kafka, Jews and justice from Agamben's Pauline reading. There are undoubtedly similarities between the perspectives of Agamben and Benjamin on the secular legal system. Like Agamben, Benjamin considers state laws inherently to be instruments of abusive sovereignty. In his essay 'Critique of Violence', he points out their mythical nature and in his writings on Kafka shows how the legal system exerts its violent power wantonly everywhere, infiltrating itself into the most personal and intimate realms of existence. Like Agamben, Benjamin sees Kafka's novels *The Trial* and even more so *The Castle* as poignant illustrations of a world where obscure legal instances inflict arbitrary, opaque and repressive regulations on individuals who remain ignorant of the laws to which they are subjected. For Benjamin the dismal world of Kafka's novels is one of unregulated, 'global promiscuity', the lowest stage of human existence. Benjamin calls this world a pre-historic swamp world (*Sumpfwelt*, GS 2.3: 1236) in which everyone is guilty and everyone is a victim of the law as well; it is, above all, 'a world that renders impossible any discriminating between right and wrong'; the world depicted by Kafka is instead constituted 'by the very impossibility of a clear decision', an impossibility which, as Rodolphe Gasché succinctly writes, 'perpetuates the order of wrong (*Unrecht*) thus also excluding the very possibility of justice'.[8]

In his essay 'Building the Wall of China' ('*Beim Bau der Chinesischen Mauer*') Benjamin shows how life in Kafka's novels is characterized paradoxically by the simultaneity of an omnipresent law and absolute lawlessness. Unlike for Agamben, this lawlessness is equally if not more responsible for the terror of Kafka's world than the tyranny of the law. It is in terms of utter lawlessness that Benjamin describes life in the village in Kafka's *The Castle*:

> Even the people in power are so lawless that they appear on the same level as those at the bottom of the pile; without any distinctions (*Scheidewände*) creatures of all realms teem together (*wimmeln durcheinander*) indiscriminately and the one and only bond that secretly unites them is a feeling of utter anxiety. (*GS* 2.2:681/ *SW* 2:498, translation modified)

This lawlessness, Benjamin writes, is a process of development. Benjamin elaborates on this development most explicitly in his outline for an essay he never wrote, '*Versuch eines Schemas zu Kafka*'. This one page text sketches a miniature theory of history and civilization. It describes the world in Kafka's novels as the pre-historical swamp world, which, Benjamin writes:

> Kafka, in his books, confronts with the lawful one of Judaism ... Its purity and dietary laws display the defense mechanisms against this [swamp] world ... In other words, only the Halachah still [ex negativo] contains traces of this [prehistoric] mode of existence of mankind that is long past.

> *Kafka in seinen Büchern mit der gesetzlichen des Judentums konfrontiert ... Die Reinigungs-und Speisegesetze beziehen sich auf eine Vorwelt, von der nichts mehr erhalten ist als diese Abwehrmaßnahmen gegen sie. Mit anderen Worten: nur die Halacha enthält noch Spuren dieser fernsten Daseinsart der Menschheit.* (*GS* 2.3:1192).

'Kafka's books', Benjamin continues, 'contain the missing Haggadah [the narrative component of the Talmud] to this Halachah [its legal aspect] … Intertwined with this Haggadic text is the prophetic dimension in his books' (*Kafkas Bücher enthalten die fehlende Hagada zu dieser Halacha. / Aufs innigste verschränkt aber mit diesem hagadischen Text enthalten seine Bücher einen prophetischen, GS* 2.3:1192).The world as it presents itself in *The Trial* and in *The Castle*, this world without distinctions and divisions, without boundaries and order, is thus both a pre-historical *Vorwelt*, and prophetically announces the return of this oppressive lawlessness in the present. Benjamin writes: 'Kafka's novels play in a swamp world. But then, this world is also our world; because we have not overcome it, only repressed and forgotten it' (*Kafkas Romane spielen in einer Sumpfwelt. Aber diese Welt ist dann auch wieder die unsere: eben darum, weil wir sie nicht bewältigt, sondern nur verdrängt und vergessen haben, GS* 2.3:1236). The lawless world of pre-history depicted by Kafka is, for Benjamin, also the index of his own present: writing as a Jew in the 1930s, Benjamin describes the legal system of his own times by way of his characterization of Kafka's swamp world in which the laws, far from ordering life, intrude into the whole of everyday life and become identical with the ultimate lawlessness reigning in an oppressive 'state of exception'.

So far, this description of the workings of state law does not seem to vary much from Agamben's view, but the major difference is that, for Benjamin, this pre-historic – as well as present – state, in which the law is 'bastardized' with lawlessness and in which all boundaries are undone is contrasted to – rather than, as in Agamben, identified with – Judaism. For Benjamin, revealed law instituted the possibility of justice. And it is only 'justice that serves as the point of departure for [Kafka's] critique of myth' (*GS* 2.2:437/*SW* 2:815). The defence against a world without boundaries, separations and distinctions would thus, for Benjamin, be Jewish law itself: not only is it distinguished from an oppressive state law-ruled by sheer power; it is – or rather would be – its antidote. In a letter to Scholem from August 11, 1934, Benjamin writes: 'Indeed, if we follow Kafka's presentation, the work of the Torah has been thwarted' (*'Das Werk der Thora nämlich ist – wenn wir uns an Kafkas Darstellung halten – vereitelt worden'*) (*BS* 167/*CS* 135, translation modified). In his preparations for this letter, Benjamin added: 'And everything that Moses once accomplished, would have to be made up for in our epoch of the world' (*'Und alles, was einst von Moses geleistet wurde, wäre in userm Weltzeitalter nachzuholen', GS* 2.3:1246).

In this surprising defence of Jewish law Benjamin differs from Agamben in opposing the mythical lawless world of both pre-history and modernity depicted by Kafka to the Halachic Jewish world. But Benjamin also makes sure to distinguish his reflections on Kafka's Halachic dimension from Jewish *theological* readings. In his outline for the unwritten essay he states: '[Kafka's] prophesy for his immediate future' – which is the state of the world in Benjamin's time itself – 'is much more important for Kafka than the Jewish *Theologumena*, which one only wanted to find in his work. The punishment [the return of the swamp world] is more important than the one who punishes. The prophesy is more important than God' (*[Kafkas] Prophetie auf eine allernächste Zukunft ist für Kafka weit wichtiger als die jüdischen Theologumena, die man allein in seinem Werk hat finden wollen. … Die Prophetie ist wichtiger als Gott', GS*

2.3:1192; emphasis added). Undoubtedly, Benjamin had Max Brod in mind, whom he elsewhere criticized heavily with respect to his Jewish theological reading of Kafka. But this comment may also be addressed to his main interlocutor in matters of Kafka, Gershom Scholem, although Scholem's theology, based on the Kabbalah, is fundamentally different from Brod's.[9]

Between 1925 and 1938 Benjamin and Scholem exchanged a stream of letters about Kafka's work that can count among its most profound interpretations.[10] In the course of their exchange, important dissonances between the two friends come to the fore (cf. BS 168–70/CS 136–8). These differences concern the role of theology in interpreting Kafka, the importance and nature of the law in Kafka's work, and the understanding of Halachah and Haggadah in this context. Encompassing all these differences is a dissimilar outlook on justice and the Jewish tradition. Surprisingly, Scholem, who is generally considered to be the more 'Jewish' thinker of the two, is further removed than Benjamin from certain core aspects of the Jewish tradition. Less surprisingly, what interests Benjamin more than Scholem are aspects of this tradition that relate to the human, more precisely the political, rather than the divine realm.

Benjamin and Scholem disagree on the justification of a theological reading of Kafka. In his reply to Benjamin's account of Kafka's world as a swamp world and its counterpart in the Torah, Scholem writes: 'The *existence* of the secret [Kabbalistic rather than Halachic] law destroys your interpretation: in the pre-historical world there hardly is this chimerical muddle, and certainly not one of the kind that announces its [persistent] existence. *There* you went much too far with the elimination of theology and threw the baby out with the bathwater' ('*Die* Existenz *des geheimen Gesetzes macht deine Interpretation kaputt: es dürfte in einer vormythischen Welt chimärischer Vermischung nicht da sein, ganz zu schweigen von der so besonderen Art, in der es seine Existenz doch ankündigt. Da bist Du mit der Ausschaltung der Theologie viel zu weit gegangen, das Kind mit dem Bade auszuschütten*', BS 154/ CS 123, translation modified). Scholem indeed regards the 'possibility of divine judgment' (*die Möglichkeit des Gottesurteils*) as the sole concern of Kafka's writings (*den einzigen Gegenstand der Kafkaschen Produktion*). Kafka's work, and in particular 'Before the law', is for him the perfect illustration of the 'inverted trace of a disappeared transcendence'. Scholem invokes Kafka as the ultimate witness of a negative theology, in which, in Stéphane Moses' words, 'all we can assert of God is the very fact of his absence'.[11] Kafka, in Scholem's view, still represents 'an instance – borderline to be sure – in the history of revelation':[12] it is – and here Kafka, for Scholem, rejoins the heretic Kabbalists – 'the nothingness of revelation' ('*das Nichts der Offenbarung*') (BS 175/CS 142).[13] While Scholem thinks in theological categories of Kafka's references to the law, Benjamin, though he acknowledges a certain 'shrouded' (*beschattete*; BS 159/CS 128) theological dimension in his own writings, is less interested in *Gott* and more concerned with the ways the Jewish Talmudic tradition, more particularly the interaction between Halachah and Haggadah, provide insights – and a possible alternative – to the dismal world depicted in Kafka's fiction and visible in the realities of Benjamin's time. Rather than seeing a Kabbalistic 'nothingness of revelation', Benjamin instead regards the 'distortion of existence' (*Entstellung des Daseins*) of the 'upcoming [political] legal system'[14] as Kafka's 'fixation' and 'one and only concern'.[15] But Benjamin nevertheless reintroduces the Jewish dimension which he deems necessary for a reading of Kafka by defining this distortion precisely in terms of a world in which the Torah 'has been thwarted' (*BS* 167/*CS* 135).

Scholem and Benjamin also have a different understanding of the Halachah.[16] Unlike Benjamin, who sees it as an antidote to the chaotic medley of the pre-historic – and present – swamp world, Scholem is sceptical of the Halachah in the name of his own views of Kafka as a heretical, antinomian Kabbalist in the tradition of Shabbtai Zevi, the seventeenth-century leader of an antinomian messianic sect. Scholem writes to Benjamin: 'Not, dear Walter, the *absence* [of the revealed law] in a pre-animistic world is the problem, but instead its *impossibility of being fulfilled*' ('*Nicht, lieber Walter, ihre* Abwesenheit *in einer präanimistischen Welt*' [*sondern*] '*ihre* Unvollziehbarkeit *ist das Problem*, *BS* 158/*CS* 126, emphases in the original, translation modified). Scholem comes close to the Pauline view of Agamben when he says of the Halachah: the 'absolutely concrete is the unfulfillable as such' ('*das Absolut-Konkrete [ist] das Unvollziehbare schlechthin*', *BS* 39/*CS* 28, translation modified).[17] This relates to Scholem's view of Kafka who, he believes, 'ceaselessly compares the concrete reality of human existence with the ideal of absolute justice, an ideal that the Jewish tradition, for its part, symbolizes in the image of divine judgment'.[18] In Judaism, however, the ideal of absolute justice, is, like the fulfilment of the law, not of this world. In presupposing the possibility of a fulfilment of the law, Scholem echoes, however faintly, the Pauline argument developed in his 'Epistle to the Romans' that the Jewish law has to be abrogated because it cannot ever be fully lived up to.[19] For Paul, Jewish law is indeed the very source of sinfulness[20]; for him, the coming of Christ and his death on the cross fulfilled the law once and for all and the 'works' – meaning the Mitzvot, the observance of the commandments – have therefore to be suspended and replaced by the interiority of divine grace and love. However, Scholem's antinomianism does not go in this direction. In his interpretation of Kafka as well as in his exchange with Benjamin and elsewhere, Scholem's anarchist impulses remain within the boundaries of Jewish antinomian Kabbalah, and Kafka remains for him a late representative of this tradition.[21]

Benjamin and Scholem also disagree on the meaning and function of the Haggadah. At first, this seems not to be the case in the most precise parallel – and distinction – Benjamin draws between the Haggadah and Kafka's stories: 'Kafka's writings', Benjamin writes in a letter to Scholem on June 12, 1938, 'do not modestly lie at the feet of the doctrine, as the Haggadah lies at the feet of the Halachah. Though apparently reduced to submission, they unexpectedly raise a mighty paw against it' ('*Kafkas Dichtungen sind von Hause aus Gleichnisse. Aber sie legen sich der Lehre nicht schlicht zu Füssen wie sich die Haggada der Halacha zu Füssen legt. Wenn sie sich gekuscht haben, heben sie unversehens eine gewichtige Pranke gegen sie*', *BS* 272/*CS* 225, translation modified). Scholem regards this passage as a confirmation of his own view of Kafka's antinomian attitude. While Benjamin's image could indeed be read in this way, Scholem's interpretation misses the nuances of the gesture described by Benjamin. Scholem indeed has a point when he objects to Benjamin that 'the antinomian nature of the Haggadic that you mention, is not a characteristic of Kafka's Haggadah alone, it is inherent in the nature of the Haggadic as such' ('*die Antinomie des Haggadischen, die du erwähnst, keine der kafkaschen Haggada alleine [ist], sie gründet eher in der Natur des Haggadischen selber*, BS 286/CS 236, translation modified). He is, however, only partly right: not only is Benjamin's image of the raised paw – as I will show – not truly antinomian, but also not all Haggadot relate to the Halachah in this way. Moshe Halbertal distinguishes between three different paradigms for the relationship between Haggadah and Halachah: 'The first and simplest', he writes, 'is when the narrative provides a basis for the law'; the second 'emphasizes the way in which the story permits a transition to a different sort of legal knowledge' and 'allows us to see how the law must be followed [as] we move from "knowing that" to "knowing how"'; it is only the third paradigm, which Halbertal calls 'the most delicate', that corresponds to Benjamin's description of the relation between Haggadah and Halachah. In this third paradigm, Halbertal writes, 'the story actually has a subversive role, pointing out the law's substantive limitations'.[22] This last paradigm is certainly the one to which Benjamin's saying about Kafka's Haggadic dimension applies, but it is crucial to distinguish this idea of subversion from an antinomian approach to the Halachah.

A closer look at the distinction Benjamin makes between Kafka's stories and the Haggadah reveals that it is far from antinomian. What is implied in Benjamin's strange image of the 'mighty paw' raised against the Halacha? It evokes the manifestation of a creaturely presence, a gesture of threat and a motion of halting off. In order to better understand the implications of this image one has to go back to Benjamin's essay 'Franz Kafka: Building the Wall of China', where he elaborates on the analogy between Kafka's writings and the Haggadah. In a passage immediately following his diagnosis of 'Kafka's fixation on the sole topic of his work – namely the distortion of existence' ('*Die Fixierung Kafkas an diesen seinen einen und einzigen Gegenstand, die Entstellung des Daseins*') – Benjamin explains that Kafka's prose resembles the Haggadah in what may 'appear to the reader like obsessiveness' ('*kann beim Leser den Eindruck der Verstocktheit hervorrufen*'), a mode of writing that exceeds any morality that could be drawn from it. Speaking of Kafka, Benjamin writes:

> We may remind ourselves here of the form of the Haggadah, the name Jews have given to the rabbinical stories and anecdotes that serve to explicate and confirm the teachings – the Halachah. Like the Haggadic, the narrative parts of the Talmud, [Kafka's] books too, are stories; they are a Haggadah that constantly pauses, luxuriating in the most detailed descriptions, in the simultaneous *hope and fear* that it might encounter the Halachic order, the doctrine itself, en route. (*Man hat hier an die Form der Haggadah zu erinnern: so heißen bei den Juden Geschichten und Anekdoten des rabbinischen Schrifttums, die der Erklärung und Bestätigung der Lehre – der Halacha – dienen. Wie die haggadischen Teile des Talmud so sind auch diese Bücher Erzählungen, eine Haggadah, die immerfort innehält, in den ausführlichsten Beschreibungen sich verweilt, immer in der Hoffnung und Angst zugleich, die halachische Order und Formel, die Lehre könnte ihr unterwegs zustoßen.*) (*GS* 2.2:678–9/*SW* 2:496; emphasis added)

Benjamin calls this hesitation, the ambivalence between hope and fear of encountering the law, 'deferral' or 'postponement' (*Verzögerung*), a term that, with a slight shift, could perfectly fit the waiting of the man at the door of the law. As in these Haggadot,

Benjamin continues, Kafka's parables 'show the true workings of grace' (*'das eigentliche Walten der Gnade'*) in the fact that [in them] 'the law never finds expression as such – this and nothing else is the gracious dispensation of the fragment' (*'Daß das Gesetz als solches bei Kafka sich nirgends ausspricht, das und nichts anderes ist die gnädige Fügung des Fragments'*, GS 2.2:679/ SW 2:497). The Haggadah avoids turning into a Halachah, much like Kafka's parables – or rather anti-parables that don't yield a doctrine or a moral. Just as the mighty paw raised against the Halachah, the Haggadah, is like Kafka's writings in the sense that it both stops short of encountering the law and also limits the law by keeping it from overstepping its boundaries which are set by creaturely, lived life itself. But it is crucial in Benjamin's image that this paw does not crush the Halachah: Its gesture is not to be confounded with antinomian transgression or abolition of a law deemed violent; it corresponds instead to the structure of dynamic interaction between Halachah and Haggadah, between narrative and the law inherent in the Jewish idea of Justice.

Notes

*   Parts of this essay have appeared in '"Before the Law stands a doorkeeper. To this doorkeeper comes a man ..."': Kafka, narrative, and the law', *Naharaim* 6.2 (2013): 175–94.

1   Cf. Theodore Ziolkowski, *The Mirror of Justice: Literary Reflections of Legal Crises* (Princeton, NJ: Princeton University Press, 1997), 224–40. Ziolkowski reads Kafka's work as a paradigmatic exploration of the crisis of the legal system in the early twentieth century, more particularly the debate about the relationship between law and ethics and the confounding of morality with law. Ziolkowski shows how Kafka's exposure to the legal controversies of his time influenced his fictional writings such as the disputes between Pure Law and Free Law and the struggle between the conservative values and antiquated laws of the Habsburg Monarchy and the more modern legal system of the German Empire since 1871. Ziolkowski convincingly shows that *The Trial* parodies the absurd procedures of the Austrian system based on Free Law where actual trials involving the possibility of defence on the part of the accused are a sham and punishment is a direct effect of power. But Ziolkowski shows how Kafka is equally dissatisfied with Wilhemine Germany's Pure Law system of supposedly rigorously rational retribution.

2   Examples of readings of Kafka in the context of Law and Literature Studies include Patrick J. Glen's essay on 'Franz Kafka, Lawrence Joseph and the possibilities of jurisprudential literature' (*Southern California Interdisciplinary Law Journal* 21.1 [2011]: 47–94), in which he insists that Kafka 'can provide a glimpse into the real and sometimes surreal world of actual legal practice' (54) and the necessity to take the multiple perspectives of the participants in legal procedures into account. A similar and equally didactic justification for reading Kafka in the context of jurisdiction is 'Franz Kafka's outsider jurisprudence' by Douglas E. Litowitz (*Law & Social Inquiry* 27 [2002]: 103–37), who emphasizes Kafka's relevance for a better understanding of the outsider who gets involved in legal matters without knowledge of its procedures. In 'Reading Kafka's trial politically: Justice – law – power' (*Contemporary Political Theory* 7 [2008]: 8–30), Graham M. Smith similarly

demonstrates how Kafka's legal narratives depict the modern subjects' anxiety in the face of the laws' inscrutability for common man; Smith focuses on modern man's vain desire for justice and his characters' inability to locate, read or *fix* the Law because, while they desire the order it would provide, they reject the necessary sovereign authority their legitimacy would require. In all these examples the specificity of the literary aspect of Kafka is kept out of the picture.

3   Cf. Carl Schmitt, *Political Theology: Four Chapters on the Concept of Sovereignty*, trans. George D. Schwab (Chicago, IL: University of Chicago Press, 2005).

4   Agamben's interpretation of Kafka's parable constitutes the last part of 'The Messiah and the sovereign' (1992), which is reproduced almost word for word in – and constitutes the backbone of – *Homo Sacer*.

5   Jacques Derrida, 'Before the law', in Derrida, *Acts of Literature*, trans. Avital Ronell and Christine Roulston, ed. Derek Attridge (New York: Routledge, 1992), 195.

6   Derrida writes in 'Before the law' of 'a sort of non-event, an event of nothing or a quasi-event which both calls for and annuls a narrative account' (198).

7   Echoing earlier interpretations, Michel de Certeau speaks of this ray of light as 'that brightness, Kafka's allusion to the Shekhina of God in the Jewish tradition' (Michel de Certeau, *The Mystic Fable: The Sixteenth and Seventeenth Centuries*, trans. Michael B. Smith [Chicago, IL: University of Chicago Press, 1995], 3).

8   Rodolphe Gasché, *The Stelliferous Fold: Toward a Virtual Law of Literature's Self-Formation* (New York: Fordham University Press, 2011), 278–79.

9   This correspondence starts with a letter from Benjamin (from July 12, 1925) in which he conveys to Scholem his admiration of the Prague author: 'Today as ten years ago his short story "Before the law" counts for me as one of the best that exist in the German language' ('*Seine kurze Geschichte "Vor dem Gesetz" gilt mir heute wie vor zehn Jahren für eine der besten, die es im Deutschen gibt*', *GB* 3:64). In a letter from July 17, 1934, Scholem takes strong exception to Benjamin's denial that the law is at the heart of Kafka's work and more particularly to what he deems to be Benjamin's 'strictly profane' understanding of the law.

10 It was Scholem who initially encouraged Benjamin to include a discussion of the 'Halachic and Talmudic reflections as they so pressingly appear in "The Doorkeeper Before the Law"' (*BS* 169/*CS* 137, translation modified) into his essay on Kafka, mainly to please the publisher Schocken whom Scholem had persuaded to invite Benjamin to submit his Kafka essay.

11 Stéphane Mosès, *The Angel of History. Rosenzweig, Benjamin, Scholem*, trans. Barbara Harshav (Stanford, CA: Stanford University Press, 2009), 145.

12 Mosès, *The Angel of History*, 145.

13 Letter of September 20, 1934. Stéphane Mosès writes that for Scholem, 'the law, in the trial appears as a parody of itself: there are tribunals seated in dark attics, penal codes concealing pornographic booklets, judges who do not judge, lawyers who no longer believe in the law, police and hangmen who resemble mediocre provincial actors. This arcane and unfathomable justice' is, Moses concludes, 'the reverse image of divine justice and the perfect representation of Scholem's negative theology' (Mosès, *The Angel of History*, 157).

14 Benjamin speaks here of the prophetic aspect of Kafka's 'Haggadic' writing, '[t]he precisely registered oddities that abound in the life it deals with must be regarded by the reader as no more than the little signs, portents, and symptoms of the displacements that the writer feels approaching in every aspect of life without being able to adjust to the new situation' ('*Die überaus präzisen Seltsamkeiten, von denen*

das Leben, mit dem es zu tun hat, so voll ist, sind für den Leser nur als kleine Zeichen, Anzeichen und Symptome von Verschiebungen zu verstehen, die der Dichter in allen Verhältnissen sich anbahnen fühlt, ohne den neuen Ordnungen sich selber einfügen zu können'). That which most explicitly refers to Kafka's vision of the situation that will become a reality in Benjamin's time is his insistence on 'the almost incomprehensible distortions of existence that betray the emergence of these new laws' (*'die fast unverständlichen Entstellungen des Daseins ... die das Heraufkommen dieser Gesetze verraten'*, GS 2.2:678/SW 2:496).

15 'Kafka's fixation on the sole topic of his work – namely the distortion of existence – may appear to the reader like obsessiveness' (*'Die Fixierung Kafkas an diesen seinen einen und einzigen Gegenstand, die Entstellung des Daseins, kann beim Leser den Eindruck der Verstocktheit hervorrufen'*, GS 2.2: 678/SW 2:496). It is interesting that Benjamin uses the word *'Verstocktheit'* when describing the aspect of Kafka's writings that reminds the reader of the Haggadah. It is the word that has been used at least since Luther to discredit the Jews who refuse to see the truth of Christ.

16 Cf. Benjamin's letter of July 20, 1934, BS 159–62/CS 128–30, and the editors' notes of the *Gesammelte Briefe*, GB 4: 462–5.

17 Quoted by Benjamin in his letter to Scholem February 28, 1933: *'Ist doch das Absolut-Konkrete das Unvollziehbare schlechtin'.*

18 Mosès, *The Angel of History*, 154.

19 In his letter of July 17, 1934, Scholem accuses Benjamin of 'regarding the law only from its most *profane* perspective' (*'die Terminologie des Gesetzes, die Du so hartnäckig nur von ihrer* profansten *Seite aus zu betrachten Dich versteifst'*), and continues: 'the *moral world of the Halacha* and its abysses and dialectic must have been obvious to you' (*'Die moralische Welt der Halacha und deren Abgründe und Dialektik lagen Dir doch offenbar vor Augen'*) (BS 158/CS 127, emphases in the original, translation modified). Scholem believes that Benjamin's interpretation of the Halachah indeed lacks a theological dimension and disregards the 'abysses and dialectic' of the impossibility of the Halachah to be fulfilled.

20 'What shall we say, then? Is the law sin? Certainly not! Indeed I would not have known what sin was except through the law', Rom. 7:7.

21 In some respects Scholem's view is clearly distinct from Agamben's – and Paul's: while considering the revealed law to be unfulfillable, he obviously rejects the notion that Christ did fulfil the law. In his letter of August 1, 1931, he compares Kafka's writings to 'the moral reflections of a Halachist who tried putting into language a paraphrase of divine judgment' (*'die moralische Reflexion eines Halachisten ..., der die* sprachliche *Paraphrase eines Gottesurteils versuchen wollte'*). But he adds: 'Here, for once, a world is put into words, in which redemption cannot be assumed. Go and explain this to the Gentiles!' (*'Hier ist einmal die Welt zur Sprache gebracht, in der Erlösung nicht vorweggenommen werden kann – geh hin und mache das den Gojim klar!'*, quoted in Gershom Scholem, *Walter Benjamin – die Geschichte einer Freundschaft* [Frankfurt a.M.: Suhrkamp, 1975], 213, emphasis in the original). For Scholem the impossibility of fulfilling the Halachah is part of his negative theology.

22 Moshe Halbertal, 'At the threshold of forgiveness: A study of law and narrative in the Talmud', *Jewish Review of Books* 7 (Fall 2011): 34.

Works cited

de Certeau, Michel. *The Mystic Fable: The Sixteenth and Seventeenth Centuries*. Translated by Michael B. Smith. Chicago, IL: University of Chicago Press, 1995.

Derrida, Jacques. 'Before the law'. In Jacques Derrida, *Acts of Literature*. Translated by Avital Ronell and Christine Roulston. Edited by Derek Attridge. New York: Routledge, 1992, 181–220.

Gasché, Rodolphe. *The Stelliferous Fold: Toward a Virtual Law of Literature's Self-Formation*. New York: Fordham University Press, 2011.

Glen, Patrick J. 'Franz Kafka, Lawrence Joseph and the possibilities of jurisprudential literature'. *Southern California Interdisciplinary Law Journal* 21.1 (2011): 47–94.

Halbertal, Moshe. 'At the threshold of forgiveness: a study of law and narrative in the Talmud'. *Jewish Review of Books* 7 (Fall 2011): 33–4.

Litowitz, Douglas E. 'Franz Kafka's outsider jurisprudence'. *Law & Social Inquiry* 27 (2002): 103–37.

Mosès, Stéphane. *The Angel of History. Rosenzweig, Benjamin, Scholem*. Translated by Barbara Harshav. Stanford, CA: Stanford University Press, 2009.

Schmitt, Carl. *Political Theology: Four Chapters on the Concept of Sovereignty*. Translated by George D. Schwab. Chicago, IL: University of Chicago Press, 2005.

Scholem, Gershom. *Walter Benjamin – die Geschichte einer Freundschaft*. Frankfurt a.M.: Suhrkamp, 1975.

Smith, Graham M. 'Reading Kafka's Trial politically: Justice – law – power'. *Contemporary Political Theory* 7 (2008): 8–30.

Ziolkowski, Theodore. *The Mirror of Justice: Literary Reflections of Legal Crises*. Princeton, NJ: Princeton University Press, 1997.

13

Expropriated Experience: Agamben Reading Benjamin, Reading Kant

Alex Murray

Recent discussions of Giorgio Agamben's engagement with Immanuel Kant have tended to focus on the critique of Kantian moral philosophy put forward in *Homo Sacer: Sovereign Power and Bare Life* (1995). In reconstructing Agamben's relationship to both Benjamin and Kant, scholarship has remained largely silent on the broader place of Kant in Agamben's project. While Agamben has revisited Kant in *Opus Dei* (2012) to provide arguably his most fulsome critique to date, this essay sets out to sketch the ways in which Agamben's earlier work from the 1970s, *Stanzas: Word and Phantasm in Western Culture* (1977) and 'Infancy and history: An essay on the destruction of experience' (1978), undertake nothing less than a revision of Kant's project, focusing on 'critique' and experience respectively. Both of these tasks are aligned explicitly with Benjamin and this essay will reconstruct the contours of that early attempt to salvage through Benjamin an idea of the experience of language that would provide an overcoming of the Kantian division between the 'transcendental subject' and the 'empirical I'. This reading offers a chance to pause over the relationship between Agamben's early and later readings of Benjamin, calling into question the ruptures and continuities in Agamben's response to the Kantian settlement.

Agamben and Kant

Surveying the reception of Agamben's work reveals that Kant is usually neglected as a foundational thinker in the development of Agamben's project. The works of Benjamin and Heidegger are clearly important, but it is usually taken as given, and therefore under-examined, that all of Agamben's work has been an attempt to work through various aporias and tensions in post-Kantian thought. Agamben's first book, *The Man Without Content* (1970), inaugurated a dialogue with Kant to which Agamben has returned throughout his work. In that early work Agamben aligns himself with Nietzsche's critique of Kantian aesthetics. In the *Critique of Judgement* (1790) Kant famously attempted to develop a series of criteria and categories for reflective judgement. The 'subjective universal' judgements of the Sublime and the Beautiful have been widely understood to be attempts to reconcile some of the tensions that emerged around questions of moral law in the *Critique of Practical Reason* (1788). In order to avoid the possibility of subjective illusion Kant develops the *sensus communis*, a '*public* sense' of the beautiful and the good to anchor judgement:

> a faculty of judging which in its reflective act takes account (*a priori*) of the mode of representation of everyone else, in order, *as it were*, to weigh its judgement with the collective reason of mankind, and thereby avoid the illusion arising from subjective and personal conditions which could readily be taken for objective, and illusion that would exert a prejudicial influence upon its judgment.[1]

Agamben's early critique of Kant is based upon his rejection of two central tenets of Kantian aesthetics, namely the disinterestedness of beauty and the elevation of the spectator (as *sensus communis*) rather than the artist as the centre of aesthetic judgement. Agamben's first book explores, following Nietzsche, the nihilism of art in modernity by examining the powerful, solipsistic, passionate interest in art from the perspective of the artist. This early rejection of Kant is, arguably, not a particularly original or radical one; it sees Kant's critical project as the foundation of modern thought, but one whose idealism is wholly unsuited to the conditions of modernity. In the final chapter of *The Man Without Content*, 'The melancholy angel', Agamben invokes the Benjaminian 'angel of history' to develop its aesthetic parallel, the 'angel of art', for which his visual model is Dürer's *Melancholia*. Whereas Benjamin's angel is driven forward by the storm of progress, the angel of art is 'immersed in an atemporal dimension, as though something, interrupting the continuum of history, had frozen the surrounding reality in a kind of messianic arrest' (*MC* 109–10). It is the first appearance of the messianic in Agamben's body of work, and the first time that he draws on Benjamin in offering a formulation of an aesthetic inoperativity. In opposition to the Kantian *sensus communis*, Agamben offers the isolated individual whose alienation refuses the principle of collective judgement that could ground both a universal art and morality. In short, he pits Benjamin against Kant from the very beginning of his corpus.

By far the greatest concentration of secondary criticism on Agamben and Kant has been concerned with the ways in which Kant is presented in *Homo Sacer: Sovereign Power and Bare Life*. Here Agamben suggests that the pure form of law in Kant, in 'being in force without significance', resembles what will become the 'state of exception' that has been key in the development of modern political nihilism. Daniel McLoughlin has suggested that this claim has been too often passed over; to accuse Kantian Moral Law of inaugurating modern nihilism is striking and tendentious. But for McLoughlin Agamben identified in Kant 'the first time in which the indeterminate ground of the normative form is brought to light'.[2] In opposition to that 'imperfect nihilism', Agamben pits Walter Benjamin's 'messianic nihilism that nullifies even the Nothing and lets no form of law remain in force beyond its own content' (*HS* 53). This messianic nihilism arguably underpins Benjamin's 'Critique of Violence' and Adam Kotsko has gone as far as suggesting that that essay supplies the 'basic structure' of the *Homo Sacer* project.[3]

There are a few comments to be made here about the differences between

Agamben's Kant in *The Man Without Content* and in *Homo Sacer*. That earlier work on aesthetics seems to uphold the rather uncontroversial epistemological break ushered in by Kant, whereas the *Homo Sacer* project has been marked by an attempt to challenge epistemological breaks, shifts and ruptures by examining certain juridical, political and governmental categories (*oikonomia*, bare life, state of exception) across seemingly irreconcilable historical divides. In the later project Kant will appear as a moment at which tensions existing within the structure of the Western political tradition are brought to light, rather than instantiated. In the two works that I will be examining here in more detail there is a return to Kant's thought as the instantiation of a modern crisis of experience, yet now that crisis has been understood in a much more fundamental, structural sense. Agamben will now turn to language as the foundation for his future philosophical project.

The island of truth

Published some seven years after *The Man Without Content*, *Stanzas: Word and Phantasm in Western Culture* (1977) arguably marked a shift in Agamben's work, and the moment at which the influence of Walter Benjamin became far more pronounced. The product of a period of sustained research at the Warburg Institute in London, the book signalled a methodological development in Agamben's work. The introduction is a dense exploration of precisely what 'Criticism' as a concept means. Agamben introduces criticism as marked by an historical paradox: 'when the term "criticism" appears in the vocabulary of Western philosophy, it signifies rather inquiry at the limits of knowledge about that which can neither be posed nor grasped' (*S* xv). The limit-point of knowledge here is Kant's, and in *Stanzas* it will be phantasy and language that lie just beyond the critical project. From the very outset then, *Stanzas* is framed – obliquely – contra Kant:

> If criticism, insofar as it traces the limits of truth, offers a glance of 'truth's homeland' like 'an island nature has enclosed within immutable boundaries', it must also remain open to the fascination of the 'wide and storm-tossed sea' that draws 'the sailor incessantly toward adventures he knows not how to refuse yet may never bring to an end'. (*S* xv)

The embedded quotations here are all taken from the third chapter of the 'Transcendental doctrine of judgment' in the *Critique of Pure Reason*, where Kant hypothesizes his famous 'island of truth' surrounded by an 'ocean of illusion'. Kant's extended use of a topological metaphor in the passage is striking for a number of reasons. First it offers such a precise level of detail to the illusory seascape that surrounds the 'land of truth': 'many a fog bank and rapidly melting iceberg pretend to be new lands and ceaselessly deceiving with empty hopes the voyager looking round for new discoveries, entwine him in adventures from which he can never escape and yet also never bring to an end'.[4] The illusion of other places, of other 'islands of truth' contains within it the suggestion that the homeland of truth on which Kant positions us is itself an illusion. Kant asks the reader to hesitate before embarking on a journey into the sea of illusion and cast our eyes instead upon a map of the land we are about to leave and to 'ask, first, whether we could not be satisfied with what it contains, or even must be satisfied with it out of necessity, if there is no other ground on which we could build; and, second, by what title we even occupy this land, and can hold it securely against any hostile claims'.[5] A map is, of course, an abstraction, and the cartographic process one of topological illusion; what would a 'truthful' map of the island of truth look like? Perhaps it would be a map akin to the Borges fragment (the conceit for which Borges borrowed from Lewis Carroll's *Sylvie and Bruno Concluded* [1893]) in which the Cartographers Guilds construct a map of the Empire that is the exact scale as the Empire itself.[6] Willi Goetschel has argued that underpinning Kant's metaphor is an implicitly political dimension, an acknowledgement that:

> colonization is what we are always already doing when we set out to determine the grounds and limits of our reason. Colonization, Kant's narrative illustrates, takes place the moment our epistemological subject acts, that is, produces knowledge. … [T]he scientific and philosophical production of knowledge can only operate within the limits of an epistemic model that takes as its model the colonization of the world of experience.[7]

This attempt to 'colonize' experience in order to produce knowledge is precisely what Agamben will, following Benjamin, expose in the Kantian critical project. But it is far from an arbitrary moment in the *Critique of Pure Reason* that Agamben isolates to introduce his alternative model of criticism. In essence the island of truth is the critical project, and Kant's message seems to be that we should stay on this island of understanding rather than seek to leave it in search of new lands, a search that seems like an endless pursuit of illusion.

As Michèle Le Dœuff has argued, this island is 'the emblem of the great Kantian enterprise', 'the self-justification of a project which is, for good measure, conducted on the very plain where that project could least readily be defended: that of the pleasure principle'.[8] For Le Dœuff, the choppy seas beyond the island are described as full of pain and suffering; illusion is seemingly a siren that could lead the sailor into pain, suffering, even death. Best then to stay on the island, which is after all enchanting (other translations will read 'seductive'), enjoying the limited pleasures rather than risking the untold suffering of venturing off it: 'one avoids the discomfort of the icy fogs, but at the cost of renouncing the dream of discovery, the call of new lands, and hope'.[9] Le Dœuff suggests that we should read Kant's secure 'island of truth' in opposition to another, more dangerous island that appears in Kant's 'Conjectural beginning of human history'. That essay concludes with a reflection upon the 'greatest ills that oppress civilized peoples', namely war, the shortness of life and finally the illusion of a utopian alternative, the 'empty longing' that is:

> [t]he shadowy image of the *golden age* so much praised by the poets, where we are supposed to be relieved of all the imagined needs with which luxury burdens us, we are satisfied with the mere needs of nature, a complete equality of human beings, an everlasting peace among them – in a word the pure enjoyment of a carefree life, dreamt away in laziness or frittered in childish play: – a longing that

makes the Robinsonades and voyages to the south sea islands so charming, but in general prove how much boredom the human being feels with his civilized life, if he seeks its worth solely in *enjoyment* and brings laziness as a counterweight to reason's reminder that he should give his life its worth through *actions*.[10]

Kant's moralizing condemnation of enjoyment and laziness is telling, as is the implicit condemnation of the novel form as an entertainment. Given Agamben's repeated exploration of the disruptive potential of play in *Infancy and History*, *Profanations* and *State of Exception*, we can see in this second island the locus of an alternative critical project. Kant's denial of pleasure – whether that be the inoperative joy of life on the south sea island of fantasy, or the potential pleasures to be found in casting off from the island of truth – is telling; the critical project seeks to exorcise illusion by sequestering itself, but from what? The intoxicating illusion that Agamben identifies here is precisely language, with all its duplicity, deception and deferred meaning. Yet there is of course an irony in Kant turning to the metaphor of the island at this decisive moment in the critical project. Kant was notoriously critical of analogical reasoning yet, as John Callanan notes, was prone to using it himself.[11] The analogy that Kant makes here between truth and an island, the metaphysician and the seafarer, is for purely rhetorical ends, yet in so doing it indicates the importance of rhetoric, presentation and metaphor in the work of criticism. If Kant – systematically rather than practically – abjured analogy and metaphor, it was to another thinker who made these tropes, along with allegory and symbol, principle in an alternative mode of criticism, that Agamben turns.

In apparent opposition to Kant's 'island of truth', Agamben introduces Benjamin. The effect is, seemingly, to align himself with Benjamin's own model of criticism (and with it that of German Romanticism), as well as to highlight the unacknowledged limit-point of Kant's own thought:

> For the Jena group, which attempted through the project of a 'universal progressive poetry' to abolish the distinction between poetry and the critical-philological disciplines, a critical work worthy of the name was one that included its own negation; it was, therefore, one whose essential content consisted in precisely what it did not contain. The European critical essay in the present century is poor in examples of such a genre. ... [T]here is strictly speaking perhaps only a single book that deserves to be called critical: the *Ursprung des deutschen Trauerspiel* of Walter Benjamin. (*S* xv)

Apart from outlining the importance of Benjamin's study (which Agamben does not discuss further here or anywhere else), this statement puts forward a definition of criticism, one which, arguably, mirrors Agamben's own critical project. Here it is the tension between philosophy and poetry that produces criticism; poetry grasps language without knowing it, philosophy knows language yet cannot grasp it, and criticism is the space in which a knowledge of language is enacted in the work itself: 'In the West the word is thus divided between a word that is unaware, as if fallen from the sky, and enjoys the object of knowledge by representing it in beautiful form, and a word that has all seriousness and consciousness for itself but does not enjoy its object because it knows not how to represent it' (*S* xvii). Here the fundamental division is between representation and epistemology. Philosophy knows but is incapable of representation, of presenting its object of knowledge. Here Agamben very self-consciously echoes Benjamin's words in the 'Epistemo-Critical Prologue' to the *Trauerspiel* where Benjamin states of his work:

> Its method is essentially presentation [*Darstellung*]. Method is a digression. Presentation as digression – such is the methodological nature of the treatise. The absence of an uninterrupted purposeful structure is its primary characteristic. Tirelessly the process of thinking makes new beginnings, returning in a roundabout way to its original object. This continual pausing for breath is the mode proper to the process of contemplation. For by pursuing different levels of meaning in its examination of one single object it receives both the incentive to begin again and the justification of its irregular rhythm. Just as mosaics preserve their majesty despite their fragmentation into capricious particles, so philosophical contemplation is not lacking in momentum. (*GS* 1.1:208/*OT* 28, translation modified)

Criticism, from the Benjaminian position, is marked by a refusal to approach its object directly, to claim the object of analysis is simply knowable and grasped as such. There will be no syllogism, no surety of perspective, no attempt to measure experience against transcendental categories. Methodologically and stylistically Agamben will follow Benjamin's outline of critical practice, certainly during this period of his work (I would suggest the influence of Debord and Foucault becomes more pronounced in the late 1980s and *The Coming Community* [1990] marks a parallel development in method from his early work).

Stylistically, Agamben takes from Benjamin an approach in *Stanzas* that attempts to perform or enact the idea through presentation rather than argumentation. While *Stanzas* is certainly not the most experimental or difficult of Agamben's work – the title for which must go to *Idea of Prose*, followed by *The Coming Community* – in many ways it represents the best example in which Agamben's work provides a focus on a clear object, the interrelation of word, melancholy and desire in Western culture, with a diffuse and heterogeneous series of essays, as well as an elliptical and circuitous style. The text has a genesis that we may consider typical of Agamben's work, with the various themes and considerations of the volume developed in earlier essays published in Italian, such as 'The dandy and the fetish' which was published in 1972, and 'The phantasms of Eros', in 1974. The completed monograph both extends these essays, yet retains the seeming autonomy of the essay form, with the myriad parts of the book holding together as a whole, yet able to be read as short reflections. Agamben is unwilling to unite them under a coherent 'argument', instead allowing the relations between the disparate parts to create diffuse forms of reflection. How one may relate the later sections on Lévi-Strauss to the earlier reflections on Medieval melancholy in the Stilnovist lyric, or the fetish nature of the commodity are debatable. Analogously, the relation in each chapter between the chapter proper and the sections variously entitled 'scholia' in section two, or the extensive discursive footnotes in sections one, three and four is at times obscure. There is then the question of how one is to relate the twenty-seven illustrations included in the book to the prose works: do they merely demonstrate the thesis contained within, or are they running a parallel, yet different series of reflections? And what precisely are we to make of the excess of images in a book devoted to the word? The answer to these questions is related to the object of the book itself.

As Benjamin's focus on allegory was used to highlight the Baroque nature of history, the intersections and interstices between the parts of *Stanzas* are designed to provide us with what Agamben terms in the introduction 'a model of signifying that might escape the primordial reflection on signifier and signified that dominated Western reflection on the sign' (*S* xvii). Agamben's book refuses to offer us any one symbolic logic or system that will offer a concrete alternative to the Saussurian paradigms he is subtly deconstructing (and with them Derrida's over-determined systematization of Saussure's thought). What emerges in *Stanzas*, ultimately, is a non-system of inoperative criticism that remains alive and attentive to the paradox of language (it communicates its own communicability through the subject), that ruminates on the erotics of critique without giving up on the desire that lies at its heart. It is then Benjamin who outlines an alternative method. While Benjamin's critique of Kant will be of decisive importance for the philosophical orientation, it is his mode of composition, his style that is, to my mind, of equal value. As Justin Clemens has noted, 'Agamben's paratactical praxis functions not only insofar as he attends to its apparition in others, nor just at the level of word and figure, sentence and paragraph – but even in the movement and presentation of his thought from article to article, from book to book'.[12] Parataxis, like the 'paradigm' that became such an important feature of the *Homo Sacer* project, works by what Agamben will describe as a 'bipolar analogical model' (*ST* 31). While Benjamin was largely critical of analogy, Agamben takes from Benjamin something like an analogical method that is presented in *Stanzas* as a model of criticism explicitly *contra* Kant.

Experience and experiment: Reading *Infancy and History*

On the occasion of the French translation of his collection of essays *Infancy and History* (first published in Italian in 1978, French translation 1989; English translation 1993), Agamben penned an essay that is striking for its synoptic clarity. Given that the collection contained one of his most challenging essays ('Infancy and history: An essay on the destruction of experience'), Agamben's preface 'Experimentum linguae' offered readers an explicit statement of his work's driving aim. In it he suggests in his work to date he has 'stubbornly pursued only one train of thought: what is the meaning of "there is language"; what is the meaning of "I speak"' (*IH* 6). The relationship between ontology and language was the decisive problem of Agamben's work and even today it underscores his work on governmentality. While *Language and Death* (1982) was to articulate that relationship in an idiosyncratic and challenging reading of Hegel and Heidegger, in this later reflective essay Agamben again returns to the relationship between Benjamin and Kant to frame his own philosophical project: 'taking Benjamin's guidelines for his project on the philosophy to come, the experience at issue here can be defined only in terms of the "transcendental experience" that was inadmissible for Kant' (*IH* 5). The text to which Agamben refers, the 1918 essay, unpublished in Benjamin's lifetime, 'On the Program of The Coming Philosophy', is Benjamin's most sustained engagement with Kant, and the place where he most comprehensively addresses the problem of experience in strictly philosophical terms. In order to understand how Agamben builds on a Benjaminian concept of experience, it is necessary to reconstruct the argument the German thinker put forward there.

Written while Benjamin was still on course for a conventional academic career, 'The Coming Philosophy' was an attempt to articulate the limits of Kantian thought, and the direction for a philosophy that was able to grasp the problem of experience in manifold registers. Approaching a coming philosophy meant necessarily jettisoning the Kantian model of experience which, according to Benjamin, floundered on its own historicity: Kant's idea of experience was 'unique and temporally limited', a 'world view' that was also that of the Enlightenment (*SW* 1:100–1). Benjamin declared it was necessary to develop a more 'metaphysically fulfilled experience', one that was able to produce a form of systematized knowledge not in spite of experience, but in harmony with it. At the heart of Benjamin's essay (and Agamben's Benjaminian reading of Kant) are the two words for experience in German: *Erlebnis* is a particular experience, something that happens to you; *Erfahrung* suggests more the knowledge gained from that experience. David Ferris suggests that it might be more useful in English to think of *Erlebnis* as experiences and *Erfahrung* as experience (that, for instance, which we communicate as a body of knowledge – 'In my experience', for example).[13] In Benjamin's essay only *Erfahrung* appears and, as Peter Fenves has noted, this is crucial to Benjamin's goal, which is to map out the possibility for a philosophy 'contra *Erlebnis*'.[14] As Benjamin begins that essay, 'the central task of the coming philosophy will be to take the deeper intimations it draws from our times and our expectation of the future, and to turn them into knowledge by relating them to the Kantian system' (*SW* 1:100). The time to come, with all its radical uncertainty, was to be key to a new philosophy because it made the 'struggle for certainty' all the more challenging for philosophy. The challenges proffered by a coming philosophy were identical to those that had faced all forms of epistemology, Kant's included. For Benjamin there were two core obstacles: 1) to develop a 'certainty of knowledge that is lasting' and 2) to 'develop the integrity of an experience that is ephemeral' (*SW* 1:100). Kant's project satisfied the first obstacle but at the expense of the second. It had to denigrate the fleeting, the ephemeral nature of experience, and in doing so abnegate its own historical specificity.

If the *Critique of Pure Reason* had to privilege the *a priori* conditions for the possibility of knowledge, it was at the cost of the *a posteriori* experience of the subject in the world; the certainty of pure reason could only achieve its 'sad significance' in isolation from experience itself. In order to understand what should be 'adopted' and 'cultivated' from Kant's critical philosophy and what should be 'rejected', it was crucial to understand his work as a product of Enlightenment thought and thus limited by it. Benjamin diagnosed a series of 'decisive mistakes' in Kant's project that were as a result of the 'hollowness of the experiences available to him' (*SW* 1:102). There were two key 'inadequacies' in Kant's philosophy: the first was to develop a concept of knowledge that was modelled on subject-object relations, and the second the ways in which he related 'knowledge and experience' to 'human empirical consciousness'. If the first was the grounds for the attempt to develop transcendental conditions of knowledge, the poverty of his understanding of the second led to the denigration of experience. To develop a new philosophy it was wholly necessary to properly confront experience in order to overcome its poverty in the wake of the Enlightenment. Experience had, according to Benjamin, remained a form of 'mythology' in Kant, as it had done for all primitive peoples:

> The commonly shared notion of sensuous and intellectual knowledge in our epoch, as well as in the Kantian and the pre-Kantian epochs, is very much a mythology … Kantian 'experience' is metaphysics or mythology, and indeed only a modern and religiously very infertile one. Experience as it is conceived in reference to the individual living human and his consciousness, instead of as a systematic specification of knowledge, is again in all of its types the mere *object* of this real knowledge, specifically of its psychological branch. (*SW* 1:103)

The coming philosophy must surmount the necessary tensions and contradictions between the epistemological and the phenomenological. The philosophy that Benjamin mapped out in this essay was to be a new form of knowledge, an 'autonomous, innate sphere' that would dissolve the existing opposition between knowledge and experience. The new 'conditions of knowledge' would then provide the basis for a 'new concept of experience'. This new concept of experience would be 'exclusively' related to the transcendental consciousness. Benjamin was at pains to stress that his concept of experience was rigorously demarcated from the work of 'Neo-Kantians', which included that of Heinrich Rickert and Hermann Cohen. Whereas the neo-Kantians had attempted to ground Kant's philosophy of knowledge by turning to science, Benjamin would ally himself, somewhat abruptly and enigmatically at the essay's conclusion, with the attempt to relate knowledge to language undertaken by Johann Georg Hamann. In order to understand the introduction of Hamann and language here it is necessary to explain Benjamin's indebtedness to the philosopher now thought of as a key 'counter-Enlightenment' figure.

Hamann and the genealogical priority of language

The influence of Hamann on Benjamin's critique of Kant (and on Agamben's engagement with Benjamin's Kant) can be most clearly seen in an unpublished essay from 1916, 'On Language as Such and on the Language of Man'. This essay more of less rehearses Hamann's arguments about language being the stumbling block to the Kantian project, drawing on many of the same examples, such as Edenic naming. Hamann, in a letter, outlined his critique of Kant's critical project as follows:

> Indeed, if a chief question does remain: *how is the power to think possible?* – The power to think *right* and *left, before* and *without, with* and *above* experience? then it does not take a deduction to prove the genealogical priority of language … Not only the entire ability to think rests on language … but language is also the *crux of the misunderstanding of reason with itself.*[15]

Hamann's claim that language has a 'genealogical priority', that it precedes and provides the very basis for the possibility of thought, was a position with which both Benjamin and Agamben concur. In his essay, Benjamin begins by unambiguously declaring that 'every expression of human mental life can be understood as a kind of language' (*SW* 1:62). The human languages that we use, 'communication in words', are only particular instances of language. Language 'as such' precedes all human languages. There is no access to this language, but that does not mean that it is not communicated, rather 'mental being communicates itself in language and not through language' (*SW* 1:63). Having distinguished between language as such and the language of man, Benjamin goes on to suggest that common conceptions of language are 'bourgeois', in which it is assumed 'that man is communicating factual subject matter to other men'. This view is both 'invalid' and 'empty', holding that 'the means of communication is the word, its object factual, and it addressee a human being'. Against this Benjamin contrasts the 'other conception of language' that 'knows no means, no object, and no addressee of communication. It means: *in the name, the mental being of man communicates himself to God*' (*SW* 1:65). Benjamin reads the Fall as the moment at which man abandoned the name and 'fell into the abyss of the mediateness of all communication, of the word as means, of the empty word, into the abyss of prattle'. The 'empty prattle' that followed Creation rendered all questions of absolute morality, of good and evil, likewise empty. This is a crucial point for Benjamin: 'The Tree of Knowledge stood in the garden of God not in order to dispense information on good and evil, but as an emblem of judgement over the questioner. This immense irony marks the mythic origin of law' (*SW* 1:72). The emptiness of language, man's lapsarian loss of language as naming, marks the beginning of law.

This is a significant point if we pause briefly to reflect on Benjamin's well-known essay 'Critique of Violence' (1921). He concludes that essay by suggesting that in order to break the 'cycle maintained by mythic forms of law' it was necessary that a 'divine violence', a 'revolutionary violence', a 'pure immediate violence' come into being (*SW* 1:251–2). The means for that 'divine violence' were, the earlier essay suggests, to be found in language, in a coming philosophy that was able to account for, and be at one with, language as such. It is in this way we can begin to understand why Benjamin's acceptance of the 'genealogical priority of language', that he takes from Hamann, is so intrinsically connected to the new modality of experience that is part of 'the coming philosophy'. Benjamin concludes that essay as follows:

> A concept of knowledge gained from reflection on the linguistic nature of knowledge will create a corresponding concept of experience which will also encompass realms that Kant failed to truly systematize. The realm of religion should be mentioned as foremost of these. Thus, the demand upon the coming philosophy can ultimately be put in these words: to create on the basis of the Kantian system a concept of knowledge to which a concept of experience corresponds, of which the knowledge is the teachings [*Lehre*]. (*GS* 2.1:168/*SW* 1:108, translation modified)

Benjamin clearly suggests that it is only an acknowledgement of the 'linguistic nature of knowledge' that will lead to the possibility of a new concept of experience, but also introduces the declaration that that knowledge will be grasped through the teachings. This claim corresponds to Benjamin's focus elsewhere in his work on a form of study. In his essay on Kafka (1934) Benjamin, reflecting on Bucephalus in 'The new advocate', suggests that in order to challenge myth, Kafka turned not to law, to some regulated, arbitrary structure of knowledge, but to study: 'the law which is studied but no longer practiced is the gate to justice. The gate to justice is study' (*SW* 2:815). Agamben will, in *State of Exception* (2005), take up Benjamin's analysis of Kafka and see in it the possibility for putting law to a new use: 'the law – no longer practiced, but studied – is not justice, but only the gate that leads to it. What opens a passage toward justice is not the erasure of law, but its deactivation and inactivity [*inoperosità*] – that is, another use of law' (*SE* 64).

Expropriation and experience

To readers of Agamben the preceding discussion of Benjamin's critique of Kant, most specifically of his extension of Hamann's claims that pure reason had attempted to purify reason by excluding language from it, should be somewhat familiar. Unsurprisingly, Agamben's most sustained engagement with Kant, 'Infancy and history', is also his most fulsome engagement with Hamann. Summarizing 'Infancy and history' is no easy task, yet there are a few key threads in it that can help us to approximate something like an exposition: Agamben announces, following Benjamin, that his object is to explore the destruction of experience in modernity or, more specifically, to uncover how experience has been 'expropriated' from 'modern man' (*IH* 15). 'Expropriated' is a singular adjective to use in this context, suggesting as it does the deprivation of property, usually for the public good. That experience has become an object, something that exists as a form of knowledge removed from language and the traditions that once sustained it, underscores that while in the past 'experience has its necessary correlation not in knowledge, but in authority', at the present time 'all authority is founded on what cannot be experienced' (*IH* 16). If experience can be expropriated, become a sort of portable property, it also suggests that it now has an exchange value, rather than being in any sense intrinsic to knowledge. Agamben's language here is in accord with the insights he was developing a little earlier in *Stanzas* on the nature of use, for instance noting the ways in which in the Universal Exhibition of 1851 witnessed 'the transfiguration of the commodity into *enchanted object*' was a 'sign that the exchange value is already beginning to eclipse the use value of the commodity' (*S* 38). Agamben's claims in later books, such as *Profanations*, that we must develop a 'new' form of use, to 'play with' and deactivate the endless processes of separation enacted by capital (*PR* 87), is prefigured in the desire to similarly render inoperative the means by which modern science, culture and thought had expropriated experience.

Before Agamben approaches the philosophical expropriation of Kant, he begins the first section of 'Infancy and history' by taking aim at the everyday expropriation of experience, offering the rather banal example of tourists preferring to photograph a great monument rather than to experience it. This is a conflation of the experiential (*Erlebnis*) with the knowledge or wisdom gained from experience (*Erfahrung*), but it is crucial for Agamben's broader project that the everyday experience of consumer society is itself the grounds on which older forms of knowledge are eroded, rendered inoperative as part of the logic of capitalism, and thus can be the space in which the new forms of experience that Benjamin anticipated in 'The Coming Philosophy' can come about. As Agamben states (noting the camera standing in for experience):

> of course the point is not to deplore this state of affairs, but to take note of it. For perhaps at the heart of this senseless denial there lurks a grain of wisdom, in which we can glimpse the germinating seed of future experience. The task which this essay proposes, taking up the legacy of Benjamin's project 'of the coming philosophy', is to prepare the likely ground in which this seed can mature. (*IH* 17)

The remainder of Agamben's essay covers, broadly speaking, three different areas in which the critique of Kantian thought and their manifestations in modernity are outlined: science, psychology, language. This schematic summary naturally fails to do justice to the bewildering range of Agamben's references and examples, particularly in the 'Glosses' that follow each chapter, but the three broad areas do highlight the means by which Benjamin provides a key to the philosophical horizon beyond Kant that Agamben seeks to map.

If modern consumer culture (symbolized by the modern tourist, whom Agamben will chastise with great regularity in his works) has sold our inability to experience back to us, it is modern science that first witnessed this process of expropriation. Modern science was responsible for separating experience from knowledge; science, at its origins, demonstrated a great 'mistrust of experience'. Agamben uses the example of Galileo's telescope, which produced the 'doubt' of experience that led to Descartes's deceiving demon (*IH* 19–20). The scientific experiment was thus ultimately responsible for the distrust of experience that would lead to its appropriation:

> The scientific verification of experience which is enacted in the experiment – permitting sensory impressions to be deduced with the exactitude of quantitative determinations and, therefore, the prediction of future impressions – responds to this loss of certainty by displacing experience as far as possible outside the individual: on to instruments and numbers. (*IH* 20)

Scientific quantification and modelling is anathema to experience, which is itself 'incompatible with certainty': it cannot be measured or quantified, for as soon as it does so it 'immediately loses its authority' (*IH* 20). What passes for experience after Bacon, Galileo and Newton has no grounding in lived experience and the forms of fable, story and myth that were the bedrock of pre-modern experience.

From modern science's expropriation of experience, to Kant's transcendental subject – so removed and so foreign to the forms of lived, local experience that preceded it – is but a short jump. In fact Kant's early work emerged out of Newtonian natural science. A crucial step on the path towards developing the Critical System of the late works is found in Kant's *Universal Natural History and Theory of Heavens* (1755). In this work Kant speculated on the possibility of negotiating between transcendental knowledge – which the Universe recreates infinitely – with empirical knowledge, what we can know of nature. While the tension between these two methods was seemingly irreconcilable, it was in his Critical project that their unification would be realized. *The Critique of Pure Reason* was the final moment, according to Agamben, in which 'the question of experience within Western metaphysics is accessible in its pure form' (*IH* 36–7). Kant, of course, outlined a 'transcendental subject' that was beyond the direct knowledge of an object (for it has limited sensory experience), and so was therefore only able to think the object. Kant, in formulating the relationship between thought and experience anew, would declare, according to Agamben, that experience (as a form of knowing) was 'inexperiencable' (*IH* 36). One of the most important consequences of the denigration of *Erlebnis* is that philosophy 'delegates' the task of 'comprehending' the experiential to poetry and mysticism (*IH* 41). Philosophy would instead continue, through Husserl and others, to search for 'pure experience', something 'anterior both to subjectivity and to an alleged psychological reality' (*IH* 42). In opposition to this fracturing of *Erlebnis* into the realms of poetry on the one hand, and of a quest for pure experience in Husserl's critique of empirical psychology on the other, Agamben will attempt to recast the problem of experience as a problem of language in the final section of 'Infancy and history'.

Agamben's starting point for exploring language in relation to experience is, like Benjamin, Hamann. In outlining the critical project's location of knowledge in a 'mathematical model' and therefore its failure to discern 'the original place of transcendental subjectivity within language', Hamann opened up a critique of Kant which Benjamin and Agamben would endeavour to extend and, in some senses, complete (*IH* 50). The mathematical-geometrical model that had dominated theories of knowledge from antiquity to the present must come to terms with the unacknowledged role of language within it: 'it is in language that the subject has its site and origin, and that only in and through language is it possible to shape transcendental apperception as an "I think"' (*IH* 51). In support of Hamann's 'intuition', Agamben draws on the French linguist Émile Benveniste. Benveniste's work on subjectivity in language offers Agamben the framework for extending Hamann's insight, so he can declare that '*[t]he transcendental subject is nothing other than the "enunciator", and modern thought has been built on this undeclared assumption of the subject of language as the foundation of experience and knowledge*' (*IH* 53, emphasis in the original). Accordingly, the primary task of Agamben's early work would be to restore the subject of language to the central place in modern thought. Yet this is far from some linguistic triumphalism; Agamben posits 'infancy' as the originary 'experience' of language, yet we can never gain access, or return to this moment or mode: 'this in-fancy is not something to be sought, anterior to and independent of language, in a psychic reality of which language would be the expression' (*IH* 54). Instead infancy 'coexists with the origins of language', and is the moment in which language is both 'pure' and in a process of becoming semantic, that is becoming a mode of human expression. That infancy and language emerge with simultaneity, means that language can never be removed from being. Infancy is then a limit-point, one of those 'threshold' figures that characterize Agamben's thought.

As Thanos Zartaloudis has explained, infancy, the 'fact that language exists', indicates 'the pure exteriority of language *within* language, a perfectly empty dimension of pure experience that can be experienced and shown only through an experience *in/with* language'.[16] Infancy then becomes the name for the peculiar experience of language, the sense in which the human is both articulated by, but anterior to, linguistic being: 'in terms of human infancy, experience is the simple difference between the human and the linguistic. The individual as not already speaking, as having been an infant, that is experience'. Yet, as Agamben goes on to emphasize, the individual 'experience' of the difference between language and being has its most pronounced manifestations in language itself; infancy 'rules out language as being in itself totality and truth'; 'infancy, truth and language are limited and constituted respectively in a primary, historico-transcendental relation' (*IH* 58). This 'historico-transcendental' apparatus will develop to become a central tenet of Agamben's work in the *Homo Sacer* series, in which a series of archaeological investigations will map the contours and conse- quences of our linguistic expropriation in the juridico-political sphere.

Conclusion: Discontinuous being

The object of 'Infancy and history', as I have been mapping it so far, is to examine the consequences of articulating the genealogical priority of language as the inoperative heart of the Kantian transcendental subject. Yet Agamben, following Benjamin, will uncover the consequences of this operation in the ground of history. For infancy – 'the difference between language and speech' – 'opens the space of history'. In so doing Agamben gives experience an explicitly political dimension. The 'destruction' of experience in modernity was a consequence of language becoming increasingly instrumentalized, a tool for the organization of knowledge that lay outside of it. In a sense, the emptying out of language and the emptying out of experience are one and the same thing. To experience again, however, does not mean that it is necessary to recover some pre-Babel pure language. On the contrary it means grasping the essential division between language and speech that characterizes the human.

Human history will then not be made up of an unshakeable movement towards reason, the unstoppable path to progress, but those moments of rupture: 'History, therefore, cannot be the continuous progress of speaking humanity through linear time, but in its essence is hiatus, discontinuity, *epochē*. That which has its place in infancy must keep on travelling towards and through infancy' (*IH* 60). Language is then the ground on which we will experience anew: it is the location and essence of the human as fractured, removed, disarticulated from being. The coming experience must emerge from the negative ground of language. Agamben would go on to make this fundamental paradox the key to *Language and Death: The Place of Negativity* (1982), but it is in 'Infancy and history' that we can see the development of inoperativity as the process by which the ineluctable contradictions at the heart of being become the ground for those strategies and tactics that can exacerbate the inherent contradictions of their manifestations in law, politics and life. The discontinuity of speaking humanity is the essence of experience, and the 'germinating seed' for a new experience.

Notes

1   Immanuel Kant, *Critique of Judgement*, trans. James Creed Meredith (Oxford: Oxford University Press, 2007), 123, 377

2   Daniel McLoughlin, 'In force without significance: Kantian nihilism and Agamben's critique of law', *Law and Critique* 20.3 (2009): 246.

3   Adam Kotsko, 'On Agamben's use of Benjamin's "Critique of Violence"', in *Telos* (2008): 120.

4   Immanuel Kant, *Critique of Pure Reason*, trans. and ed. Paul Guyer and Allen W. Wood (Cambridge: Cambridge University Press, 1999), 339.

5   Kant, *Critique of Pure Reason*, 339.

6   Jorge Luis Borges, 'On exactitude in science', in *Collected Fictions*, trans. Andrew Hurley (London: Penguin, 1999), 325.

7   Willi Goetschel, '"Land of Truth – enchanting name!" Kant's journey at home', in *The Imperialist Imagination: German Colonialism and Its Legacy*, eds. Sara Friedrichsmeyer, Sara Lennox, and Susanne Zantop (Ann Arbor, MI: University of Michigan Press, 1998), 329.

8   Michèle Le Dœuff, *The Philosophical Imaginary*, trans. Colin Gordon (London: Continuum, 2002), 11.

9   Le Dœuff, *The Philosophical Imaginary*, 12.

10 Immanuel Kant, 'Conjectural Beginning of Human History', trans. Allen W. Wood, in Immanuel Kant, *Anthropology, History, and Education*, eds. Günter Zöller and Robert B. Louden (Cambridge: Cambridge University Press, 2007), 174.

11 See John J. Callanan, 'Kant on analogy', *The British Journal for the History of Philosophy* 16.4 (2008): 747–72.

12 Justin Clemens, 'The Role of the Shifter and the Problem of Reference in Giorgio Agamben', in *The Work of Giorgio Agamben: Law, Literature, Life*, eds. Justin Clemens, Nicholas Heron and Alex Murray (Edinburgh: Edinburgh University Press, 2008), 51.

13 David Ferris, *The Cambridge Introduction to Walter Benjamin* (Cambridge: Cambridge University Press, 2008), 111.

14 Peter Fenves, *The Messianic Reduction: Walter Benjamin and the Shape of Time* (Stanford, CA: Stanford University Press, 2011), 155–7.

15 Johann G. Hamann, as quoted in Gwen Griffith-Dickson, 'Johann Georg Hamann', in *The Stanford Encyclopedia of Philosophy* (Summer 2013 edn), ed. Edward N. Zalta, http://plato.stanford.edu/archives/sum2013/entries/hamann/

16 Thanos Zartaloudis, *Giorgio Agamben: Power, Law and the Uses of Criticism* (London: Routledge, 2010), 253.

Works cited

Borges, Jorge Luis. 'On exactitude in science'. In *Collected Fictions*. Translated by Andrew Hurley. London: Penguin, 1999, 325.

Callanan, John J. 'Kant on analogy'. *The British Journal for the History of Philosophy* 16.4 (2008): 747–72.

Carroll, Lewis. *Sylvie and Bruno Concluded*. In *The Complete Illustrated Works of Lewis Carroll*. Edited by Edward Guiliano, illustrated by John Tenniel. New York: Avenel Books, 1982.

Clemens, Justin. 'The role of the shifter and the problem of reference in Giorgio Agamben'. In *The Work of Giorgio Agamben: Law, Literature, Life*. Edited by Justin Clemens, Nicholas Heron and Alex Murray. Edinburgh: Edinburgh University Press, 2008, 43–65.

Fenves, Peter. *The Messianic Reduction: Walter Benjamin and the Shape of Time*. Stanford, CA: Stanford University Press, 2011.

Ferris, David. *The Cambridge Introduction to Walter Benjamin*. Cambridge: Cambridge University Press, 2008.

Goetschel, Willi. '"Land of truth – enchanting name!" Kant's journey at home'. In *The Imperialist Imagination: German Colonialism and Its Legacy*. Edited by Sara Friedrichsmeyer, Sara Lennox, and Susanne Zantop. Ann Arbor, MI: University of Michigan Press, 1998. 321–36.

Griffith-Dickson, Gwen. 'Johann Georg Hamann'. In *The Stanford Encyclopedia of Philosophy* (Summer 2013 Edition), edited by Edward N. Zalta, http://plato.stanford. edu/archives/sum2013/entries/hamann/

Kant, Immanuel. *Critique of Pure Reason*. Translated and edited by Paul Guyer and Allen W. Wood. Cambridge: Cambridge University Press, 1999.

—'Conjectural beginning of human history'. Translated by Allen W. Wood. In Immanuel Kant, *Anthropology, History and Education*. Edited by Günter Zöller and Robert B. Louden. Cambridge: Cambridge University Press, 2007, 160–75.

—*Critique of Judgement*. Translated by James Creed Meredith. Oxford: Oxford University Press, 2007.

—*Universal Natural History and Theory of Heavens*. Translated by Ian Johnston. Arlington, VA: Richer Resources Publications, 2012.

Kotsko, Adam. 'On Agamben's use of Benjamin's "Critique of Violence"'. *Telos* 145 (2008):119–29.

Le Dœuff, Michèle. *The Philosophical Imaginary*. Translated by Colin Gordon. London: Continuum, 2002.

McLoughlin, Daniel. 'In force without significance: Kantian nihilism and Agamben's critique of law'. *Law and Critique* 20.3 (2009): 245–57.

Zartaloudis, Thanos. *Giorgio Agamben: Power, Law and the Uses of Criticism*. London: Routledge, 2010.

Appendix

On the Limits of Violence (1970)

Giorgio Agamben
(trans. Elisabeth Fay)[1]

Fifty years after the publication of Walter Benjamin's 'Critique of Violence', and more than sixty years after Georges Sorel's *Reflections on Violence*, a reconsideration of the limits and the meaning of violence stands little risk of appearing untimely.[2] Today, humanity lives under the constant threat of its own instantaneous destruction by a form of violence that neither Benjamin nor Sorel could have imagined, a violence that has ceased to exist on a human scale. However, the exigency of rethinking violence is not a question of scale; it is a question of violence's increasingly ambiguous relation to politics. Thus, this critique diverges from Benjamin's exposition of violence's relation to law and justice, seeking instead to determine its relation to politics, and in so doing, to uncover the question of violence in and for itself. In other words, we aim to determine the limits – if such limits exist – that separate violence from the sphere of human culture in its broadest sense. These limits will allow us to address the question of the only violence that might still exist on a human scale: revolutionary violence.

At first glance, the relation between violence and politics appears a contradiction in terms: European history itself is predicated on the notion that violence and politics are mutually exclusive. The Greeks, who invented most of the concepts we use to articulate our experience of politics today, used the term *polis* to describe a way of life founded on the word, and not on violence. To be political (to live in the *polis*) was to accept the principle that everything should be decided by the word and by persuasion, rather than by force or by violence.[3] The essential characteristic of political life was thus *peitharkhia*, the power of persuasion; it was a power so revered that even those citizens condemned to death were persuaded to die by their own hand.

The Greeks' association of politics with language – and their understanding of language as essentially non-violent – was so pervasive that anything outside the *polis*, including encounters with slaves or barbarians, was defined *aneu logou*: a phrase that did not refer to actual physical deprivation of the word, but exclusion from the only way of life in which language alone had meaning.

The idea that language precludes any possible violence, as Benjamin rightly notes, is borne out by the fact that lying was not punishable under any ancient legal code. Political life as *peitharkhia* depended upon a particular understanding of language's relation to truth: namely, the belief that truth, in and of itself, could exert persuasive power on the human mind. The Greeks did not view 'persuasion' as a specific technique such as sophistry, but rather as an essential characteristic of truth. From its origins, Greek philosophy was in conflict with the political sphere, where truths seemed to be losing the power to persuade – one need only think of Plato's bitterness as he helplessly watched his master Socrates condemned to death. Feeling increasingly exposed to the threat of violence, philosophers began seeking truths outside the politico-temporal sphere, truths radically removed from any possibility of violence. Seen in this light, our experience of politics is unlike that of the Greeks: we know first hand that Greek philosophers were right to suspect that truth in politics cannot persuade against violence. Furthermore, today we are witnessing the proliferation of a form of violence totally unknown to the ancients, as more and more lies are introduced into the political sphere.

We can thus say that the association of language with non-violence no longer holds up to scrutiny. Indeed, the dissolution of this relation forms a dividing line between our experience of politics and that of the ancients; any political theory founded on Greek suppositions is inevitably unreliable today.

The modern age can claim the dubious honour of moving beyond a simple recognition of language's suggestive power, enacting a calculated plot to introduce violence into language itself. Today, organized linguistic violence aimed at manipulating consciousness is such a common experience that any theory of violence must address its expression in language. Moreover, linguistic violence is no longer limited to the political sphere: it has entered the daily realm of human *divertissements*. The explosive diffusion of pornography at the end of the eighteenth century was nothing other than the discovery that the experience of certain linguistic constructions can, in certain contexts, provoke reactions entirely removed from the will of the individual. Language can influence the body's instincts, overpowering the will and reducing humans to nature. Language can do what violence does: language can arouse. In short, the appeal of pornography is its ability to introduce violence into the realm of non-violence: language.

To this end, the Marquis de Sade, a serious and coherent scholar of pornography, devised a deliberate project (a perfect counterpart to the Kantian project seeking a maxim for action that could be elevated to universal law) to find a form of violence that:

> would go on having perpetual effect, in such a way that so long as I lived, at every hour of the day and as I lay sleeping at night, I would be constantly the cause of a particular disorder, and that this disorder might broaden to the point where it brought about a corruption so universal or a disturbance so formal that even after my life was over I would survive in the everlasting continuation of my wickedness.[4]

Sade found his universal catalyst in linguistic violence. And yet, careful analysis reveals that pornography shares some essential qualities with another form of linguistic expression, one that usually occupies the highest position in any hierarchy of cultural values: poetry. It is no accident that Sade's search for a universal catalyst within linguistic violence coincides with Hölderlin's description (the first of many to use figurative violence to articulate the experience of poetry) of the tragic word's violence, where 'the word seizes the body so that it is the latter which kills'.[5]

In many ways, the idea that violence inheres in poetic language can be traced back to Plato. Curiously, few have grasped the motive behind his much-debated ostracism of the poets. In some respects it is a perfectly explicit manifestation of the belief that persuasion should never be violent, one of the cornerstones of *maieutika*, the Socratic theory that regards free linguistic relations among human beings as a 'midwife's art'. Maieutics is incompatible with violence: as violence is an irruption of the outside that immediately denies the liberty of its victim, it cannot reveal inner creative spontaneity, only bare corporeality. Poetry introduces a form of persuasion that does not rely on truth, but rather on the peculiar emotional effects of rhythm and music, acting both violently and bodily – Plato was thus bound to cast the poets out of the city.

Perhaps the greatest divide between our experience of politics and that of the Greeks lies in our awareness that persuasion itself becomes violence in certain forms and circumstances, specifically when persuasion goes beyond the free linguistic relation of two human beings, and is taken up by modern techniques of reproducing spoken and written language. This is the essence of the only widespread form of violence that our society can claim to have invented, at least in its modern form: propaganda.

Here it is necessary to confront another of our society's inventions, namely, the theory of violence that has emerged in our era, completely upending traditional ideas. In this theory, violence is not at all incompatible with the midwife's art, as Plato believed. Rather, it is, as Marx writes in *Capital*, 'the midwife of every old society pregnant with a new one'.[6] This phrase is noteworthy, not only because one could argue that all modern discussions of violence are simply attempts at exegesis, but because Marx's characterization of politics and society reveals his understanding of the relation of violence to politics. Of course, the above observation was not meant to be applied to all kinds of violence; the violence that demolishes an old social order by exercising maieutic action upon a new one is distinct from the violence that preserves existing law, opposing change of any kind. The problem lies in identifying a just violence, a violence oriented towards something radically new, a violence that can legitimately call itself revolutionary.

The most common criterion employed to identify this violence is drawn from a kind of historical Darwinism. This theory – often mistakenly associated with orthodox Marxism, but actually derived from bourgeois sociological constructions of history influenced by Darwin and developed in the late nineteenth century – configures History as a linear progression of necessary laws, similar to the laws governing the natural world. Accordingly, the Marxian conception of man and nature, and the radical transformation contained therein (their *Aufhebung*, in dialectical terms), is clumsily construed as reducing History to prevailing ideas of nature in nineteenth-century science.[7] In this theoretical framework, the Hegelian reconciliation of liberty and necessity – which Marx consistently criticized – becomes the precondition for establishing a reign of mechanistic necessity that contains no space for free and conscious human action.

Within this framework, identifying just violence is no problem at all: if violence is the midwife of history, it need only hasten and facilitate the (inevitable) discovery of History's necessary laws. Violence that serves this end is *just*; violence that resists this end is *unjust*. To appreciate just how clumsy this interpretation is, we need only consider that it paints the revolutionary as a naturalist who discovers a plant species destined for extinction and then uses everything in his power to hasten its demise so that he may realize the laws of evolution. This was precisely the model adopted by totalitarian movements in the twentieth century, whose self-proclaimed exclusive right to revolutionary violence fostered involutional processes within authentic revolutionary movements. This was exactly what happened in Nazi Germany with the deportation of the Jews, and what happened in Russia with the great purges of 1935, when whole Soviet populations were deported – the only difference being that Hitler sought to 'hasten' the realization of a natural law (the superiority of the Aryan race), while Stalin believed he was 'hastening' the institution of an equally necessary historical law.

Even if we could ignore the disastrous political consequences that this theory of violence has wrought, we would still be able to identify its true defect: namely, that it situates the justification for violence *outside* of violence itself. In other words, it simply places violence within a broader theory of means that justify a superior end; the end is the sole criterion to determine the justice of the means. Benjamin correctly noted that, while such a framework can justify the application of violence, it fails to justify the principle of violence itself. Ultimately, any theory that defines the legitimacy of revolutionary means through the justice of their end is as contradictory as legalistic theories that guarantee a just end by legitimizing repressive means.

Violence in nature may only be called just by those who believe in cosmic plans and divine providence; human violence may only be called just by those who believe that history is a steady advancement along the predetermined route of linear time (the vision of vulgar progressivism). In European culture, the need for theodicy – the philosophical justification of God – arose only when the capacity to reconcile history's cruelty with divine goodness had been lost, extinguishing immediate faith in divine justice. Likewise, the need to justify violence arose only when all consciousness of violence's original significance had been lost. A theory of revolutionary violence is meaningless within historical theodicy, which paradoxically renders the revolutionary into a kind of Pangloss, convinced that everything is happening for the best, in this best of all possible worlds.

In light of all this, we do not seek to identify a *justification* of violence (the means to a just end). Rather, we are searching for a violence that needs no justification, that carries the right to exist within itself. As Sorel and Benjamin reflected on possible theories of revolutionary violence, they both recognized the necessity of breaking the vicious cycle of means and ends in order to discover a form of violence that would, by its very nature, be irreducible to any other. Sorel distinguishes between *force*, which aims at authority and power – in other words, the creation of a new state – and proletarian *violence*, which aims at abolishing the state. For Sorel, proletarian violence had been misunderstood primarily because Marx, while offering a detailed and thorough description of the capitalist order's violent evolution, had been quite sparing in his account of the proletariat's organization:

The consequence of this inadequacy of Marx's work was that Marxism deviated from its real nature. The people who pride themselves on being orthodox Marxists have not wished to add anything essential to what their master has written and they have always imagined that, in order to argue about the proletariat, they must make use of what they have learned from the history of the bourgeoisie. They have never suspected, therefore, that a distinction should be drawn between the force that aims at authority, endeavouring to bring about an automatic obedience, and the violence that would smash that authority. According to them, the proletariat must acquire force just as the bourgeoisie acquired it, use it as the latter used it, and end finally by establishing a socialist State which will replace the bourgeois State.[8]

Benjamin expands upon the Sorelian theory of a general proletarian strike, finding his model of revolutionary violence in the distinction between mythic violence, which imposes law and may thus be called dominant, and 'pure and immediate' violence, which seeks to impose no law, not even in the form of *ius condendum*. Instead, pure and immediate violence ousts both law and the force that upholds it, the State, thereby inaugurating a new historical age.

However, in both cases the objective of finding a violence that contains its own principle and justification remains only half fulfilled. Ultimately, the criterion remains teleological: the end of ousting the State and instituting a new historical order is the determining factor. Despite this, both Sorel and Benjamin push themselves to an outlying threshold from which we can begin to perceive the outlines of a theory of revolutionary violence. After all, what is violence that imposes no law? Isn't violence divorced from the assertion of power a contradiction in terms? What gives revolutionary violence the miraculous ability to blast open the historical continuum, beginning a new era? These questions will guide our approach as we consider a possible theory of revolutionary violence.

A violence that deliberately refrains from enforcing law, and instead breaks apart the continuity of time to found a new era is not as inconceivable as it initially seems. We know of at least one example of such violence, though it is situated outside our 'civilized' experience: sacred violence. Most primitive peoples celebrated violent rituals designed to rupture the homogeneous flux of profane time. These rituals resurrected primordial chaos, making humans contemporaries of the gods and granting them access to the original dimension of creation. Whenever the life of the community was threatened, whenever the cosmos seemed empty and vacant, primitive peoples would turn to this regeneration of time; only then could a new era (a new revolution of time) begin.

Curiously, these rites of regeneration were often celebrated among peoples commonly considered to be the creators of history: Babylonians, Egyptians, Hebrews, Iranians, Romans. It is almost as though these peoples, no longer bound to a way of life determined by purely cyclical and biological temporality, felt more keenly the need to periodically regenerate time, ritually reaffirming the violence at the origin of their history.

The desire to reintroduce the time of original creation through sacred violence did not arise from a pessimistic refusal of life or reality. On the contrary, it was precisely and only through the sudden irruption of the sacred and the interruption of profane time that primitive humans could fully engage with the cosmos, asserting power through the extreme act of spilling their own blood. In this way, they regained the authority to participate in the creation of culture and a historical world.

The conception of the *polis* lent a special urgency to Greek examinations of sacred violence, which articulated its unsettling power in the figure of Dionysus, a god who dies and is reborn. Sacred violence reveals itself where humans intuit the essential proximity of life and death, violence and creation; it emerges when humans discover that the experience of this proximity is rebirth and the generation of new time. Seen in this light, the closing words of Euripides's *Bacchae* become significant. The tragedy, which tells of the conflict between the god's sacred violence and the tyrant's profane violence, concludes with an expression of man's eternal faith in a new, unexpected possibility: the possibility of restarting time.

> Many things the gods accomplish
> unexpectedly. What we waited for does not come to
> pass,
> while for what remained undreamed the god finds ways.[9]

In *The German Ideology*, Marx draws an explicit connection between the proletarian experience of revolution and the ability to restart history and found society along new lines. He writes that 'the revolution is necessary, therefore, not only because the *ruling* class cannot be overthrown in any other way, but also because the class *overthrowing* it can only in a revolution succeed in ridding itself of all the muck of ages and become fitted to found society anew'.[10] The ability to open a new historical age belongs solely to a revolutionary class that experiences its own negation in the negation of the ruling class. Applying Marx's characterization of the revolutionary experience to the question of violence will reveal the criterion necessary to our inquiry.

Revolutionary violence is not a violence of means, aimed at the just end of negating the existing system. Rather, *it is a violence that negates the self as it negates the other; it awakens a consciousness of the death of the self, even as it visits death on the other*. Only the revolutionary class can know that enacting violence against the other inevitably kills the self; only the revolutionary class can have the right (or perhaps, the terrible imperative) to violence. Like sacred violence before it, revolutionary violence can be described as *passion*, in its etymological sense: self-negation and self-sacrifice. When seen from this perspective, it becomes clear that repressive violence (which enforces law) and delinquent violence (which defies law) are no different from the violence aimed at establishing new laws and new power: in each case, negation of the other fails to become negation of the self. Executive violence is fundamentally impure, regardless of its objective – as conventional wisdom recognizes, vilifying both the hangman and the cop – because it always excludes the only hope of redemption, it refuses to negate the self as it negates the other. Revolutionary violence alone can resolve the contradiction that Hegel described as a basic dissonance in the concept of violence: 'force or violence destroys itself forthwith in its very conception. It is a manifestation of will that cancels and supersedes a manifestation or visible expression of will'.[11]

Thus, there is but one criterion by which violence may call itself revolutionary. Experience tells us that our society is hardly ever conscious of the fundamental contradiction of the violence it enacts. Most violent revolts against the dominant class do not bring about revolution, just as most doses of medicine do not bring about miraculous cures. Only those who *consciously* confront their own negation through violence may shake off 'all the muck of ages' and begin the world anew. Only they may aspire, as revolutionaries always have, to call a messianic halt capable of opening a new chronology (a *novus ordo saeclorum*) and a new experience of temporality – a new History.

Revolutionary violence must be understood in light of its relation to death, a fact that allows us to extend our inquiry to revolutionary violence's relation to culture. Every culture aspires to overcome death. Everything that humankind has thought, known, written, or created as 'culture' has been created, written, known, and thought with the aim of making peace with death. This is the basis of our perpetual inclination to separate violence and language: language is, first and foremost, the power we wield against death, the only possible space for reconciliation. To the eternal question 'why is there something, rather than nothing', culture responds by exploring the mystery that Benjamin once called 'that object, to which in the last instance the veil is essential' (*SW* 1:351); culture transports us to a region where 'nothing' and 'something', 'life' and 'death', 'creation' and 'negation' reveal themselves as inextricably bound, bringing us to the very limits of language's possibilities. Once it has led us to the threshold of what cannot be known through language, culture exhausts its function. Because it aims at reconciling us to death, culture can go no further without negating itself.

Revolutionary violence alone may cross this threshold. It occurs in the stunning realization of the indissoluble unity of life and death, creation and negation. This realization can only occur in a sphere beyond language, which radically disturbs and dispossesses humankind. Violence, when it becomes self-negation, belongs neither to its agent nor its victim; it becomes elation and dispossession of the self – as the Greeks understood in their figure of the mad god. The living cannot recognize their own essential proximity to death without negating themselves, and this contradiction acts as the seal guarding the most sacred and profound mystery of human existence.

As an experience of self-negation, revolutionary violence is the *arrheton* par excellence, the unsayable that perpetually overwhelms the possibility of language and eludes all justification. It is precisely by going beyond language, by negating the self and powers of speech, that humanity gains access to the original sphere where the knowledge of mystery and culture breaks apart, allowing words and deeds to generate a new beginning.

At the dawn of every history aimed at ensuring security and making peace with death, it shall be written: 'In the beginning, there was the word'. At the dawn of every new temporal order, however, it shall be written: 'In the beginning, there was violence'.

This is both the limit and the insuppressible truth of revolutionary violence. By crossing the threshold of culture and occupying a zone inaccessible to language, revolutionary violence casts itself into the Absolute, validating Hegel's observation that the most profound representation of truth is contained in the violent image of the 'Bacchanalian revel in which no member is not drunk'.[12]

Notes

1   First published in Italian as 'Sui limiti della violenza', *Nuovi argomenti* 17 (1970): 159–73. The present translation previously appeared in *diacritics* 39.4 (2009): 103–11. The editors would like to thank Giorgio Agamben, *diacritics* and Elisabeth Fay for permission to reproduce the translation, and Lorenzo Fabbri and William Watkin for helping secure the permission.

2   Modified from the original to correct a reference to the publication date of Benjamin's 'Zur Kritik der Gewalt' (1921). Trans. [The Italian says 'Twenty years after'; Agamben might have referred here to the 1955 edition of Benjamin's *Schriften* (2 vols., eds. Theodor W. and Gretel Adorno, Frankfurt a.M.: Suhrkamp), the first volume of which opened in fact with 'Zur Kritik der Gewalt'. – eds]

3   See Arendt's description of the Greek concept of politics in *The Human Condition* (Chicago, IL: University of Chicago Press, 1998), Chapter 1.

4   Marquis de Sade, *Juliette*, trans. Austryn Wainhouse (New York: Grove, 1968), 525.

5   Friedrich Hölderlin, *Essays and Letters on Theory*, trans. Thomas Pfau (Albany, NY: State University of New York Press, 1988) 114.

6   Karl Marx, *Capital: A Critique of Political Economy*, trans. Samuel Moore and Edward Aveling (New York: Modern Library, 1906), 824.

7   It is well known that contemporary science, having abandoned this idea, no longer derives natural laws from a mechanistic model of the world.

8   Georges Sorel, *Reflections on Violence*, trans. Thomas Ernest Hulme with Jeremy Jennings, ed. Jeremy Jennings (Cambridge: Cambridge University Press, 1999), 169–70.

9   Euripides, *The Bacchae*, trans. C. K. Williams (New York: Farrar, 1990), 86–7.

10 Karl Marx and Friedrich Engels, *The German Ideology*, trans. Clemens Dutt, W. Lough and C. P. Magill (New York: Prometheus, 1998), 60.

11 G. W. F. Hegel, *Philosophy of Right*, trans. S. W. Dyde (New York: Cosimo, 2008), 33.

12 G. W. F. Hegel, *Phenomenology of Spirit*, trans. A. V. Miller (Oxford: Oxford University Press, 1977), 27.

Works Cited

Arendt, Hannah. *The Human Condition*. Chicago IL: University of Chicago Press, 1998.
Euripides. *The Bacchae of Euripides*. Translated by C. K. Williams. New York: Farrar, 1990.
Hegel, G. W. F. *Phenomenology of Spirit*. Translated by A. V. Miller. Oxford: Oxford University Press, 1977.
—*Philosophy of Right*. Translated by S. W. Dyde. New York: Cosimo, 2008.
Hölderlin, Friedrich. *Essays and Letters on Theory*. Translated by Thomas Pfau. Albany, NY: State University of New York Press, 1988.
Marx, Karl. *Capital: A Critique of Political Economy*. Translated by Samuel Moore and Edward Aveling. New York: Modern Library, 1906.
Marx, Karl, and Friedrich Engels. *The German Ideology*. Translated by Clemens Dutt, W. Lough and C. P. Magill. New York: Prometheus, 1998.
Sade, Marquis de. *Juliette*. Translated by Austryn Wainhouse. New York: Grove, 1968.
Sorel, Georges. *Reflections on Violence*. Translated by Thomas Ernest Hulme with Jeremy Jennings. Edited by Jeremy Jennings. Cambridge: Cambridge University Press, 1999.

Index

angel of 139
continuum of 216
end of 156, 165, 166 n.8
natural 75, 93, 100, 101, 111
philosophy of 73, 92, 142
Hitler, Adolf 234
Hobbes, Thomas 111
Hoffmann, E. T. A. 31 n.17
Hölderlin, Friedrich 30 n.15, 117, 233, 238 n.5
Holocaust 135–6 n.4
Homer 61, 62, 63, 68 n.35, n.37
homo sacer (concept) 6, 8, 116, 125, 128, 130, 132, 133–4, 136 n.4, 144, 147, 148, 193, 194, 195, 196, 198, 202
Homo Sacer (project) 6, 113, 161, 216, 217, 221, 228
Honneth, Axel 4, 5, 11 n.15, n.19, 12 n.25
Horkheimer, Max 3
humanity 30 n.9, 55 n.16, 67 n.5, 80, 86, 98, 126, 130, 131, 157, 178, 188, 203, 228, 231, 237
Husserl, Edmund 227
Hyginus 61, 63

idealism 216
identity 153, 155, 165, 174, 181, 182, 183
ideology 60, 67 n.18, 197
illusion 100, 175, 201, 216, 217–21
immanence 92, 99, 100, 102, 112, 169, 170, 171, 172, 174, 182
absolute 170, 173
imperative 78, 159, 180, 182, 183, 201, 236
categorical 182
indeterminacy 20, 21, 39, 40, 58, 62, 64, 82, 95, 114
index, historical 1, 52, 55 n.16, 207
indifference 27, 57, 139–52, 170, 171, 173
indistinction 128, 146, 176, 194
zone of 116, 144, 145, 146, 171, 172
infancy 179, 181, 227–8
innocence 62, 64, 76, 77, 79, 81–2, 86, 87, 111, 151, 177
inoperativity 8, 131, 132, 149–51, 167 n.17, 170, 172, 180, 181, 182, 183, 216, 219, 221, 225, 226, 228 *see also* *désœuvrement*; deactivation

instrumentality 155, 156, 190 191
irreparable/irreparability 153–5, 157, 165, 166 n.5, 180, 181

Jaffé, Edgar 2
Jena group 219
Jesi, Furio 176, 184 n.11
Jewish tradition 9, 66, 86, 111, 112, 129, 201, 202, 204, 205, 207, 208, 209, 212 n.7
Judaism 129, 136 n.5, 202, 206, 207, 209
judgement 85, 86, 87, 94, 96, 187, 215, 216, 224
aesthetic 216
collective 216
divine 96, 201, 208, 209, 213 n.21
ethical 87
reflective 215
teleological 10 n.3
juridical order 21, 22, 23, 26, 29 n.3, 92, 93, 97, 116, 127, 147, 193
juridification 171, 174
jurisprudence 34 n.43, 146, 195
justice 3, 8, 19, 22, 23, 32 n.23, 77, 85, 87, 91, 94, 96, 97, 98, 103, 105 n.11, 112, 131, 134, 136 n.9, 147, 158, 163, 164, 171, 172, 175, 176, 177, 178, 201, 202, 205, 206, 207, 208, 211, 212 n.3, n.13, 225, 234
absolute 209
divine 148, 163, 177, 181, 212 n.13, 234
human 177, 181
law and 23, 103, 147, 157, 158, 162, 167 n.11, 231
natural 163, 177
pure 182
universal 162

Kabbalah 202, 208, 209
Kafka, Franz 3, 9, 65, 70 n.44, 167 n.14, 201–14, 225
Kant, Immanuel 4, 9, 9–10 n.3, 35 n.54, 88 n.10, 161–2, 170, 172, 177, 184 n.14, n.15, 215–30, 232
Kelsen, Hans 193
Klages, Ludwig 88 n.4
Klee, Paul 25
Kojève, Alexandre 131

religion 136 n.5, 153, 155, 165, 167 n.14, 181, 224
resistance 164, 187–200
retribution 40, 42, 43, 44, 48, 49, 53, 58, 141, 190, 211 n.1
revelation 45, 49, 50, 51, 52, 59, 75, 130, 203, 205, 208
reversal, messianic 203–4
revolt 3, 12 n.30, 27, 93, 94, 95, 98, 176, 237
revolution 10 n.11, 51, 96, 156, 165, 176, 178, 179, 192, 235, 236, 237
Rickert, Heinrich 110, 111–12, 119 n.11, n.12, n.13, n.14, n.15, 223
Romanticism 30 n.11, 101, 104, 119 n.18, 219
Rosenzweig, Franz 35 n.53, 175, 184 n.10
rule 36 n.56, 42, 46, 100, 116, 117, 126, 128, 133, 145, 165, 170, 171, 175, 193, 194, 197, 198, 199, 200, 203
  of law 94, 142, 145, 173, 194
  monastic 161

sacratio 116
sacredness 77, 87, 147, 148
  of life 6, 130, 133, 134
sacrifice 8, 66, 77, 78, 82, 125–37, 148, 157, 160, 165, 178, 179, 180, 183, 236
Sade, Marquis de 232, 238 n.4
Salomon-Delatour, Gottfried 3
salvation 49, 50, 65, 101, 129, 180, 183, 196, 199
Sappho 61
Saussure, Ferdinand de 221
Scheerbart, Paul 2, 9 n.3, 25, 33 n.34, 35 n.48
Schiller, Friedrich 110, 118 n.4
Schlegel, Friedrich 110, 118 n.5
Schmitt, Carl 4, 6, 8, 11 n.16, n.17, n.20, 19, 113, 116–17, 121 n.34, n.36, 127, 134, 136 n.13, 143, 145, 146, 149, 152 n.11, 170, 171, 173, 178, 184 n.8, 193, 197, 198, 201, 212 n.3
Scholem, Gershom 2, 10 n.4, 74, 88–9 n.11, 184 n.12, 185 n.19, 202, 203, 205–13
secularization 99, 139
Shakespeare, William 167 n.14, 36 n.56, 82

Shekhinah 205
signature 120 n.26, 139, 140, 142, 143, 145, 147, 148, 149, 151, 152 n.8, 193
Simmel, Georg 119 n.15
sin, original 65, 91, 92, 98, 99
Social Democracy 96
society 29 n.5, 55, 94, 95, 127, 144, 159, 171, 233, 236, 237
  bourgeois 156
  classless 156
  consumer 226
Socrates 232
Sombart, Werner 2
Sophocles 61, 63, 99, 104 n.2
Sorel, Georges 2, 4, 10 n.11, 11 n.19, 31 n.17, 35 n.52, 96, 160, 191, 231, 234, 235, 238 n.8
sovereign 36 n.55, 99, 100, 127, 128, 133, 144, 145, 146, 149, 152 n.11, 169, 170, 177, 188, 192, 201, 203, 204, 212 n.2
  decision 4, 19, 28, 128, 130, 132, 133, 145, 146, 147, 149
  exception 116, 147
  law 113, 116, 171
  power 103, 113, 130, 131, 132, 133, 134, 137, 141, 144, 146, 178, 189, 193, 201
  rule 169, 170
  violence 137, 145, 146, 147, 148, 149, 173
sovereignty 4, 6, 8, 9, 98, 117, 133, 134, 144, 145, 146, 173, 178, 187, 188, 189, 192, 193, 194, 195, 196, 197, 198, 206
Spartacist revolution 96, 112
Spinoza, Baruch 170, 182
Stalin, Joseph 234
state 21, 26, 30 n.9, n.11, 30–1 n.15, 31 n.16, 94, 96, 97, 103, 140, 141, 142, 143, 144, 146, 150, 151, 152 n.7, 157, 160, 163, 175, 187, 190, 191, 192, 195, 200 n.3, 234, 235
  bourgeois 235
  capitalistic 160
  colonial 160
  dictatorial 164
  modern 20, 21, 22, 160, 170, 201

CPSIA information can be obtained
at www.ICGtesting.com
Printed in the USA
LVHW081926030222
710074LV00004B/182

9 781474 241892